DEATH AND THE CLASSIC MAYA KINGS

The Linda Schele Series in Maya and Pre-Columbian Studies

DEATH AND THE CLASSIC MAYA KINGS

JAMES L. FITZSIMMONS

UNIVERSITY OF TEXAS PRESS
Austin

This series was made possible through the generosity of William C. Nowlin, Jr., and Bettye H. Nowlin, the National Endowment for the Humanities, and various individual donors.

Requests for permission to reproduce material from this work should be sent to:
Permissions
University of Texas Press
P.O. Box 7819
Austin, TX 78713-7819
www.utexas.edu/utpress/about/bpermission.html

♾ The paper used in this book meets the minimum requirements of ANSI/NISO Z39.48-1992 (R1997) (Permanence of Paper).

Library of Congress Cataloging-in-Publication Data

Fitzsimmons, James L.
  Death and the classic Maya kings / by James L. Fitzsimmons. — 1st ed.
      p.   cm. — (The Linda Schele series in Maya and Pre-Columbian Studies)
  Includes bibliographical references and index.
  ISBN 978-0-292-71890-6 (cl. : alk. paper)
  1. Mayas—Kings and rulers—Death and burial.   2. Mayas—Funeral customs and rites.   3. Mayan languages—Writing.   4. Tombs—Mexico.
5. Human remains (Archaeology)—Mexico.   6. Mexico—Antiquities.
I. Title.
  F1435.3.F85F57 2008
  393.0972′0902—dc22
                                                            2008014909

for Rebecca

CONTENTS

LIST OF FIGURES AND TABLES xi

A NOTE ON ORTHOGRAPHY xv

ACKNOWLEDGMENTS xvii

CHAPTER 1: CELEBRATIONS FOR THE DEAD 1
Anthropology and Death Rituals 3
The Classic Maya Case 7
Methodological Concerns 10
Kingship and the Ancestors 15

CHAPTER 2: DEATH AND THE AFTERLIFE
IN THE LOWLANDS 17
Earth 18
Maize 22
Mortality 24
Writing Death 25
The Self and the Soul 39
Breaths of Life and Death 42
Way 44
To the Afterlife 48
Celestial Bodies and Maize Gods 52

CHAPTER 3: ROYAL FUNERALS 61
Waiting for Interment 61
Gravemakers 64
Tombs as Underworld Surfaces 68
Tombs as Caves 71

Tombs as Houses 72
Timing and the Ritual Process 72
Embalming and Processing 74
Dressing and Bundling the Corpse 76
Painting 81
Arranging the Body, Arranging the Furniture 83
Sealing the Tomb 101

CHAPTER 4: DEATH AND LANDSCAPE 105
K'inich Yax K'uk' Mo' 107
Lowland Founders and Local Variations 112
Cults of Personality 117
Bird Jaguar IV 120
Gods and Orchards at Palenque 123
Souls within Buildings 130
Ancestor Shrines 134

CHAPTER 5: ENTERING THE TOMBS
OF THE CLASSIC MAYA KINGS 142
Patterns of Reentry at Piedras Negras 145
Fire in the Motmot Burial 156
Fire and History at Tonina 160
Family Affairs 161
False Reentry 162
Painting, Drilling, and Bone Peeling 164
The Portable Dead 166

CHAPTER 6: THE DEAD KING AND THE BODY POLITIC 170
Royal Funerals: Public or Private? 178
Bodies and Monuments 180
Corpses, Souls, and Mourners in Transition 181

GUIDE TO APPENDIXES 185

APPENDIX 1: BURIAL STRUCTURES AND CONTEXTS 188

APPENDIX 2: BODY PREPARATIONS
AND FUNERARY ACTIVITIES 194

CONTENTS

APPENDIX 3: GRAVE GOODS 202

NOTES 209

REFERENCES 227

INDEX 261

LIST OF FIGURES AND TABLES

A section of color plates follows page   154

Fig. 1. The Maya area   8

Fig. 2. Piedras Negras Panel 2   9

Fig. 3. An Underworld scene   14

Fig. 4. The death of Wak Chan K'ahk' and the Seven-Black-
Yellow-Place of Tonina Monument 69   19

Fig. 5. Chaak, God A, and the Jaguar God of the Underworld   20

Fig. 6. Hun Ajaw and Yax B'alam   21

Fig. 7. Crocodile from Copan Altar T   21

Fig. 8. Waxaklajuun Ub'aah K'awiil as the Maize God on
Copan Stela H   23

Fig. 9. Maize personified on the Temple of the Cross   24

Fig. 10. The "death" verb *cham*   26

Fig. 11. Section of Tikal Altar 5 that describes a woman as deceased   27

Fig. 12. Breath escaping from nostrils as *t'ab'ay*   27

Fig. 13. Variants of *k'a'ay u sak* "flower" *ik'il*   28

Fig. 14. *Sak,* "white," glyph as an exhaling flower on Stela 14,
Yaxchilan   29

Fig. 15. Phrase *k'a'ay u sak* "flower"   30

Fig. 16. Mok Chi (God A') on an unprovenanced vessel   32

Fig. 17. *Ochb'ih* and *och haj*   33

Fig. 18. Excerpt from Quirigua Zoomorph G, west   34

Fig. 19. Iconography on Tikal bones from Burial 116   36

Fig. 20. Iconography from Early Classic Rio Hondo vase   36

Fig. 21. Examples of *och b'ih* and *och ha'* on Tikal Stela 31   37

Fig. 22. Onyx vessel from Hix Witz   38

Fig. 23. Glyph for *u b'aah*   41

Fig. 24. Classic Maya *way* killing other *way*   45

Fig. 25. Lords of the Underworld as captives   51

Fig. 26. Yax Ehb' Xook as K'inich Ajaw   54

Fig. 27. Kan B'alam as the Jaguar God of the Underworld   54

Fig. 28. Detail of Figure 6 from the tomb of K'inich Janaab' Pakal I   56

Fig. 29. Detail of K'inich Janaab' Pakal I on his Sarcophagus Lid   58

Fig. 30. Detail from the Palenque Sarcophagus Lid and Yax
K'uk' Mo' on the Rosalila Structure at Copan   59

Fig. 31a. Maya lord with mourners   62

Fig. 31b. Maya lords being reborn as trees   62

Fig. 32. Río Azul Tomb 1 paintings   69

Fig. 33. Tikal Burial 23   73

Fig. 34. Río Azul Tomb 19   77

Fig. 35. Two examples of bundles in Maya art   79

Fig. 36. Tikal Burial 195   80

Fig. 37. Piedras Negras Burial 82   86

Fig. 38. Socketed bloodletter from Piedras Negras Burial 82
and deified bloodletters from Tikal Burial 116   89

Fig. 39. Tikal Burial 116   91

Fig. 40. Tikal Burial 10   94

Fig. 41. Piedras Negras Burial 5   95

Fig. 42. Death and transformation on K1182   99

Fig. 43. Plan view of K'inich Janaab' Pakal I's tomb   102

Fig. 44. The Copan site core, showing Temples 26 and 16   109

Fig. 45. The west side of the Rosalila structure   110

Fig. 46. The Tikal site core   113

Fig. 47. Tikal Burial 125   114

Fig. 48. Seibal Tablet VI   116

Fig. 49. Yaxchilan Stela 4   121

Fig. 50. The Sarcophagus Lid at Palenque   124

Fig. 51. Sides of the Palenque Sarcophagus Lid   126

Fig. 52. Lady Olnal (Figure 7) from the tomb of
K'inich Janaab' Pakal I   128

Fig. 53. The "Dazzler" vessel from Copan Burial XXXVII-4   134

Fig. 54. Caracol B-19-2nd tomb showing sealed capstones   136

Fig. 55. Yaxchilan Lintel 25   138

Fig. 56. Map of Yaxchilan showing Structure 23   140

Fig. 57. Caracol Stela 6 excerpt   143

Fig. 58. K'inich Yo'nal Ahk I   147
Fig. 59. Yaxchilan Lintel 14   148
Fig. 60. A scene of sacrifice from K4013   150
Fig. 61. Piedras Negras Stela 1, right   153
Fig. 62. The Motmot marker at Copan   157
Fig. 63. Tonina Monument 161   161
Fig. 64. Tikal Altar 5 and Stela 16   165

TABLES

Table 1. Liminality   4
Table 2. Known Deified or Celestial Ancestors   55
Table 3. Death and Burial Dates of Classic Maya Rulers   63
Table 4. "Founders" of the Classic Maya Lowlands   107
Table 5. Reentered Royal Tombs of the Classic Maya Lowlands   144
Table 6. Death and Accession Dates at Classic Maya Sites   173–175

A NOTE ON ORTHOGRAPHY

The hieroglyphic orthography used in this book largely conforms to that used in *Reading the Maya Glyphs* by Michael Coe and Mark Van Stone. The one exception involves words bearing the consonant *b:* given that all other glottal sounds are represented in this text, and that *b* is universally glottal, I have chosen to use prime to represent the sound *b'* as well.

Author's Note: Figures 2, 4, 48, 55, 56, 59, and 61 are from the Corpus of Maya Hieroglyphic Inscriptions and are reproduced here courtesy of the President and Fellows of Harvard College. The CMHI is an active research archive and ongoing recording program of the Peabody Museum of Archaeology and Ethnology, Harvard University, devoted to the recording and dissemination of information about all known ancient Maya inscriptions and their associated figurative art.

ACKNOWLEDGMENTS

Death and the Classic Maya Kings is a book about the ties between what is archaeologically observed—the "death" in material culture as represented by burials, funerary architecture, and grave furniture—and what was recorded by the Classic Maya scribes. In the course of writing this book, an adaptation of my Ph.D. dissertation, numerous foundations and institutions provided me with generous financial and logistical assistance during my fieldwork at Piedras Negras and Zapote Bobal, as well as throughout the trajectory of my graduate and postgraduate studies.

Without financial aid from the Department of Anthropology, Harvard University; the U.S. Department of Education (Foreign Languages and Areas Studies program); the Whiting Fellowship Foundation; the Center for World Religions (Harvard University); the Owens Fund; the Mellon Foundation; and, in large part, Middlebury College, this book would not have been realized. Research at Piedras Negras was carried out as part of the Proyecto Piedras Negras and generously supported by a number of the above institutions and funds. In addition, the project received generous donations and support from the Universidad del Valle, Guatemala; Ken Woolley and Spence Kirk, of Salt Lake City; the Foundation for the Advancement of Mesoamerican Studies, Inc. (FAMSI); the Ahau Foundation; the National Science Foundation; the Fulbright Fellowship Program; Fulbright-Hayes; the Heinz Foundation; the Rust Fund of Brigham Young University; and the Albers Trust of Yale, along with research funds from former Dean Clayne Pope and Vice President Gary Hooper of Brigham Young University. My field and laboratory efforts no doubt benefited from these august institutions and individuals.

I thank all the members of the Proyecto Piedras Negras not only for their support and academic assistance but also for their friendship. I wish to especially thank the Instituto de Antropología e Historia (IDAEH) and project codirector Héctor L. Escobedo, who, along with Stephen D. Houston, provided me with the opportunity to excavate and research at the site. Likewise, David Webster, Kitty Emery, and Lori Wright imparted crucial insights both inside and outside the field, particularly with respect to the Piedras Negras Burial 82 materials. Personal correspondence with several other project members was likewise critical in the development of this work. Particularly the efforts of Mark and Jessica Child, Charles Golden, Zachary Hruby, Amy Kovack, A. Rene Muñoz, and Andrew Scherer to clarify and explain the results of their excavations—as well as my own—afforded me avenues of inquiry that I would otherwise have ignored. Special thanks go to Zachary Hruby and Heather Hurst, whose drawings continue to serve in all things related to Piedras Negras archaeology.

I also extend my appreciation to all of the Guatemalan archaeologists who have worked with the Proyecto Piedras Negras over the years. Excavations realized by Tomás Barrientos, Carlos Alvarado, and Marcelo Zamora, working under the auspices of Escobedo, were of specific import to this book. Likewise the efforts of Lillian Garrido and Ernesto Arredondo Leiva to provide me with insights into the functions of structures overlooking the West Group Plaza cannot be ignored. At the same time, I would like to extend my appreciation to all the workers and support staff of the Proyecto Piedras Negras: without their tireless endeavors, the project would have soon collapsed. Heartfelt thanks also go to Srs. Joaquín Aguilar and José "Arnoldo" Ramírez. Although they may not ever read this, these individuals are never far from my thoughts of Piedras Negras.

In addition, I would like to thank all the members of the Proyecto Petén Noroccidente Hix Witz (Zapote Bobal) for their continued support and insight. In particular, Laura Gámez, Véronique Breuil, Melanie Forné, Edy Barrios, Edwin Roman, Franz Lauer, Bryan Carlo, and Charlotte Arnauld have contributed directly to the information presented in this book, either from research at La Joyanca, Zapote Bobal, or both. Their moral and intellectual support, together with that of the people of Vistahermosa, Guatemala, has been—and continues to be—an inspiration.

Beyond these projects, I must acknowledge the efforts of all the archaeologists and epigraphers referred to in this work; without their publications, correspondence, and expertise, the archaeology of Classic Maya death would be confined to a much smaller work. Specifically, the insights of Wendy Ashmore, Harvey and Victoria Bricker, Jane Buikstra, Karla Davis-Salazar, Barbara Fash, R. Jeffrey Frost, Ian Graham, Takeshi Inomata, Rosemary Joyce, George Lau, Patricia McAnany, Gordon Rakita, Nora Reber, Izumi Shimada, and Karl Taube have, over the years, contributed greatly to my ideas about the archaeology of the Americas, ceremony, epigraphy, and iconography. In addition to those mentioned above, I would like to thank the many individuals and institutions who generously contributed to the photographs and images in this work, including the Corpus of Maya Hieroglyphic Inscriptions (Harvard University), the Foundation for the Advancement of Mesoamerican Studies, Inc., the Penn Museum (University of Pennsylvania), Arlen Chase, Diane Chase, Barbara Fash, Grant Hall, Stephen Houston, Justin and Barbara Kerr, Merle Greene Robertson, and David Stuart. Doubtless there are others. To these people I extend my apologies for their omission.

This project could not have been written without the generous institutional support of Dumbarton Oaks, Washington, D.C., and the Sainsbury Research Unit of the University of East Anglia. The majority of my dissertation revisions took place at these institutions; I thank them for providing me with superb library access as well as accommodations during my years there. In particular, I would like to thank Jeffrey Quilter, Steven Hooper, and Joanne Pillsbury not only for their support but also for their faith in me as a scholar. I would also like to thank Charlene Barrett and Ann Nottingham for their logistical assistance subsequent to my time at these institutions. Moreover, I would like to extend my gratitude to the editorial staff at the University of Texas Press.

David Stuart, William L. Fash, and Stephen D. Houston have sacrificed countless hours guiding me through my academic career. Working with David Stuart on all things hieroglyphic has been a rewarding experience: I cannot emphasize enough his contribution to my understanding of—and enthusiasm for—Classic Maya writing. With an ability to recall and explain almost any inscription, David Stuart was formative in the development of this thesis. In addition to providing me with the opportunity to work at Copan, William L. Fash was instrumental to my academic growth at Harvard University and continues to extend a helping hand through all the numerous "crises" in graduate and postgraduate life. Stephen D. Houston has, along with Escobedo, played an integral role in my archaeological research at Piedras Negras (as well as in the publication of that material). I benefited from Houston's encyclopedic knowledge of Classic Maya inscriptions throughout the course of writing this book. I am particularly indebted to the above individuals for their tireless support, for their criticisms as well as their congratulations.

My final acknowledgments go to my family, who have supported me personally and professionally over the course of my time at Harvard University and in my postgraduate career. With me they have endured the frenetic life of an academic in the final stages of turning a dissertation into a book, from panic and despair to relief and (subsequent) lethargy. In addition to my parents, Kevin and Teresa Fitzsimmons, I would like to thank Laura Fitzsimmons as well as Clara, Molly, and Lena. Lastly, I wish to thank my wife, Rebecca Bennette, whose tireless devotion surprises me every day of my life.

DEATH AND THE CLASSIC MAYA KINGS

ONE

CELEBRATIONS FOR THE DEAD

Rituals surrounding death are informed not only by biological concerns but also by social and religious norms of behavior. As a primary focus in sociocultural anthropology, the study of death witnessed an explosion in theoretical refinement and scope over the last few decades of the twentieth century, expanding far beyond its modest nineteenth-century origins in the study of social organization to address broad philosophical and anthropological issues.[1] Archaeology has followed a similar path, with speculative, chronological, and cultural approaches to burials supplanted by the concerns of processual and postprocessual theory.[2] Yet most analytical approaches to death have at their theoretical roots the work of early-twentieth-century sociologists such as Robert Hertz and Arnold van Gennep, themselves the by-products of a larger, late-nineteenth-century tradition initiated by Émile Durkheim and published in *L'Année sociologique*. Through their work, we see death reflecting and shaping social values,[3] ideas that find resonance even among the tombs and temples of Classic Period Mesoamerica.

The crux of van Gennep's thesis, originally formulated for societies in Madagascar and Indonesia, is that death rituals—part of a class of rituals concerned with the transition from one status to another, such as initiation or marriage—consist of a tripartite structure. These involve a separation from the original status, a liminal period, and a reincorporation of the individual into a new social status; a "death" and subsequent "rebirth" into a new identity are characteristic of each of the three stages.[4]

Hertz dealt with a similar situation in Borneo: his fieldwork revealed a number of societies that did not see death as instantaneous. One notable example from his research involves a period when the body is neither alive nor fully dead. Set rituals are undertaken, including secondary burial and feasting, to bring the dead out of the liminal stage into a new social status, that of an ancestor.[5] Although Hertz did not categorize or even number these stages, his concern with the liminal phase of death rites has, along with van Gennep's approach, set the standard for subsequent elaborations and refinements of the anthropology of mortuary ritual.[6] More important for the present study, however, has been his idea that the changing state of the body during these ceremonies often reflects the changing state of the soul. Viewing these states from three sides of death—corpse, soul, and mourners—Hertz pioneered a new form of comparative analysis that continues to be used in modern research.

As can be surmised, the application of these ideas—or their subsequent elaborations—to archaeological contexts presents a difficult problem. Lacking living participants in ancient death rites, archaeologists are denied *direct* access to ceremony outside of ethnographic or ethnohistoric information. Attempting to view "the three sides of death" is far more difficult when all of the participants have expired! Nevertheless, traditional approaches to rank and status are today complemented by studies addressing death in all its symbolic and sociological roles, including cultural attitudes toward mortality as well as ideas about the afterlife.[7] In Mesoamerica, works by van Gennep, Hertz, or other more recent theorists have had a lesser impact; in the Maya lowlands, there have not been many attempts to reconcile the anthropology of death with artifactual remains in a systematic way.[8]

For the Classic Maya (AD 250–900), the works of Alberto Ruz Lhuillier and W. Bruce M. Welsh remain the foremost analyses of burial practice. The former's focus on grave goods, orientation, and patterns in mortuary practice was adopted in subsequent studies of the Maya area and at Teotihuacan.[9] Documenting the widespread presence of specific grave goods and burial patterns for the Classic Maya, Ruz Lhuillier synthesized information from numerous sites throughout the lowlands, building upon interpretations from site reports and attempting to reconstruct elements of Classic Maya religion and ideology. The task of reconstructing elements of Classic Maya religion has since been met in a variety of ways, ranging from specific analyses of underworld supernaturals to generalized treatments of belief systems.

The more technical study by Welsh established firm grave typologies for the Maya lowlands and dealt with grave orientations, social implications of grave goods, and general burial practices based on patterns in such behavior as skeletal mutilation or human sacrifice among elite as well as household interments. As he did not examine epigraphic or iconographic data, Welsh proposed general patterns of Pan-Maya and regional practice based on archaeological evidence augmented by references to ethnography and ethnohistory. Despite these limitations, his work continues to be relevant to scholars of Classic Maya mortuary analysis.

Recent developments in hieroglyphic and iconographic decipherment have changed the way Classic Maya religion is studied, to the point where such issues as perceptual psychology, ancestor worship, and the sociopolitical aspects of "tomb entering" rituals can be viewed textually in the words of ancient Maya scribes and their kings. Elaborate rites of death, spanning from days to hundreds of years, have been identified for specific individuals and support the existence of multiple stages of death and rebirth, in some ways similar to those noted earlier for Indonesia and Madagascar. Moreover, knowledge of these rituals is now beginning to be applied to archaeological examples.[10] In light of these developments, a broader anthropological analysis of Classic Maya remains seems justified.

The "language" of royal Classic Maya burials—as a material, textual, and iconographic entity—is the focus of this work. Viewing this language through a lens of developments in contemporary Mesoamerican archaeology and anthropology, I examine how royal written and iconographic records of Classic Maya mortuary rituals accord with archaeological evidence. Although this study focuses primarily on examples from sites where mortuary epigraphy, archaeology, and iconography converge, I have used supporting data from sites where one or more of these are in evidence. Testing the archaeological record with examples from text and iconography does not presume superiority of one over the other for understanding Classic Maya religion, but rather explores the continuities and discontinuities that can be gleaned from existing data. Moreover, although examples from text are used to posit models for royal mortuary ceremonialism, significant inter- and intrasite variations exist. Investigating these sheds light not only on individual or local strategies for interment but also on the sociopolitical and religious climate that brought about ceremonies for the dead.

ANTHROPOLOGY AND DEATH RITUALS

In a widely cited work on the use of ethnographic parallels in archaeology, Peter Ucko has pointed out that multiple analogies are a crucial factor in the explanation of material remains. In the case of a burial, aspects such as orientation, grave goods, or tomb construction do not necessarily imply belief in an afterlife and therefore require supporting data.[11] This is precisely why combining archaeology, epigraphy, iconography, and multiple lines of ethnographic inquiry appears to be the most rigorous methodological approach to the Classic Maya case. Nevertheless, we might analyze the ways in which these lines of ethnography fit within broader anthropological theory. In looking at ethnography to provide meaning, we may overlook the theoretical context of an ethnographic example within the anthropology of death itself. To provide this framework for the current research, I have drawn upon models first constructed—and subsequently revised and elaborated upon—in the early part of the twentieth century. Influenced in large part by Durkheim's notions of self and society, these models involve rites of passage and changes in societal state. Criticized as "vague truisms" but vindicated in the same breath,[12] they require a brief explanation as well as a defense of their applicability to the present work.

Focusing on the opposition between individual autonomy and societal integration, Durkheim was instrumental in shaping the sociology of religion. He

TABLE I

LIMINALITY

I.	Marriage	Childbirth	Death
II.	Single/Married (engaged)	Pregnancy/Birth	Alive/Dead
III.	Single→Engaged→ Married	Pregnancy→Pregnancy/Birth→ Birth	Alive→Dying→Dead

Source: After Metcalf and Huntington 1991, fig. 1.

saw religion as a collection of commonly held beliefs uniting individuals within society and, at the same time, defining separate identities within that whole.[13] This tension between society and autonomy plays out in the work of van Gennep, where various aspects of the death ceremony draw lines between, divide, and reintegrate corpse and culture. In his schemes, ceremonies involving transition, such as those performed for marriage, pregnancy, or death, are characterized by a tripartite structure. These are illustrated in Table 1,[14] where states are broken up into three schemes: (I) single distinctions; (II) two categories; and (III) three "ceremonial" stages.

The first stage of scheme III involves rites of separation, preliminal rites, which divorce individuals from their previous status. In childbirth rites among the Toda of India, for example, van Gennep notes a separation of the expectant mother from her village and all sacred places, imbibing ritual drinks and marking herself with burns. The second liminal, or threshold, rites involve a transitional state—in the case example, this is a return to her home, the performance of appropriate rites, and a waiting period ending in the delivery of the child. The final postliminal rites require the incorporation of the individual into a new status, ceremonies once again changing the role of the individual within society. For the Toda, mother and child leave the house to live in a special hut two or three days after childbirth. Rites are performed for the departure from the house, departure from the hut, and the return to the house, identical to those marking the preliminal period. While lacking the elaboration of the pre- and postliminal rites, death rituals among the Toda accentuated the liminal period, a characteristic noted by van Gennep for a number of societies in India, Indonesia, and Madagascar.[15]

Although van Gennep was concerned with a wide array of rituals marking transition, Hertz limited his study to funerals and secondary burials in Indonesia, particularly those performed by the Berawan in Borneo. Concentrating on the "intermediary period," which is roughly analogous to the liminal in van Gennep's work, Hertz observed a period, lasting anywhere between eight months and ten years, when the deceased was in between life and death.

Within a temporary burial place, in many cases a miniature wooden house raised on piles or a roofed platform, the corpse remained in state until its flesh was gone. At this time, the village prepared a "great feast" (magnitude determined by length of decay), and the bones were processed and reburied at a new location. Combining these rituals with observations on religious practices in Borneo, Hertz proposed that the fate of the body in these death rites was analogous to the fate of the soul. The corpse, in the process of decay and putrescence, was a model for the soul: during the "intermediary period," the soul was homeless and an object of dread, unable to enter the afterlife. The feast, he observed, marked the end of this period and the celebration of the soul's arrival into the land of the dead, indicated by the now-dry bones and the reestablishment of more "friendly" social relations with the deceased.[16] Stressing the interrelationship of corpse, soul, and mourners, Hertz provided a case study and model for future analyses of burial rites and secondary burials.

Scholarship since these two seminal works has illustrated their strengths as well as their weaknesses. As noted by Peter Metcalf and Robert Huntington, van Gennep's initial idea—that rituals have a beginning, a middle, and an end—appears simplistic. The merit of his analysis, as they assert, is in demonstrating the similarities between the preliminal, liminal, and postliminal rituals; each involves a symbolic "death" of the old status and the construction of a new one.[17]

With respect to death rituals, the liminal phase has been a topic of much elaboration. For example, in exploring the concept of "liminality" in the death rites of the Ndembu of southern Africa, Victor Turner developed the view that liminality was a "state of transition" whereby the deceased was "betwixt and between" normal societal roles. Extending this analysis outside of southern Africa, Turner saw the liminal period as a static, autonomous point in the death process.[18] Metcalf and Huntington have criticized this view, cautioning that the static view of liminality divorces it from larger processes of change and transformation. Liminality, they argue, should be explained in terms of change, process, and passage.[19] Yet even van Gennep observed that liminality in death rites could be somewhat static:

A study of the data . . . reveals that the rites of separation are few in number while the transition rites have a duration and complexity sometimes so great that they must be granted a sort of autonomy.[20]

Likewise, some of the most influential modern mortuary studies have drawn upon van Gennep's tripartite arrangement to analyze the relationship between funerary ritual and social structure. Occasionally we see a disparity between mortuary behavior and social status, a problem facing archaeologists in the field as well as sociocultural anthropologists. As observed by Jack Goody and Peter

Metcalf in West Africa[21] and Borneo, respectively, this disconnection can take the form of ennoblement, where corpses of politically unimportant or marginal individuals are dressed in royal finery or set within elaborate mausoleums. Death provides an excuse for a leader to consolidate power, as per Metcalf, or a social group to direct attention to its prosperity in the form of a dressed body, as among the Lo Dagaa in West Africa. While this ennoblement may not be relevant to royal funerals among the Classic Maya,[22] the idea that a tripartite or similar arrangement can be manipulated to serve political ends will be a central theme in this book.

Despite these adaptations of van Gennep's work, his basic tenets remain widely used in the anthropology of death. Wary but admiring of the application of his ideas to multiple societies, Metcalf and Huntington have provided the best criticism and defense of van Gennep to date:

> Van Gennep's notion that a funeral ritual can be seen as a transition that begins with the separation of the deceased from life and ends with his or her incorporation into the world of the dead is merely a vague truism unless it is positively related to the values of the particular culture. The continued relevance of van Gennep's notion is not due to the tripartite analytical scheme itself, but to the creative way it can be combined with cultural values to grasp the conceptual vitality of each ritual.[23]

The model of preliminal, liminal, and postliminal rites *must therefore be culturally embedded to be analytically useful.*

Equally important are critiques and revisions of the model provided by Hertz. The idea that the passage of the soul is comparable to the decay of the body may indeed be an "invariate universal,"[24] but exceptions have been observed. In Madagascar, for example, Bara funeral customs lack the concept of a journeying soul, whereas clearly defined conceptions of an afterlife are characteristic of Merina funeral rites.[25] Moreover, Hertz did not take into account issues of differential status in his work, a just criticism[26] equally relevant to sociocultural and archaeological anthropology.

Focusing wholly on these exceptions and refinements, however, ignores the scope and intent of Hertz's work. The majority of his ideas did not address "universal" theories of death like van Gennep; he limited his work to a set group of cases within a clearly defined culture area. The true value of his approach to scholars outside Indonesia can be found in the idea that one can review the symbolism of death rites to find mirrors in changing societal roles and relations. It is the idea that the fate of the body *can* mirror the fate of the soul—or a change in the relationship between deceased and society—and not that it *will*, that can be applied outside the Indonesian context. As Catherine Bell has pointed out, the body is not necessarily the "mere physical instrument of the mind" but can represent the social person; as such, we should compare the rites and attitudes associated with the physical body in order to understand changes to the social one.[27]

Therefore, the purpose of this book is *not* to force the models of van Gennep, Hertz, Turner, or others onto the Classic Maya example, but to examine their more general tenets within the context of Maya archaeology, epigraphy, and iconography. Karl Taube was the first to apply the idea of liminality to Mesoamerican examples in his work on Yucatecan New Year festivals;[28] further efforts to tie Mesoamerican archaeology to such models have been made, for example, by Shirley Mock in her study of termination rites.[29] The present work builds upon their initiatives by drawing on models of liminality and body-soul equivalency to explain Classic Maya mortuary behavior. To illustrate how these ideas can be investigated with respect to the Classic Maya, it is perhaps useful to take an example from one of the largest and best-known cities of tropical lowland Mesoamerica.

THE CLASSIC MAYA CASE

Flourishing within the lush jungle of the southern Yucatán Peninsula (Figure 1), the great Maya cities of the Classic Period rose and fell in a period roughly bounded between AD 250 and AD 909.[30] Among the palace complexes, administrative buildings, and temples at the heart of these centers, Maya rulers commissioned monuments bearing hieroglyphs and portraits illustrating themes of dynastic succession, conquest, and courtly life. One of the best-known polities, centered at the site of Piedras Negras on the Usumacinta River, has been pivotal to our understanding of the Maya inscriptions. As the setting for two major archaeological projects, Piedras Negras has likewise served as a focal point for investigations into nearly every aspect of Classic Maya society, from art and architecture to political economy. Several years ago, I examined the ways in which royal anniversaries—events commemorating births, deaths, and other aspects of personal life—were observed by the Piedras Negras dynasts. The twenty-year anniversary of the death of a ruler, for example, might be marked by a special dance; it might even be celebrated by a "visit" to the tomb so that his survivors could gain access to his remains. Discussing similar practices at the sites of Copan and Seibal, I noted that the time between an initial event—death—and subsequent rites varied within and between sites throughout the Classic Maya lowlands.[31]

In the case of K'inich Yo'nal Ahk I (Ruler 1) of Piedras Negras, who died on February 6, 639 (9.10.6.2.1 5 Imix 19 K'ayab), the interval was approximately twenty years; our next record of events begins on October 11, 658 (9.11.6.1.8 3 Lamat 6 Keh). On this day the tomb of Ruler 1 was "censed," that is, burning torches, incense, or both were brought within the burial chamber. Six days later, on the one-*k'atun* (ca. twenty-year) anniversary of the death of his father,

FIGURE I. *The Maya area (after Fash 1991b, fig. 4)*

Ruler 2 received a number of royal helmets. Mimicking a rite that took place hundreds of years prior to the occasion and is mentioned on Piedras Negras Panel 2 (Figure 2), this second phase was overseen by the Maya god of lightning (Chaak), an unknown entity (1-Banak 8-Banak), and a figure dubbed the "Jaguar God of the Underworld." Conjured to witness this occasion, these gods were probably complemented by a retinue of earthly subordinates. Clearly, this was an important event in the history of Piedras Negras, where political and religious events converged at precisely recorded times.

The events surrounding these activities are well known. Following the death of K'inich Yo'nal Ahk I, his son waited almost four months to take office. As I demonstrate in subsequent chapters, he may have waited almost a week to lay his father to rest; his successors and contemporaries in the Maya area spent varying—sometimes copious—amounts of time waiting to inter their dead.[32] Thus for the lords of Piedras Negras, we have discrete, dated ceremonies occurring on ritually significant days attached to the death of a ruler. Numbered

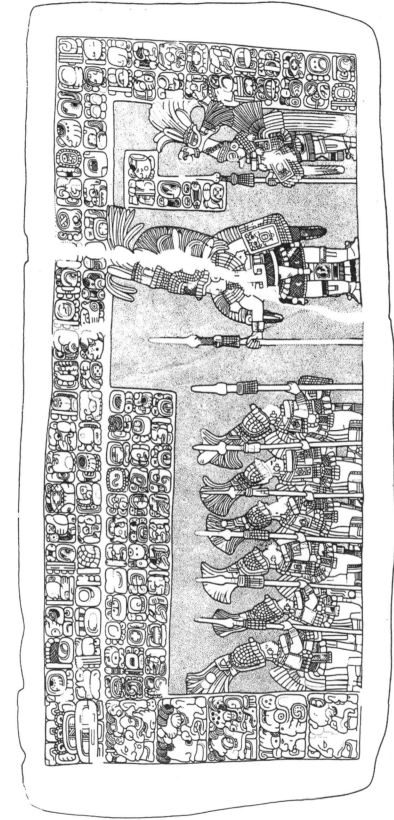

FIGURE 2. *Piedras Negras Panel 2 (Stuart 2003; from the Corpus of Maya Hieroglyphic Inscriptions, Vol. 9, Part 1: Piedras Negras)*

lapses in time, involving kingship and reigns of rulers, as well as a rich assortment of items recorded on monuments, are complemented by archaeological information confirming a pattern of "tomb firing" at Piedras Negras. Completing this picture is an assortment of scholarly literature on Classic Maya beliefs in the underworld and a wealth of ethnographic data on afterlives, ancestors, and episodic funerary behavior.

From this brief introduction, we might find a series of events that *could* spell "stages of death" for the Classic Maya rulers of Piedras Negras. The length of time involved in the mortuary rites for K'inich Yo'nal Ahk I suggests practices not unlike those observed by van Gennep and Hertz for radically different societies, involving a "middle period" when royal society at Piedras Negras was in transition. But while it is tempting to try to fit the death of Ruler I into a tripartite scheme or other universal, it seems more useful to analyze the Classic Maya example as an entity unto itself. As Metcalf and Huntington note:

> It is necessary not merely to apply an old formula to new rituals, but in a sense to create anew the rites of passage in a dynamic relationship among the logic of the schema (transitions need beginnings and ends), biological facts (corpses rot), and culturally specific symbolizations.[33]

By examining the Classic Maya case for archaeologically, textually, and iconographically represented rituals, we can begin to reconstruct models for how the Maya conceived of death and, perhaps more importantly, how mortuary rites were carried out from beginning to end. In creating these models, we might find that the sociocultural anthropology of death—as represented by the ideas of van Gennep, Hertz, and their successors—and the archaeological anthropology of the Maya are two halves of a greater conceptual whole.

METHODOLOGICAL CONCERNS

The royal focus of the Classic Maya inscriptions presents limitations for this study of ancient rites of death and burial. Written by and for a ruling minority, the texts were a form of communication shared between select individuals in polities throughout the Classic Maya landscape. Given that this study is a comparison of what can be gleaned from the archaeological, epigraphic, and iconographic records of kings in combination, I focus out of necessity on the royal sector of Classic Maya society, as defined by the burials of rulers or their immediate families. That royal sector in turn is limited to those sites—largely confined to the southern lowlands—that historically bore a tradition of strong, centralized kingship. As these burials were not, for the most part, the result of human sacrifice, I do not generally focus on this concept, a topic requiring separate volumes for its importance in Classic Maya history. The ideas and conclusions expressed in this book thus center on a fairly small segment of Classic Maya society in space and time. Nevertheless, burials from all segments and geographic areas of the Classic Maya world are available for study and comparison, and where applicable, I use their data for analogy to the royal situation.

There is clear evidence that many sites shared common beliefs about the afterlife and the process of death. These commonalities are most observable in the phrasing of death (e.g., *k'aay u sak* "flower" *ik'il*, "it finishes, his white flower breath," or *ochb'ih*, "road-entering") on Maya monuments and in the use of conventions in grave construction, grave goods, symbolism, and site layout. The "ideology" of a Maya tomb, as Michael Coe has described,[34] *is* somewhat universal. The problem lies in the application of these broad views on death to individual contexts:[35] most of the burials to be discussed, even within a single site or narrow time frame, display variations on common themes of descent, rebirth, and flowery paradises. Where appropriate, I deal with these variations and commonalities epigraphically as well as archaeologically. We might look to wider sociopolitical developments in the lowlands to explain this variation: changing power relationships between and within sites certainly affected the dissemination of ideas. Likewise, religion itself is an evolving, changing entity. Fashions come and go and are not always explainable through the lens of politics or social aggrandizement. Where possible, I have used archaeology and epigraphy to delve into this problem, pointing out situations where motives or changing modes of belief are evident.

Another methodological concern lies in the use of the term *royal* to describe interments. Two publications have defined criteria by which interments, barring epigraphic evidence, can be identified as royal. The first of these, by Estella Weiss-Krejci and T. Patrick Culbert, addresses a broad lowland sample of Maya burials and defines royal burials by the statistical frequency of tombs, ceramics in large quantity (>13), red pigments, earflares, stingray spines, jades in large quantity, pearls, obsidian blades, and mosaics. In this study, there is a broad correlation between the first six of these categories, with smaller frequencies of the latter three. The second publication, limited to Piedras Negras and by Fitzsimmons et al., identifies a royal burial based on a series of similarities with other high-status interments at the site. In this case, the similarities include a carved bloodletter, a large number of jade artifacts, a jade stingray spine, the presence of a vaulted tomb, and hieroglyphs identifying its occupant as "royal." Yet no pearls, obsidian eccentrics, or mosaics were recovered; only one vessel was found within this tomb. Clearly there are some discrepancies between these definitions of royalty.

However, we must remember that sites were discrete entities, and kings, the rulers of distinct—and oftentimes independent—polities. Alberto Ruz Lhuillier (1968) and W. B. M. Welsh (1988) have noted a series of significant regional and local patterns, including:

1) a relative paucity of grave ceramics in Palenque and Piedras Negras interments;

2) a comparatively small number of bowl-over-skull burials at Copan, Piedras Negras, Palenque, and Tonina;

3) the reuse of graves for successive interments at Tonina and Palenque;

4) a predominantly northern head orientation for graves at Piedras Negras, Palenque, Tonina, Tikal, and Uaxactun; and

5) a predominantly eastern head orientation for graves at Uaxactun (temples only), Dzibilchaltun, Seibal, Altar de Sacrificios (northern in residences), Copan, and Altun Ha (only in residences).

Thus while a broader model of royalty is both necessary and useful for comparing funerary behaviors at sites, we must keep in mind local patterns as well. What is identifiably royal at a site like Tikal—where royal burials adhere to or even exceed all qualifications of royalty heretofore provided—cannot be wholeheartedly applied to qualify or disqualify royal interments elsewhere, particularly at sites like Palenque or Piedras Negras. Consequently, I primarily limit the sample of this study to individual interments identified epigraphically, iconographically, archaeologically, or contextually as royal by their excavators. At the same time, I have designated as "royal" a small number of burials that, while falling within the Weiss-Krejci and Culbert parameters for royalty, clearly stand apart from other local or regional interments. The result is a conservative list of royal burials, which appears as Appendix 1, that takes into account individual site peculiarities. The burials in this appendix do not represent all of the known royal burials in the Classic Maya lowlands; instead, they represent a sample of burials about which enough information is published or readily accessible to provide insights into the kings and queens of the Classic Maya world.

A final methodological concern involves the applicability of ethnographic and ethnohistoric data. Conceptions of death drawn from these sources are set within a context of syncretic pre- and postcontact ideas ranging between God and indigenous supernaturals. Ethnohistoric accounts from Yucatan, for example, display an amalgamation of Christian and native conceptions of the afterlife:

They said that this future life was divided into a good and a bad life—into a painful one and one full of rest. The bad and the painful one was for the vicious people, while the good and the delightful one was for those who had lived well according to their manner of living. The delights which they said they were to obtain, if they were good, were to go to a delightful place, where nothing would give them pain and where they would have an abundance of foods and drinks of great sweetness, and a tree which they call there *yaxche*, very cool and giving great shade, which is the ceiba, under the branches and the shadow of which they would rest and forever cease labor. The penalties of a bad life, which they said that the bad would suffer, were to go to a place lower than the other, which they called Metnal, which means "hell," and be tormented in it by the devils and by great extremities of hunger, cold, fatigue and grief.[36]

Thus, it is difficult to draw the line between pre- and postcontact developments with certainty; we cannot divorce this "heaven" and "hell" of sixteenth-century Yucatan from what *we* identify as "native" in postcontact accounts. Nowhere is the problem of analogy more evident than in our own conceptions of the Classic Maya Underworld (Figure 3), largely based on a postcontact version of the Quiche *Popol Vuh*. To draw absolute correlations between the Classic and the Colonial is to deny seven hundred years of indigenous religious change that developed through the influx of Christianity, Central Mexican, lowland, and highland ideas.

However, even in examining ethnographic and ethnohistoric sources it is clear that there are widespread similarities crossing ethnic, temporal, and linguistic boundaries. For example, central to many conceptions of illness and death among the modern and historic Maya is the idea of "soul-loss," a concept observed among the Lacandon, the Zinacantecos, and a number of highland Maya groups. Death is the result of "fright" from the gods, the death of an animal spirit-companion, or the sale of the soul to the "Earth Lord" (*witz*).[37] Similar ideas are represented in the ethnohistoric literature by such texts as *The Book of Chilam Balam of Chumayel* and *The Ritual of the Bacabs*.[38] For these groups, the soul is thought to leave the body at the point of death, eventually joining a pool of ancestors worshipped at the community or individual level. There is clear evidence that similar ideas are represented in the archaeology and epigraphy of the ancient Maya.

Illustrating this point are two examples of soul-loss and ancestor worship from Classic Maya texts. The idea that the soul is removed from the body as a cause and function of death is represented textually by the use of the word *ik'*, synonymously translated as "breath," "life," "spirit" in death phrases on monuments and pottery: *k'a'ay u sak* "flower" *ik'il*, "it ends, his white ? breath." Visually, this breath is depicted as "traveling" on pottery, where death's heads appear with ascending *ik'* glyphs pouring from their nostrils. While there are no concrete associations of *sak ik'* in Ch'orti', the closest modern relative to the language of the Classic Maya, *sak-ik'* in Colonial Yucatec is translated as a "wind coming from the west."[39] This direction, in turn, has long been associated with the solar mythology of the Classic Maya Underworld. This "traveling" soul appears to have been one of many souls residing in the Classic Maya body. The

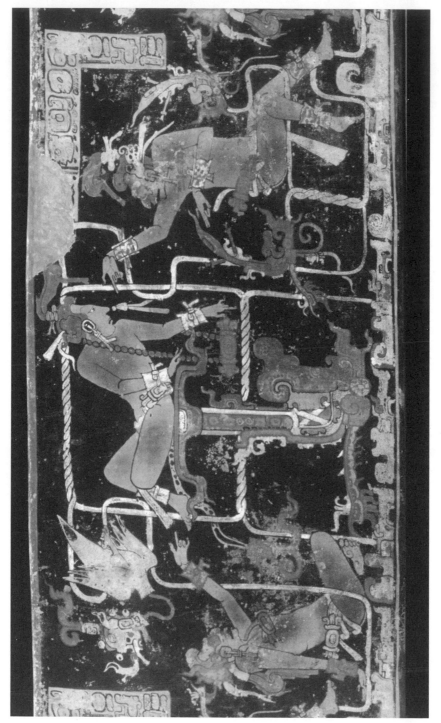

FIGURE 3. *An Underworld scene (#688 © Justin Kerr)*

idea of multiple souls is preserved today in highland societies in the form of animal spirit companions or souls, who share the fate of the soul corresponding to the Classic Maya *ik'*.

A second example concerns the use of *ch'ab'-ak'ab'*, "penance-darkness,"[40] a phrase observed on a number of monuments in the Peten. Associated with the conjuring of ancestors in a variety of situations, *ch'ab'-ak'ab'* rituals involve a number of archaeologically recoverable items of penance, including stingray spines and bloodletting bowls. In ethnohistoric accounts, *ch'ab'-ak'ab'* is a phrase used in the curing of sicknesses, conjuring ancestral and supernatural entities to perform their healing task:

> Removed is creation (*ch'ab*), removed is darkness (*akab*), from the bond of its force at the place [o]f Ix Hun-pudzub kik, Ix Hun-pudzub-olom. There he took his force, at the place where he vomited water, [if] not water, then clotted blood.[41]

Similarities such as these cannot be ignored; that both ancient and colonial sources mention the conjuring of ancestors and supernaturals indicates some continuity in theology. Therefore, remembering their distance in time, we can look to further parallels between ancient, colonial, and modern rites to gain insight into Classic Maya mortuary ceremonialism.

KINGSHIP AND THE ANCESTORS

In any discussion of death and the rituals surrounding it, notions of an afterlife must come into play. Despite an abundance of iconographic depictions of the Maya Underworld, few texts even come close to describing the Classic Maya conception of it. As noted earlier, analyses of ceramic or monumental depictions of the Underworld have traditionally focused on imagery from the *Popol Vuh* or other Colonial Period sources,[42] despite the fact that no known glyph for Xibalba, or the Underworld, exists. While a complete study of the Underworld is far beyond the scope of this work, some basic theories on how the afterlife was conceived are necessary, particularly with respect to a widespread facet of Classic Maya life—ancestor worship. Setting up this afterlife will be the task of the following chapter, although as a pivotal concept the afterlife does factor into many interpretations and analyses. It is particularly relevant when we deal with the relationship between dead kings and their successors. Far from being a paradise divorced from earthly concerns, the royal hereafter was all too often yet another stage involving consultations, oversight committees (albeit supernatural ones), and other forms of episodic contact.

Numerous ways in which ancestors were perceived, summoned, and used have surfaced in recent years. Addressing the nature of ancestor worship in

Living with the Ancestors (1995), Patricia McAnany has done much to raise our awareness of reverential behavior in Classic Maya archaeology.[43] Since that publication, items such as Classic Maya heirlooms, elaborate rituals of conjuring, and volumes of "fired" tombs throughout the lowlands have come to light. Although disturbed burials were initially viewed as signs of disrespect, we now accept many of them as signs of reverence or political manipulation.[44] Ancestors are today viewed as having an even more "active" role in Classic Maya elite life: "dancing" on his son's birthday, a deceased Ruler 2 of Piedras Negras exemplifies this line of thought.[45]

Given that this study primarily examines royal rituals of death, the process by which a ruler is turned into an ancestor is of great concern. As noted by van Gennep and Hertz, the transition from a living individual to an ancestor is a transformative one. This process is in evidence for the Classic Maya, as noted by Linda Schele and Peter Mathews, in such visual media as the Sarcophagus Lid of Pakal at Palenque, where its famous ruler, K'inich Janaab' Pakal I, is shown in ascendance with a "garden of ancestors" flanking his rise.[46] Despite the clarity of iconography depicted in this example, there is some question as to what happens to the institution of kingship when a ruler dies. It is clear that at some point the status of ancestor is reached, whereupon the ruler is engaged as an ancestor in a variety of religious and politically motivated rituals. It is the point between death and dynastic succession, mentioned earlier for Piedras Negras Ruler 1, that is troubling. Exploring why sites have long interregna brings up issues of the body politic versus the body natural, itself a topic of wide anthropological and historical concern.[47]

Research into the nature of death rituals and ancestor worship among the Classic Maya kings has implications for the study of the burials of elites and commoners. Being able to reconstruct not only the rituals involved but also the ideas that drove them highlights the similarities and differences of a belief system spanning the Maya lowlands. While Classic texts were written by and for native and visiting dignitaries, some of the largest results of royal mortuary practice—in the form of temples and other large-scale monuments—were visible to individuals outside the royal sector. In a sense, the way in which Classic Maya kings represented death communicated it to others. This is not to say that belief systems were wholly shared between royal, elite, and nonelite groups, but it is at least probable that commoners learned where their rulers were going after death. Some of the same burial practices, in terms of grave goods (albeit on a much smaller and poorer scale), were indeed shared on a number of status levels. Accordingly, general concepts of an afterlife, whatever the status of the individual, were probably active for the descendants of the dead. Whether this Underworld was viewed as the horrific Xibalba or a place of "food and drinks of great sweetness"[48] will be discussed in the sections to come.

TWO

DEATH AND THE AFTERLIFE
IN THE LOWLANDS

As observed by Alfredo López Austin in his seminal work, *The Human Body and Ideology*,[1] Central Mexican peoples of the Colonial Period saw mortality as an acquired attribute. It was a stigma procured during sex or maize consumption: ingesting maize and participating in sexual activity were ways of consuming death and incorporating it into the body. In eating maize, they brought what was born of the earth—of the realm of death—into their bodies and hence began participation in a larger life cycle.[2] Knowing *in teuhtli, in tlazolli,* "the dust, the filth," of sex was likewise viewed as a willing surrender of oneself to the things of the earth. For all save nursing children, these activities would eventually result in death and one of many afterlives; babies simply returned to heaven to await "successful" birth once more. The implication here is that human beings, were they able to refuse the earth, would live forever. We see this in the treatment of Aztec children in the Florentine Codex, who do not die in the traditional sense: "[They] were the ones who never knew, who never made the acquaintance of dust, of filth . . . they become green stones, they become precious turquoise, they become bracelets."[3] Instead of reaching Mictlan, they go to Tonacacuauhtitlan to await a second birth, nursed under the branches of a World Tree. Gonzalo Fernández de Oviedo y Valdés cites an alternative view for the Nicaraos, who believed that children who died before eating corn would resuscitate and return to earth as men.[4]

Unfortunately, we do not have similarly detailed information for the Classic Maya; it is easier to discuss stages of Classic Maya death than ancient conceptual rationales for mortality. There are no indications that sex, in the Classic Maya worldview, was causally connected with mortality. Maize, however, may have been viewed as a source of death—as well as life—for the Classic Maya. To make this case, it is necessary to review Classic Maya beliefs about the earth as a realm of death, and its relationship to the mythological and symbolic attributes of maize. In examining Classic Maya rationales for mortality, we bring ourselves closer to understanding the epigraphic and archaeological practices surrounding death. We must keep in mind, however, that much like the Nicarao example, there may have been concurrent—but not necessarily contradictory—models of death during the Classic Period. As a result, the following can only provide a general framework for death as we know it from Classic sources.

EARTH

Throughout space and time, Mesoamerican peoples have considered the earth to be a living thing. It is a kind of divinity personified. Mountains are analogous to heads, caves to mouths or wombs, and rocks to bones.[5] Far from being humanoid, the earth in Classic Maya times was represented by a number of different metaphors, though turtles (tortoises) or crocodiles, floating upon a primordial sea, are usually the creatures featured. Tonina Monument 69, for example, displays a deceased ruler sitting atop the glistening, stylized head of a crocodile (Figure 4).[6] Natural features were supernatural in aspect. Breathing clouds or eating sacrificial victims (Figure 5), caves and mountains were ubiquitous, facially expressive subjects of Maya art and architecture.

This lack of distinction between the supernatural and natural worlds is further complicated by the fact that Mesoamerican peoples consider the earth to be a place of death. "Lineage mountains" and caves play a significant role in contemporary Maya ancestor worship,[7] and they clearly served a similar purpose during the Classic Period. Constructing mountain temples within their cities, the Classic Maya created houses for their dead[8] bearing images of new life, vegetative (maize) growth, and nature personified. Caves, either natural or replicated within funerary structures, were similarly portrayed: whether burying their dead in caves or carving vegetative and Underworld themes into stone, scribes and their lords brought the anthropomorphic earth and death together visually as well as physically. At El Peru, a site in the northwest Peten, they are brought together textually. El Peru Stela 3 describes a deceased lord named K'inich B'alam who spent fifty-two years—a complete Calendar Round— within the "heart of the turtle," *'ol ahk*.[9] This rare insight into the El Peru mindset recalls the anniversaries of Piedras Negras. When viewed in the context of Classic Maya burials, it reminds us that tombs are collections of ideas as well as material remains.

A further elaboration on these themes has been provided by Michel Quenon and Geneviéve Le Fort,[10] who have outlined a sequence of events on monuments, vessels, and unprovenanced ceramics involving the death and resurrection cycle of a Classic Maya Maize God. Although there are a number of variations in this mythology, representing local or regional theological differences, the basic sequence of events remains the same. The death of the Maize God, represented by his image sinking below the surface of the watery Underworld, is followed—after an indeterminate length of time—by his naked rebirth from a "fish-serpent," one of a host of serpentine creatures that act as conduits for supernatural beings.[11] The god is then dressed in all his finery by several female

FIGURE 4. *The death of Wak Chan K'ahk' and the Seven-Black-Yellow-Place of Tonina Monument 69 (Mathews 1983)*

attendants and placed in a canoe. Piloting this canoe are two figures nicknamed the Paddler Gods, the same figures who ferried him into the Underworld. Presumably paddled to his final destination, the Maize God then emerges from the carapace of a turtle (Figure 6). Chaaks, or the Classic equivalents of the Hero Twins of the *Popol Vuh,* assist him in this endeavor, cracking open the turtle carapace with lightning weapons or watering him so that he will sprout. Stephen Houston has interpreted these Hero Twins as primordial cultivators who act in a fashion similar to those featured on Copan's Altar T (Figure 7).[12]

Parallels can be drawn between the Maize God and the individual from El Peru. They are both inside the "turtle" at some point; the Maize God is reborn, but not yet resurrected within that space. When he is resurrected, it is from a place of death. The implication is that he is reborn—but still dead—until the carapace is cracked and he is allowed to grow. This fits nicely with the

FIGURE 5. *Chaak, God A, and the Jaguar God of the Underworld (#4011 © Justin Kerr)*

FIGURE 6. *Hun Ajaw and Yax B'alam (#K1892 © Justin Kerr)*

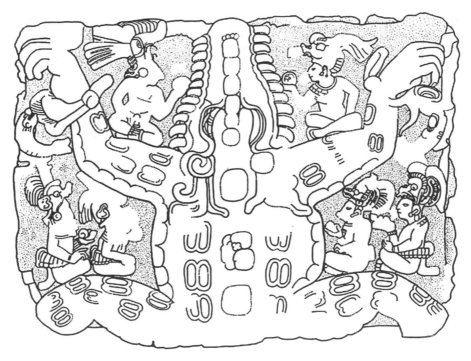

FIGURE 7. *Crocodile from Copan Altar T (after Schele and Miller 1986, fig. 22)*

distinction between rebirth and resurrection drawn by Quenon and Le Fort: rebirth is the animation of the deceased in the Underworld, whereas resurrection is the reanimation of the deceased outside the Underworld.[13] In the case of the Maize God, this resurrection involved his return to the surface of the earth through the back of the "turtle."

MAIZE

As a metaphor for the annual agricultural cycle, the story of the Maize God goes far beyond ancient conceptions of landscape. Karl Taube has made a case for these events describing not only the origins of corn in Mesoamerica, but also the creation of mankind:

> Although it is not mentioned in the early colonial Popol Vuh, the resurrection of the maize god by the hero twins and the Chacs adds an important insight into the underlying meaning of the journey of the hero twins in search of their father [as mentioned in the *Popol Vuh*]. In addition to vengeance, their mission is to resurrect him from the underworld and thus bring maize to the surface of the earth . . . in the Quichean Popol Vuh, the search for maize immediately follows the vanquishing of Xibalba and the partial revival of Hun Hunahpu and Vucub Hunahpu. This maize is the source of the modern race of humans, the people of corn.[14]

The idea that the Classic Maya, like their colonial and modern descendants, saw themselves as "people of corn" is an important one.[15] It implies a special relationship between the Classic Maya and their landscape, suggesting a parallel between the Maize God cycle and the human experience. Certainly Maya kings sought to demonstrate this relationship, portraying themselves as Maize Gods on stelae such as Copan Stela H (Figure 8). In doing so, kings like Waxaklajuun Ub'aah K'awiil (18 Rabbit)[16] placed themselves at the center of a mythology characterized by agricultural death and renewal. We may see a more subtle reference to "people of corn" in the Classic Maya term for "adolescent," *ch'ok*[17] (sprout), although in modern Ch'orti' it is used in conjunction with terms for "young beans," "maize," and "moons" (*ch'okb'u'r, ch'oknar,* and *ch'ok e katu',* respectively).[18] Mary Miller and Karl Taube have suggested a pervasive extreme form of maize mimicry by the Classic Maya rulers; they cite the form of cranial deformation used as equivalent to the elongated form of the maize ear.[19] A subsequent work has compared the "thick, lustrous hair" of the Maize God to corn silk, an idea that has implications for how the Maya viewed physical beauty.[20]

The best evidence for parallels between the human and maize cycles, however, comes from depictions on Maya monuments and from the use of maize iconography in Classic Maya tombs. We find human heads sprouting as ears

FIGURE 8. *Waxaklajuun Ub'aah K'awiil as the Maize God on Copan Stela H (drawing by Linda Schele, © copyright David Schele, courtesy of Foundation for the Advancement of Mesoamerican Studies, Inc., www.famsi.org)*

from maize plants (Figure 9), funerary temples covered in iconic corn, offerings of maize plants and images in watery locations, and artifacts in Maya tombs illustrating portions of the Maize God cycle. Such imagery suggests that death, like life, was thought to be a vegetative process; we see parallels of this maize-to-life imagery in the *Popol Vuh*, where stalks of maize dry out when the Hero Twins are "killed" by the lords of Xibalba. We might thus argue that mortality—for the Classic Maya—was viewed as a product of the maize cycle, in which people were born from death in order to live and die again.

Maize, of course, was not simply a crop grown for comparative or religious purposes. As *the* major food source for the Classic Maya, maize was an integral part of life in the lowlands. In addition to being deified, maize was also hu-

FIGURE 9. *Maize personified on the Temple of the Cross at Palenque (drawing by Linda Schele, © copyright David Schele, courtesy of Foundation for the Advancement of Mesoamerican Studies, Inc., www.famsi.org)*

manized, as can be seen in examples from Palenque, where cobs of corn were interchangeable with human heads. This iconographic convention can be seen later in Postclassic highland Guatemala and Central Mexico, where representations of corn are provided with eyes and teeth.[21] A similar attribution of human qualities to maize is an integral part of modern Maya religion. Evon Vogt notes that for the Tzotzil, maize plants, like humans, are believed to have "inner souls," *ch'ulel,* in the ear and heart of each kernel, just as they are found in the heart of each person. Ruth Bunzel observed similar beliefs among the Quiche in Chichicastenango.[22]

MORTALITY

Given the symbolism associated with maize, both as represented by the Maize God and in the humanized aspects of maize in Classic Maya iconography, we might picture the Maya as eating more than just food when they consume corn. As mentioned earlier, various portions of the landscape were believed to be alive and connected to death; maize, as born from that death and eaten by an individual, is anthropomorphized in a variety of contexts. If this anthropomorphism and modern Maya beliefs in souls for maize are any indication of Classic Maya ideas, then we can view this consumption as "soul eating" or, more properly, "death eating." While imitating the properties and supernatural associations of maize on an ideological level, the Maya were eating maize and incorporating it into their bodies. In principle, the concept of eating "of the earth" or *ch'uhlel*, for the Aztecs and Tzotziles respectively, is not altogether different from the idea of "god eating," a term coined in the nineteenth century to identify aspects of Christian practice. In any event, eating maize may have involved a kind of anthropophagy and, by the arguments listed above, was a means of imbibing death and incurring mortality. Perhaps the Classic Maya situation was analogous to that of the modern Tzotzil:

> Man needs to eat in order to live; but in order to eat he sees himself forced to kill other beings. When he eats, he incorporates death into his organism, and so his life, which depends upon death, becomes death.[23]

John Monaghan has spelled out this relationship, echoed in contemporary Quiche, Kekchi, and Central Mexican mythology, as a kind of mutual obligation or covenant: two sides, agreeing to suffer and die for one another (things of the earth consumed, and humans consumed by the earth) make "agriculture and civilized life" possible.[24] Thus, we might postulate that the royal rationale for death arose from two distinct but compatible ideas: (1) it was part of the maize cycle, where the individual is maize, growing and proceeding from death in order to return to it; and (2) it was a function of eating maize, eating of the crocodile, turtle, or other substance wherein death had been planted, thereby *becoming* more like maize and its growth cycle.

Of course, the above rationales for Classic Maya mortality are not explicitly spelled out in the inscriptions. Likewise, although death and rebirth are often depicted in vegetative terms, with Maize God mythology manifested in the tombs and temples of Maya royalty, royal ancestors are not usually depicted as the Maize God resurrected. Instead, they are shown as human-god hybrids, as celestial bodies, or in more abstract forms. The reasons for this are not immediately clear, but they will be elucidated through an examination of ideas about souls and animating entities, royal conceptions of the afterlife, and the ways in which death was phrased on Maya monuments. In short, we must address that ultimate of questions: Where did the Classic Maya rulers believe they went after death? It is to this concern that we will now turn, although I necessarily save a detailed examination of the maize-celestial dichotomy for the end of the chapter.

WRITING DEATH

The Classic Maya kings referred to death in a variety of ways. Perhaps the most basic verb describing death, one that continues in use in a variety of Mayan lan-

FIGURE 10. *The "death" verb* cham *(drawing by James L. Fitzsimmons)*

guages today, is the word *cham-i* or *cham* (Figure 10).[25] In modern and colonial Mayan languages, the root word *cham*, "die," has a number of cross-cultural associations, the most notable of which are: (1) as a root, *cham* is used for words involving sickness or ill health in Ch'orti' and Tzotzil; (2) *cham* is used as a root for words involving the afterlife in Kanhobal and Jakalteko; (3) combined with other nouns, *cham* is used for changes of state in both Kanhobal and Tzotzil, or—perhaps most important in light of what has already been reviewed—as the term for "dried-up corn silk" (*cham-hol* in Tzotzil).[26] Although *cham* is not the primary word for "death" in a number of Mayan languages, it or a permutation of it can be found throughout the highland languages in connection with sickness or mortuary practice.

During the Classic Period, this word for "death" was represented in the inscriptions by a fleshless skull, modified by the syllable -**mi** and the % symbol for death as an infix; this % symbol appears in a variety of iconographic and glyphic contexts on Classic Maya monuments and ceramics. First appearing on a circular altar from Tonina dating to the Early Classic, *cham*, "[he] dies," appears in a variety of Late Classic and Postclassic contexts modified with both -**mi** and -**aw** postfixes. Given the use of -**mi**, it can be argued that the *cham* verb is actually *cham-i*, but we do not have enough information at present to determine which reading is correct;[27] in general, I use *cham* unless -**mi** is specifically used in an inscription. A possible use of *cham* as a descriptive noun can also be found on the famous Tikal Altar 5 (Figure 11), where it describes the defunct, fleshless Lady Tuun Kaywak.

During its time of use, the *cham* glyph was modified to include either a "death-eye" prefix (no syllabic or phonetic value) in the monumental inscriptions or a visual representation of breath, with the glyph *ik'*, "breath, wind," escaping from the nostrils of the skull and depicted on ceramics. This use of the glyph *ik'* in death phrases has been observed in a variety of contexts, both glyphic and linguistic.[28] Given that the living soul is identified as breath or wind throughout Mesoamerica, the implication of the *ik'* form of the *cham* glyph is that a soul is escaping from the nostrils of the skull.[29] Even more telling is the fact that the *cham* glyph, when modified by *ik'*, reads *t'ab'ay*, "[it] ascends"; (Figure 12). *T'ab'ay* usually occurs in a wholly different form, but both variants refer to the raising, literally "ascending," of Classic Maya monuments.[30] Souls, exhaled from dying bodies, rose in much the same way.

Stephen Houston and Karl Taube,[31] illustrating the connection between breath, souls, and fragrant flowers, have suggested that the placement of breath escaping from the nose, rather than the mouth, "alludes to the olfactory quality of the breath-soul, sweet air in contrast to the stench of death and decay." Further developing these ideas in a circulated manuscript, David Stuart has likened these tendrils of breath on ceramics to floral stamens. This would symbolically transform the face of death into that of a flower, exhaling the "perfume" of the soul.

Such ideas are supported by the fact that the hieroglyph for "lord," *ajaw*, began its life as a flower: Stuart has documented a chain of developments spanning the Early and Late Classic Periods that transformed the *ajaw* glyph stylistically

FIGURE 11. *Section of Tikal Altar 5 that describes a woman as deceased (drawing by Linda Schele, © copyright David Schele, courtesy of Foundation for the Advancement of Mesoamerican Studies, Inc., www.famsi.org)*

FIGURE 12. *Breath escaping from nostrils as* t'ab'ay *(#K4572 © Justin Kerr)*

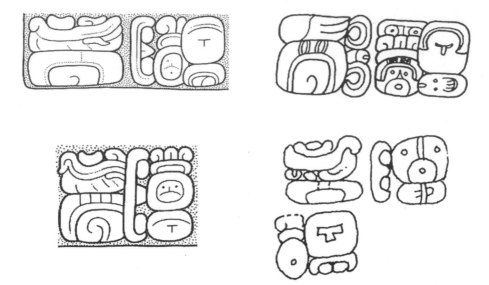

FIGURE 13. *Variants of* k'a'ay u sak *"flower"* ik'il *(clockwise, from top left: Yaxchilan Lintel 27, A2–B2, after Graham and von Euw 1977; Dos Pilas Stela 25, after illustration by Linda Schele [fig. 4.2] from Freidel, Schele, and Parker 1993; Tonina MNAH Disk, after Schele 1982, 136, fig. 11; and Yaxchilan Lintel 27, G2, after Graham and von Euw 1977)*

from flower to face.[32] Residuals of this transformation may also be seen in the Central Mexican equivalent of the Ahau day name, which is Flower, and in the use of *ajaw* glyphs on jade flowers in the Classic Maya lowlands.[33] If we think of the Classic Maya as "composed of" maize, likening their life and death processes to the maize plant, then perhaps these equations of lords and flowers refer more to the souls of individuals rather than to their physical bodies. In death, the body-as-maize may have been transformed into the metaphor of an exhaling flower. The death of a Classic Maya lord could be thought of as putrescent, represented by his decaying body, and as sweet, the manifestation of the breath-soul leaving his lifeless body. As has been observed elsewhere, floral fragrance was symbolic of the vitality of kings—even deceased ones—and as such makes its way into the written and iconographic language of Classic Maya tombs.[34]

This equation of "soul" with "flower" is even more manifest in another phrase for "death," *k'a'ay u sak* "flower" *ik'* (or *ik'il*), "it finishes, his white flower breath" (Figure 13), first identified as a death expression by Tatiana Proskouriakoff in the 1960s.[35] Barbara McLeod deciphered the first part of this verb on the Copan Hieroglyphic Stairway in the phonetic spelling of **k'a-a-yi;** from this, David Stuart was able to link the Classic Maya *k'a'ay* to the colonial Tzotzil phrase *ch'ay ik'*, "extinguished breath."[36] Since this discovery, *k'a'ay* (sometimes *ch'ay*) has been widely glossed as "to end, terminate, or finish." It is perhaps interesting to note that the root *k'a* also occurs in modern Ch'orti'; we can find it in a word referring to a type of illness (*k'a'* or *granos,* literally "grain disease") and in the verb *k'a'pes* (to terminate, finish, or arrest). Other modern adaptations of *k'a'ay* illustrate an association with losing and forgetfulness, as in Tzotzil, although there are a few phrases that connect it to "putting an end to" disputes or lives.[37]

Subsequent scholarship has revealed that *k'a'ay u sak* "flower" *ik'* refers to the expiration (*k'a'ay*) of a flower, incorporating the glyph for "white," *sak*, with the stylized *ajaw* flower mentioned earlier and the glyph *ik'*, "wind, breath." Iconographically, the fact that fragrant smells often emanate from *sak*, "white," glyphs only strengthens the analogy between death and floral issue (Figure 14). Houston and Taube have suggested that the agent of this issue is the fragrant white plumeria (*Plumeria alba*),[38] known as *sak nikte'* in Yucatec; the flower is best known for its use in leis or other floral arrangements in the Pacific islands and the Americas.[39] Houston and Taube have likewise noted the association between the plumeria and "wind" in Yucatec. There is no known translation for this glyph; *sak nikte'* does not occur in the inscriptions, and for the time being we must view the "flower" as a specific species probably ending in *k*, based on the suffixes that sometimes accompany the "flower" glyph.[40]

Epigraphically, *k'a'ay u sak* "flower" *ik'* is represented in a variety of ways. It appears to describe the final flowery exhalation of an elite; it is a description of the visual information recorded for the *cham* glyph. Somewhat problematically, the syntax of *k'a'ay u sak* "flower" *ik'* varies between and within sites. In an example from Tonina, the *k'a'ay* glyph is followed by the aforementioned "flower" glyph suffixed by **-ki** and then *sak ik'il*, or "it finishes, his flower white breath." Another example from Palenque seems to be missing the *k'a'ay* verb

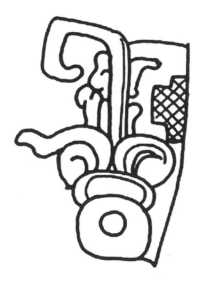

FIGURE 14. Sak, *"white," glyph as an exhaling flower on Stela 14, Yaxchilan (after illustration by Linda Schele [fig. 4.2] from Freidel, Schele, and Parker 1993)*

FIGURE 15. *Phrase* k'a'ay u sak *"flower"* ik' u tis chan ahk hixwitz ajaw b'akab', *"it ends, his white 'flower' breath, his flatulence, Chan Ahk, Lord of Hix Witz, b'akab'"; drawing by Stephen Houston)*

and possessive pronoun; in perhaps this most interesting use of this phrase, the words *juuntahn sak* "flower" *ik'*, "precious white flower breath," are used to describe the deceased K'inich Janaab' Pakal I of Palenque following a string of *juuntahn* phrases.[41] As such, the *k'a'ay u sak* "flower" *ik'* phrase might actually be a couplet:[42] "it finishes, his flower, his white breath." Whether this separates the death of the "flower" and[from?] the death of the white breath (*sak ik'*) is at present unclear; differences in ideas about death at Tonina and Palenque may be manifested by such variations in phrasing.

In one example of the *k'a'ay u sak* "flower" *ik'* phrase, on a looted onyx bowl, there is an addition to the usual death expression: *k'a'ay u sak* "flower" *ik u tis*, "it finishes, his flower breath, his flatulence" (Figure 15). David Stuart has identified and contrasted these two breaths, one as oral and sweet, the other as anal and foul.[43] Given the obvious biological associations of flatulence with death, it is possible that the contrast between these two breaths is really a contrast between the breath of life and the breath of death. The word *kis,* analogous to the *tis* of the inscriptions and found in various forms in modern Mayan languages as the word for "flatulence" or "excrement" (e.g., *kiis* or *kisiij* in Quiche, *tsis* in Tzotzil, or *tis* in Ch'orti'), can be found as a root in the name of one of the Classic Maya death gods, known as Schellas God A, in the Madrid Codex. It is also the name of a Death God among modern Yucatec and Lacandon populations, who is glossed as the rather unfortunate "flatulent one."[44]

Visual analogies to this noxious quality in Classic Maya death gods can be found in iconographic representations of God A', versions of which have been identified as Akan or Mok Chi (Figure 16). Tied to the Classic Maya version of Xbalanque of the *Popol Vuh,* Mok Chi is usually shown as a reclining figure with a distended belly who bears the same *ak'b'al,* "darkness," vase around his neck as Schellas God A.[45] Aside from his closed eyes, which are replicated on *cham* glyphs and dead individuals throughout the corpus of hieroglyphic inscriptions, his distension is almost certainly an allusion to death. Gods and mortals (*sitz' winik*) are sometimes shown dying in this distended, reclining position; their swollen bellies likely result from a buildup of internal gases.[46] Distending the stomach and navel, these gases are in contrast to the flowery exhalation: just as *ik'* is the breath of life, the other exhalation is the breath of death. They combine to produce a duality in phrasing that places the body of the deceased, in this case Chan Ahk of Hix Witz, in transition. This breath of life may be further fragmented. It is difficult to say whether the "ending" refers solely to the flowery exhalation or to both, although the contrast here is clear. More on these exhalations will surface in the forthcoming discussion of Classic Maya souls.

Two major death phrases used by the Classic Maya are verbs of "entering": *ochb'ih* and *och ha'* (or possibly *ochha'*), commonly glossed as "road-entering" and "water-entering," respectively. Much like the phrase *och k'ahk',* "fire-entering," used either with *tu yotot,* "in his house," or *tu muknal,* "in his tomb," these verbs involve an act of transformation. In the case of "fire-entering," it seems clear that the objects or structures involved undergo a change of state; building phases are "killed" by fire in termination rituals, new structures are made habitable or "alive," whereas the occupants of tombs at certain sites undergo physical transformation during "firing."[47] In modern Tzotzil, *och,* "to enter," is associated with such phenomena as "becoming" or "changing," as in *och-k'on,* "beginning to yellow [corn]," or *och ta xavon,* "be turned into soap." It is likewise used to refer to curing ceremonies, as in *och kantela* or *och limuxna,* "[to] hold [a] curing ceremony," and entrances into religious posts or the rainy season are referred to as *ochebal.*[48] Perhaps most important for the present discussion, however, are its uses in house dedication: *och kantela na* or *och limuxna na,* practices that have been well documented in Zinacantan during *hol chuk,* "good heart," and *ch'ul*

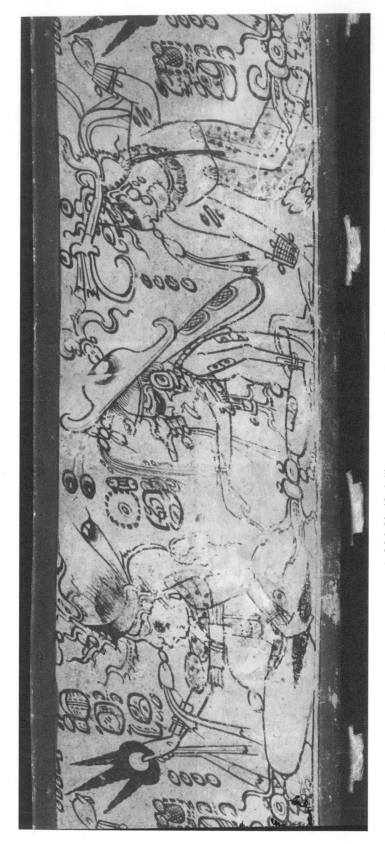

FIGURE 16. *Mok Chi (God A') on an unprovenanced vessel (#K2286 © Justin Kerr)*

FIGURE 17. Ochb'ih, *"road-entering," and* och haj, *"water-entering"; after Schele 1999, 40, and Jones and Satterthwaite 1982, 409)*

kantela, "holy candle," ceremonies.[49] Conceptually, however, the closest phrase to these "entering" verbs occurs in Colonial Yucatec, where *okol k'in* is described as "sun-entering," a phrase used for the death of someone old or infirm.[50] This phrase, of course, has implications for the way in which the Yucatec—and perhaps the Classic Maya themselves—viewed the process of death.

The phrase *ochb'ih,* "road-entering," first identified by David Stuart[51] and often tense modified with **-hi** and **-ya** suffixes, is metaphorically easy to explain in light of modern beliefs but difficult to link definitively with Classic Maya ritual and practice (Figure 17). In literal terms, there are no clear iconographic depictions of roads that incorporate death imagery for the Classic Maya, although there are numerous references to such roads throughout the colonial era *Popol Vuh.* Modern survivals of *bih,* "road," make it clear that this word is associated with paths, roads, ways, and journeys in both common and ritual speech. In Ch'orti', *b'i'r* is not only "road" but also "gap" or "opening," while in Tzotzil, the root word for "road," *b'e,* can be modified by nouns or particles to describe tunnels and entrances to natural features as well as the body. Hence we find phrases like *b'e 'unen,* "vagina," (literally "road of the child"); *b'e sim,* "nostril" (road of mucous); or *b'e-o',* "ravine, ditch" (road of water).[52] Similar associations with channels and trenches can be found in Yucatec (*beel ha',* "canal") and Quiche (*ub'eeja',* "road of water") as well as Mam (*tb'ee waa'ya,* "road of water, canal"; derivatives of *b'ej* in Jakalteko are used to describe "falling" (*b'ejtzo'* and *b'ejtzo'ayoj*).[53] *Ochb'ih* might thus be the beginning of a transformative journey into the darker places of the earth,[54] represented spiritually by the Classic Maya Underworld, along a road of some kind. Stephen Houston has suggested that the Classic Maya *sakb'ih,* or "white road," found at sites like Caracol or Tikal, may be death related. He cites the roads terminating in what are clearly mortuary complexes or pyramids at Caracol, suggesting that movements along these might replicate the movements of the dead in their final journeys.[55]

There is some evidence to suggest that the *ochb'ih* death phrase does not always refer to the demise of the physical body. As I noted in a previous work (1998), there is a record at the site of Piedras Negras of an *ochb'ihiiy,* "[he] road-entered," event for Ruler 2 that postdates his death. There seems to be some disagreement on the original death date, as his *cham,* "death," is recorded as having

Y   Z   A'   B'

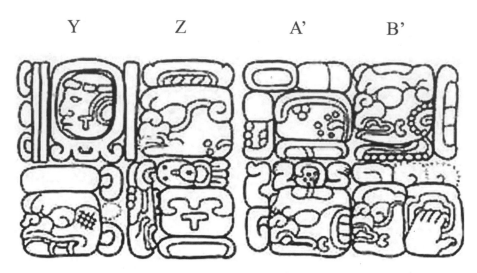

FIGURE 18. *Excerpt from Quirigua Zoomorph G, west (after Looper 1996, fig. 3)*

been on November 16, 686 (9.12.14.10.13 11 Ben 11 K'ank'in) while his *k'a'ay u sak* "flower" *ik'il,* "death," is one day later. This is the only example from the corpus of hieroglyphic inscriptions that incorporates all three "death" expressions for the same individual. While the one-day discrepancy could be attributed to scribal error, it is almost certain that the *ochb'ihiiy* event—six or seven days off—refers to something else.

Simon Martin and Nikolai Grube have suggested that this discrepancy involved the burial of Ruler 2; in their scheme, *ochb'ihiiy* would refer to the burial of Ruler 2 and not his death.[56] This is an important distinction, for it makes *ochb'ih* less of a "death" verb, as it has widely been regarded in the past, and more of a "burial" verb. *Ochb'ih* is therefore an entering into not only a "road" but also a tunnel, gap, or opening; it describes the placement of the body in a tomb a certain number of days after death. How many days this was seems to have varied on a case-by-case basis, ranging from the next day to more than a week after the event (see Chapter 4); presumably some of this was related to grave preparation, although there may have been religious reasons as well.

Yet we already have a verbal phrase, *muhkaj,* "he/she is buried," used at Piedras Negras and elsewhere for burials. *Ochb'ih* would seem a bit redundant. Moreover, at Quirigua there is an example of *ochb'ih* eventually followed by *muhkaj,* on Zoomorph G (Figure 18). In one context, however, *ochb'ih* and "flowery" death are combined: *och'ihiiy u sak* "flower" *ik',* "[the] road was entered [by] his white "flower" breath." There the "breath" has not ended or terminated, but has actually gone on a journey. This may be why we have a discrepancy between the *cham, k'a'ay,* and *ochb'ih* dates at Piedras Negras: there is a split between the physical and spiritual sides of death!

With the transformative properties of the *och* verbs, then, it may be more appropriate to conceptualize *ochb'ih* as encapsulating a variety of implied meanings, elements of religious belief that describe the change of an individual into part of the physical landscape. In its character, *ochb'ih* seems to describe a single action, "road-entering," which is why I have departed from the usual *och b'ih* found in the literature. It is also often a passive phrase, taking a single suffix **-aj** to create *ochb'ihaj*, glossed literally as "[the] road is entered." This makes it fundamentally different from *och k'ahk'*, the active entering of fire into something (bringing fire into a building, for example), a phrase that never uses passive constructions.[57] *Ochb'ih* is something that happens to an individual; the deceased does not enter the road, but rather the road is entered by the deceased. The landscape is changed by the dead.

Phrases like *ochb'ih* or *och k'ahk'* probably had implied meanings beyond the acts of descent or "firing." "Entering fire" is somewhat nonsensical without an underlying knowledge of what that process involves; in our case, some of this knowledge is not transparent, but inferences can be made based on when and how these processes occur. *Ochb'ih* is an example of what I would describe as "embedded mythology," a phrase in the script that implies meaning outside of its literal translation; it involves Classic Maya ideas about the dead in relationship to the landscape and the process of death itself. A better example of this can be found in the second death expression involving *och*, "enter," which is *och ha'*, or "water-entering."[58] Like *ochb'ih*, *och ha'* provides evidence that death was a process instead of a single event.

Only a handful of references to *och ha'* have been identified. Nevertheless, it appears to denote a process of transformation and travel much like *ochb'ih*, For, unlike that verb, there is a wealth of "water-entering" iconography to support the idea that *och ha'* refers to the travel of the soul into the watery Underworld. The watery associations of the Classic Maya Underworld have been extensively documented by Nicholas Hellmuth and elaborated upon in a variety of publications.[59] Perhaps the most visually important description of a deceased individual entering water is found on the bones recovered from Tikal Burial 116 (Figure 19), where the dead Maize God and a host of animals are taken under the surface of the water by individuals dubbed the Paddler Gods. The enigmatic "canoe" glyph sometimes paired with these scenes seems to be related to the action of this "entering," although it seems to be used as a possessed noun (*u* "canoe" *b'aak*, "his 'canoe' bone"). It does occur as a verb in certain contexts, although its meaning is clearly separate from *och ha'*.

In their seminal *Classic Maya Place Names*, David Stuart and Steven Houston have identified the location where the Maize God is going as *u'uk ha' nal*, "Place of Seven Water,"[60] and it is presumably to a similar locale that *och ha'* events are directed. Comparable watery resting places can be found on a variety of ceramic vessels depicting both gods and mortals, where individuals are seen either being thrown by the personified Death God into a watery cave, as on the aforementioned Kerr 4011, or winding around watery bands and being reborn

FIGURE 19. *Iconography on Tikal bones from Burial 116 (after Schele and Miller 1986, fig. VII.1)*

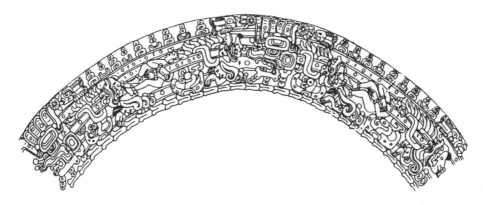

FIGURE 20. *Iconography from Early Classic Río Hondo vase, showing humans clinging to water bands (after Quenon and Le Fort 1997, fig. 17)*

from shells (Figure 20). One notable example from the site of Río Azul, a place that in Early Classic times was under the suzerainty of Tikal, displays an entire tomb decorated in such bands; the death of the lord within the tomb is actually described as his birth, recalling the Maize God resurrection sequence. *Och ha'* is a means of stating that an individual is going into these watery places. Like *och b'ih*, it appears to involve a radical change in the location of the soul.

That the two statements are comparable in their theoretical base is evidenced in part by Tikal Stela 31, where both phrases are used (Figure 21). *Och ha'* is written as the death expression for Chak Tok Ich'aak I (Jaguar Paw), the first well-known ruler of Tikal, while *ochb'ih* is mentioned in the death of Siyaj Chan K'awiil II (Stormy Sky). As the son of Siyaj K'ahk' (the hilariously nick-named Smoking Frog), Siyaj Chan K'awiil II was probably not originally in line for the throne; Siyaj K'ahk' seems to have led a Teotihuacan-related coup over Chak Tok Ich'aak I and placed his son on the throne.[61] Since Chak Tok Ich'aak I met his death by violent means, one wonders whether the difference in phrasing—*och ha'* versus *ochb'ih*—for him was intentional. Certainly there is nothing overtly violent in other examples of *och ha'*, but perhaps the use of these two phrases on the monument was a subtle way of differentiating the victor from the victim in this conflict. At the very least, we are dealing with a kind of substitution, although the nuances in meaning may never be clear.

Research on the aforementioned "canoe" glyph has added an interesting twist to the death phrases described above. Initially proposed to be a death glyph on the aforementioned Tikal bones,[62] the "canoe" glyph seems to be related to the process of watery descent. It is a logographic depiction of the boats used by the Paddler Gods featured on ceramics and other artifacts, and appears to end in -**k,** based on its suffix. These Paddlers are hieroglyphically represented by glyphs incorporating *k'in* and *ak'ab'* main signs at sites like Ixlu, Jimbal, Tonina, and Naranjo.[63] They appear to have been mythologically involved in the transportation of a deceased individual to and from the watery Underworld, as outlined earlier. The "canoe" glyph on the Tikal bones (albeit a possessed noun) is clearly related to downward transport; the dead are descending below the watery surface of the Underworld. As no glyph for rebirth (ascent) involving the Paddlers has yet been identified, it is assumed that the "canoe" verb on Kerr 4692 (the same vessel described earlier for the *k'a'ay u sak* "flower" *ik'il u tis* couplet) represents descent as well.

If we look closely at the phrasing on this vessel (Figure 22), it becomes apparent that three death phrases are involved: (1) the aforementioned death of the Hix Witz *ajaw*, the latest event on the ceramic; (2) the "canoe" glyph phrase; and (3) a third *cham-i* event. Although we cannot read the glyph following the "canoe," it appears to be the same place-name written after the *cham-i ti ? tuun*, reading something like "at/to (the) ? stone"; this phrase also occurs on a fragment from Site Q. The significance of the circular glyph following the first *tuun* is likewise unclear, although Stephen Houston has suggested it is **nu-,** employed here as disharmony lapses.[64] Lacking another name or date for the second *cham* event, the implication is that it refers to the same person being set in the "canoe."

Writing each event as taking place at the same location could mean a variety of things. One option is that both journeys began in the same place at the same time; another is that *ti ? tuun* was merely the starting point. A third, more

FIGURE 21. *Examples of* och b'ih *and* och ha' *on Tikal Stela 31 (after Jones and Satterthwaite 1982, fig. 52)*

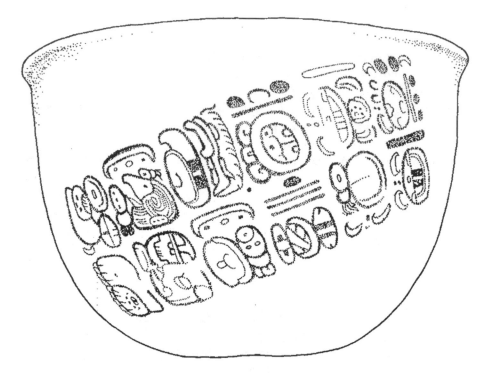

FIGURE 22. *Onyx vessel from Hix Witz (drawing by Stephen Houston)*

unlikely in light of the syntax used with *cham–i*, is that *ti ? tuun* is a place in the Underworld. Given what I have already noted about *ochb'ih* and death as a journey with multiple stages, both at Piedras Negras and in contemporary Maya societies, I find that *ti ? tuun* as a starting point for the journey is the most tenable interpretation. Houston has suggested that *ti ? tuun* is similar to the phrase *och witz* at Tonina, a type of entering conveying a journey into the darker mountain passages of the earth.

In summation, we might view the "death" verbs as being of essentially three classes: (1) verbs that describe changes in the physical body at the point of death, illustrating the escape of the breath of life (and death) from an individual and represented by *cham–i* and *k'a'ay u sak* "flower" *ik'il;* (2) verbs that equate the placement of the physical body into the earth with a spiritual journey to the Underworld, represented by *ochb'ih* and *och ha';* and (3) verbs that largely describe purely physical processes (*muhkaj*) or purely spiritual ones (the "canoe" glyph). Drying up, withering, and sickness are the hallmarks of this first class, whether by implication in the verb *cham–i* or by being visually represented by the dying flower of *k'a'ay u sak* "flower" *ik'il.* Traveling and transformation appear to link those verbs of the second category, while the third category appears to require one of the previous two in its phrasing. Elements from each of these categories, as noted above, can be found in modern-day words for "death" in a variety of contemporary Maya societies. In large part, both categories are concerned with souls, whether they are "escaping" or "entering" into the mythological places of the Underworld, and it is toward an examination of Classic Maya souls that the discussion must now turn.

THE SELF AND THE SOUL

Numerous studies have grappled with the concept of the soul in contemporary Mesoamerica.[65] As John Monaghan has noted, the human soul is often seen as an animating force that can also be possessed by animals, manufactured items, and even buildings.[66] Although the majority of ethnographies involving souls and traveling souls are Central Mexican in origin, there are some notable exceptions, particularly for Tzotzil and Kekchi communities. Nevertheless, it has been observed that in most contemporary Maya communities, including Mam, Tzeltal, Tzotzil, Tzutujil, Lacandon, and Quiche, there is a belief in at least two types of souls, corresponding to an "inner soul" and an "animal spirit companion"; God or the ancestral deities impart these to the individual.[67] Similar beliefs, as well as the widely recognized Central Mexican concept that the body dissolved into various "portions" after death, may have existed among the Classic Maya.[68] To argue this point it is necessary to look at contemporary notions of souls and their relative place in the Mesoamerican worldview.

As observed by Vogt for the Tzotzil Maya, the human body is composed of two separate spiritual parts, the *ch'uhlel* and *ch'anul* (or *wayhel*), corresponding to the "inner, personal soul" or "shadow" and the "animal spirit companion." The first of these has thirteen parts and is centered in the heart, although one source cites that it is air, of a gaseous nature. The loss of some or all of these parts (soul-loss) can lead to sickness or death. This soul-loss is caused by a variety of factors, traditionally involving problems at home or in the civil-religious hierarchy. Death is the result of the most serious forms of loss, and is caused by the gods, by the death of the animal spirit companion, by the sale of the soul to the "Earth Lord," or by accidents and murder.[69] Similar beliefs have been observed for the Quiche, Kekchi, and Lacandon Maya, although in the case of the Kekchi, who, like many groups, ascribe souls to humans, houses, saints' images, maize, bodies of water, and mountains, soul-loss does not result from any connection to an animal spirit.[70]

In addition to being "lost," Tzotzil souls are also thought to travel outside the body, particularly when the individual is unconscious, drunk, ill, having sex, or sleeping. In some cases, a part of the soul, lost in travel, may actively not wish to come back: Calixta Guiteras Holmes notes a common Tzotzil fear that parts of the *ch'uhlel* will actually be happier outside the body, thus causing intentional "soul-loss." Even more fragmentary divisions of the *ch'uhlel* necessarily occur during one's lifetime: parts of the body that share the characteristic of rapid growth and a need to be cut, such as hair or fingernails, contain portions of the soul.[71] These divisions have the result of forcing a human being to leave portions of his soul wherever he has lived.[72] Despite these divisions, however, the *ch'uhlel* is believed to be ultimately indestructible. As Guiteras Holmes relates, upon death, this soul is believed to associate with the grave for a period of time corresponding to the number of years lived on earth; the soul spends this time gathering up the fragmented pieces of *ch'uhlel* spread over the landscape so as to reintegrate itself. It then is believed to rejoin a larger "pool" of souls kept by the gods, to be used eventually for another person. Something similar has been observed among the Quiche, although in that case, there is a soul that becomes an ancestor and another reincarnating entity that loses its prior identity after atoning for the sins of its host.[73]

Alfredo López Austin has identified the Tzotzil *ch'uhlel* with the Central Mexican concept of "shadow," or *tonalli*. In Central Mexico, this is a type of animating (animistic) entity that is linguistically associated with ideas of "heat" and culturally identified as a "center for thought, independent of the heart," one's personal link to the world of the gods. This personal link can be observed in modern meanings of the word *ch'uhlel* and its root, *ch'uh*, as "holy" and "god" respectively. The *tonalli* makes up a person's individuality and has its own desires that need to be satisfied, either through food and drink or by a person's interaction with the things he/she desires. Much like the Tzotzil concept of "soul-loss," the *tonalli* can be seduced by lures during periods of absence comparable to those mentioned for the Tzotzil; it can likewise be taken captive and held against its will by the gods or the dead, to whose world the *tonalli* often travels. According to López Austin, the *tonalli*, like the *ch'uhlel*, is made up of multiple parts; although these total twelve, they can likewise be left in hair, fingernails, and such spread over the landscape and must be collected by the *tonalli* after death. Other characteristics shared between the Tzotzil and modern as well as contact-era Central Mexican populations include: (1) the representation of the *ch'uhlel* and *tonalli* as air, which in the Nahuatl case is the invisible "breath" of the gods; (2) the belief that the *tonalli*, "shadow," or *ch'uhlel* is present in many living things, including plants and hills; and (3) the idea that *ch'uhlel* and *tonalli* are "personal" qualities, ones that are tied to an individual's sense of self and being.[74] Interestingly enough, the Central Mexican concepts of *tonalli* focus on this soul as springing forth from the *head*, not the heart of Tzotzil *ch'uhlel*.[75] Laurencia Alvarez Heidenreich notes, however, that in one modern Mexican community, the "shadow" is believed to withdraw closer to the heart when an individual is injured.[76]

As is the case with the Tzotzil Maya, Aztec and modern Central Mexican traditions hold that the *tonalli*, following death, wanders the earth to gather its disparate parts; one source also has it wandering to restore and repair the goods enjoyed by the individual during life. Following these actions, the Aztec "shadow," for example, entered a box where an effigy drawing the various por-

FIGURE 23. *Glyph for* u b'aah, *"himself, his person, his head," a concept tied to the Central Mexican* tonalli? *(after Graham and von Euw 1977, 15, Lintel 2)*

tions of the *tonalli* was kept with two locks of hair, one saved from the individual at birth and the other from the crown of the head after death.[77]

Available evidence from Classic Maya epigraphy and iconography points to the concept of *b'aah*, "self, person, head" (Figure 23), as being the closest to the Central Mexican concept of *tonalli* and the Tzotzil one of *ch'uhlel*. As Stephen Houston and David Stuart have demonstrated, the glyph *b'aah* has three documented uses: (1) as a literal reference to "self," "person," or "head"; (2) as a metaphor for the "head" or "top" individual of a particular social or political hierarchy; or (3) as an allusion to a physical image that represents the "self." They argue that the emphasis of the *b'aah* "on the head, on surfaces, on partible personalities" points suggestively to a belief that parallels the *tonalli*.[78]

But can we equate the Classic Maya notion of "self" and "image" with an animating spirit? As Houston and Stuart note, the comparison with the *tonalli* is an imperfect one at best. Likewise, there are other Classic Maya concepts that overlap with the "shadows" and *ch'uhlel* of Central Mexican and Tzotzil lore. For example, the Classic Maya words *k'uh*, "god," or *k'uhul*, "holy," linguistically analogous to the Tzotzil *ch'uhlel*, might be considered.[79] Like the Tzotzil *ch'uhlel*, *k'uhul*, "holy," is linked to the blood. It is depicted iconographically as beads of blood dripping from a precious material—such as shell, jade, or bone—or from a variety of colors (typically *k'an*, associated with vegetative growth). Drained during autosacrifice, it is something offered to the gods or ancestors, a portion of the self that is used in conjuring the supernatural. Yet *k'uhul* is tied more to kingship, to an institution, than to an individual: glyphically, the right to use *k'uhul* in a title was confined to Maya rulers, and then only upon accession to office. *B'aah* seems far more universal, a reference to one's own individuality, essence, and personal qualities.

The idea that *b'aah* is a kind of Classic Maya soul is further supported by ethnohistoric and archaeological information from the Maya lowlands. As in the Central Mexican case, mortuary effigy boxes—where wooden images of the deceased were kept—were used in sixteenth-century Yucatán. Following the death of nobles, their cremated ashes were placed within hollow clay statues, put within jars, and kept below temples, while those of "important people" were placed within a receptacle in the *head* of a wooden statue and then placed "with a great deal of veneration among their idols."[80] They were heirlooms, inherited property; Patricia McAnany has likened these images to material symbols of the rights of inheritance, visual evidence of one's ancestry and proper reverence for the deceased.[81] Similarly "curated" cranial bones and wooden effigies have been observed in the Classic Maya lowlands, at Postclassic Chichén Itzá, in the Madrid Codex, and in nineteenth-century Yucatán.[82] Steven Houston and David Stuart have also identified Classic Maya heirlooms bearing the names of ancestors in shell and jade.[83] Perhaps these are in some way connected to concepts of the "shadow" or "self." Indeed, caring for physical representations of ancestors is a common theme in Maya religion. Given the historic concern for physical remains or effigies of ancestors, it seems likely that bones and heirlooms retained some small measure of a soul or "self," an idea we shall return to in later chapters.

Yet the most ubiquitous representation of the Classic Maya "self" argues against the equation of *b'aah* with "soul," at least in the Western conception of the word.[84] Portraits of rulers, in the form of stelae, *are* physical images that represent the self. They may have served in much the same way as the god images or sacred surfaces of contemporary Mesoamerica; as John Monaghan has noted, what makes a god a god in Mesoamerica is usually the "skin," the "bark," the "head," the "face," or the "mask."[85] These surfaces can be images—like wood or stone carvings—or even places such as caves, which for the Kekchi are the faces of the *tzuultaq'as,* or "earth deities."[86] In a sense, we might view a monument such as Copan Stela H (see Figure 8) as a faithful replica of the "self"—in this case of Waxaklajuun Ub'aah K'awiil (18 Rabbit)—even though it was created when that king was alive. That images such as these can be "faithful replicas," however, implies a kind of supernatural quality, and although it is difficult to unequivocally equate this with "soul," it is clear that *b'aah* has *some* of the hallmarks of the souls of contemporary Zinacantan and Central Mexico.

Even partially linking *b'aah* with *tonalli* or *ch'uhlel* raises some interesting questions for the previous discussion of Classic Maya death verbs. Perhaps the most obvious of these is that if the Central Mexican "shadow" and the Tzotzil *ch'uhlel* are "air" or "breath," is the escape of *ik'* depicted for the *k'a'ay u sak* "flower" *ik'il* and *cham* glyphs really the Classic Maya equivalent of "shadow"? Are the discrepancies between the dates for *och b'ih* and *cham* (or *k'a'ay u sak* "flower" *ik'il*) somehow related to journeys of the "shadow" over the earth? These are difficult questions to answer, as there are at least three other candidates for souls or soul-like entities in Classic Maya thought.

BREATHS OF LIFE AND DEATH

The Spanish term *ánima,* corresponding to the Classic Maya word *ik',* has long been linguistically identified with the Central Mexican concept of *teyolia.*[87] *Teyolia* is an animistic entity that, for Central Mexican peoples, resides in the heart and is associated with vitality, knowledge, inclination, and fondness; upon death, this soul is the one to undertake an arduous journey to one of the various afterlives. Like the *tonalli*, the *teyolia* remains on the surface of the earth for a number of days. The *tlatoani* of the Aztecs, for example, could be conversed with up to four days after a person's death, at which time the body was cremated, only to wait another four days before beginning the journey to Mictlan. A similar belief in this kind of soul, apart from the "shadow," has been identified for the Quiche, who place this type of "personal soul" in the heart. It has elsewhere been noted that there appear to be two kinds of animistic entities bearing the name *ch'uhlel* for the Tzotzil, one that is the same as the *tonalli* and resides in the head, and another that is similar to the *teyolia* and resides in the heart.[88] Although it may not be appropriate to divide the Tzotzil *ch'uhlel* in this way, there are changes in the activities of *ch'uhlel* after death that do suggest different stages. The *ch'uhlel* first gathers up its component parts, remaining on the earth for a number of days, like the *tonalli*, and then it begins its journey to the afterlife, much like the *teyolia* of Central Mexican theology.

Beyond the above Quiche and Tzotzil examples, many modern Maya groups conceive of the soul as undertaking an afterlife journey of some kind.[89] Lacking clear evidence of a distinction between the "shadow" and the *ánima* in the Classic Maya inscriptions, it is difficult to say whether these two concepts were conflated or divorced in ancient views of the soul and the self. The glyphs for voyages of transformation outlined earlier, *ochb'ih* and *och ha'*, appear to be associated with processes occurring after the point of death, whereas the *k'a'ay u sak* "flower" *ik'il* and *cham* glyphs appear to be more involved with activities at death itself. Clearly, *ochb'ih* and *och ha'* are involved with movements similar to those outlined for the Central Mexican *teyolia*; it is an open question as to whether the same soul shown escaping from the nostrils of the *cham* glyph is the one involved in that journey.

A further wrinkle in this situation is provided to us by the *u tis*, "his flatulence," glyph. For the Aztecs, another type of soul escaped the body at death, the *ihiyotl*, today represented by the modern Central Mexican concept of "night air" or "death air." Located in the liver, as opposed to the head (*tonalli*) or heart (*teyolia*), this animistic entity is thought by modern communities to be responsible for a variety of feelings and properties, including life, vigor, passions, and feelings. For the Aztecs, it was responsible for appetite, desire, and cupidity, and it was a source of energy that could be used for one's own good, the good of another, or (with less beneficial or wanton intents) damage to an individual. In a variety of contexts, including modern Central Mexico, Aztec, and modern Ch'orti', this "night air" is associated with a noxious smell (interchangeable with the word for "fart" in Nahuatl) and an almost visible gas.[90] López Austin notes that a strong odor of this substance is, for the Ch'orti', associated with those people who are envious, angry, upset, or physically exhausted.[91] For the Ch'orti', *teyolia* is known as *hijillo*, an evil emanation from the dead; a possessor of a strong *hijillo* has the power to cause the evil eye or an injury stemming from desire or envy.[92]

43

At death, this *hijillo, ihiyotl,* or "night air" becomes a harmful emanation, a force capable of hurting the living. López Austin has linked this "night air" among the Aztecs to depictions of ghosts and has demonstrated that, for the Aztecs and their modern descendants, the fate of "night air" is linked to that of the "shadow," or *tonalli.* He notes that in modern communities of Central Mexico, the "night air" is thought to be incapable of existing without a covering, needing the *tonalli* to envelop it so that it can exist and do harm to mortals.[93] This belief, of course, implies that the harm being done by the "night air" is accomplished while the *tonalli* seeks out its missing parts. For the modern and Colonial Period Maya, the fate of the *hijillo* is not clear; it is simply described as the evil force that the dead possess, which is to be avoided at all costs with precautionary measures involving who is allowed to be near the deceased or involved with their possessions. Among the Tzotzil, for example, women will beat the floors of the house of the deceased to eliminate the person's presence, and up to three days (or nine) after burial is considered a dangerous time for the living, when the dead seek to return.[94] A lingering of souls occurs for even longer periods among other Maya groups; Oliver LaFarge and Ruth Bunzel have observed that the soul is believed to remain on earth for seven (Kanhobal) and nine (Quiche) days respectively.[95]

In its identification earlier as the "breath" of death, the *tis* glyph shows remarkable similarities to the "night air" or "death air" of modern Central Mexico and eastern Guatemala (Ch'orti' Maya). The pairing of the *tonalli* with the *ihiyotl* for the Central Mexican example is suspiciously similar to the pairing observed earlier for *k'a'ay u sak* "flower" *ik'il* and *u tis. Tis* is the word for "fart" in Ch'orti', and although *hijillo* is used separately for "night air" in the Maya example, "night air" and "fart" were interchangeable for the Aztecs. *Tis* is a visual emanation from the dead in Maya iconography,[96] and it corresponds closely with modern Ch'orti' concepts as well. If we view this glyph as a written representation of a Classic Maya soul, then perhaps the "breath of life," or *k'a'ay u sak* "flower" *ik',* is a reference to souls as well, this time in the form of *ik,* "breath, wind, life." *Ik'* in this context would seem to be closer to the Central Mexican idea of *tonalli* than to *teyolia;* rather than interpret *ik'* in terms of Aztec ideas, however, we must take "breath, wind, soul" on its own Maya terms. For the Classic Maya, *ik'* is perhaps most transparently a soul proper.

WAY

The last Classic Maya spiritual entity to be discussed is the *way,* a concept that has been closely compared with modern Maya views of "coessences" or "animal spirit companions" (Figure 24). Initially identified by Houston and Stuart (1998), the *way* glyph designates a particular creature as a "coessence," which is tied to a specific individual. The various uses of this glyph, and the creatures

FIGURE 24. *Classic Maya way killing other way. Note the victorious way of the ajaw of Calakmul (#K791 © Justin Kerr).*

identified as *way,* have been expounded upon at length by Nikolai Grube and Werner Nahm as well as Inga Calvin.[97] Much of what Mayanists believe about the *way* stems from the Tzotzil concept of *ch'anul.* In this worldview, humans are composed of two spiritual parts, the *ch'uhlel* and the *ch'anul,* and the *ch'uhlel* is shared between the person and the *ch'anul,* a forest or nondomesticated animal determined by the ancestral gods. These animals are kept within a "spirit corral" located within a mountain, which for the Tzotzil of Zinacantan is *bank-likal muk'ta vits,* "senior large mountain," from which they are let out at night by the ancestors. Wandering during the night, they are returned to their corrals by the ancestors during the day. Individuals can communicate or interact with their *ch'anul* during sleep. The *ch'anul,* however, are in constant danger of being neglected by the ancestors, escaping from their corrals into the forest and correspondingly causing illness. Whatever happens to the *ch'anul* happens to the individual sharing their soul.[98] Their destinies are shared. Extending to the sociopolitical sphere, those who have strong animals as their *ch'uhlel* are at the top of the scale, while less ferocious animals mark individuals of lesser status or power. Such is the rationale for human inequality.[99]

As Calvin has pointed out, we do not have enough information on the *way* of Classic Maya belief to make a one-to-one correlation with the *ch'anul.* Clearly, there are differences between the two. As she asserts, the *way* of Classic Maya iconography are supernatural in character, composites of two or more animals with frightening anthropomorphic characteristics; they are sometimes linked to deceased individuals, lineages, or locations with supernatural or real place-names. *Wayoob'* are often depicted in an Otherworldly atmosphere—including what we regard as the Classic Maya Underworld—and are engaged in decidedly humanlike activities such as sacrifice or dancing. The *ch'anul* of Tzotzil belief, or the "animal spirit companion" of other highland Maya communities, is typically just a single animal, possibly with an extra paw or digit, that does not engage in behavior uncharacteristic of wild animals.[100] Where the modern *ch'anul* is natural, the *way* are supernatural; they are grotesque figures seemingly in communication with the lords of the Underworld on Classic Maya ceramics.

The idea that places or sites had souls (or *way*) is likewise reflected in modern beliefs, particularly with respect to the Mam concept of *naab'l.*[101] We might compare this to the example of a spirit companion described as the *way* of Palenque, the *sak b'aknal chapat,* "white bone house centipede," of the site. Despite the fact that *way* are mentioned as the "spirit companions" of supernatural entities, such as *k'awiil* on Yaxchilan Lintel 12, we do have examples of *way* that are tied to specific "living" individuals, as on Yaxchilan Lintel 14. In short, the available evidence points to *way* as the alter egos of not only supernaturals and places but also the Maya nobility.[102]

Perhaps the most interesting examples of *way* tied to specific individuals, in light of the present discussion of Maya souls, are found on two unprovenanced ceramic pieces in a private collection. The first vessel (K791) has a list of *way* identified with the rulers of Tikal, Calakmul, and Caracol, represented by a sequence of animals and composite figures that interact loosely around the piece.[103] This demonstrates that the Classic Maya lords believed that their individual *way* could and did interact with *way* from other sites. The second vessel (K1560) shows a different form of interaction. On it, a host of *way*, some of which share attributes with the Quiche Hero Twins, are shown killing others of their kind. At least one of the victorious *way* is depicted as a *way* of the ruler of Calakmul, while the loser is the *way* of an unknown *ajaw*, represented as a variant of the Classic Maya Death God. Although there is no hieroglyphic evidence, one has to wonder if the so-called Frieze of the Dream Lords from Tonina represents a similar *way*-killing spree, set in an Otherworld with scenes related to the *Popol Vuh*. If one *way* could kill another in the Classic Maya worldview, then perhaps the idea that the individual and the *way* share fates, as per the Tzotzil *ch'anul*, was one conceptualized by the Classic Maya as well. Thus, when the *ajaw* of K1560 died in real life, perhaps as the victim of the real lord of Calakmul, his death was played out in an Otherworld with a *way* victor and victim. As noted by Guiteras Holmes for the Tzotzil, the animal soul "wanders during slumber and is either a victim or a victimizer."[104]

A less violent sequence involving the death of *way* is found on the Tikal bones from Burial 116, mentioned earlier in connection with the death of the Maize God. The fact that the Maize God has multiple *way* opens up the possibility that some individuals had numerous animal alter egos. That the *way* are shown descending into the boat with the Maize God demonstrates not only their shared fate, but the beginning of a death journey for both, the *och ha'* event detailed above. Beyond this, there are no known depictions of *way* being reborn or resurrected, as the Maize God was; the *way* are not featured in his resurrection cycle on Maya ceramics. Likewise, there is little known about the eventual fate of the *ch'anul* for the Tzotzil (or for other "spirit companions"). According to Calixta Guiteras Holmes, the body of the *ch'anul* is "eaten" when it dies, by a "*wayhel* eater" who is always "standing by ready to eat";[105] presumably because the human and *ch'anul* share the same *ch'uhlel*, there is only one journey to the afterlife.

In summation, evidence suggests that there was a general conception that the Classic Maya body and "self" comprised multiple spiritual or supernatural entities, four of which seem to be the most widespread. First is the *b'aah*, "self, person," a term corresponding loosely to the Central Mexican *tonalli* and Tzotzil *ch'uhlel*. Second is *way*, "spirit companion, alter-ego," a term referring to one or more creatures that represented the individual in an Otherworldly setting. Given what I have discussed for the *k'a'ay u sak* "flower" *ik'il* glyph, and the parallelism between it and *u tis* both in the inscriptions and in modern analogues, it seems likely that *tis* corresponds to the "shadow" as well. The third concept, "night air," or *ihiyotl* of Central Mexican theology, is possibly a more restricted phenomenon, as there is only one known occurrence of it, on a vessel presumably from Hix Witz, a polity now known to correspond to the sites of Zapote Bobal and El Pajaral (perhaps La Joyanca) in the northwestern Peten.[106] A fourth entity, corresponding to the Central Mexican *teyolia* and other aspects of the Tzotzil *ch'uhlel,* may be the one physically depicted in cycles of rebirth and resurrection on Classic Maya vessels, although it is unclear whether this soul is really the same one represented textually by *k'a'ay u sak* "flower" *ik'il.* In terms of souls, *b'aah, tis,* and possibly the images of individuals traveling in boats or on journeys represent actual parts of the individual, portions that left for an afterlife or, in some cases, remained with the body. A *way* was probably more of a creature sharing the fate (and possibly the soul) of that person.

TO THE AFTERLIFE

The Underworld, with all its mythological characters and ties to Classic Maya art and architecture, is a boundless topic for epigraphers and archaeologists alike. While studies have been made of its general properties and inhabitants, there continues to be some confusion as to what is properly an Underworld motif versus a supernatural one. In the last decade of the twentieth century, the term "Otherworld" gained currency in place of "Underworld." This has led to vagaries regarding the world of the *way* as a place of "dreams" and has contributed to a further general confusion of the boundaries between the Classic Maya Otherworld, the Underworld, and Postclassic Quiche Maya Xibalba.[107] Problems defining these places highlight the fact that we do not yet have a clear—or uniform—grasp of the Classic Maya Underworld.[108] Linda Schele and David Freidel have provided the most complete analysis to date of the Underworld-versus-Otherworld question.[109] Further studies taking into account these problems would be welcome and sorely needed additions to the literature. While this work cannot address the Underworld in its entirety, my concern with mortuary ritual must address some basic aspects of this place (or places) in order to link funerary practice with belief.

The following will provide us with a general description of what we know about the afterlife as well as the journeys taken by the souls represented on Classic Maya pottery and monumental iconography. These journeys are further complicated by the fact that there may have been an "Upperworld" in addition to an Underworld proper, that is, the "heavens" of what Schele and Freidel describe as the three layered domains of the Maya world. Christian influences aside, there is some small evidence that certain individuals joined the ranks of the gods in that heavenlike atmosphere. This discussion will focus first on the various "worlds" in Maya cosmology, followed by the final destination(s) of the Classic Maya elite.

As numerous scholars have pointed out, the Classic Maya probably conceived of layers of the Underworld, much as the majority of Central Mexican peoples did at contact.[110] From the Codex Vaticanus, we know that the Aztecs conceived of nine levels of the Underworld and thirteen layers of the Upperworld, in addition to a mortal realm of human beings. Nine-level pyramids in the lowlands, such as Tikal Temple I, the Temple of the Inscriptions at Palenque, or the Castillo at Chichén Itzá, might reflect a similar conceptualization of nine levels of the Underworld.[111] Further evidence supporting a nine-part scheme can be found in the inscriptions. The best-known example comes from Glyph G of the Lunar Series (Thompson's "Nine Lords of the Night"; the nine permutations of this glyph, as part of a cycle linked to the *haab'*, have not yet been deciphered).[112] More circumstantial evidence for a compartmentalized Underworld comes from Classic Maya place-names, where mythical locations such as Ho-Noh-Chan appear in conjunction with scenes of death and Underworld gods. Names like Uk-Ek-K'an from Copan, Tonina, and Tikal or Bolon-K'uhnal from a number of locations at Copan have been tied to supernatural "portals," ancestors, and tombs.[113] And while not all numbered place-names refer to the Underworld, a multileveled place of death resonates nicely with what we know from the Quiche *Popol Vuh*, where there are numerous "houses," such as the House of Bats or the House of Knives, within greater Xibalba.[114] Perhaps the night sun, in its own travels to the Classic Maya version of Xibalba, had to pass through these houses in order to rise the next day.

What we know about the Classic Maya Underworld stems largely from ceramic evidence; correlates of Underworld imagery abound in burial furniture, but actual depictions of life after death are quite rare in the material record. Numerous scholars have outlined the attributes of this place as well as its gods, although as yet there is no identified glyph for Xibalba,[115] a word derived from the *Popol Vuh* whose root means "fear," "terror," "trembling with fright."[116] It is the origin of all diseases, characterized by the stench of rotting flesh and decay, with landscapes, architecture, and houses for a number of supernaturals:

> The Xibalba of the Classic Period was different in one way from the Popol Vuh version of Hell. It was a watery world that could only be entered by sinking beneath the water or by passing through a maw in the surface of the earth . . . The inhabitants of Xibalba are numerous and varied: they include anthropomorphs, zoomorphs, animals and skeletal creatures of the most distasteful countenance. Many of the leading Xibalbans are shown with very old, toothless human visages, and some are transformational, combining male and female features. Xibalbans are named for the various causes of death, such as disease, old age, sacrifice, and war, and are often depicted with black marks, representing decaying flesh, as well as bony bodies and distended bellies. Their jewelry consists of disembodied eyes that come complete with the hanging stalk of the optic nerve. Xibalbans are pictured emitting farts so pungent that they emerge in huge scrolls, and their breath is so foul it is visible.[117]

These creatures of the *Popol Vuh* trick protagonists into dying; we see similar views of death as supernatural (as opposed to natural in the Western sense) among the Tzotzil and the gods of death and disease on Classic Maya ceramics. Although the rationale for Classic Maya mortality detailed earlier does provide a reason for why life is fatal, it does not explain individual, immediate causality. The various death gods, for example, likely influenced the reasons why a specific individual died due to disease or old age; death was probably not "natural" in the Western sense. But the degree to which the Classic Maya kings saw death as the causal result of trickery, soul-loss, or active choice by a specific god is unknown. We do not have as clear-cut a situation as we do for the Aztecs, for example, and as the Underworld is fleshed out in future publications, we may find the Maya situation less deterministic.

To date no attributes of particular levels of the Underworld have been described. In keeping with the idea of a compartmentalized Underworld, a number of unprovenanced vessels (some from the Río Hondo area of Mexico) depict humans clinging to watery bands; a vessel depicting a woman traversing a sky-band (K1485) seems to depict levels of another supernatural location (possibly an Upperworld). In those ceramics depicting Underworld or death themes, a number emphasize a watery place, with watery bands, creatures swimming (or engaging in other activities) in the foreground, or skulls below water. The fish-serpent of the Maize God resurrection cycle belches forth his issue in a watery place; presumably, ceramics depicting this action mark the beginning of the resurrection sequence. Many of the other actions involved in that resurrection take place in a watery realm as well: the subsequent dressing of the Maize God as well as his placement in a canoe (with the Paddlers who initially brought him to the Underworld) both take place underwater.

Other locations in the Underworld are recognizable solely by their supernatural inhabitants. In a limited series of vessels, these inhabitants are highlighted by an emphasis on the Underworld as a dark place (see Figure 3), with ropy serpentine creatures marking the boundaries of the scene. Many of the cast of Underworld characters on these vessels are *way;* their cosmological role needs to be addressed in future works. The lords of the Underworld appear as seated rulers or vanquished foes (Figure 25). This is in keeping with their positions in the *Popol Vuh* as judges and defeated members of a supernatural landscape.

From what we know of the Underworld, then, it was a multilevel place with watery, noxious, dark attributes; while there were probably local variations and embellishments on the attributes/characters of this place, the majority of Maya ceramics seem to bear out these general Underworld characteristics. It is to this nasty place that Maya rulers, elites, and probably commoners were directed when they died. In some cases, this initial journey may have involved a cast of creatures in addition to (or in place of) the Paddlers. Some vessels show dogs or other animals—one of these, the avatar of God L, or 13 Sky Owl, appears to serve as a messenger—involved with the lords of death.[118] Similarly to the way

FIGURE 25. *Lords of the Underworld as captives* (#K3560 © *Justin Kerr*)

the summons from the lords of Xibalba to the Hero Twins worked, these super-natural animals may have played a role in getting the deceased to his or her next destination. Further evidence for this stems from Aztec sources, which cite a dog as the means of Underworld transportation, and from contemporary Tzotzil mythology, which holds that a black dog ferries the deceased across a river; a rooster—with a detached head—directs the soul to its next destination.[119]

CELESTIAL BODIES AND MAIZE GODS

Of the possibly thirteen-layered Upperworld, we have little evidence from the Classic Period. It appears to have been conceptually bridged to the Underworld, although the nature of that bridge is by no means clear.[120] The number thirteen abounds in Maya sculpture, architecture, and epigraphy, from the steps of pyramids to day names. There is clear ethnographic and ethnohistorical evidence of a Maya belief in multiple Under- and Upperworlds, however. In Lacandon mythology, the Upperworld is a place of gods, divided into three realms of celestial, creator, and outer gods, respectively. When they die, humans are sent to one of the Underworlds and cannot transcend to the realm of the gods, although they are judged as "good" or "bad." The good are sent to Mensabak, where they live in the house of the Rain God until the creators destroy the world, and the bad go to live in the house of Kisin, who immerses them in fire and cold.[121] Tzotzil mythology is similar, with deceased human beings who are good—directed by the rooster—going to one of the "heavens" of *vinahel,* while the bad go to a place called *k'atin bak.* The bad are tortured and their bones burned, and the good live much as they did in life but are punished mildly if they did not strictly adhere to Zinacanteco conceptions of religious or social duty.[122] Landa's description of the Yucatecan afterlife was similarly bifurcated, with Kisin in charge of meting out punishment to errant souls. The "heavens" of Landa's account are far more like Western traditional conceptions of paradise.[123] In many situations, the decision of whether a person is good or bad rests on one or more tests. The idea of gods examining souls is a common one in Maya ethnography and can be found in Central Mexican communities as well.[124]

A similar type of final judgment—as mentioned earlier—appears in the *Popol Vuh.* The Hero Twins enter the Underworld (Xibalba) and must pass tests meted out by the lords of death; they die only to beat the Xibalbans and gain new life. The Classic Maya versions of the Hero Twins and their father, the Classic Maya Maize God,[125] are depicted in a variety of similar situations in which they defeat death and promote the emergence of the father from the surface of the earth. The visual representation of these "tests" on Maya funerary ceramics has led numerous scholars to liken the trip to the Classic Maya Underworld as a series of tasks that must be overcome, with the story of the *Popol Vuh* being a model for the trials that each human being faces at death.[126] That we can link the Maize God resurrection cycle to Classic Maya beliefs about death only strengthens this position. If we view this cycle or the Quiche story of the Hero Twins as a journey taken by Classic Maya royalty, then the Underworld cannot have been the final stop in their journeys of the soul. The tests may have been taken and passed, but to what end? Is the Underworld (or the Otherworld) really the final destination for rulers and their families?

At this point we have come full circle to the question posed earlier: Where did the Classic Maya rulers believe they went after death? Certainly, many were familiar with elements of the Maize God resurrection cycle; most sites bear victorious Maize God imagery in some form, with monuments like Copan Stela A (and its associated altar) a prime example. Likewise, we know that this story is of great antiquity in the Maya lowlands, for events on the Preclassic murals of San Bartolo display the adornment and rebirth of the Maize God in virtually the same format as on Classic Maya ceramics.[127] Yet rulers were transformed by death into something else: when depicted on monuments as ancestors, they are usually celestial bodies or are impersonating deities other than the Maize God.[128] For example, the Late Classic rulers of Yaxchilan depict royal men and women inside solar and lunar cartouches, respectively; each emanates sunlight or moonlight as a celestial body.[129] At Tikal and Copan, ancestral images of Yax Nuun Ayiin and K'inich Yax K'uk' Mo' are likewise solar (both are shown as K'inich Ajaw, the Sun God), and at Palenque, dead rulers are shown "impersonating" the Jaguar God of the Underworld and Chak Xib Chaak (Figure 26). Other depictions of deceased royalty at that site involve their rebirth as fruit trees, and there are clear indications of solar cartouches and solar rebirth.

It seems likely that these individuals escaped the Underworld to someplace else. One could probably not remain a celestial being, especially the Sun God, in the Underworld. As for the Palenque dead, they are sometimes depicted in scenes of adornment, with the kings K'inich Kan B'alam II and K'inich K'an Joy Chitam II being prime examples (Figure 27). This resonates with what we know about the Maize God resurrection cycle: belched naked from a fish-serpent, the Maize God is adorned with finery and prepared for his escape from the watery Underworld by two or more women. The Hero Twins of the *Popol Vuh*, having died themselves, rise from the water as ignoble beggars and transform into heavenly bodies. This idea of finery and change seems integral to the escape from the Underworld; that the Classic examples demonstrate a change of dress and godlike qualities suggests that some individuals have escaped (or will escape) the Underworld to another location.

Table 2 provides a list of unequivocally deified or celestial ancestors and their contexts, and stands as a testament to the fact that such things were rarely depicted, save, as it seems, at Palenque during the reigns of K'inich Kan B'alam I and K'inich K'an Joy Chitam II.

FIGURE 26. *Yax Ehb' Xook as K'inich Ajaw (after Jones and Satterthwaite 1982, fig. 51c)*

FIGURE 27. *Kan B'alam as the Jaguar God of the Underworld (after Schele and Miller 1986 and Miller 1986, fig. VII.2). Note the phrase* och u ch'een, *"[he] enters his cave."*

TABLE 2
KNOWN DEIFIED OR CELESTIAL ANCESTORS

Ancestor	Form	Site	Monument and Date	Protagonist
Chak Tok Ich'aak?	Solar?	Tikal	Stela 29, 292	Foliated Jaguar?
Yax Ehb' Xook	Solar	Tikal	Stela 31, 445	Siyaj Chan K'awiil II
K'inich Yax K'uk' Mo'	Solar/Itzamnaaj	Copan	Rosalila, 571	Moon Jaguar
Stela 5 Ancestors	Solar	Caracol	Stela 5, 613	Knot Ajaw
Stela 8 Ancestor	Solar	Yaxchilan	Stela 8, >658	Bird Jaguar III or Itzamnaaj B'alam II
Yoaat B'alam	Tlaloc/Aj K'ak' O' Chaak	Yaxchilan	Lintel 25, 681	Lady K'ab'aal Xook and Itzamnaaj B'alam II
K'uk' B'alam I	PAL Triad	Palenque	TOP, 683	K'inich Kan B'alam II
"Casper"	PAL Triad	Palenque	TOP, 683	K'inich Kan B'alam II
B'utz'aj Sak Chiik	PAL Triad	Palenque	TOP, 683	K'inich Kan B'alam II
Ahkal Mo' Naab' I	PAL Triad	Palenque	TOP, 683	K'inich Kan B'alam II
K'an Joy Chitam I	PAL Triad	Palenque	TOP, 683	K'inich Kan B'alam II
Ahkal Mo' Naab' II	PAL Triad	Palenque	TOP, 683	K'inich Kan B'alam II
Kan B'alam I	PAL Triad	Palenque	TOP, 683	K'inich Kan B'alam II
Lady Olnal	PAL Triad	Palenque	TOP, 683	K'inich Kan B'alam II
Aj Ne' Ohl Mat	PAL Triad	Palenque	TOP, 683	K'inich Kan B'alam II
K'inich Janaab' Pakal I	GI	Palenque	TOP, 683	K'inich Kan B'alam II
K'inich Kan B'alam II	GIII	Palenque	T14 Tablet, 705	K'inich K'an Joy Chitam II?
House A Quatrefoils	Solar	Palenque	House A, 720	K'inich K'an Joy Chitam II
K'inich K'an Joy Chitam II	GI	Palenque	DO Panel, 722	K'inich K'an Joy Chitam II
Itzamnaaj B'alam II	Solar	Yaxchilan	Stela 11, 752	Bird Jaguar IV
Lady Ik' Skull	Lunar	Yaxchilan	Stela 11, 752	Bird Jaguar IV
Stela 16 Ancestor	Solar	Tikal	Stela 16, 771	Yax Nuun Ayiin II

The nine stucco figures from the tomb of K'inich Janaab' Pakal I at Palenque (Figure 28) are particularly interesting, for they appear elsewhere in different guises on his famous Sarcophagus Lid. Each of these seminal figures in the history of the site bears a *k'awiil* scepter and a circular shield, emblematic of GII and GIII of the Palenque Triad, respectively; over each of their mouths is a rectangular mosaic that Linda Schele and Peter Mathews have tied to the Classic Maya Maize God, otherwise known as GI at Palenque. In their portraiture, the dead are thereby combining elements from the primary gods of Palenque and evoking the Maize God resurrection sequence at the same time.

Yet if the Maize God resurrection cycle was so important to the Classic

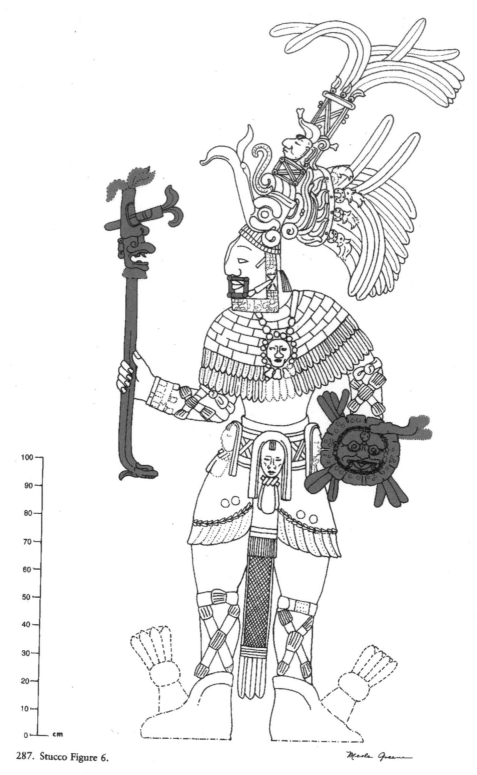

287. Stucco Figure 6.

FIGURE 28. *Detail of stucco figure (Figure 6) from the tomb of K'inich Janaab' Pakal I at Palenque (after Robertson 1983; © Merle Greene Robertson, used with permission)*

Maya, why do we have these other forms of rebirth shown in the table? As I stressed earlier in the chapter, the Maize God resurrection cycle was a metaphor for life and death. As a representative of maize, and thereby a likely component of all human beings, the Maize God can be seen as the embodiment of the natural process of growth, death, and renewal. That this character can be found throughout Maya burials indicates that this process was important for Classic Maya attitudes toward death. Eating maize, and therefore death; referred to as "sprouts" during their youth; and impersonating the Maize God in royal ritual, the Classic Maya kings emulated this god and his journey in life and in the tomb.[130] But the Maize God was not the only deity impersonated by rulers and their families. In the Great Plaza at Copan, for example, Waxaklajuun Ub'aah K'awiil (18 Rabbit) puts himself in the guise of no less than four different gods on four different stelae. Rulers and nobles throughout the lowlands wear garb identifying themselves as Chaak, God A, the Jaguar God of the Underworld, and a host of other deities. Abandoning this practice in death would therefore be inconsistent, given the daily ritual life of a Maya lord. Thus it would be internally consistent—in the Classic Maya sense—to follow the maize cycle but individually wear the guise of another deity. Whether this was personal preference or the result of changes in Classic Maya religion is an open question, unlikely to be resolved in the near future.

There is at least one example where the Maize God cycle and other deifications overlap, however. Returning to Palenque (Figure 29), the Sarcophagus Lid shows a deceased K'inich Janaab' Pakal I wearing garb belonging to the Maize God as well as *k'awiil* (perhaps another veiled reference to the Triad). Although his journey on that monument has traditionally been described as a fall into the Underworld, David Stuart has suggested the reverse, that is, a rise into an Upperworld or out of the Underworld. This idea is further supported by Pakal's fetal positioning, a sign of rebirth on Classic Maya ceramics. Given the skybands on two sides of this monument, what we may be seeing is Pakal rising like the Maize God—but into the celestial heavens. A similar concept is reflected in the iconography of a vessel in the Museum für Völkerkunde in Berlin. On this pot, death occurs in two parts, with the deceased—possibly a version of the Classic Maya Maize God—reborn as both a cacao tree and a celestial entity.[131]

Despite illuminating aspects of royal afterlives (and perhaps raising even more questions), these deification ideas only address part of the original problem. There is an obvious difference between a reborn ancestor-as-tree and a deified Sun God. Likewise, there are clear differences between the kinds of "deified" ancestors shown in Maya iconography. We might draw one line between those ancestors that appear human, such as those of Copan Altar Q or Palenque Tablet XIV, and those that have squared eyes or other attributes linking them to deities proper. Remembering the discussion of Mesoamerican surfaces and identities, it may be more appropriate to conceptualize some of these "ancestors" as deities *in the guise of* deceased rulers or vice versa in the case of the

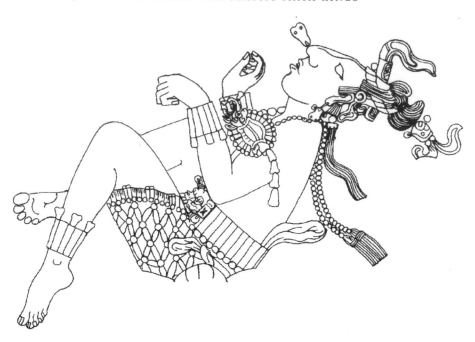

FIGURE 29. *Detail of K'inich Janaab' Pakal I on his Sarcophagus Lid at Palenque (after Robertson 1983, fig. 99)*

stucco Palenque figures. Others, such as the more "human" figures at Yaxchilan, seem rather to join the Sun God as members—but epigraphically nameless members—of the celestial sphere.[132] Such an idea calls to mind the aforementioned Quiche and Tzotzil ideas of "pools" of souls kept by the gods, the *okol k'in* concept in Colonial Yucatec, and passive versus active passages of souls into Underworld locations.

Some aspects of ancestors, particularly those from the Sarcophagus sides at Palenque, seem even more terrestrial.[133] They bear names (and sometimes fruits!) and could almost pass for living beings. We can find these at sites with "deified" ancestors, even in different depictions of the same person; for example, one can see a clear contrast between the solar and humanistic K'inich Yax K'uk' Mo's of Copan's Rosalila Temple and Altar Q, respectively (Figure 30). It is difficult to say whether these differences reflect changes in belief or style over time (the Altar Q depiction far postdates the Rosalila one). Another possibility, and one supported by the idea of multiple souls and multiple "deaths" for Classic Maya royalty, is that we are seeing the manifestations of different souls and soul identities; this would certainly explain the differences between Lady Olnal in stucco and on the Palenque Sarcophagus Lid, respectively. The more terrestrial figures may be analogous to the ancestral gods of the Zinacanteco past, who reside in the earthly domains of mountains and hills.[134] These questions may be answered in coming years, but for the moment it seems clear that our picture of ancestors cannot be a monolithic one. It is likewise certain that royal ancestors enjoyed a kind of afterlife following the Underworld.

Unfortunately, not everyone can be reborn as (or reworked into) a celestial being, Chak Xib Chaak, or K'inich Ajaw. One would hope that individuals of lower status had a myth of the soul victorious. Certainly there are nonroyal elite interments that emulate—to a degree—the themes and ideas reflected in this chapter. Beyond this, it is difficult to say what nonroyals could expect in the afterlife. Given that modern Maya ethnographies involve an afterlife of work or daily life similar to that "enjoyed" on earth, it may have been the case that the Classic Maya afterlife was not the playful location relished by Teotihuacanos in their afterlife murals.[135] Likewise, the Aztec situation probably does not apply; the "good" death for the Aztecs involved warriors, women who died in childbirth, drowning victims, and other notables going to different places. By contrast, the afterlife in the Maya area, Classic and beyond, seems to be one of tests and successful navigations through the Underworld.

There is little indication that those killed by enemies went to places different from where high elites went who died in their sleep. While some of this is probably due to the limitations of inscriptions and archaeology, there does appear to have been a belief that death itself was a form of sacrifice. The aforementioned Sarcophagus Lid at Palenque, for example, displays the celebrated

FIGURE 30. *Detail (top) from the Palenque Sarcophagus Lid (after Schele and Miller 1986, Plate 111e) and Yax K'uk' Mo' (bottom) on the Rosalila Structure at Copan (after Fash 1991b, fig. 52)*

Pakal lying on a sacrificial plate in death; he is offered up and eaten by the earth as a sacrificial victim, part of the phagohierarchy illustrated above. A visually more sophisticated version of death as sacrifice occurs on a series of ceramic vessels bearing images of Itzamnaaj: the dying god transforms into—and is surrounded by—fat, succulent deer, the quintessential sacrificial animal of the Classic Maya world.[136] His change of state, from living god to sacrificial deer, echoes Van Gennep (1960) and ideas of death as phased; transformation makes his death palatable, creating an acceptable situation in which his death is like other deaths in the Classic Maya world.

To be sure, some deaths were more important to the royal court than others. Death was not a "great equalizer," and some ancestors were more prominent in courtly life than others. We have only to look at ancestors like K'inich Yax K'uk' Mo' of Copan, Yax Ehb' Xook of Tikal, or K'inich Janaab' Pakal I of Palenque, whose tombs were pivotal in future architectural efforts at those sites,[137] to see ancestral inequality. Unfortunately, public remembrance was—and continues to be—at the mercy of politics and society. Individuals who were prolific, or who had others to be prolific for them, were chief figures in the afterlife of the public.

THREE

ROYAL FUNERALS

As can be expected, funerary rites are not generally depicted from start to finish. Perhaps the best encapsulation of behaviors associated with death, burial, and rebirth comes from the aforementioned Berlin vessel (Figure 31). On it, a deceased lord is wrapped within a bundle inside a funerary temple, with mourners outside crying and gesturing toward the pyramid. Although his burial is not shown, it is implied: his bones sit amid watery bands, indicating his entry into the Underworld. He reappears in two forms, as an anthropomorphic cacao tree and as an abstract lunar deity. Even this vessel, however, does not start at the beginning of the funerary rite. For that we must rely solely on hieroglyphic materials, although subsequent portions of these rites can be viewed through the lenses of archaeology, iconography, and epigraphy. The following is an attempt to reconstruct each *possible* step of royal funerals, taking into account known temporal and spatial variations. In doing so, we see that certain ideas and behaviors saw popularity and decline among the royal populations at lowland sites.

WAITING FOR INTERMENT

The Late Classic Period was a time of great social change in the Maya lowlands. Populations reached their height, and the fall of the Central Mexican city of Teotihuacan around AD 600 brought with it vast realignments in economic and political networks.

The next two hundred years would see ancient Maya civilization reach its highest artistic and intellectual point. It is during this era that we find the most elaborate references to death rites and rituals. Such references are far from commonplace, however, and it is largely due to the archaeology of Maya sites that we have the ability to describe and reconstruct the activities that took place during a funeral. The first possible steps in death rites were, of course, the preparations leading up to interment. Although they are not many, there are a few references to Maya burials that describe a lapse of time between the death

FIGURE 31A. *Maya lord with mourners (after drawing by Nikolai Grube in Eberl 2000, 312)*

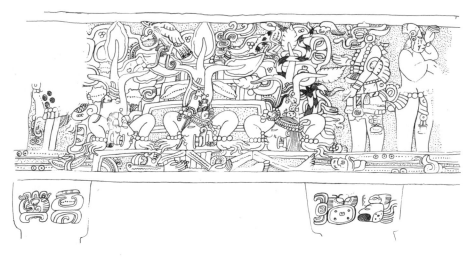

FIGURE 31B. *Maya lords being reborn as trees (after drawing by Nikolai Grube in Eberl 2000, 312)*

and the interment of Maya kings. Overall, the time period seems to have been rather short: three days for Piedras Negras Ruler 4 and Smoke Imix (God K) of Copan, and four days for Itzamnaaj K'awiil (Ruler 2) of Dos Pilas. Piedras Negras Ruler 2 presents an interesting problem, for as we saw in Chapter 2, there is a period of eight or nine days between his *cham,* "death"; his "flowery" *k'a'ay* "death"; and his *ochb'ih,* "road-entering." The funeral for Picdras Negras Ruler 2 may have reflected these distinctions, perhaps in the manner of a rite performed for one of the most colorful kings of Classic Maya history, K'ahk' Tiliw Chan

Yoaat (Cauac Sky) of Quirigua. His funeral stands in marked contrast to those of these august rulers of the Classic Maya lowlands.

For much of its history, the Motagua Valley site of Quirigua was a provincial client state under the "overkingship" of the rulers of Copan. Excavated by Robert Sharer from 1974 to 1980, Quirigua remained a minor center until the middle of the eighth century, when K'ahk' Tiliw Chan Yoaat transformed it into a leader in political and economic affairs. After capturing his overking, Waxaklajuun Ub'aah K'awiil (18 Rabbit), he tried to rewrite the history of Quirigua with himself as a type of mythical ancestor.[1] Although Quirigua never came close to the size or splendor of its one-time master, its imitation of Copan—and attempts to outdo it—in architectural and monumental prowess transformed it into a capital of the Motagua River Valley in its own right. For unknown reasons, K'ahk' Tiliw Chan Yoaat created affiliations between Quirigua and Underworld place-names in his monuments, drawing an iconographic relationship between himself and places named "black hole" and "black body of water."[2]

Certainly, K'ahk' Tiliw Chan Yoaat's death would have been a momentous event in the history of Quirigua. The date traditionally associated with this is July 31, 785 (9.17.14.13.2 11 Ik 5 Yax), recorded by his successor, Sky Xul, on Zoomorph G (see Figure 18):

ochb'ihiiy u sak "flower" *ik'(il) tu(y) ahk tuun,* "[the] road is entered [by] his white 'flower' breath, into the turtle stone."

Although some of the glyphs immediately following have yet to be deciphered, subsequent passages involve a witness (an enigmatic figure nicknamed Sunraiser

TABLE 3
DEATH AND BURIAL DATES OF CLASSIC MAYA RULERS

Ruler	Verb	"Death" Date	Burial Date
Ruler 4 of Piedras Negras	*k'a'ay u sak* "flower" *ik'il*	9.16.6.11.17 7 Caban 0 Pax, or November 30, 757	9.16.6.12.0 10 Ahau 3 Pax, or December 3, 757
Smoke Imix of Copan	*k'a'ay u sak* "flower" *ik'il*	9.13.3.5.7 12 Manik 0 Yaxk'in, or June 18, 695	9.13.3.5.10 15 Ok 3 Yaxk'in, or June 21, 695
Itzamnaaj K'awiil of Dos Pilas	*k'a'ay u sak* "flower" *ik'il*	9.14.15.1.19 11 Cauac 17 Mac, or October 24, 726	9.14.15.2.2 1 Ik 0 K'ank'in, or October 27, 726
K'ahk' Tiliw Chan Yoaat of Quirigua	*ochb'ihiiy u sak* "flower" *ik'*	9.17.14.13.2 11 Ik 5 Yax, or July 31, 785	9.17.14.13.12 8 Eb 15 Yax, or August 8, 785

Jaguar) and the burial itself (*muhkaj*), which took place at the "13 Kawak House" ten days after his "road-entering."[3]

Aside from the entry of his soul into a "turtle," a likely reference to the earth, as described in Chapter 2, the most fascinating aspect of this passage is the burial date. As Simon Martin and Nikolai Grube have noted, ten days is a long time for a dead body to be exposed in a tropical environment, and this would have required elaborate preparations. Given what we have already learned about the various death dates for Piedras Negras Ruler 2, it seems entirely possible that K'ahk' Tiliw Chan Yoaat ceased to breathe days before his "road-entering" journey. In the extreme view, we are looking at a time period of eighteen or nineteen days. Retarding the inevitable putrefaction may have been a desirable—if not necessary—part of the funeral ceremony, particularly in the transportation of his remains to the 13 Kawak House. Perhaps, as has been suggested, the ancient Maya occasionally engaged in embalming, the removal of viscera, or other preservative practices.[4] Archaeologically, however, such efforts have been difficult to discern.

What other types of activities could have occurred during this "waiting period"? Assuming that *muhkaj*, "[he/she] is buried," refers to the sealing of a tomb or, at the very least, the placement of the body within a funerary chamber, the waiting period between death (in all its forms and permutations) and burial probably involved aspects of grave preparation and body ornamentation. As yet, we do not have enough information to say how much time was required to prepare bodies and tombs; even a conservative energetics model would make three or four days for a royal tomb an impossibility. It is to these unsung—but archaeologically observable—endeavors that we now turn our attention.

GRAVEMAKERS

Following the classification schemes for Maya burials developed by Robert E. Smith and Augustus L. Smith,[5] scholars have grappled with terms like *cist*, *crypt*, and *tomb*. Separate classifications have been published for sites like Tonina, Copan, Seibal, Dzibilchaltun, and Piedras Negras,[6] each with its own merits and problems. Broader studies have drawn hard lines between types on the basis of grave height and the presence of vaulting or plaster.[7] The Classic Maya had no such overarching models, and they produced burials whose characteristics varied over space and time, even from one king to the next. As a result, what qualifies in one classification as a "tomb" is often a "crypt" in another. For the present study, I find the general classification produced by A. L. Smith to be the most useful, with crypts and chambers characterizing the majority of royal interments in the Classic Maya lowlands. I therefore follow his definition of a *crypt* as "a carefully walled grave with capstones, sometimes a plastered floor, and which may or may not have been filled with earth."[8] Unfortunately, the same cannot be done with *chamber*. Given the currency of the term *tomb* in Mesoamerican archaeology, I present a modified version of the Smith typology: a tomb is a large stone-lined or rock-cut chamber, specially constructed for mortuary purposes, which is capped by either a flat roof or a vault.

These two constructions were but an elite part of a larger Classic Maya funerary program. Perhaps the best studies of this wider curriculum—from nonelite burials to royal tombs—are the works by Alberto Ruz Lhuillier and W. Bruce M. Welsh. These two scholars have outlined a number of pan-lowland Maya practices, many of which cross-cut royal, elite, and nonelite contexts.[9] They include:

1) a vast preference for bodily inhumation within structures, as opposed to cremation or interment within caves, *cenotes, chultunes,* or ceramic vessels, which together become more fashionable by the Postclassic;

2) the preferential use of structures located on the eastern sides of plazas for interments;

3) the placement of royal burials within temples, ceremonial platforms, or household shrines, which frequently have superimposed altars, benches, stairs, or other structures directly overhead;

4) a preference for single over multiple interments, although high-status burials can contain additional individuals;

5) the removal of skulls or faces, not all of which indicate human sacrifice;

6) the use of a bowl or shell over—or under—a skull;

7) a preference for a specific skeletal position, flexed or unflexed, at lowland sites, with extended being dominant in larger crypts and tombs;

8) prevailing head orientations, although such orientations vary between sites;

9) the use of similar grave furniture, although items like stingray spines, jade mosaic masks, and shell figurines are exclusive to high-status interments, while items like clay whistles tend to be in child interments; and

10) a general similarity between male and female interments of similar status, although those of adults are typically better furnished.

These basic principles seem to have guided the construction of the majority of burials in the Classic Maya lowlands. When cutting an intrusive pit into a preexisting structure or creating a walled grave as part of a new construction plan for the royal dead, however, architects tended to prefer tomb and crypt locations directly inside temple-pyramids or frontally and axially at their bases, as shown in Appendix 1. The types of crypts housing royal individuals were elaborate, often lined with plastered stone slabs and occasionally bearing stone floors, niches in walls, or benches along the sides. Occasionally, they display artifacts and reflect behavior on a par with royal tombs.

The three burials located directly beneath the floor of Temple 18 at Palenque are cases in point. Discovered by Ruz Lhuillier in the 1950s,[10] they may house the remains of individuals tied to K'inich Ahkal Mo' Naab' III (Chaacal III, Akul Anab III). This king, reigning from ca. AD 721 to AD 736, remodeled Temple 18 and decorated it with texts relating his birth and accession. His series of stuccoed glyphs, which had fallen out of order within the structure, have been reconstructed by William Ringle[11] and mention the deaths of his father, Batz Chan Mat, and grandmother, Lady Tz'akb'u Ajaw, the widow of the great K'inich Janaab' Pakal I. One of the first two of these individuals was likely the occupant of the central burial, which was located on axis with the structure and contained far more grave furniture than the others, although each was placed at around the same time. In addition to objects of chert and obsidian similar to those discovered in the Temple of the Inscriptions, the central grave held jade and shell artifacts bearing texts and images of martial and supernatural supremacy. As for the other burials, one had been looted or disturbed in antiquity, and the other was characterized by jade and shell artifacts, including an effigy of the Sun God, K'inich Ajaw. Despite their royal associations, however, each of the three burials was housed within a crypt surmounted by cut and dressed capstones, a less-than-royal way to bury someone. Between them, set at approximately the same time, were disarticulated whole skeletons; similar disarticulated individuals have been found in Tomb 1 of Temple 18-A and in the tomb of K'inich Janaab' Pakal I.[12] The fact that all of the interments were located directly underneath the surface of the temple suggests that the burials occurred simultaneously or over a period of time obscured by the handiwork of careful grave and floor architects.

Such handiwork was magnified in the preparation of a chamber for a royal tomb. Those carved from bedrock appear to have enjoyed a limited phase of popularity. Welsh defines a rock-cut tomb as a "large chamber cut out of bedrock, complete with shaft and steps leading to [the] tomb entrance," where the walls and ceiling are usually decorated with plaster and line paintings.[13] Graves of this type were often irregularly shaped, not truly vaulted, and covered with capstones. As represented in Appendix 1, they are perhaps best exemplified at Early Classic Tikal and Río Azul, for such notables as Tikal's Siyaj Chan K'awiil and Yax Nuun Ayiin.[14]

Over time, though, the basic idea of carving a tomb from bedrock seems to have been reinterpreted. The Late Classic Tikal Burials 195 and 116, as well as Dos Pilas Burial 30, all belonging to known kings of those sites, were carved from bedrock, partially or wholly lined with stones, and then vaulted. In this hybrid form between rock-cut and stone-lined varieties, we find even more subtle uses of bedrock. In the only known Early Classic royal burial at Piedras

Negras, as well as in the Late Classic Tomb 3 of Temple 18-A at Palenque, grave architects excavated down to bedrock and simply stopped, making use of the bedrock as a floor for the tomb. At Palenque, the architects laid large flat stones upon the bedrock floor and placed the body thereupon.

Many of the burials in this study, however, are nowhere near bedrock. This was not due to any lack of effort on the part of the grave architects: one of the most complex of all Maya royal tombs, the tomb of K'inich Janaab' Pakal I in the Temple of the Inscriptions at Palenque, was located on or slightly above the ground surface. For K'inich Janaab' Pakal I, the architects created a long, corbel-vaulted staircase leading from the top of the Temple of the Inscriptions to deep in the interior, on axis with the structure and approximately on level with the temple base. Midway down the stairway they created two "ventilation ducts" leading from the stairway to the west side of the temple. At the base of the stairway they created a vaulted chamber supported by wooden beams, plastering the entirety and covering the walls with stuccoed figures.[15] Such activities were but a small part of the erection of the Temple of the Inscriptions, which seems to have been wholly created for the purpose of interring K'inich Janaab' Pakal I.

Similar activities above bedrock—albeit not as grandiose—were performed at nearly every Classic Maya site, especially where vaulted tombs were set within preexisting structures, forming the basis of new structures, or were placed in alignment with large temple-pyramids. Such construction might seem to be a significant departure from the Early Classic Tikal and Río Azul examples, that is, from the irregularly shaped rock-cut tombs to the opposite extreme of K'inich Janaab' Pakal I's tomb. Yet both are consistent with the model of the Classic Maya earth as detailed in Chapter 2. As the carapace of a turtle or the back of an alligator, the Classic Maya earth was a setting of anthropomorphic natural features; creating a temple was merely the imposition of a new mountain upon the landscape, yet another feature of the supernatural, natural world. In carving a chamber from the bedrock, the Classic Maya were cutting into the turtle carapace, the alligator's back. In setting a body within this space, the Classic Maya were "sowing" versions of the Maize God, "planting" the seeds of future ancestral rebirth. If we liken the life cycle of Classic Maya nobles to that of maize, then burial was simply a planting with an intended result: the rebirth of a noble into an ancestor. The noble, of course, was not resurrected as the Maize God, but underwent a transformation from the dead state into the ancestral state.

Intrusive burials within temples or below plaza floors can also be viewed as sowing or planting acts. They involve a cut into previously existing elements of the site topography, the existing surface of the site at that time. In a sense, the fill of such structures as the Temple of the Cross at Palenque or the Mascarones Structure at Copan[16] *was* bedrock, and allowed the placement of intrusive tombs and capping architectural phases. Even those royal burials that are "original," in that they were constructed as the foundation for a new structure or plaza floor, conceptually overlap the intrusive interments. They too are set within sacred mountains and earthworks that raise the topography to incorporate a deceased individual within the surface of the earth. Making a new surface for the earth—or cutting into a preexisting surface—was likely an act that required a degree of ceremony as well as hard labor. If what makes a god a god in Mesoamerica is usually the "skin" or "bark," as I mentioned in Chapter 2, then perhaps what made a temple or a tomb a part of the earth was its surface—and not its fill—with subsequent construction phases creating new faces for mountain temples. If that is the case, the creation of new features on the landscape may have been viewed as a sacred affair. Beyond the creation of a space for "planting," however, tomb construction involved the generation of a location that was symbolic on a variety of levels. To the Classic Maya rulers, tombs were centers of religious and political activity; they were caves, watery environments, houses, and even places of worship. As such, the excavation of a tomb was only the first step in a larger physical and metaphorical program. Central to this program was the overall appearance of the tomb interior and the body of the deceased.

TOMBS AS UNDERWORLD SURFACES

Elsewhere I have referred to *och ha'*, "water-entering," events, in which a soul descends into water. Epigraphically, this event is found at Tikal, Río Azul,[17] and Resbalón, and on unprovenanced ceramic vessels, although it seems clear that tombs throughout the lowlands are designed to reflect entrance into a watery realm. Watery bands in the royal tombs at Río Azul as well as the proliferation of marine objects and themes in such royal burials as Burial 5 at Piedras Negras or Burial XXXVII-4 at Copan mirror themes of watery descent we have seen on Classic Maya ceramics. Spatially, an Early Classic royal tomb from Río Azul provides the best example of watery iconography complementing archaeology.

Located far to the northwest of the sites of Tikal and Uaxactun, Río Azul is perhaps best known for its painted tombs, produced over a period of a few hundred years from the Late Preclassic to the Early Classic. Of the more than thirty tombs investigated at the site, Tombs 1, 19, and 23 are the most famous; sadly, Tomb 1 and many of its contemporaries were looted before excavations began here in the 1980s. Nevertheless, enough remains of Tomb 1, characterized by niches and plastered walls painted in hieroglyphs, to gain crucial insights into the minds of its builders. Grant Hall has divided the paintings in this tomb into Panels, numbered 1–9 (Figure 32). The text located in Panel 5 provides an Initial Series of 8.19.1.9.13 4 Ben 16 Mol (September 29, AD 417) as well as a Lunar Series followed by the verb for "birth" (*siyaj*) and an unidentified name, presumably a reference to the occupant of the tomb.[18] Richard E. W. Adams

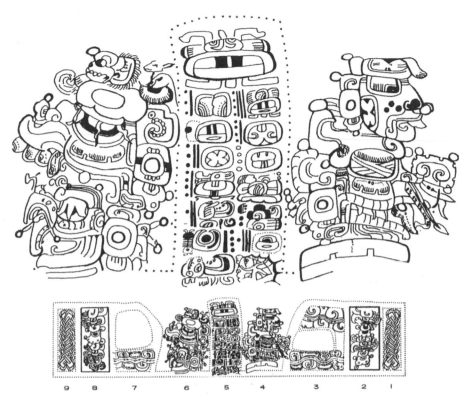

FIGURE 32. *Río Azul Tomb 1 paintings (after Hall 1989, figs. 37 and 38)*

has proposed that this birth refers to the literal birth of the tomb occupant. He speculates, based on site chronology as well as radiocarbon dating from an adjacent tomb in the C complex (Tomb 19), that the individual in Tomb 1 was between thirty-three and sixty-three years of age. However, the iconography of Tomb 1 tells a story that casts doubt on whether the architects of this tomb ever meant to provide the literal birthday of what Adams calls "Ruler X."[19]

Bordering the text on each side of Panel 5 is a zoomorphic head. The head of Panel 6 appears to be an avian Jester God wearing a headdress consisting of a "monster" associated with watery places as well as the earth (note the stones in its teeth). The creature, in turn, wears an unidentified glyph in its headdress; another motif, also probably glyphic, is located above its earflares and consists of a deer surmounting the glyph for "water" (*ha'*). The head of Panel 4 is more reptilian in character and also sports a headdress; this time the headdress is that of an "earth monster" surmounted by K'inich Ajaw as the Night Sun. In short, both of these figures deal with death thematically in a variety of ways, displaying such familiar characters as the Night Sun in the Underworld (GIII), the watery "earth monster," and a Jester God associated with death, in addition to more obscure elements such as the avian aspect or the deer. The deer, of course, is traceable to images of a dying elderly figure sometimes seen on Classic Maya ceramics; perhaps the "deer-over-water" is an evocation of that theme.

Beyond these figures, on Panels 7 and 3, are a series of watery bands. They are bordered by elaborate renditions of sacred *k'uhul* space in Panels 8 and 2, as well as evocations of rulership represented by mat (*pop*) signs. If we remember that a body was placed inside these watery bands and images, then we have a situation similar to that represented on Classic Maya ceramics where, as mentioned in Chapter 2, deceased individuals cling to the surface of the watery Underworld. That the tomb is a watery place is clear, lending credence to the idea that Ruler X was believed to be descending below the surface of the water, as in the bones from Tikal Burial 116, *and* being reborn from that surface. This fits with the larger pattern of rebirth and renewal represented in the Maize God resurrection cycle. The Maize God descends below the surface of the watery underworld only to be reborn and eventually emerge victorious from the surface of the earth. It can thereby be argued that the "birth" reference here is to Ruler X's own rebirth in water. Perhaps he too was believed to emerge from a fish-serpent, dressed in his finery and prepared for apotheosis.

This blend of iconography, archaeology, and landscape is repeated in a much later royal interment from the site of Copan, within the Late Classic Burial XXXVII-4; it has been identified as the tomb of Smoke Imix, who ruled that site from AD 628 to AD 695.[20] Here there was no painted plaster. Instead, there were series of marine objects like sea urchins, sea star and brittle star, fish vertebral bones, fragments of a sea fan, tiny pearls, clam shells, a sea sponge, and several small river stones bound within a bundle. This bundle was set near the bottom of a raised platform topped by the skeleton of Smoke Imix. William Fash and others have interpreted these marine objects as representations of a level of the Classic Maya cosmos (the Underworld), citing comparative evidence from the Aztec Templo Mayor in Mexico City:

> Similar to the positioning found here, in the offerings at the Aztecs' Templo Mayor, the marine fauna were invariably placed at the bottom of the assemblage, as the substrate upon which all other layers of the world were symbolically represented by other types of offerings.[21]

What we are probably seeing in the Copan burial is a body physically represented as rising from the Underworld. Much like the Maize God, K'inich Janaab' Pakal I, or the Night Sun emerging from death, Burial XXXVII-4 provides us with an apotheosis, in this case, physical evidence of emergence. The individual is rising out of the platform and up toward the superstructure of Temple 33 (Chorcha phase), his funerary monument.

At other sites, we see tombs iconographically drawn as portals, the "hcarts" of turtles as at El Peru, or other types of supernatural entranceways, as depicted on the marker for the Early Classic Motmot burial at Copan. It may thus be appropriate to conceptualize the floors of tombs as watery surfaces, *entrances to the Underworld but not the Underworld per se.* In the case at Río Azul, tomb painters have set a body beneath water; the Copan example shows the beginning of an escape from that realm. A Classic Maya royal tomb is thus set below the first band of water depicted on Classic Maya ceramics, which houses the physical remains of kings and nobles as they are subjected to *och ha',* "water-entering." Broken layers of jadeite underlying burials at Caracol or offerings of jade and shell within subfloor burial caches at Altun Ha may reflect a similar idea. As observed by David Pendergast, most tombs at Altun Ha bear one or three caches beneath the floors of their burial chambers.[22] Such caches or similar offerings may represent watery bands, setting the body of a noble atop an entrance to the Underworld.[23]

TOMBS AS CAVES

In most pre-Hispanic Mesoamerican cultures, caves were recognized entrances to the Underworld. Their parallels to Classic Maya tombs are clear: both tombs and caves were among the places where the Classic Maya interred their dead. For royal tombs, the overlap is not only implied but also inscribed: Peter Mathews has noted a reference to the burial of the Late Classic king Itzamnaaj K'awiil of Dos Pilas "at night" inside a *ch'een,* "cave."[24] This "cave" has tentatively been identified as Burial 30 of Structure L5-1.[25] The overlap is likewise iconographic, as evidenced by a representation of Yax Pasaj Chan Yoaat—the last king of Copan—standing over the open, cavernous maw of his likely funerary monument, Temple 18.

The hieroglyphic phrase *och ch'een,* "cave-entering," probably refers to interment or the journey of a soul into a tomb. At the site of Dzibanche, east of Calakmul, the phrase *och ch'een,* "cave-entering," occurs in the context of a human sacrifice, a rather violent "interment" that calls forth images we have seen in Chapter 2, where GIII is hurled into a cave on a number of unprovenanced ceramics. On the Palenque Temple 14 tablet (see Figure 27), *och u ch'een,* "[he] enters his cave," seems to refer to the entry of K'inich Kan B'alam into a cave, whose place-name has yet to be deciphered (D6), on 9.13.13.15.0 9 Ajaw 3 K'ank'in for a Period Ending rite; he had been dead for approximately three years at this point, but this type of return seems to fit with the images of K'inich Kan B'alam standing atop the watery surface of the Underworld layers. Entering the cave implies that he had been away from it; perhaps this cave refers to his tomb, and his image is the soul of K'inich Kan B'alam returned from the Underworld. David Stuart has suggested a relationship between *och ch'een* and human sacrifice, however, so this argument is tentative.[26]

Caves are also the intended setting for Tomb 2 of the Temple of the Cross at Palenque, where stalactites are housed with the body. A cave is portrayed monumentally as the entrance to Structure B20-2nd at Caracol, a building housing numerous bodies as well as one within the stylized maw of its exterior. Architecturally, we can add to this list the Temple of the Inscriptions and Temple 18-A at Palenque, as well as structures that have interior passages linking the chambers of rooms to the tomb, such as the Margarita complex at Copan.[27] In their construction, the passages and entranceways resemble artificial tunnels within a cavern; in practice, they allowed entrance into a symbolic cave system where the watery surface of the Underworld could be accessed. Stalactites can also be found in stelae caches at Copan, although not in tombs;[28] perhaps there is an idea that stelae also emerge from symbolic caves at that site.

TOMBS AS HOUSES

Grave architects, as they worked, would have been standing within the surface of the anthropomorphic earth as well as the place where a soul of the deceased could descend into water, but they were also creating a "house" for the physical remains of the deceased. Michael Coe has dealt in depth with the theme of tombs as houses, citing similarities between grave and domestic constructions in pre-Columbian and ethnographic contexts.[29] We can also see the parallels epigraphically in phrases such as *el naj tu mukil,* "house censing at his tomb," which are also used to describe dedicatory rites for Maya dwellings.[30] Tombs may also have been thought of as ballcourts at Late Classic Palenque, as represented in the Temple of the Inscriptions: Linda Schele and Peter Mathews have compared the layout of the tomb of Janaab' Pakal to a stylized playing field.[31] Of course, ballcourts are associated with the Underworld as well; the idea that ballcourts set players within an Underworld location is well documented for Maya sites, where the Classic Maya court emphasizes "a cosmological passage through the earth's surface and into the Underworld."[32] Of course, this association would place Pakal's tomb within the Underworld and not above it. Yet the I-shaped "ballcourt" of Pakal's tomb is more akin to Mexican ballcourts, where the alley symbolizes the surface of the earth rather than an Underworld location.[33]

TIMING AND THE RITUAL PROCESS

Knowing exactly when—and where—bodies were prepared and ornamented is often impossible. Not knowing how much of the tomb was finished before the deceased was interred makes it difficult to reconstruct an order of events for tomb construction. The excavation or creation of the funerary chamber was clearly the first part, but after that point the picture becomes less clear. One example, Burial 23 at Tikal (Figure 33), clearly demonstrates that tomb

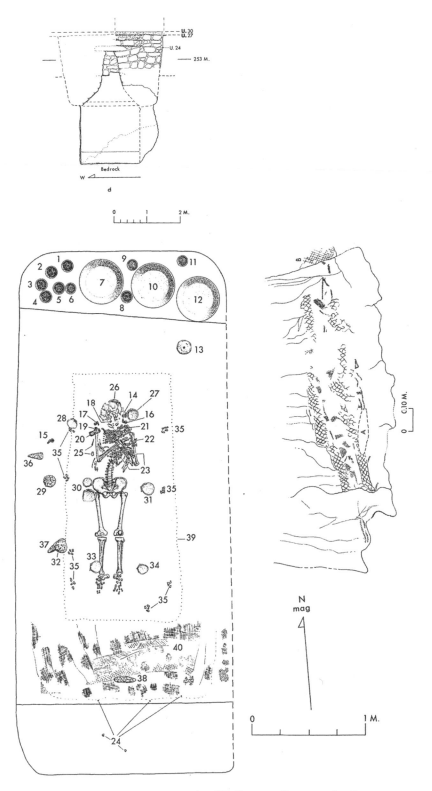

FIGURE 33. *Tikal Burial 23 (W. Coe 1990, figs. 172 and 176)*

plastering, artifact arrangement, and possibly inhumation could take place at the same time.

Created during the reign of Jasaw Chan K'awiil I (AD 682–734; Ruler A), Burial 23 was excavated deep within Temple 33, the original funerary monument to Siyaj Chan K'awiil II (Stormy Sky). It was intrusive into the previously existing Structure 4D-33-2nd and well below bedrock level, south of the tomb of that Early Classic ruler. This set Burial 23 off the central axis for the original structure, much like other multiple burial sites at Tikal. Cutting an access stairway as well as a vertical shaft downward into the structure, the grave excavators eventually converted portions of the stairwell into benches. A vault from dressed stones was supported by beams and topped with capstones, and the walls of the tomb proper were plastered over. There is evidence that the grave was being stocked as it was being plastered, for a number of the polychrome tripod plates and fluted cylinders—but not the body—displayed plaster splash. William Coe notes that in their haste, the excavators actually left a flint pick within the tomb and destroyed a jade bead, which was located far from the body and was apparently the only fragmented item in the burial. Added to this picture is a possible cloth drape laid over the deceased; there is no evidence of plaster on the drape's remains, but such an item would have protected the body as workers labored inside the tomb.[34]

Such a hurried picture, however, is in direct contrast to most royal burials in the Maya area, which contain carefully laid arrangements of shells, ceramics, or other grave goods and motifs. It is likely that specific body treatments, such as embalming, dressing, painting, or bundling, took place wholly or partially outside graves, particularly in the case of royal crypts. It is to these archaeologically observed practices that we now turn our attention.

EMBALMING AND PROCESSING

The possibility that some of the Classic Maya dead were embalmed or otherwise processed has been explored most extensively by Estella Weiss-Krejci. In looking at evidence for cremation, evisceration, the disposal or storage of internal organs, and other body processing, Weiss-Krejci has pointed out that cuts, missing skeletal elements, or other situations traditionally associated with human sacrifice, disease, or taphonomic processes could—in select cases—be the result of intentional preservative activities.[35] At present, however, it is difficult to point out definitive examples of such behavior. In the Classic Maya lowlands, there are a few cases of cremation at Dzibilchaltun and possibly at Hatzcap Ceel, but such practices seem only to have gained wide currency among the Maya in the Terminal Classic and Postclassic.[36]

Evidence for royal evisceration or the removal of certain parts of the body before inhumation is somewhat more solid, given that bones often display evidence of cut marks or skeletal remains are found lacking specific parts, such as faces, heads, hands, feet, fingers, or even long bones. In royal interments, cut marks have often been attributed to human sacrifice. For example, the tomb of the Red Queen in Palenque Temple XIII-sub had a complementary female interment whose lower thoracic vertebrae had been cut repeatedly. These cuts are usually produced by the removal of abdominal or thoracic viscera and are conventionally attributed to human sacrifice;[37] while this may be the case in the tomb of the Red Queen, there is always the possibility that such cuts would arise from postmortem treatments.[38] As yet there is no evidence that royal individuals bear such cuts, however.[39]

Royals missing body parts, including faces, have been observed by Welsh at sites like Calakmul, Tikal, Uaxactun, and Dzibilchaltun.[40] As Weiss-Krejci points out, many of these bones were missing from otherwise complete individuals; assuming that not all of these were the result of royal sacrifices or warfare, the natural conclusion might be some practice of body processing. Such activities would clearly not have been driven by a desire to protect the corpse against decay, and to the author, they seem to be more motivated by a concern for heirlooms or ancestral relics (see Chapter 5). For preservation purposes, removing or destroying the viscera would have been far more effective. Weiss-Krejci notes patterns of Classic and Postclassic burning at Uaxactun, Dzibilchaltun, Nebaj, Altar de Sacrificios, and Topoxte, where charcoal was recovered near feet, pelves, and heads subjected to limited fire damage. Some of the burials she cites are high-status ones, and the Altar de Sacrificios interment (Burial 128) was almost certainly royal. She notes that

> the recurring presence of charcoal in the pelvic region may suggest either direct subjection of the viscera to fire, the replacement of cremated viscera into the corpse or filling of the corpse with ashes for the purposes of desiccation.[41]

Certainly, there are references by Diego de Landa to "burning half the body" of corpses during funerary rites in colonial Yucatán.[42] But as Weiss-Krejci mentions, there are over one hundred highland and lowland burials, royal and otherwise, that contain charcoal or ash that is not directly associated with the body. Clearly there are other possible interpretations, including activities related to the closing and sealing of interments (see "Sealing the Tomb," below). Yet there is enough information to warrant further investigation, particularly in light of the fact that the Classic Maya were experimenting with resins, bundles, and clays in their mortuary rites. There is at least one example from Calakmul that supports the use of preservative resins in royal interments.[43] Bundling and the use of clays, however, are much more common phenomena; they were part of the larger process of dressing and preparing the corpse for interment.

DRESSING AND BUNDLING THE CORPSE

Preservation conditions often work against the recovery of cloth and other per-ishable remains from ancient tombs. As a result, the degree to which a royal corpse was dressed is usually unclear, with remains of headdresses, bracelets, necklaces, and other finery suggesting a more elaborate arrangement of per-ished textiles and other materials. At the surveyed sites, there is only one burial devoid of grave goods or decorations, a fact that prompted the excavators of Tikal Burial 125 to conclude that the primary skeleton—posited as the remains of Yax Ehb' Xook of Tikal—was disrobed and interred. Whether or not this burial is indeed the Preclassic crypt of the "founder" of dynastic Tikal, it is clearly significant architecturally. Burial 125 and its associated cache mark a new axis for all subsequent construction efforts in the North Acropolis, the royal "necropolis" for Preclassic and Classic era Tikal.[44] Given this significance, to be buried *completely* naked would have been unusual, if not downright insulting: during the Classic Period, the only individuals depicted as naked were war cap-tives or humiliated gods. Even in the aforementioned Maize God resurrection sequence, where the god is belched from a fish-serpent and dressed by atten-dants, no one truly appears without clothing.

Nevertheless, there are only two royal burials in the Classic Maya lowlands where the remains of worn textiles have been physically observed; perhaps they originally appeared like the textiles of Piedras Negras Stela 40, on which a woman wearing textiles and bound in cloth reclines in her underground tomb. In his work at Río Azul, Robert Carlsen produced a series of remarkable finds in Tombs 19 and 23. The men lying in these tombs, after having been painted with cinnabar while naked, were dressed in a variety of cloth and leather goods. In Tomb 19, the corpse was subsequently wrapped in a cinnabar-painted bundle; plant leaves, identified as allspice or pimienta (*Pimienta dioica*), were placed over the corpse and within the wrapping (Figure 34). Padding and knotted cords were also noted in association with the body, although none of these materials were found near his head: that section bore a headdress and would have poked outward from the wrapped bundle,[45] much in the manner of the image on the Berlin pot.

Evidence for this kind of bundling, or even for the covering of corpses in pelts or other textiles, is far more common. We have evidence that corpses were wrapped in both the Early and Late Classic, although Río Azul Tomb 19 pro-vides the only clear Early Classic royal example. As represented in Appendix 2, Late Classic bundled corpses appear in royal interments at Tikal and Copan; there are also cases of bundling in high-status interments at Tonina as well as Calakmul, although in the Calakmul example, the bundle contains a flexed rather than an extended corpse.[46]

Annabeth Headrick[47] has proposed that these bundles are analogous to

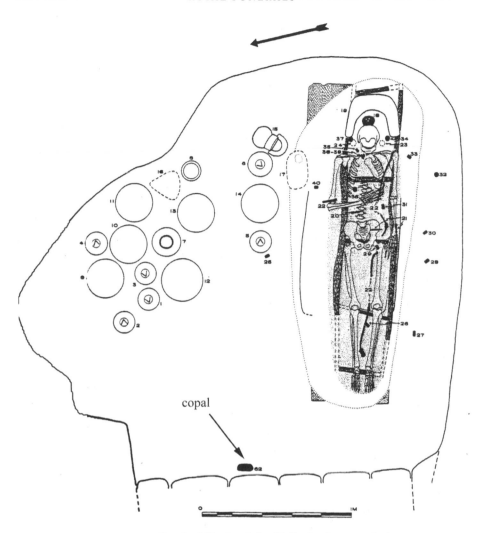

copal

FIGURE 34. *Río Azul Tomb 19 (after Hall 1989, figs. 14 and 17)*

mummy bundles at Teotihuacan, where seated masked bundles may have served as oracles or effigies of deceased ancestors within open funerary shrines. She argues that the preparatory and reverential processes involved in historically documented cases of mummy bundling are applicable to the Teotihuacan example, drawing parallels to a depiction of a Classic Maya bundled corpse on Piedras Negras Stela 40. Using documentation from Tarascan and Mixtec sources, she provides a model for bundle preparation that may be compared to evidence from the Classic Maya area.

According to Headrick, the Tarascans would prepare the bodies of their deceased kings by taking their corpses—at night—to an area where firewood and pine needles were distributed. The body of a king, dressed in finery, would be taken around this unlit funeral pyre four times to the music of trumpets; with singing, they would place him on the pyre to light it, subsequently sacrificing with clubs a number of intoxicated retainers and burying them. By dawn, the king and his finery were reduced to ashes. The ashes and the remains of his gold and jewelry would then be set within a cloth bundle and bound; the bundle was then decorated with a funerary mask and further items of gold, feathers, turquoise, and shell.

Remains of cremated bundles have been found in western Mexico, and records of similar mummy bundles are ubiquitous in highland Mesoamerica.[48] For the Mixtecs, cremated kings within bundles appear to have been used as oracles as well as "battle standards" or protective effigies; John Pohl cites a concern with the capture and destruction of ancestral effigies in war as a way of removing the power base of dominant lineages.[49] For the Aztecs, ancestor bundles served a similar purpose: after his death, the Aztec king Tlacaelel was embalmed, set on a litter, and brought forth in a battle to subdue the site of Tliliuhquitepec. Huitzilopochtli himself is reported to have been bundled, conversed with, and taken to war on numerous occasions; as the supreme "ancestor" of the Aztecs, he was mummified and wrapped as a deceased Mexica king. Huitzilopochtli was not the only god to be treated in this way; we have numerous examples from Postclassic codices where various Mexica gods are wrapped as bundles, wearing masks and embalmed in cloth.[50] We know that for the Aztecs, these god bundles represented the funerary bundles of gods who had sacrificed themselves in fire for the creation of the Fifth Sun at Teotihuacan.[51] Perhaps the cremation of Aztec lords was related to this sacrifice, a replication of the gods' sacrifice in death.

Returning to the Classic Maya, we have numerous iconographic examples of god bundles (Figure 35). Typically, they are not the reclining bundles recovered from burials but small bound packages similar to the Aztec, Mixtec, and Tarascan examples above, rough iconographic correlates of the burial within Tomb 1 of Calakmul Structure VII. Yet the Maya examples differ in that the heads are not covered but are glaringly exposed. Tikal Burial 195 may also have housed a similarly wrapped body. Jorge Guillemín describes three matrices of sediment (representing cloth) around the corpse, one of which clearly represents bound material around the postcranial skeleton.[52] Thus a "layering" may have taken place, with the first layer being a tightly bound cloth around the body, excluding the head, followed by two others, creating a cigar-shaped bundle. Copan Burial XXXVII-4 provides an interesting twist on this type of wrapping: the entire body appears to have been encased in an unfired clay matrix. Similar clay casings have been excavated in high-status Early Classic burials at Zaculeu, Zacualpa, and Lamanai.[53]

The Maya examples of bundled royal corpses also differ in that the majority

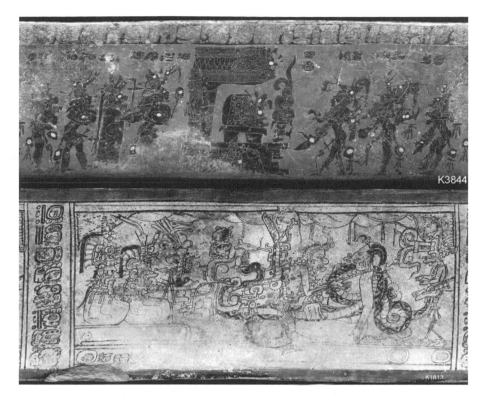

FIGURE 35. *Two examples of bundles in Maya art (#K3844 and K1813 © Justin Kerr)*

are extended, not flexed. Bundling appears to have been more a part of a preparatory rite for interment rather than a means for increasing corpse portability. Nevertheless, there are examples of secondary or even seated bundled interments in high-status and royal burials: Tonina Burial IV-6, a site of repeated reentry and interment, consisted of several bundled corpses, while Tikal Burial 48, the tomb of Siyaj Chan K'awiil II (Stormy Sky), may represent a secondary and bundled version of the king himself.[54] As Patricia McAnany has noted, seated bundles replicate the positioning of lords on their thrones: one such example is the Early Classic Burial C1 at Uaxactun, which has an adult male set upon a platform and supported by a stuccoed backrest.[55]

It is unclear whether such bundles served a function outside the tomb. At Piedras Negras, the dead clearly played a role in wedding and birthday celebrations, although their presence may have been metaphorical rather than physical.[56] Lest these suggested uses seem more frivolous than the Aztec or Mixtec examples, we may remember that Classic Maya rulers carried god effigies into battle. During the protracted wars between Tikal and Calakmul—or its allies—Jasaw Chan K'awiil I (Ruler A) captured the Calakmul deity *yajaw maan* in his victory over Yuknoom Yich'aak K'ahk'.[57] It is not inconceivable that

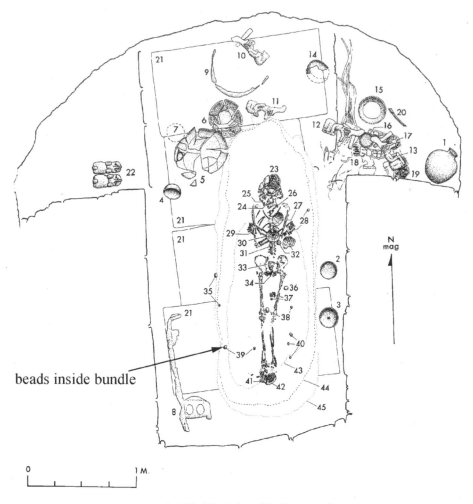

beads inside bundle

FIGURE 36. *Tikal Burial 195 (W. Coe 1990, fig. 198)*

the Classic Maya, much like the Postclassic Aztecs, also carried ancestor bundles with them against their enemies. The Classic Maya could also have used these bundles in migrations and pilgrimages: their Postclassic descendants the Quiche carried around a bundle representing their deceased ancestor B'alam Quitze as well as another icon of the god Tohil on their migrations.[58]

Bundling in the Maya case appears to have involved the incorporation of artifacts—as well as the corpse—within tightly packed cloth tied with cord (Figure 36). The ruler or royal individual would be adorned in jade, shell, lithic, or other artifacts and provided with accoutrements of office and status, although it is often difficult to distinguish between items of dress and those impregnated in the cloth wrappings. Like the Central Mexican examples, some of these bundles had masks, including the aforementioned Uaxactun Burial C1. In fact, masked mortuary bundles in the lowlands stretch at least back to 50 BC, with Tikal Burial 80 providing one of the earliest examples.[59]

In Maya iconography, mortuary bundles are characterized by their large knots and overlap with depictions of god bundles and "sacred bundles," rounded tied bags containing unknown—but perhaps precious—materials marked *icatz* (bundle, burden). Classic Maya monumental inscriptions and iconography also portray tying or wrapping in conjunction with Period Endings.[60] It is generally accepted that a *tuun,* used as a unit of time but literally meaning "stone," was wrapped or bound at discrete intervals within the Maya calendar at a variety of lowland sites; at Copan, for example, we have monumental versions of wrapped stones. This *tuun*-binding was accompanied by the erection of a stela as well as bloodletting rites or ancestral rites. In producing these stylized, wrapped monumental stones, the Classic Maya appear to have been encapsulating the end of a time period within an object; we might view mortuary bundling in much the same way.

Deceased rulers were the focus of ceremonial and political activities within Classic Maya polities; each was a *k'uhul ajaw,* "holy lord," whose power had ended, yet the importance of the royal body and deceased personality required the construction of tombs or elaborate funerary monuments. Wrapping the body is a means of localizing the remains of a deceased ruler to a finite space; perhaps it was also a means of creating a finite space for his ritual and political power, deceased though he was.

PAINTING

The painting of certain royal bodies is something that has received scant attention in the literature. William Coe, Alberto Ruz Lhuillier, and Estella Weiss-Krejci have done the most to document this occurrence in the Maya area; Rebecca Storey has proposed a correlation between so-called red-paint burials and royal tombs.[61] Painting of bodies appears to occur in a variety of contexts, from the moments *before* bundling and wrapping to well after the body has been set in its tomb. The clearest cases of prewrapping paint on bodies occur at Río Azul: Grant Hall and Robert Carlsen have documented two cases where corpses were painted red prior to being dressed and—in Tomb 23—bundled.[62]

In a number of examples throughout the lowlands, bundles are not reported but paint is. Aside from Río Azul Tombs 19 and 23, the other burials listed in Appendix 2 as bearing red paint display evidence that cinnabar or hematite was painted or sprinkled over bodies that may never have been bundled. Of these, K'inich Janaab' Pakal I of Palenque and Yax Nuun Ayiin of Tikal were clearly provided with red paint during the burial rite; the high-status occupants of Tonina Burials VII-1a and VIII-2 likewise received this treatment. All of these bodies appear undisturbed and in primary context, with Pakal and Yax

Nuun Ayiin displaying clear evidence that the rulers were sprinkled—and not painted—with the substance. Río Azul Tomb 1 likely fits within this category as well, although due to looting, we may never be sure. For the Margarita Burial at Copan, Robert Sharer and others[63] have reported evidence for the painting and sprinkling of bones after interment, during a tomb reentry rite; based on this information, the similarly disturbed Hunal tomb may have seen the use of cinnabar or hematite solely in postinterment ceremonies.

Positionally, the red paint generally occurs all over the skeleton, although the aforementioned Tonina burials, Tikal Burial 10, and possibly Río Azul Tomb 1 may present evidence that heads or skulls were accorded primary importance for decoration with cinnabar or hematite. It is possible that in cases of bundling, the bundles themselves were painted and the red color on the bones is the result of leaching. Archaeologically, it is very difficult to determine the difference between direct application to skin or bones and such indirect means of coloring.

But what is the significance of the "red-paint" burials, which occur outside the sample context to include other sites spanning the Preclassic to the Late Classic? Alberto Ruz Lhuillier has suggested that the red paint was applied to make the deceased appear more lifelike, much like a rouge.[64] Another hypothesis is that the cinnabar or hematite served as a preservative; metal-based liquids, absorbed into the skin, can serve as a poison or deterrent for insects and microorganisms. But the red paint is never in a liquid form, such as mercury, that could be absorbed and thus serve in the embalming process. A third idea is that the red paint was designed to convey a sense of resurrection. If we look at the significance of the color red in Classic Maya hieroglyphs, it is universally associated with the east, the direction of the rising sun and one that surely played into notions of Maya rebirth, particularly in the generation of solar and celestial ancestral bodies. Red is also the dominant color of Classic Maya monumental architecture.

David Stuart has suggested that the cinnabar or hematite is symbolic blood, conceptually related to the concept of Tzotzil *ch'uhlel* and the Classic Maya *k'uhul*.[65] As outlined in Chapter 2, *k'uhul* is represented by droplets of blood and seems to serve as the essence of what was sacred in Maya society. Coating a body with symbolic blood would seem to be a powerful statement, one that is perhaps related cross-culturally to the use of red ochre in the burials of late Archaic and post-Archaic North America. There ochre is sprinkled over bodies much in the manner of Mesoamerican cinnabar or hematite (to which red ochre itself is analogous).[66]

Like the North American cases, however, we have no *direct* evidence linking blood to cinnabar or hematite. Yet the idea that cinnabar and hematite are linked to rebirth may provide a clue in the decipherment of red-paint burials. Death is often represented as a kind of birth: the example from Río Azul Tomb 1, mentioned in Chapter 2, illustrates the "birth" of what was likely an Early Classic ruler of that site. K'inich Janaab' Pakal I of Palenque is displayed in the fetal position on his famous Sarcophagus Lid; his positioning is mirrored in rebirth imagery on Classic Maya ceramics. Looking at the physical process of human birth, we see blood everywhere: infants emerge from the womb covered in that substance. Taking into account this image and comparing it to Classic Maya east-west imagery, references to deaths as births, and ideas about *k'uhul* and sacred essences, it seems likely that coating a body with cinnabar or hematite after death signified rebirth.

Although the two materials do not properly dissolve, if one mixes cinnabar or hematite with water, the result *is* a bloodlike liquid. As Harriet Beaubien has suggested, it seems likely that the Classic Maya would have had many uses for this blood substitute, particularly in mortuary contexts.[67] Coating a body with symbolic blood would create a parallel between the physical and spiritual aspects of death as per Hertz; this practice has implications for how the Maya at different sites saw the process of rebirth itself. It should be mentioned here that some of the royal burials at Palenque, Tikal, and Tonina were provided with cinnabar or hematite *prior* to inhumation, whereas some of the royal burials at Copan were painted at least once *after* primary interment (see Chapter 5).

ARRANGING THE BODY, ARRANGING THE FURNITURE

As mentioned earlier in this chapter, Classic Maya burials share certain characteristics in both their construction and implementation. In terms of grave furniture and body orientation, Welsh has noted a number of regional or site-specific practices: in the southern lowlands, prevailing head orientations and skeletal positions, in addition to grave reuse, are observed in frequencies suggestive of localized burial customs. He has posited that there were regional traditions throughout the lowlands; Welsh has likewise observed a rough correlation between these regional mortuary customs and local architectural styles.[68] More research on the regional, and particularly the temporal, nature of Maya burials as a whole is needed to support these views, but they serve as an interesting baseline for comparison with royal interments. As can be seen in Appendix 2, royal interments do seem to share in the broader orientation and positioning patterns; artifactually, they share the wider practice of placing a jade or stone bead within the mouth of the deceased. Among the other artifacts from royal tombs, we find both items shared with other sites and local innovations.

As mentioned in the introduction, royal burials have previously been defined according to statistical frequencies of certain architectural and artifact types, including large numbers of ceramics, red pigments, earflares, stingray spines, jades, pearls, obsidian blades, and mosaics (including funerary masks); to these categories we might add the prevalence of inscribed or painted hieroglyphic objects, such as ceramic vessels or shell artifacts.[69] One broader set of categories includes:

> codex remains, cinnabar, mirrors, stone vessels, jadeite jewelry, jadeite earflares, jadeite masks, jadeite pendants, jadeite or stone tinklers, ceremonial bars, certain rare shells, textual remains, and perhaps stingray spines.[70]

"Royalty" has likewise been defined by Fitzsimmons and others according to complexes of artifacts specific to particular sites, that is, items that together define a burial as "royal." Instead of defining Pan-Maya criteria, such as minimum numbers of ceramics or jades, for royal interments, they see royalty as a relative phenomenon particular to each individual site.[71] There is, of course, significant overlap between these models: most of the royal burials listed in the appendixes (see Appendix 3) do in fact contain high frequencies of ceramic, jade, obsidian, and similar artifacts. Approaching the various meanings embedded within such furniture is a difficult task; doubtless several books on each category would not suffice to explain patterns and variations. Nevertheless, we can make some basic observations from artifact form and placement. The following paragraphs focus on common regional and local patterns in grave furniture divided by type or form, with particular attention given to patterns that reveal stages of funerary arrangement.

Textiles and Other Layering

One of the shared characteristics of royal burials is found in the Maya practice of layering tombs with textiles, mats, pelts, or cloths. Such materials often provide us with a sense of chronology for tomb activities. Knowing when an artifact was set within a tomb is often impossible, given variations in tomb conditions, excavation techniques, recording practices, episodic tomb reentry, and other human factors past and present, but in the case of textile layering, we do gain a sense of artifact sequence. We can view when and where artifacts were set during the layout of the funerary chamber, based on their presence above or below textiles and other perishables. The aforementioned Tikal Burial 23, for example, contained a cinnabar-painted litter surmounted by jaguar pelts; these formed the foundation, in turn, for the royal corpse and sequential layers of shells as well as other marine objects. Similar behavior can be found in other Late Classic royal interments at Tikal (Burials 116 and 196) and Copan (Burial XXXVII-4).[72]

Another form of layering can be seen at Palenque in the Temple of the Cross. Each of the three Late Classic burials (Tombs 1–3) appears to have been completely covered with textiles following the arrangement of goods within their funerary chambers.[73] We might think of this as makeshift "wrapping" or an effort to prevent falling debris from touching the bodies as floors were made and burials sealed. Tikal Burial 23 may also have had a similar layer, placed above the aforementioned body; it is not clear, however, whether these mats fell from the area of the ceiling.[74]

Unfortunately, aside from the Late Classic Tikal, Copan, and Palenque examples, there are no royal burials where textiles or pelts have been adequately preserved. Of course, there are jaguar phalanges or other faunal remains suggesting the presence of pelts in many royal interments, but lacking clear layering, it is often impossible to say when such artifacts were placed within the funerary chamber. When such textiles or pelts are sufficiently preserved, however, we are able to view interments stratigraphically. A similar situation can be observed when wooden or stone platforms are recovered.

Wooden or Stone Platforms

In a number of cases, we have evidence that royal individuals were set upon wooden or stone biers.[75] As shown in Appendix 2, rulers from Altar de Sacrificios, Altun Ha, Tikal, Río Azul, and Copan were placed upon litters that were sometimes decorated with cinnabar or even paint. We can imagine such funerary biers being painted in preparation for the body of the ruler, who was then arranged with jade jewelry and other finery. The examples of such biers range from the Early to the Late Classic with no particular discernible pattern, although, like layering, these platforms seem relatively rare; preservation as well as recovery techniques may mask wider distributions. The case at Copan seems noteworthy in that there may be a shift from stone-platform burials, represented by the early Classic Hunal, Margarita, and Sub-Jaguar interments, to more perishable platforms, as represented by the wooden bier in the Late Classic Copan Burial XXXVII-4.[76] As we have seen for the latter interment, the preparation of the tomb of Smoke Imix involved not only horizontal but also vertical arrangements of artifacts; surrounded by a clay matrix (see above), Smoke Imix was literally rising from the surface of his funerary chamber.

Ceramics

A tremendous range of ceramics, both in type and number, are interred with the royal dead. On one end, we have interments like Tikal Burial 125 and Piedras Negras Burial 82 (Figure 37), which contain few-to-no ceramic vessels. The reasons for this are not clear, although we might hypothesize that pertinent objects were kept or deposited at a later date; in the case of Burial 125, for example, a cache containing ceramic, jade, shell, and other high-status goods was close to that threadbare interment. At the opposite end of the spectrum are burials we have seen at places like Tikal that bear scores of bowls, plates, tripods, and other ceramic types. Aside from providing numerical statistics, the unfortunate

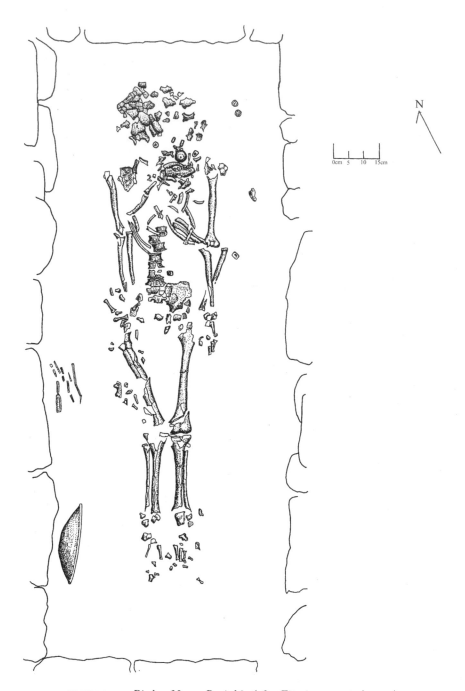

FIGURE 37. *Piedras Negras Burial 82 (after Fitzsimmons et al. 2003)*

truth is that the majority of such vessels within burial contexts served purposes unknown to us. Of course, many such vessels bear Underworld or mythological themes, and their forms and functions have been well documented: whether used for drinking chocolate, serving and storing perishables, or burning incense, such vessels sometimes bear signs of use. It has even been suggested that materials like incense or chocolate, frequent additions to grave furniture, were used to feed the dead.[77] Yet a broad systematic analysis of residues or other remains on ceramics in lowland burials has not been done.

One exception to this rule is an analysis of ceramic types and forms in lowland burials by Estella Weiss-Krejci and T. Patrick Culbert.[78] Their study is limited to the Preclassic and Early Classic, but the conclusions are startling. Corresponding roughly with the arrival of Teotihuacano warriors in the Peten at places like El Peru and Tikal, a shift in ceramic types occurred that was marked by a decrease in earlier, traditional pottery forms and the introduction of new vessel types within elite and royal lowland interments. In the Central Peten and at the site of Copan, some of these types clearly harked back to that western Mexican metropolis. Such disruption was felt not only in ceramic types but in other artifact forms as well: the frequencies and types of jade and shell artifacts, in addition to bone and particularly avian materials, were fundamentally transformed. Other such transformations will doubtless emerge as new studies are made and data processed; understanding the greater ceramic picture is crucial to future analyses of lowland Maya burials.

A small part of this greater picture is revealed at the site of Calakmul. One local, perhaps circumstantial, phenomenon that has been observed there involves the use of dishes—presumably in place of litters or stone platforms—as "beds" for royal interments. In both tombs from Structures III and VII, dated to the Early and Late Classic, respectively, individuals were placed upon a line of monochrome dishes.[79] More examples are needed to make this a practice in its own right, although the idea of using dishes as bases for interments may be related to the Tikal custom of setting bowls beneath heads;[80] to these archaeological examples we might add the iconographic use of an offering bowl to hold the defunct K'inich Janaab' Pakal I of Palenque.

Jades and Celts

Jade artifacts are worn or held in the hands in most royal interments; representing not only breath, as mouth beads, but also water, maize, and vegetation, jade held great value in the daily lives—and deaths—of Mesoamerican peoples. In terms of energy expenditure, jade beads and other artifacts were certainly among the costliest artifacts to produce; Appendix 3 details the tremendous variation in the numbers and forms of jade found within royal Maya interments.[81] Places like Altun Ha and Calakmul, for example, make other sites seem comparatively jade-poor. As is the case with ceramics, if we were to specify a minimum number or quality of jade artifacts as the criteria for "royal" interments, we would be left with far fewer interments in the sample. The picture is complicated by relatively poor interments with known ties to epigraphically identifiable rulers. Ornamented with necklaces, headdresses, mosaics, and other jade-bearing artifacts, however, the majority of Maya rulers and royalty carried these stone versions of flowers, breaths, and vegetation to the grave.

Plaques and carved ornaments likewise have a wide geographic and temporal distribution. We find representations of K'inich Ajaw, pectorals, jaguars, and even skulls in royal interments, although the forms of such items seem to be particular to individual burials. A related artifact type can be found at Palenque, where obsidian celts, or stylized axes, probably worn much like the jade or groundstone celts of Classic Maya iconography, occur in royal burials within the Temple of the Inscriptions, the Temple of the Cross, and Temple 18-A.[82] Given that obsidian was, in Classic Maya thought, a product of lightning striking the earth, the Palenque celts may be oblique references to the Maize God resurrection cycle.[83] Chaak, the Classic Storm God, is sometimes shown on Maya ceramics striking the earth with lightning weapons, thereby facilitating the emergence of new life. These celts are reminiscent of that ancient Maya myth. Of course, obsidian as a material was also used for both martial and sacrificial purposes, particularly in ritual bloodletting.

Bloodletting Artifacts

Stingray spines and other items connected to bloodletting were staples of Classic royal interments. Although not limited to royalty, their presence in royal tombs is often profound, with stingray spines, obsidian blades, or bone artifacts occurring in combination. The most extreme form of this behavior is represented by Tomb 2 at Yaxchilan, where over one hundred bone needles and spines, as well as nine carved bone bloodletters, were recovered.[84] Deified, complex bloodletting artifacts such as the latter are somewhat rare, but analogues do occur at both Piedras Negras and Tikal (Figure 38).[85] Such deification is limited artifactually to the Late Classic, although given the prevalence of these bloodletters in Maya iconography, it seems likely that similar items will surface in the larger archaeological record.

Bloodletters occur in a variety of mortuary contexts, from tomb floors and funerary biers to specific locations around the deceased. In Early Classic tombs from Tikal and Río Azul, stingray spines were placed within the hands of the deceased; a similar Early to Late Classic practice in the Central Peten involved setting one or more spines over the male pelvic area, mimicking their piercing role in bloodletting ceremonies.[86] A concern with the pelvis is manifested in the Late Classic tombs of K'inich Janaab' Pakal I of Palenque and the Margarita burial at Copan, where jade and other artifacts were set between the legs

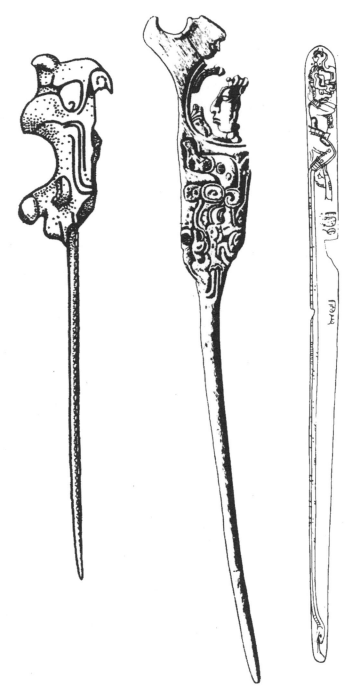

FIGURE 38. *Socketed bloodletter from Piedras Negras Burial 82 (left) and deified bloodletters from Tikal Burial 116 (center and right; after Fitzsimmons et al. 2003 and Trik 1963, figs. 11 and 8)*

of the deceased, although their role in the interment remains unclear.[87] Certainly, related bloodletting practices within interments have been demonstrated at Caracol, where we find bloodletting implements and spindle whorls within the mouth of the individual inside Structure B20; this may be a female version of the bloodletting rite within a Maya tomb.[88]

Another pattern in bloodletting artifacts is manifested by the use of boxes or possibly bags of obsidian, stingray spines, and other artifacts in Late Classic interments at Tikal and Piedras Negras, as well as at Early Classic Copan. Although no such containers have survived intact, dense clusters of bloodletting artifacts such as stingray spines, obsidian blades, jade stingray spines, or bone needles suggest these items may have been in containers similar to those recovered in the vicinity of Tortuguero and Piedras Negras.[89] Together with the pelvic and held examples, these bloodletters illustrate a desire to portray the royal dead as engaging in a fundamental aspect of Maya ceremonial life. Shedding blood to conjure ancestors and supernatural entities during life, the individuals physically—if not actually—continued to perform their ceremonial duties in death. Similar concerns with royal representation may be demonstrated by the aforementioned Caracol burial and the Margarita burial at Copan, which contain quantities of needles, spindle whorls, and other artifacts indicating an identification with weaving. Robert Sharer and Linda Schele have suggested that the weaving implements of the Margarita burial, for example, were interred to identify its occupant as a female, lunar entity.[90]

Shells and Other Marine Artifacts

Although they may identify particular qualities of individuals, marine artifacts are today recognized as objects that metaphorically transformed tombs into watery realms. Placed around bodies, within containers, and above or below corpses, shells, pearls, sea urchins, and other watery artifacts were common in royal interments and had particular currency at places like Altun Ha and Calakmul; marine artifacts create a sense that the body has been set within a cave or upon an underworld surface. Such creations were formulaic in the Central Peten, where, following its placement on a funerary bier or tomb floor, the body was complemented by successive lines of Spondylus valves. Created for the Late Classic king Jasaw Chan K'awiil I (Ruler A) of Tikal, Burial 116 provides a good example (Figure 39). Resting upon a dais covered with textiles and jaguar pelts, Jasaw Chan K'awiil I was buried with a famous cluster of bone objects as well as artifacts of jade, shell, bone, and ceramic; some of these, including stingray spines and fish vertebrae, were set immediately below his body. Covering his legs, arms, and torso—as well as the larger dais—were lines of Spondylus shells, along with other kinds of shells set at his feet, below his head, and around the chamber.[91] Such lines of shells are found in a number of royal

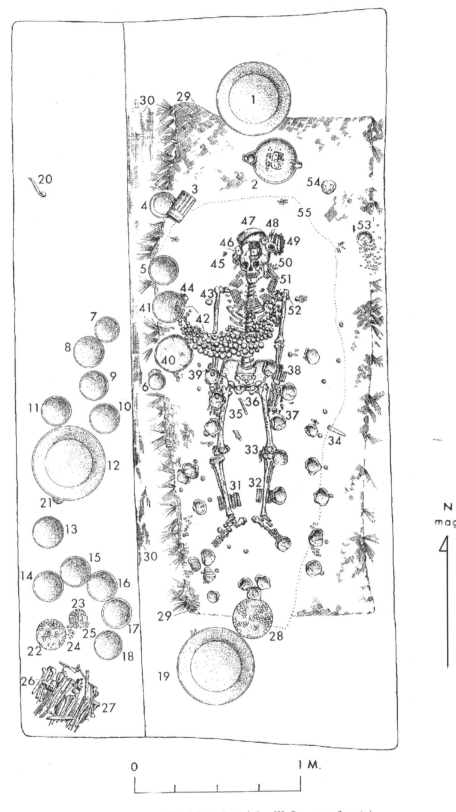

FIGURE 39. *Tikal Burial 116 (after W. Coe 1990, fig. 260)*

burials at Tikal and possibly at Uaxactun,[92] over a period of approximately three hundred years from the Early to the Late Classic.

A related practice in the Central Peten can be seen in the use of Spondylus valves to cradle or cover the head (and sometimes the feet, within and outside bundling contexts); they often occur with shell lines, and have a similar temporal distribution, but are found in royal burials at Río Azul and Dos Pilas as well as Tikal.[93] Despite their limited distribution, these practices clearly represent specialized versions of broader lowland beliefs; the large quantities of Spondylus and other shells found throughout lowland royal—and elite—burials probably represent similar ideas. The lord is physically, if not iconographically, set within the surface of the watery Underworld. In the case of shell alignments, what we may be seeing is an attempt to create iconographic watery bands within the physical limitations of the tomb.

Bowl Coverings and Masks

Ceramic vessels and masks, like shells, are often associated with crania in Maya interments. As W. Bruce M. Welsh has demonstrated, placing a bowl over or under a skull seems to have been commonplace in elite, nonelite, and royal interments throughout the Classic Period: we find skulls and bowls in residences, temples, household shrines, ceremonial platforms, and plazas, although they are most common in residential burials.[94] Among royal burials, bowls generally fall over the skull; Welsh suggests that the purpose of this practice was to protect the head.[95] He likewise notes a local pattern among elite interments at Tikal, where bowls tend to be recovered under rather than over skulls. Another pattern, perhaps limited to the Central Peten, can be found at Tikal, Altar de Sacrificios, and Seibal, where bowls with kill holes are placed over the face. That the royal Burials 128 and 116 in his sample, from Altar de Sacrificios and Tikal respectively, display this behavior suggests that the use of facial bowls spanned multiple social strata.

Mosaic masks, while covering the face, probably had less practical functions; likewise, mosaics forming pectorals or other artifacts of clothing, so prevalent in royal burials at Palenque, served more decorative or religious functions. Although masks in particular occur in only a few of the burials listed in Appendixes 2 and 3, they have a long history of use—particularly in the Central Peten—stretching back to the Preclassic. Vaguely individualistic, they overlap with ceramic vessels over skulls in a rare, albeit interesting, way. At Early Classic Uaxactun and Preclassic Tikal, there are a few examples where mosaic masks substitute for facial bones; the bones from Uaxactun Burials C1 and A20, for example, had apparently been removed at some point prior to inhumation and replaced with masks.[96] Outside the southern lowlands, at the site of Dzibilchaltun in northern Yucatán, we find a number of Classic and Postclassic elite interments where faces or whole skulls were likewise replaced, but with bowls![97]

Needless to say, the precise relationship of masks to bowls is unclear; I will deal further with these ideas, considering issues of mutilation or even ancestral veneration, in Chapter 5.

Multiple Interments

For Tikal, William Coe has reconstructed the sequence of events for Burial 10, the tomb of the Early Classic ruler Yax Nuun Ayiin I (Curl Snout).[98] This is one of the best known of all Maya interments, consisting of the remains of Yax Nuun Ayiin I and at least nine adolescents (Figure 40). Placed on his funerary bier, the king was above most of the surrounding individuals. On the basis of textile and rope imprints, Coe postulates that one of the adolescents (Skeleton J) had been wrapped as a bundle and suspended along the north wall, presumably lowered into the tomb after much of the layout had taken place. Citing a combination of skeletal, architectural, and material evidence, the excavators conclude that Skeleton J was the last individual brought into the tomb, possibly as a hurried last-minute addition. Based on the awkward positioning of Skeleton G, moreover, they propose that at least one of the individuals expired while inside the funerary chamber. The assumption has been that each of the adolescents was sacrificed for the interment of Skeleton A, although there is no osteological evidence to support premature death for any of them.

A similarly grisly picture surrounds the Late Classic body of K'inich Yo'nal Ahk II (Ruler 3) of Piedras Negras (Figure 41).[99] Following the installation of his body within Burial 5, at least one of the two present adolescent males was draped over the dead king. We find adolescent or young adult men and women in all manner of positions within other royal interments of the lowlands, from remains in boxes and bowls to groupings of crania. Other than the presence of these possibly sacrificed individuals, and the fact that they appear to have been of lesser status, we have little to go on to determine their purpose or meaning. Much like ceramics, foodstuffs, or other artifacts, many such individuals could have been interred at any time during the burial process. It seems clear that some were purposefully killed and brought to the funerary chamber; studies by Vera Tiesler Blos and Andrea Cucina clearly demonstrate sacrificial behavior in Classic Maya interments.[100] Likewise, multiple interments occur in a variety of contexts outside the royal sphere; elite burials at Uaxactun and Altun Ha, for example, contain presumably sacrificed individuals.[101] But given that Classic Maya rulers were engaged in many different burial practices, including primary and secondary burials as well as tomb reentry and reuse, it seems plausible to suggest that some cases of "sacrifice" may have been natural deaths.

Very little concrete information is available to us to explain why such secondary individuals, predominantly adolescents and young adults when identifiable, were interred with kings and their families. In death, lords are often shown

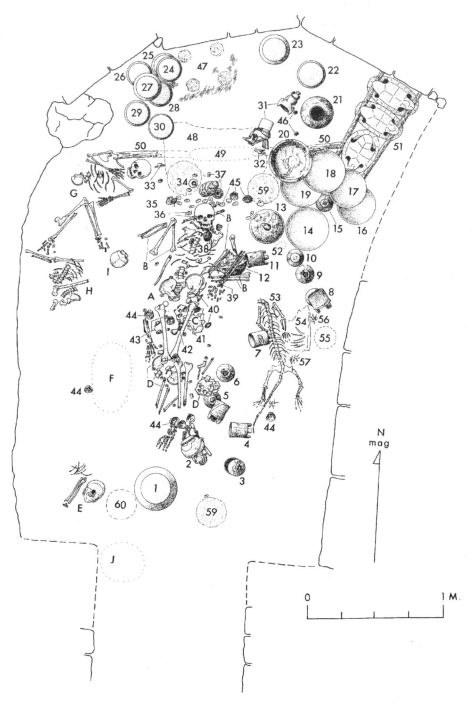

FIGURE 40. *Tikal Burial 10 (after W. Coe 1990, fig. 155)*

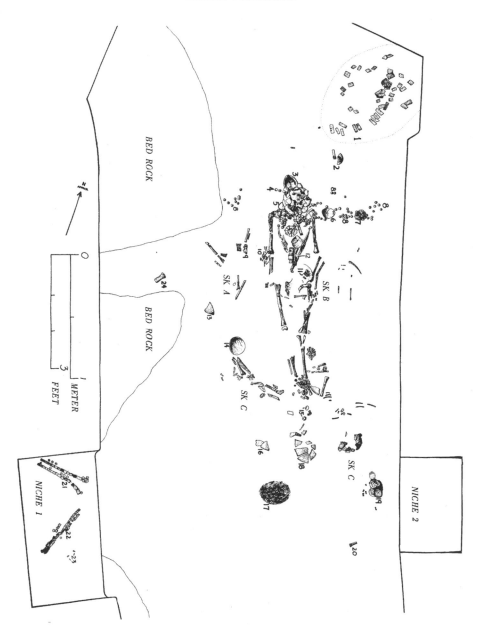

FIGURE 41. *Piedras Negras Burial 5 (after W. Coe 1959, fig. 64)*

with male or female attendants; similar attendants can be found in Maize God or other "resurrection" scenes. Perhaps these attendants are represented in multiple interments, although one might expect their numbers or genders to be standardized, which they are not, and as a result little can be said about patterning. The exception to this rule comes from Palenque, where, as will be discussed below in "Sealing the Tomb," individuals were used to seal burials from within in the Temple of the Inscriptions and Temple 18-A.

Faunal Remains

As mentioned earlier, Weiss-Krejci and Culbert have pointed out a divide in the types and frequencies of grave goods between the late fourth and early fifth centuries AD. In addition to ceramic changes, this divide was characterized by an overall increase in jade and shell artifacts and particularly by the introduction of mosaic artifacts and avian remains in royal burials. It was likewise characterized by a dramatic increase in "animal skeletons, jaguar claws, reptiles, and worked animal bones." Such worked and unworked animal bones seem comparatively rare at Early Classic Uaxactun and Late Classic Palenque,[102] however, as shown in Appendix 3. Perhaps the most noteworthy patterns of items in this class are the aforementioned bone bloodletting artifacts from Tikal, Yaxchilan, and Piedras Negras, although they by no means encompass the variety of worked objects in royal tombs. Turtleshell marimbas, anthropomorphic figures, and inscribed or iconographic bones are part of a larger host of items that were interred with Maya rulers and their families; further examples of such objects, some shared between sites, will surely surface.

Some of the faunal remains found in royal interments may be tied to individual rulers, perhaps representing *way* or other types of companions. One notable example of this occurs in the tomb of Yax Nuun Ayiin in Tikal Burial 10, where a decapitated namesake (*ayiin* means "crocodile") lies next to the dead king.[103] Other creatures like birds or even jaguars are more difficult to interpret, as we may be dealing with a multiplicity of human-animal associations and meanings.[104] We certainly find animals linked to the dead in Maya iconography, on objects such as the Tikal bones or Classic Maya ceramics, as both *way* and more naturalistic entities. Perhaps their deaths were envisioned as necessary for the aid of the deceased ruler in his Underworld journey, helping a ruler in crossing watery boundaries or negotiating the Underworld landscape, similar to the meaning of the spirits of dogs in Postclassic Central Mexico or modern highland Chiapas.[105]

Mirrors, Pyrite, and Hematite

Throughout ancient Mesoamerica, mirrors were used for a variety of purposes ranging from decoration to divination. As Karl Taube and Mary Miller have noted, mirrors represented a world that could be viewed but not passed through; basic associations with darkened caves, flaming hearths, and glistening pools of water persisted in pre-Columbian highland and lowland societies.[106] Constructed of pyrite mosaics or solid pieces of hematite, shining mirrors and beads can be found scattered throughout royal interments, perhaps in greatest quantities at Altun Ha. Some fairly interesting, if not patterned, uses of mirrors can be found at Piedras Negras and Bonampak. For the burial of K'inich Yo'nal Ahk II (Ruler 3) of Piedras Negras, William Coe reports that a large pyrite mirror had been set within the tomb at an angle, allowing the deceased to "see" himself laid out within the tomb; the burial of his successor, Ruler 4, contained a hematite mirror bearing a noteworthy captive from the Hix Witz kingdom.[107] Given the associations of mirrors with portals, it seems plausible to suggest that the lords of Piedras Negras were creating Otherworldly locations within tombs. Something comparable appears to have been going on at Bonampak, where a similar mirror was buried at its owner's feet. As Mary Miller and Simon Martin have noted, the mirror was an idealized turtle carapace, one that would have allowed its owner to see himself reborn from the surface of the world as the Maize God.[108]

Burial Sequences

In reviewing some of the major patterns and circumstances of royal tombs, we have seen motifs ranging from overlapping layers to concerns with representations and attendants. In some cases, a clear order of operations can be discerned: rows of shells, ceramic "beds," positioned mirrors, or facial bowls each had their time and place within the burial sequence. Endeavors by archaeologists to understand the order of events in burials, as related above for Tikal Burial 10 or Copan Burial XXXVII-4, provide us with detailed glimpses into the minds and actions of grave architects. Burials are collections of ideas as well as artifacts. Collected artifacts, as reflections of collective ideas, reveal not only ritual behavior but also the motivations shaping that behavior. In looking at burial sequences, we can gain a sense of the various ideas and processes that went into the arrangement of a funerary chamber. Relating such processes for each burial is impossible here, but it would be a worthy task in the reconstruction of tombs both during and after excavation.

We must remember, however, that certain types of ceremonial activities do not preserve. Presumably, actions like feasting or dancing—documented iconographically and textually for other occasions—could and did take place, potentially during many phases of death rites.[109] Fasting may likewise have been a necessary part of mortuary rites in the Maya lowlands. Although not archaeologically (nor perhaps epigraphically) observable, fasting was a necessary part of the worship of gods, a sacred duty for the Quiche of the *Popol Vuh:*

Nim ki q'oheyik Nim nay puch ki mevakik. Are loq'obal tz'aq Loq'obal pu 'ahavarem k umal. Nahatik chik x e mevahik, x e qahabik ch u vach ki kabavil. Va q'ute ki mevahibal: beleh vinaq k e mevahik, hu beleh q'ut k e qahabik k e k'atonik. Ox lahuh vinaq chik ki mevahibal, ox lahuh chi q'ut k e qahabik. K e k'atonik ch u vach Tohil, ch u vach pu ki kabavil.

Great was their essence, and great were their fasts. These were sacred buildings, and sacred was the lordship to them. For a long time they fasted; they prostrated themselves before their god. This then was their fast: 180 days they fasted, and 180 days they prostrated themselves and burned offerings. 260 days themselves. They burned offerings before Storm and before their god.[110]

Moreover, at the beginning of this chapter, scant evidence for wailing as part of the burial rites was mentioned. To this bit of information we might add what can be gleaned from a series of vessels, probably produced by the same person or at a similar location, that describe the death of an elderly man (Figure 42).[111] A woman who is consoled by an attendant wearing deer ears stands over the deceased; other figures stand around him on these vessels and, in at least one scene, are about to sacrifice a deer and throw it into a cave.[112] At some points it seems as if the only human individual in the scene—perhaps the only living one—is the mourning woman. The others appear to accompany the deceased, who in some scenes seems transformed into a deer himself. He dies inside what appears to be a residence, on a bench with drapes, and on one vessel we see flowers falling over his body.

Most royal deaths probably presented a similarly grim scene; we can imagine rulers like K'inich Janaab' Pakal I or K'inich Yo'nal Ahk dying in their homes. Lost is the information regarding where they were bundled; who bundled or handled them; how they were transported to the tomb; and what types of mourning, feasting, dancing, or musical activities took place during burial rites. Patricia McAnany has called particular attention to feasting: she has proposed banquets and even musical bands on the basis of Colonial Period analogies.[113] Certainly that ethnohistoric record is more revealing than Classic Maya texts on such behavior:

But when in time they came to die, it was indeed a thing to see the sorrow and the cries which they made for their dead, and the great grief it caused them. During the day they wept for them in silence; and at night with loud and very sad cries, so that it was pitiful to hear them. And they passed many days in deep sorrow. They made abstinences and fasts for the dead, especially the husband or wife; and they said that the devil had taken him away, since they thought that all evils came to them from him, and above all death. Once dead, they put them in a shroud, filling their mouths with ground maize, which is their food and drink which they call *koyem,* and with it they placed some of the stones which they use for money, so that they should not be without something to eat in the other life . . . Usually they abandoned the house and left it deserted after the burials, except when there were a great many persons in it, so that they with their society lost some of the fear which remained in them on account of the death.[114]

FIGURE 42. *Death and transformation on* K1182 *(#K1182 © Justin Kerr)*

In the ethnographic record, Maya death rites generally involve the use of a ritual specialist, that is, a person knowledgeable in ceremony who functions as the leader of the activities. In Chichicastenango, Ruth Bunzel has observed a series of events following the death of the head of household.[115] The men related to the deceased gather in his house, without the women, and make contributions to cover the costs of buying the rockets, the coffin, and the meat for "the funeral feast." After procuring these goods, the family and friends of the deceased hold an all-night vigil around the corpse, supplemented by feasting and drinking. The knowledgeable person, or *chuchajaw*, is called upon to make Christian responses; if he has been making defenses for the deceased (that obviously came to no avail), he burns incense in the room where the patient died, calling on the ancestors of the dead to embrace their new member. They then wash the head of the corpse and, bringing the body into the patio, clothe it and place it within the coffin with its possessions. The corpse is then taken out into the street on a funeral procession, with the *chuchajaw* beating the floors of his house and the street in front so the soul will not linger. Along the way to the burial site, the corpse is turned around in front of the church many times so the soul may lose its way from home. Burial is accompanied by drinking and the burning of rockets, and the aforementioned (see Chapter 2) count of nine days; the soul then returns to the house and sleeps for nine days on the blanket and mat on which he died.

Despite considerable variation, the basic elements of the Quiche Maya mortuary rite are repeated among the Tzotzil, Yucatec, and Kanhobal Maya: vigils, feasting, washing, dressing, processional activities, and a "waiting period" after burial or death, often between two and nine days, are common.[116] For these groups (not including the Quiche), the person or persons actually handling the deceased must be elderly. In some cases, these elderly figures are of the same sex as the deceased. The reasons given for this requirement center on the fear of becoming impotent or barren, as well as on the dread of being taken into death by the soul of the deceased. Other prohibitions range from restrictions on who can bathe the deceased to who is able to bury the body; among the Tzotzil and Kanhobal, individuals closely related to the deceased, for example, people with the same surname, cannot interact physically with the body. The mouth of the deceased should be closed or covered, along with the eyes among the Tzotzil.[117]

These prohibitions and formalized activities form a set of behaviors that we have not seen archaeologically or epigraphically for the Classic Maya, and they give us a sense of depth in funerary rites that is far more complicated than the basic outline of Classic Maya mortuary ceremonies presented above. Yet if we think of royal corpses as expired embodiments of supernatural and political power, and remember the degree to which royal ancestors were commemorated at sites via temples or other activities (see Chapters 3, 4, and 5), the hypothesis that royal corpses would not have been directly handled by commoners seems plausible. It is doubtful whether this behavior would have been appropriate during the life of a *k'uhul ajaw*, "holy lord." This is perhaps the reason why we find references to royal individuals presiding over high-status interments: the burial of Batz Chan Mat of Palenque, a member of the royal family who fathered the king K'inich Ahkal Mo' Naab III, was supervised by K'inich Janaab' Pakal I of Palenque. Perhaps Pakal served as a kind of modern *chuchajaw*, the person who oversaw (*yilah*) this death rite and who was ultimately responsible for making sure that the ancestors of Batz Chan Mat were properly notified of his coming. Unlike the modern examples, however, it seems clear that close royal family members were handling dead remains, particularly in cases of tomb reentry (see Chapter 5); we must therefore use a measure of caution in applying these ethnographic models to archaeologically unobservable behavior.

SEALING THE TOMB

At some point after grave goods and bodies were arranged, activities were terminated and the tomb was sealed. This sealing was frequently accomplished with further rites involving fire, lithics, and even sequential interments, a kind of termination ritual that—in most cases—ended the physical interaction between the living and the dead.

Fiery terminations are perhaps the most common and have been observed in royal and high-status interments in Early Classic Río Azul and Tikal, as well as in Late Classic burials at Tikal, Yaxchilan, and Copan.[118] At Tikal and Copan, copal or another substance was burned atop the capstones of the tomb, whereas at Río Azul, copal was burned within the funerary chamber. This floor burning at Río Azul was augmented by further events shown on some of the vessels in Tomb 23, as well as the placement of a wall sealing the chamber. Such burning activities were occasionally replicated outside the tombs themselves: royal ancestral shrines containing evidence of protracted, continuous burning have been located at Tikal, Copan, and Caracol (see Chapter 5).[119]

Burning also took place at the point of a structure's dedication through the "firing" of incense or other materials; we have clear, widespread epigraphic evidence for this in *och k'ahk'*, "fire-entering," or *el naah*, "house-censing," phrases accompanying the erection of a house or temple structure.[120] Given that the dead are often part of the dedicatory process in these events, either in the first construction within a new building or in an intrusive cut into an old one that is then covered over, I see the "firing" of a structure as functionally equivalent to the initial burning activities that take place outside new tombs. Both occur when the building activities are complete for the house, whether it is a tomb or a funerary structure. The "firing" of capstones may therefore signify that the tomb is not only inhabited, but also fundamentally habitable as a "house" for

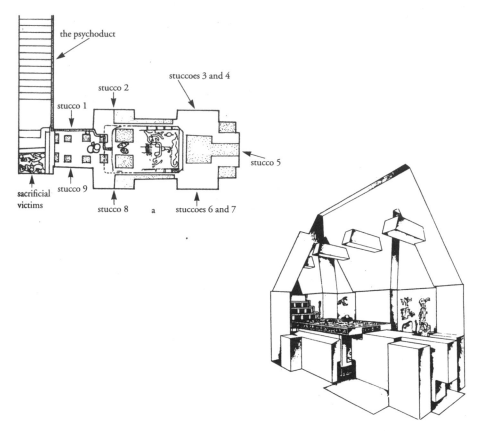

FIGURE 43. *Plan view of K'inich Janaab' Pakal I's tomb (after drawing by Linda Schele, © copyright David Schele, courtesy of Foundation for the Advancement of Mesoamerican Studies, Inc., www.famsi.org)*

the dead. As others have suggested, this "firing" may have had a dual purpose: incense, in addition to flowers and other fragrant substances, was used to "feed" the dead long after their interment at Maya sites.[121]

Also involved in sealing rites was the sacrifice or burial of individuals and precious objects outside the tomb. This type of funerary human sacrifice seems to have been most formalized at Palenque, where the Late Classic tomb of K'inich Janaab' Pakal I (Figure 43) as well as that of an unknown lord in Temple 18-A were first walled in, then augmented by at least five individuals set in stone boxes to the right of the wall.[122] Something similar may have taken place in the Early Classic Burial 125 at Tikal: the capstones were first "fired" and then augmented by the burial of a single individual who, lacking grave goods, was set to rest atop the roof of the funerary chamber.[123]

The caching of precious artifacts to seal the cut or stairwell of tombs is likewise observed in the Temple of the Inscriptions. To seal the tomb of K'inich Janaab' Pakal I deep within the heart of the temple with the aforementioned stone boxes, elites and laborers set two separate caches along the monumental stairway, backfilling the opening until they reached the summit.[124] Further caching behavior, some related to ancestral veneration, was replicated at most Maya sites; at Altun Ha, for example, caches were frequently placed both above and below funerary chambers, seemingly set there to begin and end the burial process.[125] More on such behavior will be reviewed in the succeeding chapter.

A very different type of caching behavior, but also clearly related to tomb sealing, was the widespread use of chert and obsidian flakes, boulders, debitage, blades, and eccentrics to close the cut of a tomb. Early and Late Classic tombs at Tikal, Dos Pilas, Río Azul, Caracol, Altar de Sacrificios, Altun Ha, Uaxactun, Yaxchilan, and Lamanai all make use of lithics in sealing events. Such lithics usually occur in layers (ca. 3–7 lenses), although such layers are variable on an individual basis. Although Tikal has the longest identifiable history of this practice, Grant Hall has documented the widespread chronological use of chert and obsidian levels in contexts ranging from the Protoclassic to the Terminal Classic.[126] It is perhaps significant that no such behavior has been observed outside the Central Peten, although chert or obsidian debitage can be found in a variety of termination rituals at places like Copan or Piedras Negras.[127] Obsidian may have held a special place in burial termination rites at Tikal: in the Early Classic Burials 10 and 23, only the last layer held eccentrics and debitage made of volcanic glass.[128]

Michael Coe has proposed that these chert and obsidian layers above tombs set the burials below within the Classic Maya Underworld, citing pictorial evidence from the Codex Borgia, the *Popol Vuh*, and Aztec examples in which certain layers of the Underworld are characterized by knives and sharp objects.[129] Grant Hall has offered alternative explanations for this phenomenon: (1) the chert and obsidian layers represent debitage from tools utilized to cut the tomb chamber and shaft, in other words, the "leavings" that were supported by eccentrics or other goods in caching behavior; or (2) the chert and obsidian layers represent the "teeth" of a symbolic mouth, and the shafts represent cave mouths leading downward into the Underworld of the tomb. He sees the chert and obsidian as residues or indicators of lightning,[130] a phenomenon associated with caves:

> Images of the Cauac monster may represent a cave, which was thought to be the physical source of lightning, or the lightning bolt itself; the Monster can also be the place where the lightning strikes.[131]

Hall notes that the "tendency for chert to throw off sparks when struck is a property supporting its symbolic association with lightning." I would tend to agree with his second explanation: at Piedras Negras we have clear evidence that the chert and obsidian inside caches comes not from the tools manufactured to cut their housing but from debris collected throughout the site. We might modify Hall's second interpretation to include the tombs themselves as cave entrances—and not Underworld locations, as supported by the evidence presented earlier in this chapter. The chert and obsidian, as symbolic teeth, might identify the chamber as a maw in its own right, with multiple rows of teeth represented by the layers above. A particularly bizarre example from Río Azul, perhaps supporting this hypothesis, involved the grave architects of Tomb 23 covering the tomb floor with chert debitage *prior* to interment.[132] Such an activity would have set the body directly upon the jaws of the Underworld.

Sealing a tomb is a transformative act. It is something that changes the way in which an individual can interact with human remains. In the Temple of the Inscriptions at Palenque or Margarita at Copan, individuals were housed inside temples with elaborate internal shrines and stairways. Filling these stairways with rubble altered the accessibility of tombs and limited the ability of descendants to manipulate the bones and grave goods of their ancestors or perform rites within funerary chambers. This closure was replicated time and again within funerary structures of the lowlands, oftentimes without further physical interaction. Bodies went from being inanimate but accessible to wholly inaccessible. The deceased became part of the funerary structure, even personified by that structure, rather than an individual physically—and possibly spiritually—distinct from that structure. This is what it meant to become a "founder" or axis for further constructions. Following interment, the dead became fundamental parts of a physical landscape.

FOUR

DEATH AND LANDSCAPE

Patricia McAnany has observed that creating a "genealogy of place" has been of historic concern to Maya communities. The establishment and recognition of land rights, in both colonial- and modern-era Yucatán, seems to have involved questions of inheritance, habitual encroachment, or primary occupancy. McAnany has suggested that similar ideas existed in pre-Hispanic times, with the "principle of first occupancy" defining lineage customs and conflicts in the Classic Maya lowlands. In essence, the first individuals to colonize a given area gain permanent ownership of the best agricultural lands; families who arrive later are forced to either fight for decent arable land or settle on inferior territory. Over time, she argues, severe social inequality is the result, with individuals in positions of power duly inheriting favorable properties or seizing lands dominated by weaker parties.[1]

The death of such individuals, McAnany notes, is habitually accompanied by their interment within residential platforms. These platforms are then subsequently modified and expanded by descendants, who inter their own individuals intrusively or within architecturally related structures. In other words:

> The Maya residence as the receptacle of the ancestors . . . assumes a quasi-legalistic character and stands as witness to the validity of the rights, privileges, and responsibility of its current occupants.[2]

In many ways, ancestors were intangible property, and their associated residences, places for the "curation, transformation, and regeneration of enduring social personae."[3] Whether formalized by ancestral shrines or not, these "founding" members of residential structures are common and encountered as early as the Preclassic. Populated by visible reminders of territorial inheritance, the Classic Maya landscape was modified over time to serve the needs of dominant and subordinate lineages alike.[4]

At the top of this hierarchy of power was the Classic Maya king and his lineage. Organizationally, it has been demonstrated that systems of lowland kingship and kinship were very different: as reflected by the mechanics of power, gender, and economy in these systems, kingship was clearly not "lineage writ large," but rather a centralizing force at odds with lineage authority. Semidivine charters for government, tribute gathering, labor drafts, and other forms of codified domination are, as McAnany has argued, abhorrent to lineage organization. As a result, we might expect the expression of royal concerns with territory and inheritance to be quite different, set apart from the concerns of lineage and the "principle of first occupancy."

Nevertheless, concerns with "founders" and distant ancestors exist at many Maya sites. The ultimate lineage, the family of rulers and relatives documented by large funerary temples and inscribed monuments, is often concerned with the portrayal of a "first" or temporally remote royal figure. Such figures were presumably concerned with inheriting or seizing favorable agricultural lands, and their burials may have originally served to demarcate territorial boundaries much as in the example from K'axob'. We can extend this founder model beyond agriculturalism, however. A site core, in addition to being the center of a metropolis, was likewise a part of the greater Maya landscape. In bringing a royal ancestor to rest therein, the Classic Maya kings may have sought to convey permanent ownership of the core and thereby the site. This is both an extension and a departure from the lineage model, for it asserts singular ownership while architecturally documenting that claim.[5]

In practice, these ideas were implemented to different degrees at Classic Maya sites, depending in large part upon the strength of centralized authority. In some portions of the lowlands, particularly in the Belize region, such authority seems to have been weak.[6] Nevertheless, at sites ranging from Tonina to Caracol, certain individuals—reveling in the afterlife afforded by their public display on buildings and other structures—were more dominant than others. Some were singled out as progenitors of dynasties entombed within mortuary structures or habitually mentioned on Maya monuments as distant, important ancestral figures. Epigraphically, a founder is described and defined as the "first" in an unbroken line of succession, shown "arriving" to found a new dynasty or presented as a remote, pivotal ancestor by descendants. Archaeologically, they may be found within structures whose existence dominates most future architectural alignments and programs within the site core. Table 4 provides a list of individuals who, to date, fit one or more of these criteria.

Most Maya rulers sought to demonstrate the unique nature of their reigns, and as a result, we might be tempted to supplement this list with numerous rulers who documented their cosmological or futuristic primacy, such as K'inich Janaab' Pakal I of Palenque or K'ahk' Tiliw Chan Yoaat of Quirigua. But even these great rulers traced their lines back to particular "founding" individuals of their lineages. Such founders seem to have achieved a status separate from that of their contemporaries and successors, one visible in the art, architecture, and archaeology of Maya sites: they were actual or manufactured "firsts" in the landscape of Maya politics. When encountered, their funerary structures seem to mark royal boundaries within a site as well as new "natural" features that

TABLE 4
"FOUNDERS" OF THE CLASSIC MAYA LOWLANDS

Name	Site	Date (AD)	References
Yax Ehb' Xook	Tikal	~90	Grube 1988; Schele 1992a; Stuart 1998
? Ajaw	Tonina	~217	Martin and Grube 2000
Chak Tok Ich'aak?	Tikal	292	Martin and Grube 2000
Te' K'ab' Chaak	Caracol	331	Chase, Grube, and Chase 1991
Yoaat B'alam I	Yaxchilan	359	Martin and Grube 2000
Siyaj K'ahk'	Tikal	378	Stuart 2000a
"Skyraiser"	Calakmul	<411	Martin and Grube 2000
K'an Mo' B'alam	Seibal	~415	Stuart and Houston 1994
K'inich Yax K'uk' Mo'	Copan	426	Schele and Stuart 1986
K'inich Yax K'uk' Mo'	Copan	426	Schele and Stuart 1986
K'uk' B'alam I	Palenque	431	Martin and Grube 2000
? Mo'	Tamarandito	~472	Houston 1993
Ahkal Mo' Naab'	Palenque	501	Stuart 1999; Martin and Grube 2000
"Turtle Tooth"	Piedras Negras	510	Fitzsimmons 1998
Ahkal K'uk'	Tortuguero	~510	Martin and Grube 2000
Ruler 1	Tonina	~514	Mathews 1979
B'alaj Chan K'awiil	Dos Pilas	~648	Houston 1993
Lady Six Sky	Naranjo	682	Schele and Freidel 1990
Aj B'olon Haab'tal	Seibal	849	Schele and Mathews 1998

demonstrate the "rights, privileges, and responsibilities" of rulers in relation to the subject population. One of the most visible of these dynastic founders can be found at Early Classic Copan.

K'INICH YAX K'UK' MO'

The Classic Maya site of Copan, extending to the modern town of Copan Ruinas, has been a haven for archaeological inquiry since the 1890s. Efforts by the Carnegie Institution, the Peabody Museum of Archaeology and Ethnology at Harvard, the University Museum at the University of Pennsylvania, and the Honduran Institute of Archaeology, as well as the influence of local organizations such as the Copan Association, have created a comprehensive picture of Classic Maya society extending from the activities of Classic Maya nobility to the daily lives of artisans, scribes, and agriculturalists in the site core and surrounding communities. Under the overall direction of William L. Fash and

Ricardo Agurcia, projects conducted here have made Copan one of the best-known and most extensively studied Classic Maya polities.

Like Tikal, Copan appears to have been the target of foreign intrigue and possibly militaristic expansion from Central Mexican–related powers: more than forty years after the installation of the son of Spearthrower Owl at Tikal, K'inich Yax K'uk' Mo' "arrived" (*hul-i*) at Copan. A native of the Central Peten,[7] K'inich Yax K'uk' Mo' (r. 426–ca. 437) was habitually portrayed as a Central Mexican lord, but bearing a square shield and other accoutrements that befit his connections with the great metropolis of Teotihuacan.[8] Records describe his travels from the distant "west" as well as his foundation of a new Classic Maya dynasty at Copan in AD 426. Succeeding generations of rulers thought this event so important that monuments and structures to his memory continued to be built and maintained until the demise of the site. So thorough were their efforts that the early history of Copan was—and continues to be—eclipsed, despite sparse evidence that this polity was well established long before the arrival of K'inich Yax K'uk' Mo'.[9]

Following his arrival, K'inich Yax K'uk' Mo' embarked upon a building program that was to lay the foundation for two of Copan's most important structures, Temple 16 and Temple 26 (Figure 44), with the construction of the Hunal and Yax platforms. These buildings show clear architectural ties with Central Mexico and the Peten, respectively, and are a testament to a fusion of Mesoamerican aesthetics that occurred during the reign of this enigmatic king. Hunal itself, or more properly its location, retained its importance as the heart of Copan from these humble beginnings to the site's demise; Yax, as a product of this founder, was similarly revered.[10] Dying in about AD 437, K'inich Yax K'uk' Mo' likewise remained visible in the texts and monuments of his successors, from his son to the final ruler of Copan. That son, Ruler 2, interred his father within Hunal and razed its superstructure; perhaps in a show of local resurgence, the Central Mexican Hunal was replaced by a proper, apron-molded Maya structure, similar to the style of Early Classic buildings in the Peten. This structure, known as Yehnal, was decorated with portrait masks of the Sun God K'inich Tajal Wayib' flanking its frontal steps; it was also provided with an internal access stairway leading northward, down into a burial chamber.[11]

For whatever reason, Yehnal was razed shortly after its completion, although its chamber and stairway remained intact. It was subsumed by a building nicknamed Margarita, which was decorated with painted stucco spellings of Yax K'uk' Mo's name as well as an Underworld toponym, Bolon K'uh (Nine God).[12] The empty tomb therein was put to use, housing a local elderly woman whose burial is the "richest" female interment yet discovered in the lowlands; it is believed that she was a local elite married to K'inich Yax K'uk' Mo' to cement his newfound control.[13] This woman was presumably carried past the intertwined macaws and quetzals marking this as the place of the founder and down the access stairway to the burial chamber, where she was laid to rest. After a time, the

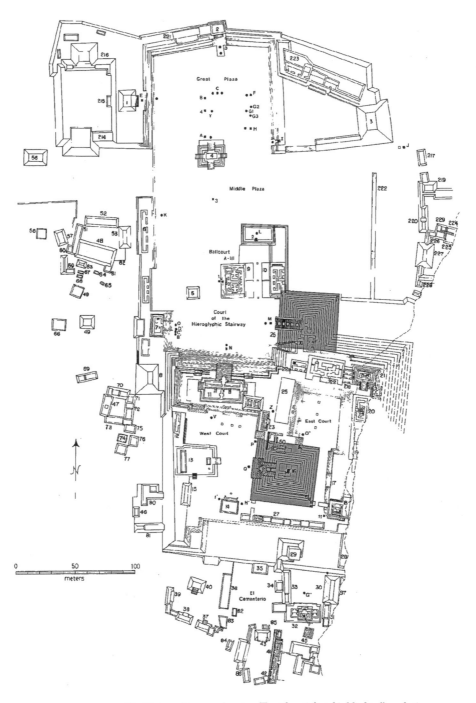

FIGURE 44. *The Copan site core, showing Temples 26 (top highlighted) and 16 (bottom highlighted; after Fash 1991b, fig. 8)*

Margarita superstructure was partially razed and an offerings chamber created, which was itself connected to the access stairway.[14] Excavators cited evidence of protracted burning activities in this chamber, which appears to have remained open even after the construction of the next building phase, Chilan. According to Sharer and his colleagues, when the chambers were finally sealed around AD 553–578, the Margarita burial received numerous new offerings, including the famous "Dazzler" vessel.[15] Reconstructed by a team of conservators led by Harriet Beaubien, the vessel displays K'inich Yax K'uk' Mo' "personified as his own mortuary shrine."[16]

Presumably the "Dazzler" and other offerings were left by the tenth ruler of Copan, "Moon Jaguar" (r. 553–578), who encapsulated Chilan within one of the most elaborately decorated temples known from the Maya area, Rosalila. Constructed over each of its predecessors as well as the bodies of the nobles housed therein, Rosalila was so revered by subsequent rulers that when it was buried over one hundred years later, it was not razed—as it normally would have been at Copan—but carefully covered with construction fill.[17] Although the iconography of its exterior has been dealt with in a variety of publications,[18] the importance of this structure as a mortuary shrine necessitates a brief review (Figure 45).

K'inich Yax K'uk' Mo' appears in the lowest register of the structure as an avian aspect of Itzamnaaj, a god who in Classic Maya times was associated with kings, scribes, and avian creatures, particularly the ancient version of Vucub Caquix of the sixteenth-century *Popol Vuh*. Above the king, versions of the Sun God are flanked by growing maize vegetation and double-headed serpents vom-

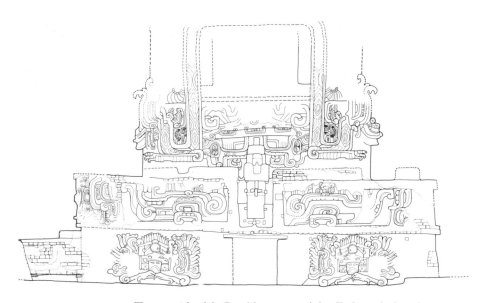

FIGURE 45. *The west side of the Rosalila structure (after Fash 1991b, fig. 52)*

iting forth unidentified humanoids. The second register repeats these serpentine themes, this time within the context of a zoomorphic mountain, or *witz*. Avian forms of Itzamnaaj on the north and south sides of Rosalila are surmounted, in the top register, by the snaking bodies of serpents winding around a skull.

The *witz* head of the second register, like those found on other temples at Copan and elsewhere in the Maya lowlands, identifies Rosalila as a stylized mountain. It is a "living" structure that, through its entranceways and holes, can be entered as if it were a cave or other portal to the Underworld.[19] The placement of the Sun God upon this mountain, but visually below the head of the mountain, may identify this as a place of the Night Sun; the sun, having entered the Underworld, is placed below the mountain. The skull of the third register is harder to interpret, but as the peak and focal point of the monument, it may allude to the burials or physical remains below. Serpents wend their way throughout the temple, the mountain, and the skull, much like those that appear on Classic Maya ceramics and monuments in connection with ancestral conjuring, rebirth, and regeneration. Similar themes are echoed in the iconography and epigraphy of Yaxchilan, Piedras Negras, and Tikal. Combined with the presence of the fused Itzamnaaj–K'inich Yax K'uk' Mo', such themes strongly suggest that Rosalila was a place for ancestral veneration—and, more specifically, conjuring—in theory, if not in practice. Given that the walls inside Rosalila are heavily blackened by smoke and that the structure was used until the reign of Waxaklajuun Ub'aah K'awiil (695–738),[20] it is probable that Rosalila was the scene of protracted ritual activities for generations, including those directed at communication or interaction with K'inich Yax K'uk' Mo'.

Of course, the story of Temple 16 does not end here. Modified by successive generations of rulers, its final version was completed by the last ruler of Copan, Yax Pasaj Chan Yoaat (r. 763–810), who not only continued to emphasize the Central Mexican attributes of the "founder" but also tied himself directly to the founding lineage with the well-known progression of rulers on Altar Q. In doing so, Yax Pasaj Chan Yoaat was simply continuing a long tradition of association between a living Maya ruler and a deceased "founding" king. This association was both architectural and physical in nature: by re-creating Temple 16 repeatedly or performing rituals therein, rulers connected themselves personally to the legacy of K'inich Yax K'uk' Mo's remains and architectural programs.[21]

Something similar appears to have been going on at Temple 26, where the Yax structure of the founder was modified over time as a testament to his Central Mexican heritage. That structure may have originally been dedicated by K'inich Yax K'uk' Mo' for an unknown woman with clear ties to Central Mexico, whose uncharacteristic shaft tomb was recovered from the accompanying plaza floor. She was obviously a contemporary and perhaps a seminal figure worthy of her own dedicatory structure.[22] Whether or not this was the case, it is clear that the Copan dynasts continued to draw upon K'inich Yax K'uk' Mo' and his Teotihuacano connections (real or imagined—it turns out he's actually from the Peten) for hundreds of years. It is to his work and his ancestral shrine that generations of rulers wedded their claims to power. In fact, long after the death of K'inich Yax K'uk' Mo' around AD 437, Temple 26 was rebuilt—in a sense "refounded"—with the interment of Smoke Imix (ca. 695), the twelfth ruler of Copan.[23] Burial XXXVII-4 made use of earlier structures associated with the founder while at the same time marking Temple 26 as the funerary monument to a Late Classic king.

LOWLAND FOUNDERS AND LOCAL VARIATIONS

How pervasive are preoccupations with founders in the lowlands? The sites of Tikal and Uaxactun also provide evidence that creating a "genealogy of place" for royal lineages was a central concern to Maya kings, but in a way fundamentally different from that of Copan. Instead of creating a funerary temple for the founder and modifying it through time with architecture, dynasts at Tikal and Uaxactun chose to create royal lineage compounds in which the grave of a founder became the locus for future regal interments. A royal necropolis was created where funerary buildings were not only spatially but also physically tied to dynastic founders.[24]

The Mundo Perdido complex, toward the western edge of the Tikal site, was one such place: its primacy in the Preclassic probably made it a natural choice for the burials of Early Classic kings wishing to subscribe to that glorious past. Scholars have suggested that it was the Classic royal burial ground between 250 and 378.[25] The gradual shift in focus from Mundo Perdido to the North Acropolis in the Early Classic (Figure 46), however, seems to have marked a desire to create a new "genealogy of place" to the northeast. The first step was characterized by the placement of the sumptuously stocked, but as-yet-unidentified, Burial 85.[26]

Another change took place with the interment of Burial 125, posited as the grave of the dynastic founder Yax Ehb' Xook (ca. 90). Although no artifacts were recovered from this primary burial (Figure 47), a feature six meters to the east—a cache in all but designation—contained a variety of goods that one would expect from a burial in the Protoclassic: elite ceramic wares, shells, and miscellaneous human bones were among the artifacts recovered. Their location, according to Christopher Jones, marked a new axis for the North Acropolis.[27] Aligned with this burial, the new axis served as a reference point for all subsequent Acropolis efforts, including most royal burials leading to the reign of Jasaw Chan K'awiil I (682–734), who seems to have initiated the construction of more separate funerary temples at Tikal.[28]

The final step in the disenfranchisement of Mundo Perdido, however, seems to have come with the entrance of Siyaj K'ahk' and his "New Order" in the Peten. Chak Tok Ich'aak I (r. 360–378) was deposed in 378 and replaced by Yax

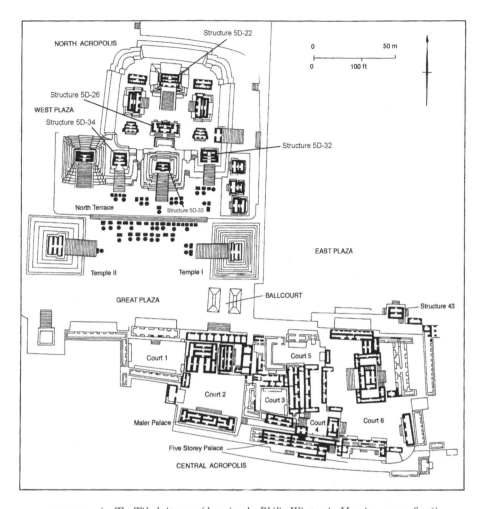

FIGURE 46. *The Tikal site core (drawing by Philip Winton in Harrison 1999, fig. 6)*

Nuun Ayiin I (r. 379–404?).[29] His lineage—and the pertinent lineage monuments in general at Mundo Perdido—presumably fell into disfavor, although subsequent incarnations of Tikal rulers (including the grandson of Siyaj Chan K'awiil II) revived his name and the history of these earlier times.[30] The competition between the Mundo Perdido and the North Acropolis, as well as the eventual success of the North Acropolis as the necropolis of kings, illustrates that drawing upon the primacy of a lineage founder—or his burial ground— was as crucial to the Tikal dynasts as it was at Copan.

Other examples of royal sacred geography can be found at nearby Uaxactun, deep within Structure A-5, and at Caracol in Structure B20. A burial found in Uaxactun Structure A-5, Tomb A29, has been identified as belonging to none other than Siyaj K'ahk', the Teotihuacano warrior whose actions led to the overthrow of ruling lineages at Tikal and its neighbors. Following Siyaj K'ahk's

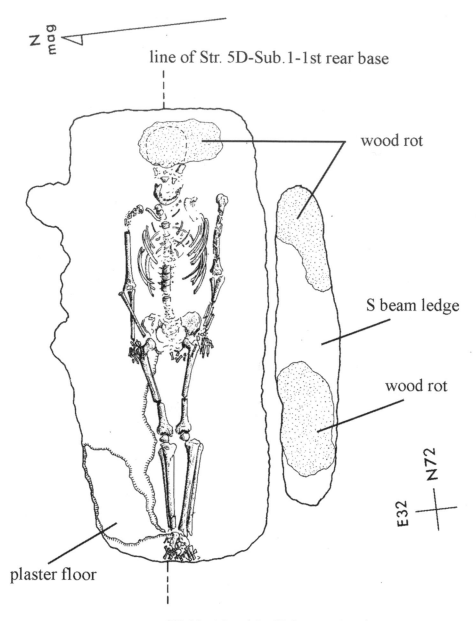

line of Str. 5D-Sub.1-1st rear base

wood rot

S beam ledge

wood rot

plaster floor

N mag

E32   N72

FIGURE 47. *Tikal Burial 125 (after W. Coe 1990, fig. 62)*

interment in AD 402, Structure A-5 became a burial ground for a number of fifth- and sixth-century kings, each of whom presumably sought to demonstrate his ties to Siyaj K'ahk' and his aging New Order in the Central Peten. At Caracol, Structure B20 was modified over time to incorporate at least four vaulted tombs. The earliest of these, Tomb 4, had an associated shrine and altar that were eventually subsumed by further interments.

Outside of these examples from the Central Peten, however, it is difficult to find polities where a single formative individual serves as the basis for a royal lineage compound. In large part this is because Tikal and Uaxactun have long histories of archaeological inquiry, with named Early Classic kings tied to numerous interments. Certainly there are many sites where dynastic founders have been tied to major construction events, as at Dos Pilas and Tonina,[31] with subsequent site developments proceeding therefrom. But as a whole, royal lineage compounds, with a clearly identifiable founder and numerous subsequent interments, tend to be archaeologically elusive. Numerous lineage compounds from nonelite contexts *have* been recovered, however, with clear parallels to structures like Mundo Perdido and Structure A-5. These include Groups 9N-8 and 10L-2 at Copan, as well as Group IV at Palenque, the compound devoted to the lineage of the *sajal* Chak Suutz'.[32] This shared tradition suggests that future concrete examples of lineage compounds will be found at both the royal and elite levels.

Yet, as McAnany has demonstrated, the lineage model does not necessarily apply to royalty in the same way that it does to nonroyals.[33] At Copan, Rosalila spatially defined the locus of ancestral veneration for the founder, but it was far from being a place for the burials of kings. In fact, founder or not, most royal burials at Classic Maya sites are not located in necropolises but scattered throughout the site core inside—or associated with—large funerary structures. Oftentimes they "founded" their own structures: at Altun Ha, for example, David Pendergast has demonstrated that high-status interments, royal or otherwise, were usually linked to new construction events.[34] Such structures were viewed as *witz* or similar natural features; they were *not* strictly thought of as human-made once constructed. They also reflect individualistic, protracted attempts to remake the terrestrial landscape. I argue that rulers asserted their hegemony over the landscape by placing their bodies therein, with dynastic founders providing the earliest and therefore best claims to a constantly changing, consistently modified site core, a place that McAnany has described as the "built environment."[35] Temples or similar structures, as natural features, were inherently territorial in nature and owned by the rulers entombed therein. Founders were merely "first" or formative individuals taking part in that process.

Far more common than architectural founders, moreover, are documentary texts and iconography naming or showing dynastic "firsts" for present rulers. Most of the individuals featured in Table 4, for example, can be found or seen in later retrospective accounts. Often these founders were used to legitimate changes to ruling power structures or to demonstrate that a given dynasty had revived. Indeed, of the founders listed in Table 4, only the unknown *ajaw* from Tonina falls outside this paradigm, a condition that is perhaps due more to our ignorance of his reign than to any lack of concern on the part of his descendants. The latest examples from Dos Pilas, Naranjo, and Seibal are, of course, cases where individuals portray themselves as founders of new dynasties; given

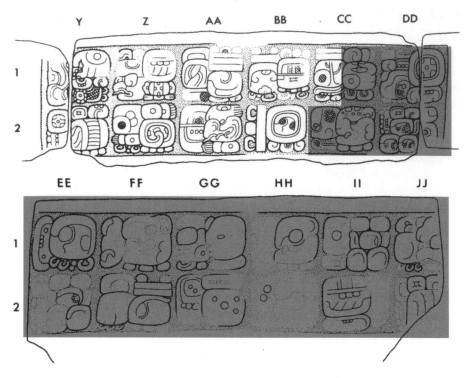

FIGURE 48. *Seibal Tablet VI (Graham 1996, 59)*

time, such kings would likely have been memorialized with further monuments by their descendants.

References to founders are assertions of legitimacy set within chiseled stone. They provide physical "proof" of family ties for future generations, even when such ties are initially questionable. An example from Seibal is a case in point. Here we find the ruler of Dos Pilas, having newly conquered Seibal, taking part in local ancestral rites (Figure 48): K'awiil Chan K'inich (r. 741–761?) designates an heir to the throne of Seibal while the tomb of a long-dead Seibal king, Kan Mo' B'alam (ca. 400), is being opened.[36] Although our knowledge of Seibal's early history is fragmentary at best, we do know that this early king died about 350 years before these proceedings:

och k'ahk' u muknal kan mo' b'alam u kabiiy yich'aak b'alam, k'uh(ul) ? ajaw utiiy wuk ? u chamaw kin? b'alam? janaab' ? ch'ok ? ajaw u kabiiy k'awiil chan k'inich k'uh(ul) mutul ajaw

"fire enters his tomb, Kan Mo' B'alam, under the supervision of Yich'aak B'alam, holy lord of Seibal, then [on] 7 Etz'nab' he receives it, Kin? B'alam? Janaab' ?, [the title of] young lord of Seibal, under the supervision of K'awiil

Chan K'inich, holy lord of Dos Pilas. (Author's translation of glyphs in Figure 48)

The text suggests that the young lord was chosen by K'awiil Chan K'inich. It also implies that the actions and references to Kan Mo' B'alam were initiated at the behest of the Dos Pilas king. Most texts referring to tomb "firing" involve direct participation between agent and patient, as in: "Fire is entered into his tomb, Kan Mo' B'alam, by Yich'aak B'alam." But here we find only "supervision," indicating that the figure here was of more use to Dos Pilas than to Seibal. Kan Mo' B'alam was a founder in the sense that his remote memory gave the young lord legitimate access to the site and its throne.

Even if Kan Mo' B'alam was not the actual progenitor of the Seibal dynasty, he was clearly a new "original" who could serve to legitimate his successors. He was the ancestor to whom the new king traced his power.

The use of founders to demonstrate lineage ties was often shameless but rarely subtle. One of the most egregious uses of founders for political gain occurs at Late Classic Quirigua when K'ahk' Tiliw Chan Yoaat (r. 724–785) slays his former overlord, the thirteenth ruler of Copan. The king of Quirigua describes himself as "fourteenth in line," a probable allusion to the Copan founder K'inich Yax K'uk' Mo' and an indication that he, and not the new Copan king, K'ahk' Joplaj Chan K'awiil, was the true heir to that Early Classic heritage.[37] A similarly disjunctive approach to ancestors may be represented on Tikal Stela 31, where Yax Ehb' Xook (ca. 90) floats protectively over an individual whose father benefited from the collapse of Early Classic dynastic rule in the Central Peten.[38] Less violent examples include the Late Classic portrayal of Yoaat B'alam I of Yaxchilan (ca. 359) on Lintel 25, who emerges from a serpent at the behest of Lady K'ab'aal Xook and Itzamnaaj B'alam II (681–742), and the lavish—if sometimes inexplicable—attentions paid to particular ancestors on Late Classic monuments at Palenque, Tamarandito, Tonina, and Tortuguero. In large part, then, dynastic founders were manufactured entities, with honors and attributes bestowed upon them long after their deaths. Nevertheless, certain prominent individuals were able to promote their own ascent—or the ascent of others—in the afterlife of the public, including our case example, K'inich Yax K'uk' Mo' of Copan, living on through the eyes and practices of the descendants that came after them. These ancestors supported future dynasts in their claims to supremacy.

CULTS OF PERSONALITY

Founders, as we have defined them here, were not the only dead of importance to the Classic Maya kings. We find numerous individuals—the recent dead, for example—who play a prominent role in the art and architecture of sites throughout the lowlands. But as demonstrated by ethnographers working in places like Africa, Asia, and the Americas, becoming a bona fide "ancestor" is often a selective process:

> The practice of ancestor veneration and the rituals surrounding the treatment of the dead are not extended equally to all members of a lineage; rather, they are employed preferentially when particularly important and influential members of a lineage die.[39]

A Classic Maya king, as the supreme head of the ruling lineage, certainly fell within the parameters for selection. As the most important and influential member of his lineage, he was usually interred with goods befitting his status inside or near large, monumental symbols of royal authority. Individuals of significant—albeit lesser—import were likewise provided with significant accoutrements and monuments. Walking on or near such symbols of authority was a fact of daily life within the site core, such that by the Late Classic many sites were veritable foothills negotiated by kings, courtiers, elites, and their subordinates.

Yet, just as these "foothills" and their occupants were ranked, with rulers occupying the choicest positions within the site core, so too were the kings themselves ranked. We have seen this in the case of the founders, who clearly attained "remembered" status as noteworthy ancestors. Similarly, politically successful rulers were probably accorded greater honors than lesser kings. Individuals like K'inich Janaab' Pakal I of Palenque or Jasaw Chan K'awiil of Tikal were probably regarded by friend and foe alike as prominent figures in the histories of their polities, and they likely attained a status equal to—if not greater than—dynastic founders. We see this nominally reflected in the tendency of their successors to make powerful names their own, as in K'inich Janaab' Pakal II and III at Palenque and Jasaw Chan K'awiil II of Tikal, who revived the names of greater kings as their sites lurched toward collapse.[40]

There are indications as to how the Classic Maya viewed such ancestral inequality. Beyond the "principle of first occupancy" or ideas of preferential treatment for remote ancestors, we might look to how the Classic Maya viewed power and the exercise of it, such as in the model proposed by Stephen Houston and David Stuart. In their analysis, they see Classic Maya power relationships as "discursive, involving both assertion and acceptance of claims to authority." Formalized by laws and regulations, power is coalesced through "individual acts that employ power, not as abstract generality, but as a set of highly specific applications which test its limits."[41] One of these "individual acts" was the conjuring of royal ancestors, an ability that required a measure of ritual power, or what David Stuart and James Fitzsimmons have identified as the *ch'ab' ak'ab'*, "creation/penance-darkness," of a ruler. In their scheme, *ch'ab ak'ab'* is a creative quality that allows a ruler to conjure an ancestor or produce progeny (i.e., sons are the *ch'ab' ak'ab'* of their fathers).[42]

Stuart and Fitzsimmons see this power as being embedded in both personality and office, similar to the authority invested in the ritual specialists in modern Tzotzil, Tzutujil, Mam, and Yucatec Maya communities.[43] As a number of ethnographies on Maya shamanism have demonstrated, ritual power has a history of being linked to office and rulership. Succession to a higher office is, among historic and modern populations, linked to the aggrandizement of ritual power, with ritual power as both the result of and cause for accession. Rulers and their families may thus have personified accrued ritual power, with the length of office or greatness of reign corresponding to the depth of ritual—as well as political—power of the individual. As Houston and Stuart have proposed, the title of *k'uhul ajaw*, "holy lord," may be a "title that accrues meaning through ritual practice, with such rulers serving as supernatural mediators and protectors of godly effigies."[44] Thus we might see certain ancestors—founders or otherwise—being accorded greater prestige as a result of heightened accrued ritual power, itself both the cause and effect of a long, fruitful reign.

Nevertheless, it is difficult to rank rulers who have not been accorded the exalted "founder" status. To be sure, the works of prolific kings transformed their sites artistically and architecturally, but these efforts were admittedly directed toward self-aggrandizement. That they were able to mobilize labor for such activities as construction or long-distance warfare is significant, but how do we compare their efforts with those of obscure kings whose burials and monuments have yet to be discovered? In addition to problems of archaeological sampling, we cannot qualitatively rank ancestors without sets of assumptions about what the Classic Maya saw as valuable.

Yet ancestors only remain important if they are remembered, if the qualities that brought them to the heights of ancestral status are maintained or reinvented through time and space. Most sites gave birth to individuals who aggressively campaigned for their legacy, as well as to situations where that legacy was intentionally destroyed. We have only to look at "Middle Classic" Tikal, the conquest stairway at Naranjo, major defeats at sites throughout the lowlands, or the widespread tumultuous events of the Terminal Classic to find instances where monuments were effaced or destroyed.[45] We might thus equate the ranking of ancestors to a struggle for remembrance in which the ability of the deceased to withstand the legacy of his or her successors was called into question. As a result, although we cannot rank the royal dead, we might view a successful ancestor as the individual remembered well beyond the immediacy of his life.

Such philosophical issues are key to the work of Paul Ricoeur, whose influential treatise on the endurance of history, *Time and Narrative,* addresses the permanence of art and architecture. Drawing upon earlier existential work by Martin Heidegger, Ricoeur has suggested that a work of art—or, by extension, any monument conveying a sense of history—remains historical "only if, going beyond death, it guards against the forgetfulness of death and the dead, and remains a recollection of death and a remembrance of the dead."[46] Competing with kings at other sites or with predecessors, each ruler may have sought to assert his importance and influence in a bid to prevent the "forgetfulness of death." Whether or not they were successful during the Classic Period is an open question, save, of course, in the case of founders. In viewing the *competition* for dominance, however, we gain insight into how kings wanted to be perceived after death. No person in Classic Maya history exemplifies this kind of aggressive competitor better than Bird Jaguar IV of Yaxchilan. Ultimately, he, like most other kings of the Classic Period, sought to litter the Maya landscape with evidence of his rights to territory and throne. One way to do this was to document who and—just as importantly—where his ancestors were.

BIRD JAGUAR IV

Coming to power under dubious circumstances, Bird Jaguar IV took the throne on May 3, 752 (9.16.1.0.0 11 Ahau 8 Zec), ten years after the death of his father, Itzamnaaj B'alam II, in 742. David Stuart, in reconstructing the history of Yaxchilan, has suggested that a puppet king, Yoaat B'alam II, may have ruled at the site during this time under the auspices of Piedras Negras.[47] Emerging from these difficult times, Bird Jaguar IV was Yaxchilan's most prolific ruler, creating over thirty monuments and *three* hieroglyphic stairways. Bird Jaguar IV seems to have spent his entire reign promoting "his own legitimacy" with accounts of his exploits as well as images of his ancestors. He created a number of retrospective monuments dedicated to his grandfather, Bird Jaguar III, and to a remote Early Classic ancestor, K'inich Tatb'u Skull II. Although he may have wished to distance himself from Piedras Negras domination along the Usumacinta River, his concerns probably stemmed in part from his parentage. Bird Jaguar IV was not the son of Lady K'ab'aal Xook, his father's principal queen, but the progeny of an obscure wife from Calakmul, Lady Ik Skull. As Simon Martin and Nikolai Grube have observed, the insecure king seems to have made a concerted effort to create his own glorious history and ancestry, leaving his mark on nearly every quarter of the site core with inscribed monuments and buildings.[48]

Some of these efforts were directed toward the construction of Structures 20 and 24, both of which were provided with numerous lintels documenting his illustrious parentage and describing funerary rites performed by Bird Jaguar IV for his ancestors. Likewise, he created numerous monuments around the site depicting remote ancestors or deceased parents. Sometimes these predecessors appear as deities within solar cartouches or as retrospective, historical human beings, either at the top or bottom registers of stelae. Bird Jaguar IV saw fit to represent his deceased father, Itzamnaaj B'alam II (r. 681–742), in each of these

FIGURE 49. *Yaxchilan Stela 4 (after Tate 1992, fig. 86)*

ways. The Itzamnaaj B'alam II of Yaxchilan Stela 11, composed well after his death, is the historical person preserved in a retrospective image, whereas his ancestral version on Stelae 1, 4, 10, and probably 6 is deified and solar in nature (Figure 49). On these latter monuments, he is with Lady Ik' Skull inside what Carolyn Tate has identified as ancestor cartouches;[49] in these scenes, the pair rest above a skyband/serpent bar from which gods such as Chaak emerge. Classic Period versions of the Hero Twins as well as Venus symbols sometimes hang from this iconographic element, and although the cartouches vary somewhat, the general idea appears to be that Itzamnaaj B'alam II and his wife are solar and lunar beings, respectively. A variant of the Classic Maya Sun God, K'inich Ajaw, holding a skeletal serpent bar, or a god associated with aquatic plants can appear in the bottom register as well. Given the watery association of the Night Sun with Underworld motifs and the cleft (split-earth) nature of its forehead, the register below the feet of Bird Jaguar IV may represent a place below the earth, a place of death.

The placement of Itzamnaaj B'alam II and Lady Ik' Skull within the sky, as both sun and moon, indicates that Bird Jaguar IV saw his mother and father—dead at the time of the commission of each of these monuments—as having undergone a transformation into "heavenly" bodies and now residing in a place with the other gods of the Classic Maya pantheon. This conflation of "god" with "ancestor" resonates in other works produced by Bird Jaguar IV, who engages in bloodletting or captive-taking below solar cartouches. Such activities call to mind phrases in which Classic Maya ceremonies are written as being "overseen" by gods or ancestors. In the case of Bird Jaguar IV, their inclusion was plainly an attempt to portray the legitimacy—as well as the ritual efficacy—of his position at Yaxchilan.

The claim that a parent has become a god not only asserts beliefs about the royal afterlife but also provides a celestial mandate for current authority. The terrestrial mandate, the "genealogy of place" represented by pivotal burials and monuments, is complemented by references to the same god-ancestors residing in a celestial sphere.

As we have seen in Chapter 2, similar assertions are spread over space and time at other sites. We do not know whether the attainment of ancestral godhood—or something close to it—was regular, temporally defined, or limited to the examples I have presented in Table 2. But inequality in representation is still inequality, even if theoretically all kings were deified in some way. Bird Jaguar IV would have probably agreed. His transparent attempts to attain "remembered" status transformed the landscape of Yaxchilan, from his questionably significant victories over minor polities to his references to deified parents. We cannot know his significance as a bona fide ancestor to later Yaxchilan dynasts, but his use of father and landscape to assert legitimacy echoes the themes we have already seen for founders and truly noteworthy ancestors at other sites.

Representing ancestors as Otherworldly gods while at the same time heightening their tangible, terrestrial nature with burials and monuments was one way in which Classic Maya kings highlighted the pervasiveness of ancestral authority. In binding ancestors to deities as well as to features like funerary temples, Classic Maya kings could theoretically derive ancestral authority from multiple facets of the natural world. Combined with what we have seen for founders at places like Copan and Tikal, for example, certain ancestors could be both outside (deified) and within the physical landscape (interred), transcending the "forgetfulness of death" and affirming their rights in multiple ways.

As I mentioned in Chapter 2, however, other cases portray deceased rulers and their families outside the solar-lunar model, as other gods, plants, or possibly nondivinities.[50] Creating a sense of place for these ancestors was, however, no less important. Deified or otherwise, depictions of the dead in prominent locations inherently guard against the "forgetfulness of death"; most stelae or other monuments with long histories of public display perform such a function, and as the living pass into the realm of the dead, their art and architecture inherently become ancestral. To be sure, the fact that some ancestors are more human or plantlike than others may reflect different conceptions about the ultimate destinies of ancestral souls; as mentioned, we do not yet have a clear picture of such multiple destinies. What is transparent through the differences, however, is the degree to which the Maya peopled their landscape with the images and bodies of the dead. An example from the western lowlands provides evidence that ancestors, no matter how they are portrayed, can define space and serve the living in asserting lineage rights over sites as well as subjects.

GODS AND ORCHARDS AT PALENQUE

Ancestors at the site of Palenque are characterized by a naturalistic quality; even in cases where ancestors are deified, they appear human, as outlined in Chapter 2. One of the most widely cited monuments involving ancestors and landscapes at Palenque is, without a doubt, the Sarcophagus Lid of K'inich Janaab' Pakal I (r. 615–683). Acceding over four months after the death of Pakal, K'inich Kan B'alam II (r. 684–702) produced this lid as part of a larger funerary program that included interring his father within a funerary chamber accessed by a vaulted, ventilated stairway as well as a psychoduct (see below).[51] Although the stairway was eventually sealed with rubble fill, there are indications that it was meant to be left open for some time: a removable stone slab, covering the stairway, afforded access deep into the heart of the structure.

Although K'inich Kan B'alam II built at least part of the Temple of the Inscriptions as well as its internal tablets, his competition for remembrance in large part rested on the Sarcophagus Lid and its companion works, which documented the illustrious deeds of his father and linked himself to an august reign. His Tablet of the Temple of the Inscriptions, for example, alludes to the supremacy of his father over all other ancestors: it not only links the accession of K'inich Janaab' Pakal II to that of a distant god 1.25 million years in the past, but celebrates the coming anniversary of that accession over four thousand years in the future. Such references make paltry the claims of Bird Jaguar IV for his father. Remembrance—whether ultimately realized or not—was definitely a

FIGURE 50. *The Sarcophagus Lid at Palenque (Robertson 1983, fig. 99; © Merle Greene Robertson, used with permission)*

concern for the Palenque dynasts. Unlike Bird Jaguar IV, however, the Palenque dynasts chose to represent the dead in multiple, almost competitive, roles. The epigraphy and iconography of the Sarcophagus Lid (Figure 50) and funerary chamber provide us with no small measure of information about these roles and their relationship to one another.[52]

Rather than denoting a single process, the Lid appears to illustrate Pakal in multiple roles: (1) as an offering to the Underworld, he rests on a personified plate within the maw of a centipede, located between the Underworld and an unidentified sacred location; (2) as that offering, a World Tree grows from his chest, much like vegetation grows within the open chests of sacrificial victims in Maya iconography (e.g., on Piedras Negras Stela 1); (3) signaling his changing roles, he is also something that can (will) be conjured, via double-headed centipede-serpents vomiting *k'awiil*s. As at Copan, the presence of the avian Itzamnaaj and *k'awiil*s suggests that Pakal is or will be the subject of conjuring. That he will be reborn is indicated by his fetal position and the turtle pectoral,[53] which represents the same kind of turtle-rebirth imagery outlined for the Maize God in the second chapter. All of this takes place between the sky, represented by the skybands, and the earth, represented by a number of individuals in quatrefoil portals. Schele and Mathews have postulated that these figures—nobles and administrators—played some role in the organization of labor for the Temple of the Inscriptions.[54] The actual location of K'inich Janaab' Pakal I on the Sarcophagus Lid is unknown, although the background imagery conflates generalized sacred space, represented by the *k'uhul* droplets, and sweatbath iconography found elsewhere at the site, particularly in the Cross Group.

The side inscriptions recount the *ochb'ih,* "road-entering," dates for eight ancestors as well as K'inich Janaab' Pakal I (Figure 51). Given what I have already written about *b'ih* serving as a "road," "path," "gap," or "opening" in various Mayan languages, it may be the case that the Palenque Sarcophagus Lid actually shows *ochb'ih,* "road-entering," taking place, with Pakal passing through the "gap" of the maw. Given his transitory state, it is debatable whether Pakal is passing upward or downward, but it is interesting to note that *ochb'ih* dates—as opposed to the other types of "deaths" recorded at Palenque and elsewhere—are significant on this monument.

The penultimate "road-entering" events deal with Pakal's mother and father, Lady Sak K'uk' and K'an Mo' Hix, who lived during a time of dynastic disruptions and military disasters for Palenque.[55] Here these disruptions are smoothed over, although the particular attention to these events in the Temple of the Inscriptions—the funerary structure for this burial—suggests that K'inich Janaab' Pakal I and his son were far more secure in their dynastic claims than was the aforementioned Bird Jaguar IV of Yaxchilan.

The "road-entering" of Pakal ensues and is recorded as having taken place on

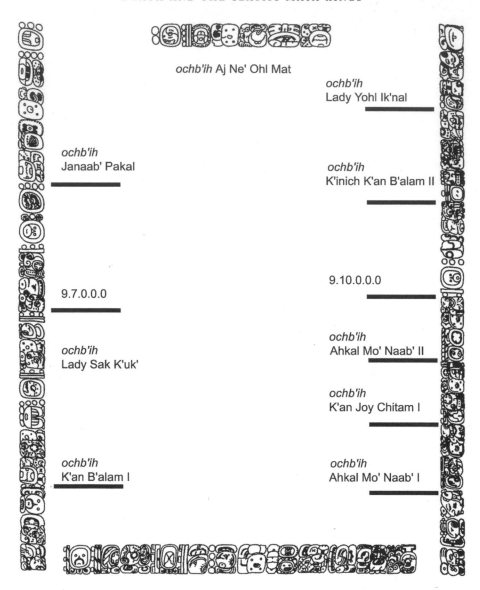

ochb'ih Aj Ne' Ohl Mat

ochb'ih
Lady Yohl Ik'nal

ochb'ih
Janaab' Pakal

ochb'ih
K'inich K'an B'alam II

9.10.0.0.0

9.7.0.0.0

ochb'ih
Ahkal Mo' Naab' II

ochb'ih
Lady Sak K'uk'

ochb'ih
K'an Joy Chitam I

ochb'ih
K'an B'alam I

ochb'ih
Ahkal Mo' Naab' I

FIGURE 51. *Sides of the Palenque Sarcophagus Lid (after drawing by Linda Schele, © copyright David Schele, courtesy of Foundation for the Advancement of Mesoamerican Studies, Inc., www.famsi.org)*

August 31, AD 683 (9.12.11.5.18 6 Etz'nab 11 Yax). Following references to Pakal's ancestors and the serpents of the Sarcophagus Lid is a curious phrase: *patb'uuy u tuunil* "God E," or "It is formed, his stone, the Maize God." As a reference to the sarcophagus and Pakal, this phrase describes the creation of the coffin for Pakal as the dying Maize God. We might liken it to a kernel of maize, planted within the heart of the mountainous Temple of the Inscriptions.

As this dying, planted god, Pakal is surrounded by iconographic representations of the ancestors mentioned in the text, who have sprouted from the earth as various fruit trees and plants. Each of the growing ancestors bears a pendant with the glyph *ik'*, "wind, breath, soul," on it, traceable to the pendants worn by other rulers at Palenque; in a sense, they wear their souls around their necks. The implication of this bizarre scene is that Pakal too will sprout from the earth, and that the Maize God imagery has been reserved for him and him alone. What is unclear is whether his emergence will bring a new addition to the orchard, or something similar to the deified or celestial ancestors of Table 2. As we saw with the Berlin vessel of the previous chapter, the latter two results—deification and vegetative regrowth—are possible when we consider multiple or divisible souls in the Maya area. Both inside and outside Pakal's sarcophagus, there are a number of competing deities and metaphors, including Chak Xib Chaak (mouth ornament), a personified tree, a possible representation of the Maize God, and accoutrements of rulership. Any of these could represent different aspects of his emergence, although one in particular—as we shall see below—stands out.

Patricia McAnany has drawn upon garden themes in her study of how the Classic Maya dynasts at Palenque viewed inheritance. She argues that orchard species were "a metaphor of royal inheritance and descent," and that the association between the various fruits within the tomb of K'inich Janaab' Pakal I was intentional. Citing botanical evidence from Cobá, she proposes that economically important orchard species, such as those represented on the Sarcophagus Lid, were highly concentrated within elite zones of settlement. As Pakal had inherited the throne, she notes, he inherited economic, ancestral, and political privileges encapsulated by the metaphor of the ancestral orchard. In short, the Sarcophagus Lid provides us with a rare glimpse into how the Palenque dynasts viewed the relationship between ancestors and the landscape.[56]

These agrarian metaphors are contrasted, however, by another ring of individuals (an example of which can be seen in Figure 52). Pakal, placed metaphorically among his own "orchard," was surrounded by other stuccoed ancestral figures.[57] Schele and Mathews have suggested that these ancestors represent the *actual* sequence of rulers preceding K'inich Janaab' Pakal I at Palenque; each bears a different headdress, and the rulers Lady Yohl Ik'nal and Ahkal Mo' Naab' II are identifiable from iconographic "spellings." Citing problems with the Palenque regime leading up to K'inich Janaab' Pakal I, they propose that nine—and not ten—individuals actually ruled at the site, and that each is depicted surrounding the dead king in his funerary chamber.[58] They are definitely *not* plants, suggesting a contrast between the actual and the dynastic families. In fact, as mentioned in Chapter 2, the mouth ornament each figure bears identifies them with attributes of the Maya god Chak Xib Chaak,[59] whereas the *k'awiil*s borne by each figure, together with visages of the Jaguar God of the Underworld on each shield, provide associations with other gods. It is perhaps

FIGURE 52. *Lady Olnal (Figure 7) from the tomb of K'inich Janaab' Pakal I at Palenque (after Robertson 1983; © Merle Greene Robertson, used with permission)*

not a coincidence that these three types of images, taken together, signify GI, GII, and GIII of the Palenque Triad.[60] These gods were worn by subsequent deified kings at the site, including K'inich Kan B'alam I and K'an Joy Chitam II.[61] It is perhaps significant that Janaab' Pakal, Lady Sak K'uk', and K'an Mo' B'alam, featured in the orchard around the Sarcophagus Lid, are not provided with similar accoutrements or featured in stucco.

Royal and (possibly) lineage-based sources of power might thus contrast and culminate in the geographically central—if deceased—ruler of Palenque, K'inich Janaab' Pakal I, within his own funerary chamber. Archaeologically, we may see this contrast within the sarcophagus itself: K'inich Janaab' Pakal I, "sown" as the Maize God within the Temple of the Inscriptions, nevertheless bears the Chak Xib Chaak (GI) ornament worn by other deceased kings at the site. His burial is thus a very local version of the same type of behavior we have seen throughout this chapter, in which individuals are surrounded by the iconographic—or physical—remains of their predecessors. Similar predecessors appear on the piers of the Temple of the Inscriptions, where humanlike ancestors hold infant forms of k'awiil. K'inich Kan B'alam II is mentioned on Pier F, in connection with these ancestors, although time has effaced his words. At the time of its construction, then, the burial and temple were clearly to the benefit of the living king. Much like Bird Jaguar IV of Yaxchilan, he subsequently built an entire group of temple-pyramids in self-glorification, linking his rule to Pakal but distinguishing himself as a k'uhul ajaw in his own right in the Group of the Cross.

One contrast that we can draw from the example of the tomb of K'inich Janaab' Pakal I is the opposition between the public face of the Temple of the Inscriptions and the relatively private nature of the funerary chamber at its heart. Most royal tombs in the lowlands were relatively private in that their creation marked the end of widespread physical or social interaction with the dead; the public face of the ancestors became monumental, expressed daily on funerary temples and other works in visible, pivotal locations. As a result of this manufactured "privacy," we might rule the actual funerary chamber of K'inich Janaab' Pakal I more as a reflection—rather than a projection—of belief. Certainly this argument would hold for the majority of the sealed chambers and tombs of kings in the Classic Maya lowlands, whose internal appearance was for grave architects and the bodies alone. But for K'inich Janaab' Pakal I and a series of other elites scattered throughout the lowlands, the tomb environment was an activity area: access stairways or episodic excavations provided a select group of individuals with entrances to chambers, remains, and representations of ancestors therein. Apart from these reentry events, which will be discussed in the next chapter, rulers transcended the manufactured privacy of the dead with less intrusive elements like psychoducts and ancestral shrines. Incidentally, the tomb of K'inich Janaab' Pakal I was provided with both an access stairway and a psychoduct, which were presumably used for different purposes at different times in the history of the structure.

SOULS WITHIN BUILDINGS

According to Linda Schele and Peter Mathews, a *psychoduct* was an architectural convention based on the idea that "the psyche or soul could move up and down the duct to communicate with the living people in the temple above." Given its form as a ropelike stone pipe and its singular association with burials, Schele and Mathews have suggested that the Classic Maya viewed the duct as a serpent, and its ropelike body mirrors depictions of serpentine conduits for supernatural creatures on Classic Maya ceramics.[62] Such ropy conduits are well documented, and they overlap conceptually with knotted breath cords on numerous monuments. Nevertheless, actual depictions of psychoducts are rare to nonexistent. Simon Martin and Nikolai Grube have suggested one possible representation of a psychoduct on Piedras Negras Stela 40, which shows K'inich Yo'nal Ahk II (687–729) scattering incense into a vent leading to the crypt of a woman, who is possibly his mother; she receives his offering and exhales a breath-soul upward through the hole.[63] However, the psychoduct here is at best stylized and could alternatively represent the results of an excavation, perhaps in part related to the reentry of her tomb.

Archaeologically, conduits like these have been recovered three times, two of them at Palenque. The famous example from the Temple of the Inscriptions is complemented by a more rigid psychoduct from the back room of Temple 18-A. Explorations by Victor Segovia in 1957 traced that psychoduct downward and uncovered a preceding construction phase for Temple 18-A; the psychoduct itself appears to have been intrusive, and it terminated in the vaulted burial chamber of an as-yet-unidentified figure.[64] Based on similarities between Temple 18-A and the Temple of the Inscriptions, the final phase of Temple 18-A probably dates to a period of time spanning the reigns of K'inich Janaab' Pakal I and K'inich Ahkal Mo' Naab' III (615–ca. 736).[65] It seems plausible to suggest that the sudden introduction of a psychoduct, where previously there was rubble fill, was the result of either a change in local status or burial practice. A further wrinkle in this story is that the Temple 18-A psychoduct was ultimately filled in during the construction of a plaster floor; what this says about changing behaviors at Palenque is unclear.

The third case of an archaeological psychoduct occurs at Early Classic Calakmul. Excavations in the palatial Structure III at Calakmul revealed the crypt of an Early Classic ruler (500–600), situated immediately beneath the floor of the centrally located Room 6. Apart from a series of jade mosaic masks and other finery surrounding the remains, the chamber was characterized by a floor-level psychoduct; beginning near the head, the duct led outside to the (left) north side of the structure.[66] Given its early date and the fact that the duct does not lead to the floor of a room, we might hypothesize that the rarely encountered psychoducts of the lowlands had slightly different functions determined by geography and time period.

Implicit in the presence of a psychoduct is the notion of a soul or animating entity *in residence,* if only for a brief time after initial burial. Creating a connection between the dead and the outside world implies that some interaction can or will take place, that the body after interment retained some measure of self that could be addressed, propitiated, or communicated with. From what we have seen in Chapter 2, a breath-soul (*ik'*) would be the likeliest candidate for such a traveling soul: as per the Calakmul example, it is associated with the head and takes the form of an exhalation, as on Piedras Negras Stela 40. Yet most of the soul types we have reviewed in previous chapters travel extensively, both before and after death, and are also divisible in nature. As a result, identifying specific souls or animating entities in connection with psychoducts is difficult. But the idea that the souls of the deceased can reside within buildings is an important one, for it makes the tomb a living space, a literal house in which a portion of the self resides, if only for a brief time. The idea that this "self" could move between the tomb and the outside world may be reflected by the psychoducts at Palenque, Calakmul, and (possibly) Piedras Negras.

Evidence for more permanent and perhaps different animating entities within buildings derives from Maya attitudes toward skeletal remains and funerary temples. As we saw in Chapter 2, multiple ideas of "self" existed in the Classic Maya lowlands, and these were not simply limited to breath-souls. One of these, *b'aah,* overlapped conceptually with the Nahua *tonalli* and Tzotzil *ch'ulel* and was represented or retained within images of kings—living and deceased—as well as skeletal elements like crania. As substitutes and embodiments of the Maya self, objects serving as *b'aah* were avatars of the royal body charged with a sacred, divine essence.[67] Like objects or features of the natural world, such items were alive and had a life force. Whether or not this life force was akin to a human soul is unclear. Scholars working throughout Mesoamerica have characterized such life force with terms like "mana," "soul," "*ixipla,*" or even "heart."[68] But structures and other human-made objects bearing this force could be manipulated in various ways, and activated and deactivated in dedication and termination rites. Human remains in particular are known to have had the power to animate or "ensoul" buildings:

> The skull, as we know from the Popol Vuh of the Highland Maya, was a primary source of regenerative power. A human skull . . . whether taken from an ancestor or a prestigious enemy, when interred in a structure could literally ensoul it . . . like a seed planted in the ground.[69]

Similar considerations involving transferring or transmitting "animateness" to buildings have been widely observed in Maya archaeology, ethnohistory, and ethnography. Building dedications often involved the death of a human or surrogate animal, through which animation was transferred from the individual—now dead—to the newborn structure. Throughout Mesoamerica, structures and objects were purified, measured, named, fed, clothed, and subjected to clear assertions of ownership, with each component of the ritual an important step in "animating the inanimate."[70] David Stuart has documented the extensive use of fire in the Maya lowlands for house dedications, in which placing a fire within a home not only created a "hearth" but also invested the house with a soul.[71]

Death and burial may have involved similar issues of ensoulment in which the body, encapsulated within its tomb and rubble fill, ultimately "animated" its tomb and accompanying funerary structure. Although practices involving "clothing" and "measuring" tombs have not been documented, tombs *are* often named, owned, "fired," and provided with structural terms, as in this example from the Panel of the Temple of the Inscriptions at Palenque:

yak'aw huntahn b'olon et naah, u k'uh(ul) k'ab'a, u mukil k'inich janaab' pakal, k'uh(ul) b'aak ajaw

[he] gives [it], protected [thing] B'olon-Et-Naah, its holy name, his tomb, K'inich Janaab' Pakal, holy bone lord (Palenque) (Author's translation)

Words like *house* or *home* are complemented with toponyms like "Nine-God" or "Seven-God," both inside tombs and on the exteriors of buildings. The house metaphor, as we have seen in Chapter 2, extends to tomb interiors with conventions like painted doors and vaulted roofs, particularly at the site of Caracol, Belize.[72] The inanimate tomb thereby became the animate cave or similar natural metaphor through a series of processes involving the body, "fire," naming, and other factors. Correspondingly, the surrounding structure was an extension of the tomb, the natural *witz* made meaningful through the introduction of the royal body. That temple too was a house, from the small "sleeping places" or "residences" of gods in model houses at Classic Copan to grandiose house-temples at places like Caracol or Palenque.[73] As Karl Taube notes, a temple was not only a house but also a metaphor for a hearth, a place of creation; its epicenter was the *axis mundi,* a ritual conduit between the levels of earth, sky, and the Underworld.[74] Such metaphors not only explain why pivotal burials are interred on axis with temples and other structures, but also support a primordial, generative aspect to the "self" interred within its tomb below. Transferring, altering, or even destroying this "self" in new construction phases was accomplished during termination rites;[75] oftentimes the goal was not to "kill" or destroy a building so much as to provide a new surface, and thereby a new or altered identity, for preexisting structures.

The interplay between "self" and temple is further manifested at sites like Tonina, Tikal, Quirigua, and Copan, where representations of temples can be worn or impersonated by both the living and the deceased. Such impersonation often takes the form of a headdress:

> As a form of reciprocal metaphor, headdresses are not only compared to miniature temples or god houses, but temples themselves frequently evoke the qualities of ritual headdresses . . . in one remarkable [Late Classic] Tikal graffito, a temple is personified as a seated man, with the roof serving as its head, the supporting platform as the lower legs and body, and the stairway as the loincloth.[76]

Headdresses likewise serve as "sentient embodiments" of rulers on a number of Late Classic ceramic vessels: we find them seated on thrones and even being addressed by subordinates as representations of rulers. They are also, as Taube has demonstrated, interchangeable with incense burners in Maya iconography. We thus have a host of associations here, from the temple as a simple monument or "house" to seemingly bizarre identifications with royal headdresses, incense burners, and living beings. If we remember that fire—and more specifically incense—was believed to make both houses and tombs "habitable," as we saw in Chapter 2, then a conflated temple-house-censer model is both probable and required for our understanding of Maya religion. Wearing such accoutrements in a headdress, Taube notes, sets the king in the world axis and "unites him to the sacred architectural landscape . . . the king becomes the living embodiment of the temple and its divine occupants."[77]

An example from Early Classic Copan takes this habitual temple impersonation one step further. The aforementioned Dazzler pot, recovered from the Margarita tomb, shows the dead king K'inich Yax K'uk' Mo' as his own funerary shrine (Figure 53).[78] He wears the Margarita structure as if it were a body, with his arms protruding outward from the headdress of the superstructure. Such a mortuary headdress serves as the "sentient embodiment" of K'inich Yax K'uk' Mo'. To wear a representation of this "embodiment" in a headdress would, according to the above analysis, involve co-opting the ancestral "self," its animating properties, and its position within the tomb at the *axis mundi* of the Maya world. I argue that this is precisely what we are seeing in the impersonation of Maya temples, where the living king substitutes for his ancestor by wearing a new surface, that of a headdress-as-temple. Monuments where this occurs, particularly frontal stelae, correspondingly substitute for the living king and serve as reminders of his own legacy years after his death.

FIGURE 53. *The "Dazzler" vessel from Copan Burial XXXVII-4 (after Martin and Grube 2000, 195)*

ANCESTOR SHRINES

Arguably, the various substitutions between Classic Maya notions of "self" and architecture lend new meaning to the presence of founders and other ancestors in the Maya landscape. Apart from being reminders of the rights of ancestry or bulwarks against the "forgetfulness of death," funerary monuments were living entities, hearths of the "self" that embody the dead in a multiplicity of ways. Walking past or entering such anthropomorphic features was a fact of royal life in the site core. Although we might identify most structures containing unequivocally remembered, venerated lords "royal ancestor shrines," some structures seem to have been singled out for particular attention—in terms of identifiable activities tied to ancestor veneration—during their history. A number of these buildings, as noted in this chapter, were modified over vast periods of time in connection with significant ancestors, particularly at the sites of Tikal, Uaxactun, Caracol, and Copan. Other structures, like the Temple of the Inscriptions at Palenque or Rosalila at Copan, saw long-term use without substantial modifications. Still more were built, as Patricia McAnany has suggested, "not so much to house the dead as to commemorate them and to celebrate the continued prosperity of the family line," as in the Margarita shrine at Copan or Temple 24 at Yaxchilan.[79]

Yet identifying buildings as shrines tells us little about how the buildings were *actually* used or the nature of the activities undertaken therein. Some of the possible activities undertaken within royal ancestor shrines include caching, feasting, fasting, bloodletting, sacrifice, and even rites designed for large-scale audiences.[80] Such behaviors are, of course, general practices and not limited to ancestral veneration. Caching, for example, seems to have involved the active definition of sacred space in new or renovated structures, a practice that was replicated on a larger, foundational scale with the entombment of a Maya king.[81] Feeding or otherwise presenting offerings to ancestors was a prime element of ancestor veneration in the Postclassic and Colonial Periods, and it is possible that some of the behaviors listed above were performed with "feeding" in mind.

Another archaeologically observable activity performed within royal ancestor shrines was burning; the burning of goods directly over ancestors seems to have been habitual, for example, at Tikal. William Coe reports that many of the burials in the North Acropolis, as well as Burial 6 within Temple I, showed signs of intentional—sometimes protracted—burning efforts; similar processes have been observed by David Pendergast at Altun Ha.[82] To be sure, not all burning events within temples need have been related to interred ancestors, but some patterns of burning are eerily suggestive. The ashy lenses of soil and charred patches on the Late Classic surface directly over Tikal Burial 10, for example, suggest that the interred Early Classic king (Yax Nuun Ayiin I; r. 379–404) was appreciated well after his remains had been consigned to the earth.

Similar practices are represented at Copan and Caracol. At the Margarita burial, burning occurred in a separate ancestor shrine connected to the tomb via an access stairway. In many ways, it seems to be a smaller version of the Temple of the Inscriptions at Palenque, although there no traces of burning have been recovered within—or directly above—the tomb. Similarly, the aforementioned Copan Burial XXXVII-4, the tomb of Smoke Imix, was subsumed by a gallery-like structure bearing charcoal as well as *incensarios* (censers) in the shapes of previous rulers. This building, dubbed Chorcha and dating to 695,

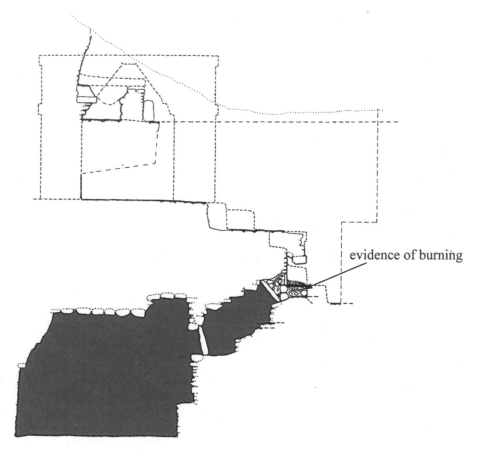

evidence of burning

FIGURE 54. *Caracol B-19-2nd tomb showing sealed capstones (after A. Chase and D. Chase 1987, fig. 20)*

obliterated earlier versions of Temple 26 that were connected to the founder of the Copan dynasty. It may have been used as an ancestor shrine for Smoke Imix until its burial by Waxaklajuun Ub'aah K'awiil in 710. At this point, it was turned into the first version of Copan's Hieroglyphic Stairway; it is perhaps no coincidence that Rosalila, the other building associated with Copan's founder, was buried at about the same time.[83]

Excavations at Caracol have also uncovered burials where burn patterns, tomb, and shrine come together (Figure 54). Within Structure B19-2nd, Diane and Arlen Chase uncovered a niche containing a series of unslipped broken wares as well as evidence of burning. As reported by Diane Chase, the back wall of this niche was removed to reveal a rough, open-air stairway leading downward through a series of slabs preventing ready access. After removing the slabs, the excavators encountered the vaulted, plastered tomb of a woman dating to AD 634. Simon Martin and Nikolai Grube have proposed that this tomb belonged to Lady Batz' Ek' of Caracol, the mother of one of the most prolific and militarily successful Caracol rulers, K'an II (r. 618–658). Similar activities have been noted by Chase and Chase in the aforementioned Structure B20, a building modified between the Early and Late Classic to house a number of high-status tombs; the building walls (interior and exterior) of Structure B20-2nd, for example, were noticeably blackened from smoke. Chase and Chase have suggested that B20 served as a prototype for later eastern ancestral shrine constructions that appear frequently in residential groups throughout Caracol.[84]

These limited archaeological cases of burning on or near royal ancestors are, of course, complemented by a wealth of data supporting a general preoccupation with the burning of incense or other precious goods throughout Maya sites spanning multiple social strata.[85] In most cases, the motives and forms of burning events are lost, although, as already mentioned, fire played a central role in dedicating or sealing buildings and tombs. Aside from the habitual burning of copal or other materials, one of the activities undertaken within buildings that would produce charred patches or lenses of burned materials was the conjuring of gods and ancestors. Conjuring appears to have been a widespread religious practice in Mesoamerican ceremonial life, involving the "grasping" or "calling" (*tzak*) of an intermediary divinity (*k'awiil*) to elicit the appearance of a god or an ancestor. In Maya iconography, such supernatural figures appear springing forth from the maws of serpents, who waft upward from the smoke of burning stingray spines, blood-spattered paper, and other precious goods. These gods and ancestors were required guests at some of the most important Maya ceremonies, ranging from kingly accessions and royal birthdays to Period Endings. It is not unreasonable to conclude, therefore, that some burn patterns over or related to burials—particularly those within large, funerary temples—represent the result of attempts to conjure supernaturals. Proximity to the ancestors vis-à-vis the *axis mundi* may have provided an additional measure of ritual efficacy for Maya conjurers. Such proximity, however, was not required.

To provide us with an idea of the character of conjuring ceremonies, as well as to illustrate this "proximity" issue, we must go to the site of Yaxchilan. For reasons unknown, dynasts at this site were particularly concerned with recording the details of such conjuring, as Yaxchilan Lintel 25 is the most elaborate representation of conjuring in the Maya lowlands (Figure 55). Taking place on October 23, AD 681 (9.12.9.8.1 5 Imix 4 Mac), the conjuring event on that panel coincided with the accession of Itzamnaaj B'alam II. The scene depicts the wife of the king, Lady K'ab'aal Xook, conjuring a warrior masked as the Teotihuacan Storm God (Tlaloc). The warrior himself is in all probability an ancestor, whose Teotihuacano costume marks him as a primordial figure in the history of Yaxchilan.[86] He emerges from a centipede-serpent; this creature, in turn, arises from blackened smoke marked by flowered *ik'* ("zero" and "breath," respectively) and *k'an* (precious) symbols. Ultimately, the entire creation derives from a bowl filled with blood-spattered bark paper, rope, and a symbol of ritual efficacy, [*chab*]*ak'ab'*, "creation," "darkness."

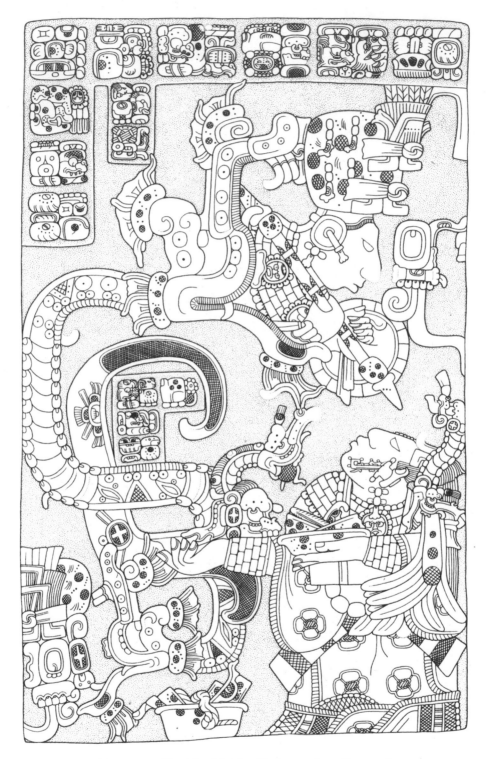

FIGURE 55. *Yaxchilan Lintel 25 (Graham and von Euw 1977)*

To accomplish this conjuring feat, Lady K'ab'aal Xook wears a centipede-serpent in her hair, while another springs forth from a skull, glancing upward at its larger twin. In addition to holding the skull, Lady K'ab'aal Xook bears another bowl filled with similar accoutrements and a headdress linking her to the Storm God and Aj K'ahk' O' Chaak.[87] Dressing as the supernaturals to be conjured and thereby engaging in sympathetic magic, Lady K'ab'aal Xook (and probably Itzamnaaj B'alam II) brought forth a centipede-serpent through bloodletting, with the remains of that process featured in the bowls of the scene. She likewise used a human skull to accomplish the appearance of Aj K'ahk' O' Chaak. We do not know whose skull was employed, although the above parallels between dress and ritual strongly suggest a link between the cranium and the emergent figure.

Presumably, there was also a verbal component; this may have been a prayer or direct address to the gods in their summoning, much like the exhortations of Blood Woman for a bundle of maize in the *Popol Vuh:*

> t at ul va 'ulok, t at ul ta k'alok
> x toh, x q'anil
> x kakav,
> ix pu tzi'a,
> at chahal r e k echa hun baatz', hun ch'oven
>
> come and eat here, come and agree here
> oh Rain Woman, oh Ripeness Woman,
> oh Cacao Woman
> and Corndough
> oh guardian of the food of 1 Monkey and 1 Howler[88]

Following this address, Blood Woman tears the tassel from the top of the maize and her net fills with ears of corn; her in-law is disconcerted but pleased. Though no gods actually appear, the basic principle of an address to gods or supernatural animals can be found time and again throughout the *Popol Vuh;* we find it again in colonial documents such as the *Ritual of the Bacabs.* These addresses to supernatural beings accomplish impossible feats for the Hero Twins or curing for the *curandero* (healer), and seem to be central to the performance of a number of ritual acts. Invocations to saints are a vital part of the rituals of modern Maya peoples as well; it is thus difficult to imagine an elaborate Classic Maya conjuring ceremony taking place in complete silence.

Lintel 25 does not mention where this event took place and only cites its date as 681. However, a later conjuring event on that lintel, dated to 726, does mention the "grasping" of *k'awiil* by an aged Lady K'ab'aal Xook "in the land of, in the cave of" Itzamnaaj B'alam II. This grasping took place as part of the dedication for Temple 23, the location of Lintel 25 as well as its companion Lintels 24 and 26. Dedicated in 726, Temple 23 was known as the *otot,* "house," of

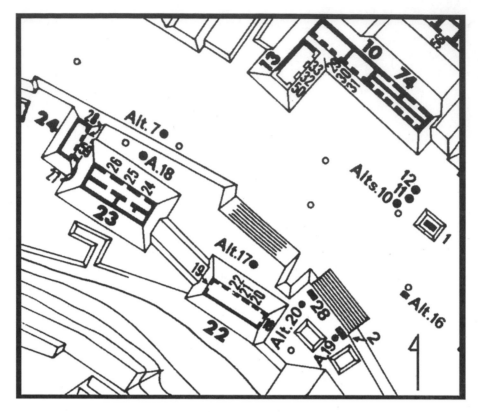

FIGURE 56. *Map of Yaxchilan showing Structure 23 (Graham and von Euw 1977, 3:6)*

Lady K'ab'aal Xook.[89] It was to become her funerary monument: an extravagant burial, identified as belonging to Lady K'ab'aal Xook, was recovered by Roberto García Moll immediately below the floor of Temple 23.[90] She died at an advanced age in 749, surviving her husband by six years.[91]

What is interesting about these dates is that during the conjuring events mentioned on Lintel 25 (Figure 56), Temple 23 was without its "proximate" ancestor, Lady K'ab'aal Xook. Although Temple 23 may indeed have been created to house the aging queen, it was to remain vacant for twenty-three years. Indeed, it was the first major structure built by her husband, Itzamnaaj B'alam II, at Yaxchilan. As the "house" of Lady K'ab'aal Xook, Temple 23 may therefore have had a number of functions, not specifically ancestral, during its history of use; given the themes on its lintels, Bryan Just has suggested that Temple 23 was a space used for conjuring supernaturals at Yaxchilan.[92] After the death of Lady K'ab'aal Xook, this space became inherently ancestral, although events in Temple 24 suggest a more complicated picture. Temple 24, which contains records of her death as well as a poorly understood burning event connected to her tomb, is probably an ancestor shrine much in the manner of connected shrine-tombs at Copan and Caracol.

This example from Yaxchilan definitively illustrates that funerary temples could be built prior to the death of their occupants; Diane and Arlen Chase have noted similar cases of tombs built long before the death of their occupants at the site of Caracol.[93] Cenotaphs likewise serve as testament to premortem planning on the part of Classic Maya architects. Unfortunately, clear-cut examples such as these are comparatively rare, with Yaxchilan Temple 24 providing the only known example where death date, dedication date, and burial come together. We simply do not know, for example, how much of a role K'inich Janaab' Pakal I played in the construction of the Temple of the Inscriptions at Palenque, perhaps the paramount example of a funerary monument in the Classic Maya lowlands.

The examples above likewise raise an important functional issue, which is the question of whether buildings like Yaxchilan Temple 23 had a "life," a different purpose, or a multiplicity of purposes prior to (and succeeding) the introduction of Lady K'ab'aal Xook to Tomb 2. Certainly we find many cases where buildings were rebuilt several times with different funerary and nonfunerary functions, as noted by Chase and Chase at Caracol or exemplified by Temple 26 at Copan.[94] If buildings, as living features, accrue ritual power and significance over time, as has been suggested by Linda Schele and David Freidel, then we might view intrusive or successive interments of kings as attempts to further sanctify ritually powerful locations. We know what buildings became upon the introduction of a royal ancestor: they became embodiments of the "self," testimonials of site ownership, and symbols of royal authority and lineage. That such buildings may have held prior significance does not change the fact that Classic Maya kings and their families sought to attach themselves to—or create anew—potent features of the natural world.

This is not to say that royal funerary temples were ever, or suddenly became, solely mortuary in nature when individuals like K'inich Janaab' Pakal I or K'inich Yax K'uk' Mo' were interred. We would not make this case for a crypt-bearing house platform or similar edifice, and thus cannot reduce such temples to being isolated "houses" for the royal dead or simply dedicatory in nature. But given their monumental scale and visibility, as well as the landscape concerns addressed thus far, it seems clear that royal funerary temples evoked a sense of place for ancestors that was reflected in nearly every aspect of daily life in the site core. The space defined by such temples was surely multifaceted, but one could not help but encounter the dead on a daily basis, vis-à-vis prominent, visible reminders of their power and presence upon the landscape. In the case of ancestor shrines, such interactions were more personal, perhaps even more private.

FIVE

ENTERING THE TOMBS OF
THE CLASSIC MAYA KINGS

Royal ancestors played a vital role in religious and political life, actively taking part in a variety of activities ranging from accessions to birthday celebrations. Dead kings occasionally "saw" or "witnessed" the activities of their descendants, overseeing events from celestial or similar positions in the manner of Classic Maya gods. Caracol Stela 6 (Figure 57), for example, mentions the scattering of incense by Knot Ajaw on the Period Ending date of 9.8.10.0.0 4 Ahau 13 Xul (July 4, 603). His actions at the Five Great Sky place are seen by his dead father, Yajaw Te' K'inich II: *yilaj ux ? [ajaw] ch'ahom yajaw te' k'inich,* "[he] sees [it], 3 *k'atun* lord dropper, Yajaw Te' K'inich II." In the same way, we might think of dead kings—as personified funerary monuments—bearing witness to the activities undertaken therein. Occasionally, however, the living sought even more direct contact with their ancestors: gaining physical access to the dead was a facet of royal ceremony at a number of sites, and this involved further interments as well as the alteration of the tomb environment. Such tombs became activity areas, and the bodies therein, portable artifacts.

Tomb reentry was a practice involving (1) the removal of capstones or other masonry elements of the tomb; (2) the subsequent modification of the grave furniture and skeleton through such activities as the burning of incense or the removal of bones; and (3) the sealing of the tomb, either permanently or temporarily. As mentioned in Chapter 3, fire was often a key element of this rite, with incense, torches, or both lit inside the burial chamber and resulting in the partial cremation or blackening of many of the artifacts and skeletal remains. This burning was often only one part of a more elaborate ceremony charged with religious and political undertones. Recorded in the most epigraphic and archaeological detail at the site of Piedras Negras, tomb reentry can nevertheless be found throughout space and time within the Maya lowlands. Based on hieroglyphic data, we have firm dates associated with tomb reentry in the lowlands spanning most of the Classic Period, from AD 441 at Copan in the eastern lowlands, to AD 799 at Tonina in the far west. Table 5 provides a list of those burials that are unequivocally royal and reentered.[1]

There are a number of cases, particularly at Caracol, where subroyal or elite burials were opened and entered by contemporaries of the Classic Maya kings.

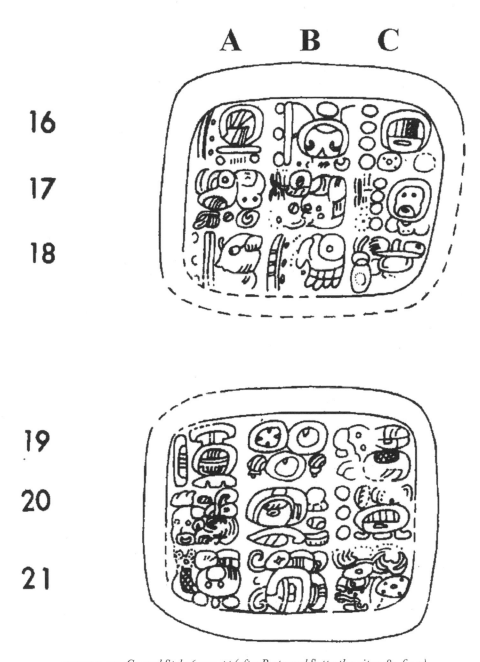

FIGURE 57. *Caracol Stela 6 excerpt (after Beetz and Satterthwaite 1981, fig. 7)*

TABLE 5
REENTERED ROYAL TOMBS OF THE CLASSIC MAYA LOWLANDS

Site	Individual or Burial	Action Taken	Date or Time Period
Copan	Motmot	*och k'ahk'*	435, Early Classic
Copan	Hunal	bones painted red, disturbed	435–455, Early Classic
Copan	Margarita	bones painted red, disturbed	435–578, Early Classic
Piedras Negras	Burial 110	new interment, missing bones	450–600, Early Classic
Caracol	Str. A34 Tomb (lower)	new interment, new offerings	>577–582, Early Classic
Tonina	Chak B'olon Chaak	*och k'ahk'*	589, Early Classic
Tonina	Burial IV-6	disturbed	>600, Late Classic
Caracol	Str. B19-2nd Tomb	disturbed	>634, Late Classic
Piedras Negras	K'inich Yo'nal Ahk I (Ruler 1)	*el naah*	658, Late Classic
Palenque	K'inich Janaab' Pakal I, TOI Tomb 1	disturbed	>683, Late Classic
Caracol	Str. A3 Tomb	disturbed	>696, Late Classic
Piedras Negras	Ruler 2	*puluuy u tz'itil*	706, Late Classic
Piedras Negras	Ruler 3	*puluuy u tz'itil*	>729, Late Classic
Tonina	K'inich B'aaknal Chaak	*och k'ahk'*	730, Late Classic
Seibal	K'an Mo' B'alam	*och k'ahk'*	747, Late Classic
Piedras Negras	Ruler 4, Burial 13	*el naah*	782, Late Classic
Tonina	Ruler 1	*och k'ahk'*	799, Late Classic

Diane Chase has documented general patterns for royal and elite entries at Caracol as follows:

> Re-entry into chambers is indicated not only by analysis of skeletal remains, but is also confirmed in the artifactual offerings placed inside chambers, as these may span a substantial period of time . . . in some cases, partial vessels and extra skeletal material were found under the primary tomb occupant even though the archaeological record makes it clear that only a single burial episode is indicated. This could suggest the possibility of the ritual inclusion of part of an earlier interment (specifically the bones and burial offerings of ancestors) to aid in the transition of a deceased individual from the world of the

living to the world of the dead . . . repeated chamber entries were facilitated by the formal entrances that exist for many of the Caracol tombs (ca. 60%). Re-entry of tombs, however, has also been documented for chambers devoid of entrances.[2]

Such patterns of reentry have not been documented elsewhere in the Maya lowlands, where elite reentries are rare or unrecognized; to this point, the best candidates for elite reentry occur in the western lowlands, particularly at the sites of Tonina and Palenque. Tonina is likewise an important location for the study of reentry for its Postclassic interments: late inhabitants of Tonina continued to inter new dead with the old well into the ninth century AD.[3]

Within the Classic Period, variations in reentry were almost certainly commonplace. Two phrases clearly associated with this practice have been identified thus far. Both of these, *och k'ahk' tu mukil* (or *muknal*), "fire enters into his tomb," and *el naah tu mukil*, "his tomb is house-censed," are conceptually tied to house dedications. It is not at all clear that these two events were the same, although archaeologically they produce similar observable results: the grave contents are typically scattered, the skeleton is blackened or disarticulated, and grave goods are either damaged or present in quantities smaller than expected for royal tombs.[4]

As of this writing, there are only two cases in the Maya lowlands where the archaeology and epigraphy of reentry overlap: the Motmot burial at Copan and Piedras Negras Burial 13 have inscriptions describing the actions taken to produce similar archaeologically observable results. It is an unfortunate fact that the most famous cases of reentry, including the example of Piedras Negras Ruler 1 presented in the introduction, are often purely epigraphic *or* archaeological. Nevertheless, we can gain insights into reentry by comparing and contrasting these sources of information. Piedras Negras provides the richest source for analysis, as there are records of habitual reentry for successive generations of kings.

PATTERNS OF REENTRY AT PIEDRAS NEGRAS

Involved in struggles with major centers such as Palenque and Yaxchilan, Piedras Negras was one of a handful of sites along the Usumacinta River to hold real regional power. Its influence was felt at sites like Bonampak, El Cayo, La Mar, Hix Witz, and Sak Tz'i; during its heyday, Piedras Negras was a cosmopolitan place sharing ideas as well as goods with numerous Maya polities, from local dynasts at El Cayo to the Central Peten. Before it met its violent end in the years after the capture of Ruler 7 by Yaxchilan (9.18.17.12.6 7 Kimi 14 Sip; March 16, 808), Piedras Negras was one of a few sites to record—in historical detail—specific aspects of political life; personal events in the lives of rulers; and, most important for the present study, ceremonial behavior.

In reviewing the mortuary aspects of this behavior, it is apparent that we have little to no information from the Early Classic Period. Struggling with other sites, particularly Yaxchilan, during the earliest years of its existence, Piedras Negras seems to have been subordinate to the distant Central Mexican metropolis of Teotihuacan. On Panel 2, an Early Classic lord of Piedras Negras (*ya ? ahk*, known in the literature as Turtle Tooth) receives a Central Mexican helmet (*ko'haw*) under the auspices of a lord called Tajoom Uk'ab' Tuun. Though the name of the "overking" is similar to one used at Calakmul, his title, *ochk'in kaloomte'*, "sun-entering ?," is often associated with Central Mexican iconography and statements that support a heritage stemming from the Mexican metropolis of Teotihuacan.[5] This heritage was confirmed in 2001 with the discovery of a wooden box from Tabasco, Mexico: the box makes reference to Tajoom Uk'ab' Tuun as a Teotihuacan lord who appears to have been a successor to the "famous Siyaj K'a[h]k' and Spearthrower Owl known from central Peten texts about 100 years earlier."[6] As a result, it would seem that Piedras Negras, like several other sites in the Central Peten, acquired—for better or for worse—a powerful "ally" in the Early Classic.

This inferior status, coupled with raids by Pomona and further subordination to Yaxchilan, probably resulted in the commission or preservation of few Early Classic monuments. Many of the major structures at Piedras Negras suffered fire damage and razing at the end of the Early Classic, including what was probably the Early Classic royal palace.[7] No doubt some inscriptions perished as a result. Those that we do have mention the erection of temples, scattering events (Panel 12), or *k'atun* endings (Stelae 29 and 30); iconographically, there is a paucity of information, none of it related to mortuary rites per se. One small hint at patterns of reentry at Piedras Negras is the Early Classic Burial 110, which seems to have been entered for the purposes of removing skeletal material as well as interring a new body;[8] future publications will refine our picture of such mortuary customs in the Early Classic.

A series of building programs literally transformed Piedras Negras in the Late Classic. During this time, perhaps to erase a memory of defeat and the ashes of the Early Classic structures, the subsequent rulers of Piedras Negras—particularly Rulers 2 and 3—embarked upon massive constructions and the production of hieroglyphic monuments throughout the site.[9] Ruling from AD 603 to AD 639, Tatiana Proskouriakoff's Ruler 1, known as K'inich Yo'nal Ahk I, embellished the South Group with monuments depicting himself in Teotihuacano garb (continuing the themes of the Early Classic) and highlighting his victories against Palenque and Sak Tz'i' (Figure 58).[10] Despite his exploits, we are more concerned with what happened to him after his death. It is on his posthumously erected Panel 4 that mortuary rituals are recorded for the first time at Piedras Negras.[11] Coincidentally, they are also the most detailed of said rites in the corpus of Maya hieroglyphic inscriptions.

FIGURE 58. *K'inich Yo'nal Ahk I (after Martin and Grube 2000, 142)*

As related in the introduction, K'inich Yo'nal Ahk I died on 9.10.6.2.1 5 Imix 9 K'ayab' (February 6, AD 639) and was interred for almost a *k'atun* (19.17.7) before his tomb was opened under the auspices of his son, Ruler 2. On the related Panel 4, his tomb—as a metaphorical house for the dead—was fumigated with smoke from burning incense (*el naah u mukil*, "his tomb is house-censed") on October 11, 658 (9.11.6.1.8 3 Lamat 6 Keh). Six days later and one *k'atun* after the death of K'inich Yo'nal Ahk I, Ruler 2 received a Central Mexican helmet in the company of a number of conjured gods. The Classic Maya Storm God Yaxha' Chaak, Waxak Banak Hun Banak (8 Banak 1 Banak), and the Jaguar God of the Underworld all make an appearance. The text of Panel 2 (see Figure 2) goes on to describe an Early Classic event, the receipt of the aforementioned *ko'haw* by Turtle Tooth under the auspices of Tajoom Uk'ab' Tuun. The iconography depicts a dominant Turtle Tooth and his heir, the otherwise unknown Joy Chitam Ahk, standing over subordinate visitors from Yaxchilan, Bonampak, and Lacanha. Given that the text promotes the two events, Early and Late Classic, as identical, we can be reasonably sure that Ruler 2 invited comparable subordinates to witness his own receipt of the *ko'haw*.

Several observations can be made about this sequence of events. First, the censing of the tomb of Ruler 2 appears to have been almost a preparatory act. They did not celebrate the anniversary of his death, only a loose approximation of a *k'atun;* this seems strange in light of the fact that Period Endings, birthdays (e.g., three-*k'atun* lord, four-*k'atun* lord), and other mortuary anniversaries at the site are measured in intervals of twenty years. Second, it would seem that opening and entering a tomb would take a considerable length of time, even for those who knew the layout and location of the burial; thus it is possible that the rituals on Panels 4 and 2 took longer than six days. Third, if the substitution of the helmet and *ko'haw* glyphs is correct, then Ruler 2 is receiving a Teotihuacano war helmet on the anniversary of his father's death, much as Turtle Tooth received his helmet under the auspices of an individual bearing titles linking him to Central Mexico. Ruler 1 is known to have occasionally dressed as a Teotihuacano, appearing on Stelae 26 and 31 wearing a war serpent headdress and bearing a classically Central Mexican square shield. Similar iconography accompanies the Early Classic lord depicted on Panel 2. Finally, the Late Classic portion of the text refers to a conjuring, the receipt of the helmet in the presence of a number of conjured gods. Is there more to the ceremony than is explicitly mentioned?

FIGURE 59. *Yaxchilan Lintel 14 (Graham and von Euw 1977)*

Conjuring at other sites, particularly at Yaxchilan, was an elaborate affair. In the previous chapter, we saw how Lady K'ab'aal Xook conjured the "flint and shield" of an ancestral deity through bloodletting, spreading blood onto bark paper strips or thorny rope, and burning these goods in a ceramic vessel. Occasionally, these kinds of activities were done in larger groups with multiple actors, as on Yaxchilan Lintel 14 or Dos Pilas Panel 19 (Figure 59). As I have already shown, conjuring may also have involved elaborate verbal or even physical gestures and, once accomplished, even whole conversations: we have numerous depictions from Yaxchilan showing mortals and supernaturals conversing. Accordingly, we might reconstruct a *hypothetical* order of events for the rituals undertaken by Ruler 2 for his deceased father (and, arguably, his own political ends):

1) Following his death in 639, K'inich Yo'nal Ahk I was buried.[12]

2) Just short of a *k'atun* (twenty years) after his death, his tomb was opened (itself no small task) and censed.

3) Another six days pass, during which time Ruler 2 and possibly others prepare for the rites at hand; vassals from other sites, if not already present at the reentry, enter into the picture.

4) On the sixth day, the actual *k'atun* anniversary of the death of Ruler 1, Ruler 2 does penance and lets blood; his blood is spread upon bark paper and burned while he invokes Yaxha' Chaak, Waxak Banak Hun Banak, and the Jaguar God of the Underworld.

5) Others are perhaps involved in this ceremony, as in cases of conjuring at Yaxchilan.

6) In the presence of his gods, and possibly vassals, Ruler 2 receives a *ko'haw* (helmet), an item that metaphorically links the king to Central Mexico.

7) If not already closed, the tomb of Ruler 1 is sealed, and Panels 2 and 4 are commissioned, coming to rest in the South Group.

From whom did Ruler 2 receive this *ko'haw*? From where? Given that bones and even offerings were seemingly removed from reentered burials in the low-lands, as at Caracol, it is tempting to think that this helmet originally belonged, or was supposed to belong, to Ruler 1 and his tomb. Certainly, Ruler 1, like many dynasts at Piedras Negras and elsewhere, had celebrated his (possibly) fictive Teotihuacano heritage. Origins notwithstanding, this helmet signifies that in death, as in life, the two rulers shared not only the office of *k'uhul ajaw yokib*, "holy lord of Piedras Negras," but also a common mythic tradition inherited from Teotihuacan and the figures represented on Panel 2.

The choice of gods summoned, as well as the days involved for this ceremony, must have been significant. As a patron of agriculture and god of rain and light-ning, Chaak can be found throughout the Maya lowlands on architecture, hi-eroglyphic monuments, and ceramics; the Jaguar God of the Underworld (GIII of the Palenque Triad), in a variety of guises, is equally ubiquitous. It is perhaps significant that Yaxha' Chaak and the Jaguar God of the Underworld appear together on looted ceramic vessels depicting sacrifice and an entrance to the Underworld (Figure 60). In these scenes, Yaxha' Chaak wields his lightning weapons and appears to be assisting the Maya god of death, Schellas God A, in hurling the infant Jaguar God into a cave or portal to the Underworld. Given that one of the forms of the Jaguar God of the Underworld is the nighttime sun, journeying below the surface of the earth to emerge the following day, we might see these ceramic scenes as metaphors for the solar journey. If Yaxha' Chaak is assisting this journey somehow, then the choice of gods on Panel 2 may have fit Ruler 1 within this mythological sequence. The significance of Waxak Banak Hun Banak is, of course, unknown.

It is no accident that the time between the death and receipt of the *ko'haw* was exactly one *k'atun* after death. It also seems plausible that the day chosen to

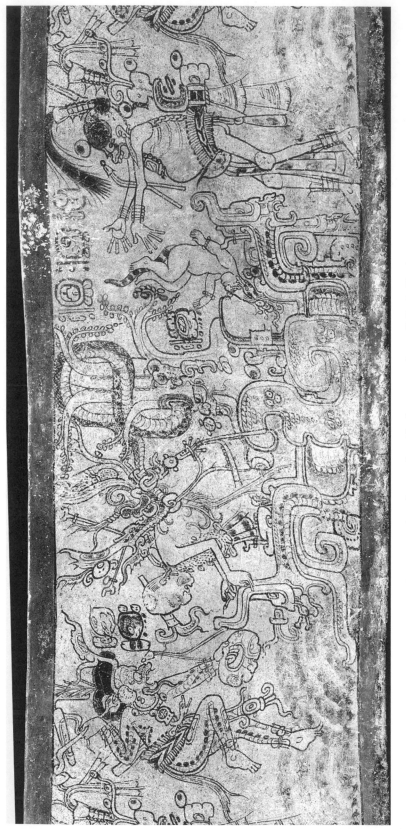

FIGURE 60. *A scene of sacrifice from K4013 (#4013 © Justin Kerr)*

open the tomb of K'inich Yo'nal Ahk I was significant, that the time between the tomb-entering and the receipt of the *ko'haw* was important. Among modern Maya peoples, day names and numbers are significant for the performance of ceremonies, public festivals, and even birthdays; many communities have ritual cycles in which "powerful" or "good" periods wax and wane with the passage of time and its days. Certain months or days are chosen for specific ritual or agricultural tasks. This time is subdivided into stages when participants—living and dead—are expected to perform different tasks:

> In the month of Pom, on the fifth day, flowers are gathered, food is prepared, an Ayuntamiento of the Dead is appointed, and church bells call the dead to partake of all that is produced by the living. On the night between the fifth and sixth, the souls of the dead visit the living, and retire before the dawn of the following day. On the tenth of Pom, the saints are taken out again in procession, and the third and last *mukta mixa* is celebrated, indicating that the year is at an end for the cultivator and the authorities. The authorities take leave of their offices and thank the deities for having been accorded the grace of living to see the end of their service. After this last one comes a period of rest, where relatives and friends gather, sing and tell stories, drink and enjoy their leisure.[13]

The timing of such events during the day was probably important as well. As mentioned in Chapter 3, Dos Pilas Stela 8 does recount the burial of a lord "at night." Passages similar to this abound in the ethnographic literature, where events are timed with morning, evening, or even specific hours of the day for efficacy, such as maize field ceremonies in Zinacantan, postfuneral rites in Chan Kom, or ritual activities in Chichicastenango:

> Morning is the preferred time for performing all ceremonies, except ceremonies of sorcery and "strong" ceremonies of protection, which are performed at night . . . important ceremonies are timed so that the final ceremonies in the mountains are performed at dawn.[14]

These daytime rites are mirrored in the Lineage of the Lords of Totonicapan, where Balam Kitze and his people pray to their gods and an ancestor, Nacxit:

> And when the day star returned they gave thanks. The lords went to their gods and taking out incense of distinctive odor they offered it saying, "Twice and three times we thank you, creators of everything around us, we thank you because we have seen the sun again and we hope to see it many times more, together with the stars, and you, our old homeland Tula, Zuyua, where our brothers are, receive our vows." So they spoke, burning the incense, and the smoke first went straight up, proving that it was agreeable to the great

god, and then inclined toward the sun, which was a sign that those offerings and those vows, born in the secret parts of the heart, had reached the presence of our father, Nacxit.[15]

We must, therefore, view the ceremonies performed by Ruler 2 as complex events, for which day names, day numbers, gods, and possibly vassals were prepared or summoned in concert. Much of this rite cannot, of course, be reconstructed at this time. But the evidence that we do have provides us with a feel for the kinds of activities that accompanied the opening of a Classic Maya royal tomb.

Ruler 1 was not the only one of his line to receive attention from his descendants. In due time, objects—or possibly bones—belonging to Ruler 2 were handled by his son and successor, K'inich Yo'nal Ahk II (Ruler 3). In what has become the most memorable prenuptial rite in the inscriptions, a dying Ruler 2 supervised the engagement of a twelve-year-old Lady K'atun Ajaw to his son on November 13, 686 (9.12.14.10.8 6 Lamat 6 K'ank'in). Although the king died two days later, this did not stop the marriage from taking place: on November 18, K'inich Yo'nal Ahk II and his bride were married, with Ruler 2 "entering the road" (*och b'ihiiy*) on November 24. One wonders how the new couple dealt with these issues.

Twenty years (one *k'atun*) after the *och b'ihiiy* event, K'inich Yo'nal Ahk II celebrated its anniversary on August 12, 706, by performing a rite limited to the inscriptions of Piedras Negras. On Stela 1 (Figure 61) a passage states:

puluuy u tz'itil "Ruler 2," u chamaw yo'nal ahk yokib ajaw ti hun ? och b'ih ahk

[it] burns his long/thin object, Ruler 2; he receives it, Yo'nal Ahk II, lord of Yok'ib', at the first *k'atun* [after the] road-entering [of] turtle [Ruler 2]

As this event does not occur outside of Piedras Negras, it is difficult to say what was actually involved; the literal translation of *puluuy u tz'itil* is "[it] burns his long object," interpreted by the author as a torch, fire-drill, or other combustible belonging to Ruler 2. It is being passed to Ruler 3, much in the manner of the *k'ohaw*, and clearly relates the father to the son—or the ruler to the successor. This "passing of the torch" may sound like a Western convention, but it is something we actually find in the Late Classic on Altar Q at Copan, where rulers show their succession via a burning torch. Following the receipt of this torch at Piedras Negras, there is no more information: we do not know for sure whether K'inich Yo'nal Ahk II opened his father's tomb or simply burned an ancestral item.[16] Yet this was not the end of Ruler 2. Eighteen years after the events of Stela 1, he resurfaces, this time "dancing" on Stela 8 as his son turns sixty (February 20, 724). Erected by K'inich Yo'nal Ahk II, Stela 8 communicates further interaction—metaphorical or even physical—between father and son.

K'inich Yo'nal Ahk II had a long and tumultuous reign, overseeing losses

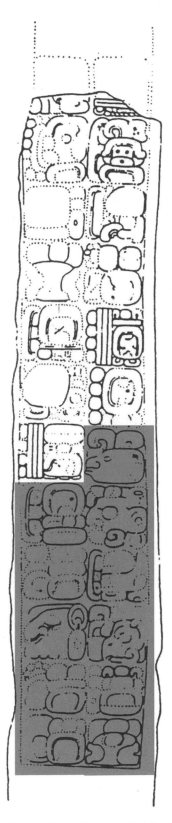

FIGURE 61. *Piedras Negras Stela 1, right (after Stuart 2003)*

to Palenque and a final victory over Yaxchilan before his death. Although we lack the actual death date, it is generally recognized that K'inich Yo'nal Ahk II expired sometime in 729. There are no inscriptions to clue us into the nature of his burial, its timing, or accompanying mortuary rites, but we have a wealth of archaeological information. His tomb, designated Piedras Negras Burial 5, was discovered by the University Museum in the 1930s; its overall appearance is similar to other royal tombs encountered at Piedras Negras, although it was never opened, "fired," or "censed."

It is nevertheless clear that *his* successor, Piedras Negras Ruler 4, continued the practice of ancestor veneration and interaction at the site. At some point after the death of K'inich Yo'nal Ahk II, for example, Ruler 4 engaged in a *puluuy u tz'itil,* "[it] burns, his long object," rite for his father. These events paralleled those performed for Ruler 2 decades earlier, and suggest that the *puluuy* rite did not involve tomb reentry for either Ruler 2 or K'inich Yo'nal Ahk II. Moreover, as related in the previous chapter, Ruler 4 seems to have scattered incense into the tomb of his mother, a figure otherwise unidentified in the inscriptions at the site; she, like K'inich Yo'nal Ahk I and Ruler 2, bears a helmet of Teotihuacano design. While the channel to this woman's tomb may indeed be a psychoduct, it seems equally likely that Stela 40 represents a true reentry event. Simon Martin and Nikolai Grube have pointed out that the day of this event, December 19, 745 (9.15.14.9.3 11 Ben 16 Pax), is exactly 83 *tzolk'in* (ca. fifty-nine years) after the death of Ruler 2, making the scattering an event performed for both his mother and his grandfather.

Following an almost thirty-year reign marked by hegemony over neighboring kingdoms as well as the mortuary rites listed above, Ruler 4 died and was interred in front of one of the largest temples at Piedras Negras, Structure O-13. The 1997 and 1998 seasons of the BYU/del Valle project at the site unearthed his burial, which had clearly been entered and had suffered considerable fire damage.

This was visible confirmation of an event mentioned on Piedras Negras Panel 3, which relates the entry of incense into the tomb of Ruler 4 by Ruler 7. As observed by a number of scholars, this entry was of great political importance to Ruler 7, for it harked back to a time when Yaxchilan and other local sites were firmly subordinate to Piedras Negras. At the accession of Ruler 7, Yaxchilan could (and did) claim mastery of much of the Usumacinta River Valley and surrounding regions. K'inich Yo'nal Ahk III and Ha' K'in Xook, the kings following Ruler 4 in the dynastic sequence, seem to have been comparatively weaker than the dynasts at Yaxchilan, erecting few monuments and only reinforcing their authority at local polities like La Mar and El Cayo. Paying attention to the present but nevertheless connecting himself to the past, Ruler 7 entered the tomb of Ruler 4 on the one-year anniversary of the death of Ha K'in Xook. He censed this ancestral tomb in much the same manner described on Panel 2 for Ruler 1 of Piedras Negras: on March 28, AD 782 (9.17.11.6.1 12 Imix 19 Sip), he "house-censed" (*el naah*).

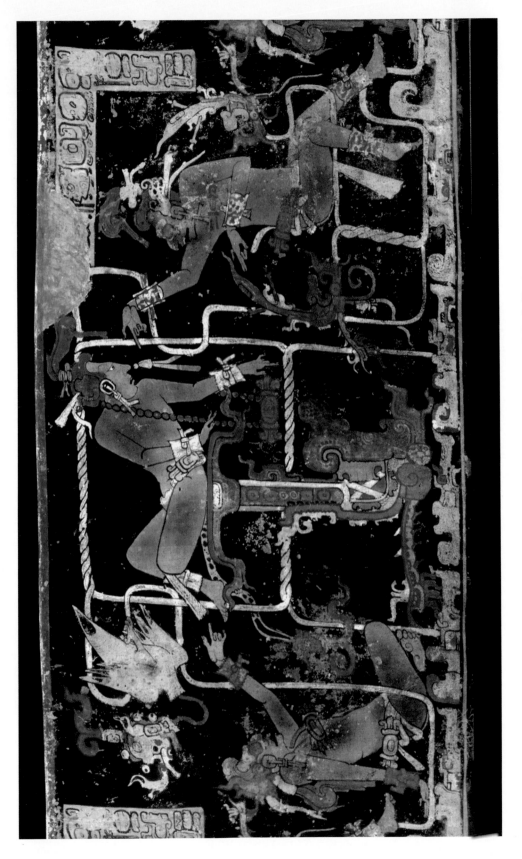

An Underworld scene (Rollout Photograph #K688 © Justin Kerr)

Chaak, God A, and the Jaguar God of the Underworld (Rollout Photograph #4011 © Justin Kerr)

Hun Ajaw and Yax B'alam (Photograph #K1892 © Justin Kerr)

Classic Maya way *killing other* way. *Note the victorious* way *of the* ajaw *of Calakmul (Rollout Photograph #K791 © Justin Kerr)*

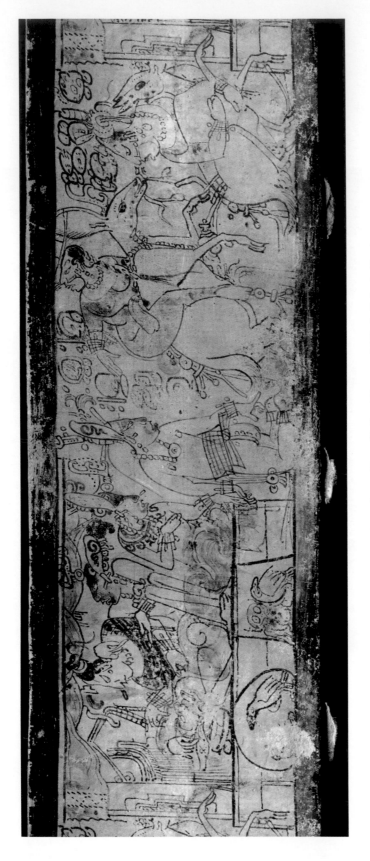

Death and transformation on K1182 (Rollout Photograph #K1182 ©Justin Kerr)

Luckily, we can observe the results of this censing. During excavations by Héctor Escobedo and Stephen Houston at Piedras Negras, a burial was unearthed in front of Structure O-13 that had fire damage. The burial contained the remains of an adult male and two adolescents, along with numerous works of jade, shell, and other materials, including a representation of a decapitated lord of the Hix Witz kingdom. As related in various publications,[17] bones were both missing and scattered throughout the tomb chamber, blackened and burned long after the flesh had decayed. Following this rite, the chamber was apparently sealed, with a new floor for the plaza obscuring the results of Ruler 7's reentry. Further publications will elaborate upon his handiwork, but for the time being, it seems that Ruler 7 was continuing a long tradition stretching back at least to the time of Ruler 1, if not to the Early Classic.

Archaeology and epigraphy at Piedras Negras therefore demonstrate a royal Late Classic tradition of ancestor veneration lasting from at least 658 to 782, with a number of tombs clearly having been opened or accessed from the outside. Rulers 1–4, as well as the woman of Stela 40, were physical and metaphorical participants in rites involving censing, dancing, and "scattering." The royal adolescent recovered from Burial 82 by the author, dating to between AD 630 and AD 680, did not receive this treatment. The reasons for this discrepancy are unknown, for a similar unidentified adolescent recovered by the University Museum within the South Group *was* "fired" sometime during the Late Classic.[18] If the rites performed for Yo'nal Ahk I are any indication of how entries like these were celebrated at Piedras Negras, then it seems likely that mortuary rites took days—if not weeks—of preparation and performance. Similar preparations may have taken place for other rites involving entry and fire at other sites, with presentation and display a central facet of ancestral veneration and the tomb reentry ceremony.

As discussed in Chapter 3, this "performance" aspect of death rites is generally not observable, as activities like fasting or dancing are largely obscured by the passage of time. In the case of postinterment rites, we do have the one example of "dancing" from Stela 8 to clue us into the kinds of behavior that went on in commemoration of ancestors. Judging from the importance of dance to Maya groups from the Colonial Period to the present day, it seems likely that dancing was an important aspect of ancestor veneration. Juan Francisco Molina Solís describes the centrality of dance to the Maya of early colonial Yucatan, noting that dancing was a part of "all their public and private festivities, religious as well as civil," and numerous authors have commented on the qualities of pre- and postconquest dance to convey drama, politics, and group dynamics.[19] Yet actual physical movement is but one part of the activities labeled as "dance" in the Mesoamerican context. An example of this is provided by Harry S. McArthur, who concludes that dance in Aguacatan, together with a host of related ceremonies, is believed to "release the deceased from a place of suffering, where they are bound with chains." Preparatory ceremonies of *sólö'n,* "unwinding," and *púhle'n alma'*, "untying the dead," are believed to free the dead, allowing them "to walk once again in the sunlight." They are considered to be part of the "dance," and in their language and performance, illustrate considerations we have seen in both pre-Columbian and postconquest settings.

> [They demonstrate] the continued subjection of the living to the dead . . . their dependence upon the dead for protection . . . their penitence for sins committed and their need to be made pure . . . their respect and care for the dead . . . and their wishes for their participation and enjoyment of the entire festival.[20]

Actual dancing, however, seems only to provide enjoyment for the dead during their release from "imprisonment" and is but one aspect of a much larger affair, much like the "dance of the drunks" within *cargo* rituals in contemporary Zinacantan or other "dances" performed in highland Maya communities. Mesoamerican rituals tend to be multivariate affairs, and it seems likely that reentry was characterized by (or was part of) a host of activities that included performance and display. Words like *och k'ahk' tu mukil* must therefore be viewed as more than simple phrases, but as conveyers of complex events potentially involving numerous participants.

FIRE IN THE MOTMOT BURIAL

David Stuart has demonstrated that phrases like *och k'ahk'* and *el naah*, while not identical in meaning, do in many ways communicate parallel events. Both involve the introduction of fiery elements into tombs and houses. Yet at Piedras Negras, there seems to have been a preference for the "censing" and burning of torches or similar objects; no tombs entered at Piedras Negras are described as "fired" per se. Censing and "fire-entering" do coexist at a number of centers, particularly with regard to house dedications. By and large, however, fire-entering seems to have been a more widespread phenomenon, perhaps reflecting, as Stuart notes, "distinct [ritual] languages in use at different sites." Luckily, there is one place where we can actually view the results of an *och k'ahk'* ceremony for comparison with the "censing" activities at Piedras Negras. The Motmot burial at Copan, unearthed near the Hieroglyphic Stairway, is the only known example where the archaeology and the epigraphy of "firing" come together.[21]

As mentioned in the previous chapter, the earliest incarnations of Temple 26 at Copan were built by K'inich Yax K'uk' Mo' and his successor early in the fifth century. In front of the second incarnation, nicknamed Motmot, archaeologists recovered the burial of an otherwise unknown woman set within a shaft tomb, much like those discovered at Teotihuacan. In a fashion similar to that of lowland Maya burials at Piedras Negras or Copan, however, the shaft tomb was opened and entered in 435.

In building this shaft tomb, the grave architects excavated a cylindrical chamber on axis with the Motmot structure and then placed a reed mat over the floor. Based on patterns of burning within the tomb, the woman was probably seated in an upright position on the mat, facing north. She was buried with a mercury-filled vessel, as well as objects of quartz and jade; three human crania complemented assorted mammal and avian bones. Following the stocking of the burial, capstones were placed above the shaft and the chamber was sealed beneath the plaza floor. As David Stuart has demonstrated, this burial may have taken place in 428. The earlier of the two dates on the Motmot marker does, however, coincide with the "arrival" of K'inich Yax K'uk' Mo' at Copan and the foundation of a new dynasty.[22]

Seven years after these events, this woman's tomb was opened to coincide with the calendrically significant Period Ending date of 9.0.0.0.0 (2 Ajaw 3 Sek). Based on events described on the Motmot marker (Figure 62), fire was

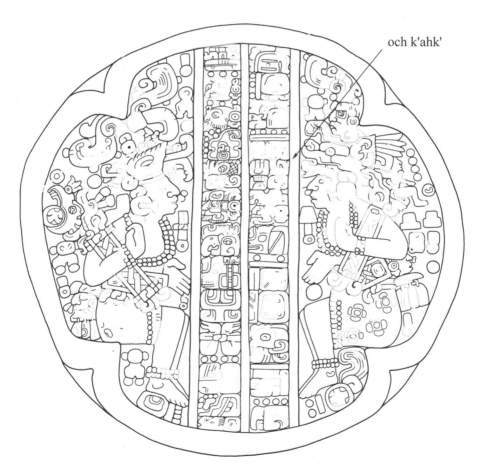

och k'ahk'

FIGURE 62. *The Motmot marker at Copan (after drawing by Barbara Fash)*

entered into her tomb. Most of her bones were displaced or suffered fire dam-age, and a deer carcass was burned atop the (eventually) reset capstones; the in-scribed Motmot marker was then set above the tomb within the plaza floor. As Rebecca Storey has noted, bodies at Teotihuacan are often interred within shaft tombs, sealed and covered by floors or other construction activities, and then "fired" from above via large bonfires.[23] Perhaps the presence of a cylindrical shaft tomb here, as well as the burning of a deer carcass, represents the use of Teotihuacano burial rites for this woman at Copan. Although the use of a deer might at first seem odd, sacrificial victims are known to have been compared to deer, particularly on Maya ceramics; deer likewise figure prominently on a series of vessels documenting the mythological death of the god Itzamnaaj.[24]

Beyond the deer burning, William Fash and Barbara Fash report the pos-sible addition of objects into the tomb, based on the lack of fire damage to some of the jades; this would represent a phase of the postinterment rite enacted prior to the sealing of the tomb and the burning of the deer. Even beyond this activ-ity, there are indications that cinnabar was set over the backfill along with fiery embers, resulting in a layer of mercury just below the Motmot capstone.[25] The significance of the mercury is somewhat unclear, although it probably relates to the "layering" aspect of Maya burials noted in Chapter 3. Similar mercury lay-ers have been observed in caches at the site of Caracol that are materially strati-fied and evidently reflect aspects of the watery Underworld.[26]

Placed above the burial to commemorate these events, the Motmot marker does not describe all these events in detail, which would have augmented our picture of the proceedings if further references and iconography had been given. The text simply notes the arrival of K'inich Yax K'uk' Mo' at Copan in 428 and the subsequent Period Ending,[27] followed by fire entering into a stone construction (*tuun*). Given the fire damage within the tomb, and that the word for "tomb" is *muk tuun* (stone burial), it is probably safe to assume that on the changing of the *k'atun*, fire was entered into the tomb of a lady of Copan.

The entry may have involved both K'inich Yax K'uk' Mo' as well as his son and successor, Ruler 2, who are featured on the marker flanking the text. These figures are engaged in the conjuring of supernaturals within a quatrefoil frame, an iconographic convention for a portal or entrance. While this portal may in-deed have been the tomb itself, there is some evidence to suggest actions tak-ing place at other locations. If we look at the Motmot marker, we see a sacred space, decorated with *k'uhul,* "holy," droplets. The stylized flowers floating in the background call to mind a variety of locations, from a Central Mexican version of the afterlife—as depicted in murals at Teotihuacan—to sweatbaths or even ballcourts. For example, Stephen Houston has demonstrated that such imagery is associated with sweatbaths in the Cross Group at Palenque; Late Classic dynasts erected temples that, in addition to being "houses" and "incense burners," served as symbolic sweatbaths.[28] Furthermore, the two kings of the markcr dress as ballplayers and stand upon toponyms similar to the house and tomb names mentioned in the previous chapter: K'inich Yax K'uk' Mo' and his son surmount the glyphs *b'olon ha'*, "9 Water," and *wuk k'an*, "7 Yellow," respectively. The nearby ballcourt, constructed during the reign of K'inich Yax K'uk' Mo' and decorated with Central Mexican feathered serpents and macaws, is thereby one of many possible locations for facets of the larger commemorative rite.[29] The overlap between sweatbaths, tombs, houses, temples, and ballcourts (not to mention incense burners) makes any complete reconstruction of this rite difficult—if not impossible.

As for the activities themselves, we find both kings conjuring supernaturals. In the case of K'inich Yax K'uk' Mo' on the left, the creature summoned appears to be a toad with a *winik*, "man," "person," glyph in its mouth. It is probably the same creature featured in Maize God resurrection imagery of the Late Classic, where it is shown emerging from a turtle carapace along with the patron of the month Pax. The creature emerging from the serpent bar belonging to Ruler 2 is not that patron, but is perhaps linked to the *chan mo'* featured in the text. Despite this difference, the action of the Motmot marker is reminiscent of other Classic Maya scenes of resurrection and rebirth involving ballplaying versions of the Hero Twins. Instead of aiding the Maize God, these Hero Twin surrogates are here serving the dead woman of the Motmot tomb. We find ideas of Hero Twins and Maize God resurrection surfacing again at Copan in later times, particularly in the interplay between the Late Classic Stela C and its altar, which were erected by Waxaklajuun Ub'aah K'awiil in the early eighth century.[30]

Combining this iconographic analysis with the archaeological reconstruction of the Motmot tomb, we can observe a series of phases to the burial and postinterment rites. Following her death, the lady within Motmot was seated in her tomb surrounded by grave goods and (perhaps) sacrificial victims. Seven years after the arrival of K'inich Yax K'uk' Mo' at Copan, the area was dug up and the capstones removed. The aging king and his son had a fire built in the shaft, causing damage to the bones and artifacts as well as displacing many of the skeletal elements. They subsequently set new items of jade inside and replaced the capstones, killing and burning a deer atop the burial. Backfilling to just below the Motmot marker, they added a layer of cinnabar and burning embers, causing a level of mercury to form before the carved Motmot marker was set in place. Fire was thus used to "fumigate" the tomb as well as seal it anew, much like the fire-sealed burials we have seen elsewhere in the lowlands; the mercury may have been a local take on the "watery" layers I have described at places like Tikal and Río Azul. Related activities may have been taking place in the nearby ballcourt or within the sacred space of the Motmot structure itself.

None of these activities relate *why* the Motmot burial, of all the other interments at Copan, was "fired." Yet if we look at the burial in its entirety, we see a number of overlapping concerns. First, the Motmot marker was dedicated around the time of the death of K'inich Yax K'uk' Mo', and although we do not know his death date for sure, it seems clear that Ruler 2 was ready and waiting to take the throne at Copan. He was involved with his father in the activities for this stylistically Central Mexican burial, thereby tying himself to two great traditions: the beginning of the Classic dynasty at Copan and an earlier tradition ultimately stemming from Teotihuacan. He also tied himself to the significant 9.0.0.0.0 Period Ending. In a sense, the Motmot marker and its burial memorialized all three occasions, and thereby may have warranted a firing. Interestingly enough, Ruler 2 was also involved in the interments of K'inich Yax K'uk' Mo' and the woman in the Margarita tomb, burials that were far more "Maya" than Motmot. Our picture of Ruler 2 must therefore be revised to accommodate a ritually adept, syncretic individual who was choosing who—and who not—to "fire" over the course of his lifetime.

FIRE AND HISTORY AT TONINA

Despite the fact that the Motmot burial provides us with the only archaeologically and epigraphically documented *och k'ahk'* event at any site, similar tales can (and most probably will) be told elsewhere in the lowlands. Sites like Tonina and Seibal present unmistakable evidence that reentered, "fired" tombs were not local phenomena at Piedras Negras or Copan. We have already seen how Itzamnaaj K'awiil of Dos Pilas used tomb firing at Seibal for his own political advantage. Although the first Early Classic tomb "firing" at Tonina is poorly understood,[31] two Late Classic examples show that dynasts at Tonina were concerned with reinforcing concepts of time, history, and succession through royal ceremony, much like Piedras Negras Ruler 7 or Copan Ruler 2. The later of these, performed for Ruler 1 by Ruler 8, ties together Early and Late Classic history; it also links the "firing" to a military victory by Ruler 8 over a longstanding enemy of Tonina, the kingdom of Pomoy.

The more elaborate of the two "firing" events (Figure 63), performed for K'inich B'aaknal Chaak, reads much like a rite that could have happened at Piedras Negras during the reigns of Ruler 4 or Ruler 7. Having lifted Tonina to the zenith of its power through successful wars against Palenque and La Mar, K'inich B'aaknal Chaak died sometime around 717. Following the short-lived reign of his successor, Ruler 4, K'inich Ich'aak Chapat took power in 723. As Simon Martin and Nikolai Grube have observed, on June 18, 730 (9.14.18.14.12 5 Eb 10 Yaxk'in), K'inich Ich'aak Chapat entered fire into the tomb of his more successful forebear. They note that the timing of this rite coincided with the 42 solar and 59 *tzolk'in* anniversary of K'inich B'aaknal Chaak's accession. Having taken power seven years prior to this event, the "new" king was establishing ties to an earlier, glorious reign and two separate calendrical cycles. K'inich

FIGURE 63. *Tonina Monument 161 (drawing by Linda Schele, © copyright David Schele, courtesy of Foundation for the Advancement of Mesoamerican Studies, Inc., www.famsi.org)*

Ich'aak Chapat seems to have been unusually concerned with such cycles, commemorating these and other forms of time throughout his reign.[32]

FAMILY AFFAIRS

A practice that overlaps with tomb "firing" or "censing," and one that is particularly evident at the Classic Maya site of Caracol, involves the single-phase or episodic deposition of human remains in large, probably familial, mausoleums. In the lowlands, such collective tombs can be traced back to the Late Preclassic, where they took the form of single, centrally located spaces that were opened and resealed to accommodate multiple individuals.[33] Clear examples of Classic Period mausoleums have been encountered at Palenque, Holmul, and Caracol. At Palenque, Franz Blom and Oliver LaFarge reported finding two Late Classic mausoleums in an area beyond the North Group that were designated (S = Sepultura, "Tomb") S-5 and S-6. The latter tomb was connected to a hallway leading to four separate funerary chambers. Within the site core, they also encountered a stairwell, an antechamber, and three vaulted funerary chambers underneath a Late Classic version of Structure 15. Given the location of this final mausoleum, ancillary to the Cross Group, it seems likely that the tomb below Structure 15 housed individuals of high rank at the site.[34]

At Holmul, Raymond E. Merwin and George C. Vaillant found a similar situation in Structure B. Human remains inside these rooms were in varying states, ranging from extended and flexed to fully articulated and even wholly disarticulated.[35] Patricia McAnany has suggested that some of the remains at

Holmul represent primary interments, while others were gathered from else-where and deposited within the rooms.[36] Unfortunately, a proper sequence for when and how these events occurred cannot be reconstructed at this time.

Diane and Arlen Chase have encountered similar Classic-era mausoleums at Caracol. One of the most common burial practices at that site, in both tomb and nontomb contexts, is the combination of primary and secondary burials in a single deposition event.[37] A variation on this theme is successive interment, whereby burials are reentered to accommodate further individuals in mausole-ums. For the royal facet of these practices, an Early Classic tomb within Struc-ture A34 serves as a typical case of death, burial, and reentry at Caracol. It appears to have originally belonged to an individual of the highest status, as it bears a hieroglyphic text mentioning its dedication by Yajaw Te' K'inich II of Caracol (r. 553–593). The tomb was found at the base of the stairway for the structure and appears to have witnessed episodic use for more than one hundred years. As described by Chase and Chase, the archaeological evidence indicates that it was reentered on at least one occasion to inter further human remains and offerings: a minimum of four individuals, as well as offerings that included ceramics, jadeite, and shell, were recovered from the tomb.[38]

Entering such a tomb requires foresight, the knowledge that at some point in the future a tomb will be opened and accessed. At Caracol, the solution to the problem of reentry seems to have been the construction of formal entranceways, with decorated, painted doors or tomb walls delineating Underworld space and symbolically separating the tomb from the outside world.[39] Such entrances were likewise used in cases where tombs were "prebuilt," that is, constructed before the death of their intended occupants. Placing a body inside a vacant tomb, or entering an occupied one, often involved descent via an access stairway or tun-nel. In a sense, Caracol grave architects literally built entry—and reentry—into the burial process. Similar considerations seem to have motivated the architects at Piedras Negras and Copan, where the aforementioned "censed" and "fired" burials, with the exception of Burial 110, were located in rather shallow, acces-sible contexts.

FALSE REENTRY

One of the most pervasive architectural decorations in the Maya area is the masked façade. As observed by David Freidel, Linda Schele, and Joy Parker, such decorations appear from the Late Preclassic to the conquest era and consist of historical portraits, anthropomorphic supernaturals, or zoomorphic figures, such as we have already seen on the Rosalila façade at Copan.[40] Doris Heyden and Paul Gendrop have traced the greatest elaboration of masked façades to the Río Bec, Chenes, and Puuc regions of Yucatán, where the doors to pyra-mids double as giant maws for creatures portrayed in the surrounding architecture.[41] People are forced to walk through the mouths of supernaturals ranging from mountains and caves to snakes and gods. Given the associations between mountains, caves, and tombs outlined in Chapter 2, the house-tomb "censing" of Chapter 3, and the personified temple-ancestors of the preceding chapter, it is likely that at least some buildings bearing *witz* or similar masks could be entered as surrogate tombs. In many ways, one cannot conceptually divorce *witz*, "openings," and actual tombs: the rare phrase *och witz*, "mountain-entering," appears to refer to a death similar to that of *ochb'ih* or *och ha'*, and Maya iconography is rife with images of dying individuals entering cavernous mountain maws. Diane and Arlen Chase have suggested that the many lowland Maya buildings with *witz* motifs

> at the base of stairs or to frame building doors reflect the concept of pyramids and buildings as portals allowing passage beyond the present world; these pyramids and buildings form not only physical entranceways for tombs but also symbolic entranceways to the underworld.[42]

Certainly all masked spaces cannot unilaterally be designated as mortuary; a wide variety of mask types and associations have been documented, many of which bear only a tenuous connection to death or ancestors.[43] Yet given the confluence of activities related to houses and tombs, it would not be surprising to find that many of the motivations and actions surrounding tomb reentry could be symbolically performed within shrines or even masked niches. The overlap between tombs, shrines, and building niches is perhaps best illustrated by Diane Chase and Arlen Chase at the aforementioned Structure B20 of the Caana complex at Caracol, perhaps the largest example of a Late Classic ancestor shrine at the site.[44]

Situated on the eastern side of the Caana "Sky Place" complex, Structure B20 witnessed repeated interments and modifications throughout the Late Classic. One of these interments, Tomb 4, was positioned at the heart of Structure B20-4th, with the entranceway to the chamber built as a large, stylized mask set into the front stairway of the structure. Both tomb and mask were covered by a successive construction phase, Structure B20-3rd, at which time a shrine room bearing extensive evidence of burning was created. As successive constructions and tombs were created, this shrine room was obscured, but by the time Structure B20-1st-B was built, nearly two hundred years after Tomb 4, Caracol architects revisited the tomb-mask theme: a large *witz* mask was set at the base of the mound and its new, accompanying stairway. According to Chase and Chase, this mask, as the mouth of the building, "symbolically swallowed the dead already interred within the construction."[45] In this way, it served as a cavernous, albeit false, entrance into the heart of the structure, its burials, and thereby the realm of death circumscribed by the original mask of Tomb 4. In a sense, the maw was an abbreviated entrance for the tombs of Structure B20, a semipermanent opening through which to access the dead, and a psychoduct combined.

Proof that this mask was viewed in this way comes from the excavation of the maw. Divorced from an actual tomb or burial, the *witz* mask was to swallow one final occupant before it was buried by Structure B20-1st A: sometime after AD 700, portions of a body were placed within the mouth-niche. A somewhat less spectacular "mouth" is represented in the aforementioned adjacent Structure B19, where a niche bearing broken ceramics and evidence of fire damage concealed a walled stairway leading to a "gullet" tomb deep in the heart of the building.[46] In many ways, the Caracol evidence calls into question the notion of "tomb reentry" and illustrates the various forms and abbreviations this behavior took during the Classic Period. We find niches as mouths and doorways, masks as openings, and tombs falsely entered and "fired" in the rooms above.

PAINTING, DRILLING, AND BONE PEELING

In addition to tomb "firing"; the custom of interring multiple, successive individuals within tombs; and the possible removal of artifacts and skeletal remains, a few other rare, oftentimes corollary practices linked to the opening of royal tombs have been attested in the Maya area. The first of these was addressed in Chapter 3 and consists of the painting and sprinkling of bones with cinnabar or hematite during reentry. The only clear case of this occurs at Copan, within the Margarita burial, as described by Robert Sharer and his colleagues.[47] As red-painted burials occur in a variety of contexts throughout the Maya lowlands, we might attribute the red paint in Margarita to a larger set of events somewhat divorced from any reentry procedure.

The second practice to be discussed occurs solely at Tikal but requires lengthy explanation in that it is the only mortuary ceremony visually depicted on a Classic Maya monument. Glyphs portrayed on Tikal Altar 5 (Figure 64) and, to a lesser extent, on Stela 16 relate the story of an otherwise obscure figure hailing from the unidentified site of Maasal, Lady Tuun Kaywak. Following the unidentified events of 691 described at the beginning of the text, the passage goes forward almost twelve years to May 28, 703 (9.13.11.6.7 13 Manik 0 Xul). A deceased Lady Tuun Kaywak is mentioned in conjunction with a curious phrase:

chum ? chamiiy ixtuun kayawak [Lady Tuun Kaywak] k'ub'ah ti ? muhkaj b'olon ajaw nah u kab'iiy chan ? b'alam maasal ajaw

[she is] seated ? death, Lady Tuun Kaywak she is consecrated by ?, she is buried at [the] Nine Ajaw House in the land of Chan ? B'alam, lord of Maasal.[48]

FIGURE 64. *Tikal Altar 5 (left) and Stela 16 (right; after Jones and Satterthwaite 1982, figs. 23 and 22)*

The root of the word *k'ub'ah, k'ub'*, serves as a verb for "consecration" in Ch'orti';[49] used here in conjunction with the "knife" verb, it seems possible that to be consecrated with a knife involved scraping bones or otherwise processing remains. It is equally plausible, however, that this consecration involved more abstract processes, particularly with regard to the creation and preparation of Lady Tuun Kaywak's tomb in the Nine Ajaw House.

Based on elements in text and iconography, Nikolai Grube and Linda Schele have identified the pair on Altar 5 as Jasaw Chan K'awiil I (on the left) and a lord (on the right) from the undiscovered site of Maasal.[50] They appear to have taken Lady Tuun Kaywak out of her original context at Maasal to interact with her remains. Grube and Schele have suggested that her bones were withdrawn from Maasal to Tikal, perhaps in response to pressures from Calakmul. In fact, a series of remains, including a cranium and long bones, were recovered by Christopher Jones beneath Stela 16, lending credence to the idea that the activities portrayed on Altar 5 occurred nearby.[51]

For whatever reason, her tomb was opened (*pasaj*, "it is opened") on November 1, 711 (9.13.19.16.6 11 Kimi 19 Mak), over eight years after her burial. Three days later, the ritual is completed and witnessed by a *kaloomte'* (*tsutsaj yichnal kaloomte'*), presumably Jasaw Chan K'awiil I of Tikal. The companion of Altar 5, Stela 16, continues from where the altar leaves off and describes the completion of the fourteenth *k'atun* by the king of Tikal. Unfortunately, the actual events of these days are omitted and we must therefore proceed to the images presented to understand the rest of the story.

All three of the figures on Stela 16 and Altar 5 wear garb appropriate to their participation in rites of death and renewal. For their participation in the opening of the tomb, both Jasaw Chan K'awiil I and the lord of Maasal dressed as the Jaguar God of the Underworld; the latter likewise donned a conical "beekeeper" hat, identifying himself as an aspect of God A, God A'. On Stela 16, Jasaw Chan K'awiil I wears similar attire, although this time he emphasizes his role in the Period Ending by wearing *tuun* glyphs and an incense bag, presumably burned or scattered at the completion of the fourteenth *k'atun*.

Perhaps the most interesting aspects of these costumes, however, are the long staffs held by the lords on Tikal Altar 5. As recognized by George Kubler and elaborated upon by David Stuart, a series of monuments combine the Jaguar God costume with long staffs as well as the trident flint, seen here in the hand of Jasaw Chan K'awiil I.[52] As Stuart has observed, these long staffs are fire drills, used in the creation of fire. Given the association between fire drilling and nocturnal activities among the Aztecs, as well as evidence from the site of Naranjo, he suggests that tomb reentry and fire making—like the behavior we have seen at Piedras Negras, Copan, and Tonina—were connected activities at Tikal.

As related above, the act of consecrating the body of Lady Tuun Kaywak may have involved cuts or similar body processing. Although the evidence at Tikal is tenuous, clear evidence for knife scraping during a reentry rite occurs within the Great Plaza of Copan in the Late Classic, providing us with our third, admittedly rare, practice connected with the opening of a tomb. Here a text on Stela A describes the *susaj,* or "bone peeling/slicing" of the remains of Butz' Chan, the long-deceased eleventh ruler of the site.[53] Dated to 731, this rite was followed sixty days later by the placement of a substela cache and the erection of Stela A. Butz' Chan's bones, though not recovered from the cache, appear to have been instrumental in the activation of that stela within the Great Plaza.[54] In some ways, this activation recalls the function of the aforementioned bones beneath Tikal Stela 16.[55]

THE PORTABLE DEAD

As discussed in the previous chapter, burials of kings and captives alike were often used to "animate" or "ensoul" buildings or new construction phases, a consideration that probably also applies to the erection of monuments, as per the Tikal and Copan examples above. Skulls or other partial skeletal elements likewise appear to have served as discrete portions of the "self," animating materials transformed and transferred to accommodate a variety of roles ranging from war trophies—literally captured identities, given the considerations of Chapter 3—to ancestral protectors. In some cases, it seems clear that these bones were taken from burials and the bodies reinterred; in others, remains were taken by the living at or near the time of death, particularly in the case of human sacrifice.

War captives, of course, were literally the *b'aak,* "bone(s)," of their owners throughout the inscriptions. After death, their heads or bones were displayed as trophies on monuments and pottery. These ideas were echoed by Landa in describing the killing of captives in the Colonial Period:

> The hands, feet and head were reserved for the priest and his officials, and they considered those who were sacrificed as holy. If the victims were slaves captured in war, their master took their bones, to use them as a trophy in their dances as a token of victory . . . after the victory they took the jaws off the dead bodies and with the flesh cleaned off, they put them on their arms.[56]

The skulls of such captives, as noted by Mock, had a power all their own in Maya ceremony.[57]

We find such skulls and other skeletal elements in a variety of contexts, from the famous skull pit at Colha' to the "finger-bowl" caches of Caracol.[58] Oftentimes the actual source of such skeletal material remains unknown. Given that these bones are not labeled with their provenance, it is difficult to say whether they were products of reentry, sacrifice, or other behavior! In Maya iconography and epigraphy, such ritually important skeletal elements are commonplace on ceramic vessels but far rarer on monuments, with the aforementioned example from Yaxchilan Lintel 25 being the most illustrative. On this monument, Lady K'ab'aal Xook uses a skull—possibly that of a royal ancestor, although the context is far from clear—to conjure the appearance of the ancestral deity Aj K'ahk' O' Chaak. A less well-known example occurs in the fallen stucco glyphs of Palenque Temple 18. In 1952, Franz Blom excavated this temple and found a number of the stucco glyphs intact; subsequent work by Alberto Ruz Lhuillier and William Ringle has revealed one of the glyphs to have originally read *u jol k'uhil,* "his skull god."[59] What this means is unclear, although one cannot help but recall the image of a lady from Yaxchilan holding aloft a human skull to conjure her ancestral deity.

More tangible evidence of bone "use" comes from royal burials at Uaxactun (Burials C1 and A20) and Tikal (Burial 48), where the heads or faces—and, in the case of Tikal Burial 48, femurs—were removed prior to final interment and mosaic masks placed as substitutes. In Tikal Burial 48, the body of the king was clearly the product of a secondary interment; his complete lack of a head was probably not the result of taphonomy or absent-mindedness! Missing heads and faces are not limited to these sites or to royalty, however. W. Bruce M. Welsh has noted similar behavior among other populations at Tikal (Burial 85), Altun Ha (C-16/22), Altar de Sacrificios (Burial 79), and in the northern lowlands at Dzibilchaltun (Burials 450-1, 385-1, 385-2, 385-3, and 57-5).[60]

Why are these elements missing? How were they used? Given what has been said about the body and its relationship to divisible souls, it seems probable that certain skeletal elements had specific associations. Certainly the face—the seat of personality—was one of the most significant aspects of the body. A mosaic mask from Calakmul Tomb 4, thought to be the tomb of Yuknoom Yich'aak K'ahk', bears a curious inscription. According to Simon Martin and Nikolai Grube, the text describes the mask as the *b'aah*, "image" or "face," of Yuknoom Cheen II, father and predecessor of Yuknoom Yich'aak K'ahk'.[61] Carrying around—or possibly impersonating—his deceased father, Yuknoom Yich'aak K'ahk' was portrayed in death bearing his father's image.[62] Such discoveries lend meaning to the removal of faces—the "images" of ancestors or significant persons—in mortuary contexts and to the interchangeability of actual faces and mosaic masks. Taking the *b'aah* of the dead may have necessitated the use of these masks or other substitutes, such as bowls.

In each of the cases of face removal, the individuals were processed or previously buried and then interred. Welsh has suggested that the faces were taken for the purpose of ancestor veneration, although it seems equally plausible that they are the result of sacrifice, transforming the time-honored ancestor into a humiliated captive whose image was co-opted by a victorious captor. Shirley Boteler Mock has argued the latter point, seeing removed skeletal objects as the embodiment of a power or life force comparable to the force encapsulated in the seizure of royal items from captured, disgraced, and sacrificed individuals.[63] Whether veneration or humiliation was involved, the end result was similar: the bones of individuals were kept as meaningful portions of the royal self. That some remains were left while others were retained suggests a hierarchical view of the royal body, with certain elements being more "useful" than others in their religious or political contexts.[64]

The use of royal faces or other skeletal elements by the Classic Maya kings need not have been tied exclusively to sacrifice, however. Such body parts certainly had other uses in the period from the conquest to the present: Diego de Landa reports the use of mortuary effigy boxes in which wooden images of the deceased were kept in sixteenth-century Yucatán. According to Landa, the cranial ashes of nobles were placed within hollow clay statues, put within jars, and kept below temples, while those of "people of position" were placed within a receptacle in the head of a wooden statue and placed, as mentioned earlier, "with a great deal of veneration among their idols."[65] In form and function, these statues are similar to effigy figurines recovered from Classic-era Teotihuacan whose backs contain holes for presumably similar materials.[66] Such objects were heirlooms, inherited property that McAnany has likened to material symbols of the rights of inheritance and visual evidence of one's ancestry and proper reverence for the deceased.[67] Alfred M. Tozzer observed analogously curated cranial bones and wooden effigies among the nineteenth-century Lacandones,[68] documenting a physical care for ancestors that mirrors a spiritual care for the dead in present-day Maya populations.[69]

Evidence of the use of skeletal remains within the Classic Maya context is far more sparse, however. The head of a certain K'ahk' U Jol K'inich of Caracol (Fire His Sun-Faced Head), for example, appears to have been carried around as a belt ornament by his descendant, much like a war trophy. As Stephen Houston and others have noted, whether the Caracol ornament is figurative or not, there was clearly a desire for portable representations of ancestors among the Classic Maya, particularly in the use of heirloom jewelry.[70] Reentered tombs, frequently missing large numbers of skeletal elements and sparsely populated with scattered grave furniture, suggest that the Maya were physically accessing and transporting ancestral remains. This is certainly the case at Caracol, where Diane and Arlen Chase have done much to clarify the widespread role of human remains in sacred contexts. Human remains there seem to have been fluid in their transport over the landscape; in the royal sphere, Chase and Chase have documented a number of burials that seem to have been repeatedly entered and to have had human remains removed as well as interred.[71] Judging from their former connections to royal life and the various uses of human remains, heirlooms, and ancestral images outlined in this work, it seems plausible to suggest that royal remains would have held a special significance for the Classic Maya, useful in royal ritual and ancestral veneration. This seems to have been the case at Terminal Classic Ek' B'alam in the northern lowlands. A recent tomb dating to the 790s bore the remains of a lord, Ukit Kan Le'k, holding a carved human femur. Part of the text on this femur states that it was "the (physical) bone" of Ukit Kan Le'k, an individual thought to be the father of the Ek' B'alam lord. Held in the left hand of the deceased, this bone may represent the only known, labeled relic in the Maya area.[72] Time will tell if similar obviously reverential items are recovered among the southern Classic Maya.

SIX

THE DEAD KING AND
THE BODY POLITIC

As Peter Metcalf and Richard Huntington have pointed out, divine kings and their relatives are natural symbols of the perpetuity and authority of the social order.[1] Nowhere in Classic Maya society was this perpetuity more important than in the personage of the king; the divine king embodied a force ultimately responsible for the maintenance of his polity religiously as well as politically. His fortunes were intimately linked with the fate of his site: his capture or sacrifice, admittedly the probable result of military or economic misfortunes, was the symbolic collapse of what Stephen Houston and others have termed "moral authority."[2] Likewise, the death of his subordinates could present a significant problem—if not a major crisis—for the symbolic authority at a site. *Sajal*s, (nobles), royal heirs, wives of kings, and subordinate *ajaw*s (lords) were significant players in court politics and site administration. We have only to look at the ways in which subordinates were conceded power (via monuments, control of secondary centers, etc.) in the Late Classic to see how their deaths might affect hierarchical authority. The removal of one or more of the members of this hierarchy was a critical moment in power relationships between governors and governed.[3]

Stephen Houston and David Stuart have proposed a model for how the Classic Maya conceived of royal power. In their analysis, Classic Maya power relationships are "discursive, involving both assertion and acceptance of claims to authority." Formalized by laws and regulations, power is coalesced through "individual acts that employ power, not as abstract generality, but as a set of highly specific applications which test its limits."[4] Keeping this in mind, we might remember the qualities of *ch'ab' ak'ab'* described in Chapter 4, with rulers personifying accrued ritual power augmented through repeated exercise. Rulers who lived to see their fourth or fifth *k'atun* (e.g., 60–100 years) may have thereby been regarded as particularly powerful and effective rulers in their time, repositories of ritual power whose death needed to be addressed in very specific ways.

Houston and Stuart have identified another way of viewing royal power; they postulate that royal power was conceived of as "a fiery essence, hotter than the hearth, coursing through the blood and scorching the breath." In their scheme, the Maya and other Mesoamerican peoples clearly viewed the ruler as "more poetic, fragrant, and refined than others, and thus well-deserving of tribute and obedience."[5] His court was the arbiter and embodiment of an aesthetic theory of rule, housing a "moral authority" that was based on shared precepts between rulers and ruled.[6] When the symbols of "moral authority" and ritual power at a site died and sank into putrescence, Classic Maya society had to adjust. The "shared precepts" needed to be affirmed or they would fall into oblivion; the ritual power was suddenly diminished or even extinguished. In this final chapter we will explore the Maya solution to this issue, which involves two of the three perspectives of Robert Hertz—corpse and mourners—involved in the production of the third (soul) for reincorporation into Maya society.

The Classic Maya solution to the problem of royal death entailed institutionalized transfers of power through which rulers or subordinates claimed legitimacy via ancestral authority; this was a form of political manipulation involving ancestor veneration that has been extensively documented by Patricia McAnany.[7] On the most mundane level, the crisis was "solved" via the following argument: the lord is dead, but he and his ancestors have selected *me* to take his place. In the case of a royal heir, the ancestral "safety net" set the moral authority of kingship ultimately in the hands of the ancestors. Heirs could reason that there was no crisis, because the ancestors had already made their selection. Claiming affiliation to living or deceased kings, heirs could honor their ancestors through dedicatory monuments and reverential—albeit self-serving, as one could not be *too* dependent on ancestral primacy—inscriptions describing their blood ties to deceased ancestors. We might view the production of royal monuments and royal identities much like the tautology of ritual power described earlier. Because the kingly successor could raise monuments to his ancestors, he was fit to hold office; as a result of his abilities in office, he could raise monuments to his ancestors. We have seen this behavior in other chapters, particularly with respect to founders or singularly important ancestors; these heroic individuals were encapsulated in buildings serving as loci of ceremonial and political activities.

This most simplistic of explanations, "the ancestors said so," is further refined by a rare phrase at Piedras Negras and Quirigua, *yaktaaj ajawlel,* which reads as "the leaving/transferring of his kingship."[8] At Piedras Negras, the phrase describes the transfer of power from the weak ruler Ha' K'in Xook to Ruler 7. At Quirigua, the burial of the aforementioned K'ahk' Tiliw Chan Yoaat at the "13 Kawak House" was followed by *yaktaaj ajawlel* on August 10, 785 (9.17.14.13.12 8 Eb 15 Yax); his successor, Sky Xul, did not actually take office until October fifteenth of that year, over two months after the institution of kingship had been "left" or "transferred." What does this say about the institution of kingship in Classic Maya society?

Without this example, we might view the crisis of abandoned kingship as one mediated by the idea that the king continued to theoretically rule after his death until the coronation of a successor, perhaps as a mummy bundle similar to those used among the Aztecs or the Inca. Such a model would portray kingship among the Classic Maya as an office inherent to the individual rather than an abstract idea. This conflict between individual and theoretical views of kingship often defines mortuary rituals in societies worldwide, and it is one that needs to be examined with respect to the Classic Maya. Peter Metcalf and Richard Huntington have perhaps summarized world attitudes toward kingship and its transfer best, using examples from Europe and Africa to demonstrate the ways in which transfer can be accomplished. We are perhaps most familiar with their English royal model, where kingship in the Tudor court was separated into a body politic and a body natural; the king literally had two royal bodies, one of which was immortal and incorruptible and the other, natural and subject to decay. The death of the living king—even by execution—could not harm the immortal kingship. In Renaissance France, by comparison, the state was the living king and his family. Upon his death, however, royal power would theoretically pass to an effigy, in whom the state resided until the burial of the dead king and the accession of a new lord; France was literally governed by an image rather than a living person during the interim. In the practical sense, of course, the French state was ruled—barring a power struggle—by the successor during the interregnum. In addition to these "multiple kings" and "king as office" solutions to the problem of royal death, we might look to a famous model of divine kingship used in the Sudan. As elaborated by Sir James George Frazer, Edward E. Evans-Pritchard, and others, the Shilluk of the early twentieth century employed a system whereby kingship was concentrated in an ancestral spirit (Nyikang). The living king was simply a vessel for this ancestral spirit, and upon his death, the spirit passed for a time to an effigy, until such time as Nyikang entered the body of the successor. This "there is no king" scenario provides us with yet another example of the variations with which interregnums could be addressed.[9] But how did the Classic Maya understand this situation? Certainly, the use of effigies, ancestral spirits, and quasi-divine kingship *sounds* Mesoamerican in theory.

What we know of royal transitions among the Classic Maya suggests that extended interregnums were fairly common.[10] At many Maya sites with a tradition of strong, centralized kingship, interregnums lasted months, if not years. Table 6 provides a list of known death and subsequent accession dates in the Classic Maya lowlands.

From the table, it almost seems as if some interregnums were formalized, as at Copan, with around the same amount of time elapsing between the deaths and accessions of many of its rulers. From the dates and times listed, the normal time between the death of a ruler and the accession of an heir at most sites seems to have been from one to three months.

TABLE 6
DEATH AND ACCESSION DATES AT CLASSIC MAYA SITES

Site	Outgoing to Incoming Ruler	Approximate Death Date of First Ruler	Accession Date of Second Ruler	Time Elapsed
Caracol	K'an II to K'ahk' Ujol K'inich II	9.11.5.15.9 2 Muluk 7 Mol July 24, 658	9.11.5.14.0 12 Ajaw 18 Xul June 25, 658	0.0.0.1.9 29 days before death
Copan	Moon Jaguar to Butz' Chan	9.7.4.17.4 10 K'an 2 Keh October 26, 578	9.7.5.0.8 8 Lamat 6 Mak November 19, 578	0.0.0.1.4 24 days
Copan	Butz' Chan to Smoke Imix	9.9.14.16.9 3 Muluk 2 K'ayab January 23, 628	9.9.14.17.5 6 Chikchan 18 K'ayab February 8, 628	0.0.0.0.16 16 days
Copan	Smoke Imix to Waxaklajuun Ub'aah K'awiil	9.13.3.5.7 12 Manik' 0 Yaxk'in June 18, 695	9.13.3.6.8 7 Lamat 1 Mol July 9, 695	0.0.0.1.1 21 days
Copan	Waxaklajuun Ub'aah K'awiil to K'ahk' Joplaj Chan K'awiil	9.15.6.14.6 6 Kimi 4 Sek May 3, 738	9.15.6.16.5 6 Chikchan 18 K'ayab June 11, 738	0.0.0.1.19 39 days
Copan	K'ahk' Joplaj Chan K'awiil to K'ahk' Yipyaj Chan K'awiil	9.15.17.12.16 10 Kib 4 Wayeb February 4, 749	9.15.17.13.10 11 Ok 13 Pop February 18, 749	0.0.0.0.14 14 days
Dos Pilas	Itzamnaaj K'awiil to Ruler 3	9.14.15.1.19 11 Kawak 17 Mak October 26, 726	9.14.15.5.15 9 Men 13 K'ayab January 10, 727	0.0.0.13.6 76 days
Dos Pilas	Ruler 3 to K'awiil Chan K'inich	9.15.9.16.11 13 Chuwen 14 Xul June 1, 741	9.15.9.17.17 13 Kaban 0 Mol June 27, 741	0.0.0.1.6 26 days
Palenque	Ahkal Mo' Naab' I to K'an Joy Chitam I	9.4.10.4.17 5 Kaban 5 Mak December 1, 524	9.4.14.10.4 5 K'an 12 K'ayab February 25, 529	0.0.4.5.7 1,547 days
Palenque	K'an Joy Chitam I to Ahkal Mo' Naab' II	9.6.11.0.16 7 Kib 4 K'ayab February 8, 565	9.6.11.5.1 1 Imix 4 Sip May 4, 565	0.0.0.4.5 85 days
Palenque	Ahkal Mo' Naab' II to Kan B'alam I	9.6.16.10.7 9 Manik' 5 Yaxk'in July 23, 570	9.6.18.5.12 10 Eb 0 Wo April 8, 572	0.0.1.13.5 625 days

(*continued*)

TABLE 6
(*continued*)

Site	Outgoing to Incoming Ruler	Approximate Death Date of First Ruler	Accession Date of Second Ruler	Time Elapsed
Palenque	Kan B'alam I to Lady Yohl Ik'nal	9.7.9.5.5 11 Chikchan 3 K'ayab February 3, 583	9.7.10.3.8 9 Lamat 1 Muwan December 23, 583	0.0.0.16.3 323 days
Palenque	Lady Yohl Ik'nal to Aj Ne' Ohl Mat	9.8.11.6.12 2 Eb 0 Mak November 7, 604	9.8.11.9.10 8 Ok 18 Muwan January 4, 605	0.0.0.2.18 58 days
Palenque	Aj Ne' Ohl Mat to Muwaan Mat	9.8.19.4.6 2 Kimi 14 Mol August 11, 612	9.8.19.7.18 9 Etz'nab 6 Keh October 22, 612	0.0.0.3.12 72 days
Palenque	K'inich Janaab' Pakal I to K'inich Kan B'alam II	9.12.11.5.18 6 Etz'nab 11 Yax August 31, 683	9.12.11.12.10 8 Ok 3 K'ayab January 10, 684	0.0.0.6.12 132 days
Palenque	K'inich Kan B'alam II to K'inich K'an Joy Chitam II	9.13.10.1.5 6 Chikchan 3 Pop February 20, 702	9.13.10.6.8 5 Lamat 6 Xul June 3, 702	0.0.0.5.3 103 days
Piedras Negras	K'inich Yo'nal Ahk I to Ruler 2	9.10.6.2.1 5 Imix 19 K'ayab February 6, 639	9.10.6.5.9 8 Muluk 2 Sip April 15, 639	0.0.0.3.8 68 days
Piedras Negras	Ruler 2 to K'inich Yo'nal Ahk II	9.12.14.10.13 11 Ben 11 K'ank'in November 18, 686	9.12.14.13.1 7 Imix 19 Pax January 5, 687	0.0.0.2.8 48 days
Piedras Negras	Ruler 4 to K'inich Yo'nal Ahk III	9.14.18.3.13 7 Ben 16 K'ank'in November 13, 729	9.16.6.17.1 7 Imix 19 Wo March 14, 758	0.1.8.13.8 10,348 days
Piedras Negras	Ha' K'in Xook to Ruler 7	9.17.9.5.11 10 Chuwen 19 Sip March 28, 780	9.17.10.9.4 1 K'an 7 Yaxk'in June 4, 781	0.0.1.3.13 433 days
Quirigua	K'ahk' Tiliw Chan Yoaat to Sky Xul	9.17.14.13.2 11 Ik' 5 Yax July 31, 785	9.17.14.16.18 9 Etz'nab 1 K'ank'in October 15, 785	0.0.0.3.16 76 days
Tikal	K'inich Muwaan Jol to Chak Tok Ich'aak I	8.16.2.6.0 11 Ajaw 13 Pop May 24, 359	8.16.3.10.2 11 Ik' 10 Sek August 8, 360	0.0.1.4.2 442 days

TABLE 6
(*continued*)

Site	Outgoing to Incoming Ruler	Approximate Death Date of First Ruler	Accession Date of Second Ruler	Time Elapsed
Tikal	Chak Tok Ich'aak I to Yax Nuun Ayiin I	8.17.1.4.12 11 Eb 15 Mak January 16, 378	8.17.2.16.17 5 Kaban 10 Yaxk'in September 13, 379	0.0.1.12.5 605 days
Tikal	Yax Nuun Ayiin I to Siyaj Chan K'awiil II	8.18.8.1.2 2 Ik' 10 Sip June 18, 404	8.18.15.11.0 3 Ajaw 13 Sak November 27, 411	0.0.7.9.18 2,718 days
Tikal	Siyaj Chan K'awiil II to K'an Chitam	9.1.0.8.0 10 Ajaw 13 Muwan February 4, 456	9.1.2.17.17 4 Kaban 15 Xul August 9, 458	0.0.2.19.17 917 days
Tikal	Chak Tok Ich'aak II to Lady of Tikal	9.3.13.12.5 13 Chikchan 13 Xul July 26, 508	9.3.16.8.4 11 K'an 17 Pop April 21, 511	0.0.2.13.19 999 days
Tonina	K'inich Hix Chapat to Ruler 2	9.11.12.9.0 1 Ajaw 8 Kumk'u February 8, 665	9.11.16.0.1 1 Imix 9 Mol August 23, 668	0.0.3.9.1 1,261 days

Times when this is not the case do often coincide with known problems at sites: for example, the time between Ruler 4 and Ruler 7 at Piedras Negras has been well documented as a point when the dynasty was in flux.[11] The death of Itzamnaaj B'alam II of Yaxchilan in 752, though not listed in Table 6 for lack of a firm date for his successor, is the most famous example of postmortem dissension. The lack of any inscriptions at Yaxchilan for Yoaat B'alam II, a possible puppet of the lords of Piedras Negras, and the proliferation of legitimacy claims at the site by the productive Bird Jaguar IV, has sparked the idea that a protracted political conflict transpired.[12] Similar postmortem conflicts have been identified in *The Book of Chilam Balam of Chumayel* by Patricia McAnany, who identifies a "pretender to the throne" and all of the sentiments and problems surrounding him.[13]

Equating Classic Maya times of trouble with long interregnums would make Tikal seem unusually troubled and Copan unusually stable; indeed, many of the interregnums at Tikal came at points when the dynasty was facing serious problems, such as the arrival of foreign Teotihuacanos or the "Middle Classic." Yet Copan seems to have weathered the capture of Waxaklajuun Ub'aah K'awiil with scarcely an incident: roughly the same amount of time passes between his death and the subsequent accession of K'ahk' Joplaj Chan K'awiil as for the other known death-accession periods at Copan. Of course, more rocky transfers of power are concealed by our lack of solid death and accession dates; for example, when K'inich K'an Joy Chitam II of Palenque was captured or killed, it was ten years before a successor took office. Nevertheless, the Copan example is rather striking and seems to provide evidence of formalized behavior.

The case of K'ahk' Tiliw Chan Yoaat of Quirigua suggests that dead kings there did not symbolically rule during an interregnum. K'ahk' Tiliw Chan Yoaat transferred or left his office immediately after his burial but before Sky Xul could take the title of *k'uhul ajaw*. That the office of *k'uhul ajaw* was "transferred" after the burial of K'ahk' Tiliw Chan Yoaat supports the idea of a liminal period both in kingship and in death. The example from Caracol in Table 6 demonstrates another important, highly different expression of the system of kingly succession: K'an II was still alive when his successor, K'ahk' Ujol K'inich II, took the throne. At Caracol, it would seem, the office of *k'uhul ajaw* was not inherent to the person—once coronated—but was an institution that could be transferred from one living officeholder to another (however unwillingly). Thus we are left with a "movable" office that is retained by an individual, presuming he holds the title at death, until his burial. Hence, the term *interregnum* may refer at Caracol to the time between the burial of a dead king and the accession of his heir.

But where did this office go? To whom was it transferred? In some sense, the choice was undoubtedly approved or mediated by the ancestors, if we are to believe the efforts of rulers like Yaxchilan's Bird Jaguar IV; we have no idea, however, if kingship was theoretically transferred to an effigy or similar object. Practically, however, sites without a crowned *k'uhul ajaw* needed administration. In cases where the succession was disputed, we might hypothesize a greater influence of petty nobles and court figures in domestic affairs. Simon Martin and Nikolai Grube have proposed that the greater prominence given to petty nobles during the reigns of "disputed" rulers, such as K'inich Ahkal Mo' Naab' III of Palenque, might reflect their "key role" during the interregnum.[14] Where the interregnum seems to have gone more smoothly, as at Copan, the formal period when no ruler was evident could have been characterized by the informal "rule" of an incoming king. There is some evidence, however, of regents or interim leaders taking the stage before the formal coronation of a new *k'uhul ajaw:* these are individuals without the title that seem suddenly to take a role in administrative and religious affairs.

One example is Siyaj Chan K'inich of Tikal, who appears to have performed a Period Ending rite for 8.19.10.0.0 on the so-called Hombre de Tikal statue. According to Martin and Grube, the Hombre de Tikal describes events in AD 403 and AD 406 that are shared between Yax Nuun Ayiin of Tikal and a subordinate called K'uk' Mo'.[15] That Stela 31 suggests that Yax Nuun Ayiin died in AD 404, coupled with the fact that he is not listed on that monument as participating in the Period Ending rite, has prompted Martin and Grube to propose that Siyaj Chan K'inich was an interregnal figure, presiding over Tikal in preparation for the accession of Yax Nuun Ayiin's son Siyaj Chan K'awiil II in AD 411. Other examples include Yoaat B'alam II and Great Skull of Yaxchilan. Each of these appears to have taken on the duties of *k'uhul ajaw*ship without the actual title. Yoaat B'alam II could have been in power for ten years, a long time to reign as an interim leader. If he was ever a true *k'uhul ajaw*, his monuments elude us; Martin and Grube have proposed that Bird Jaguar IV may have had something to do with that fact at Yaxchilan.[16] Great Skull, who is seen on Bird Jaguar IV's last monument engaging in a flap-staff dance—an event normally reserved for heir apparents—is mentioned as the *yichaan ajaw*, "uncle of the lord," of Chel Te' Chan K'inich, the young boy who would become Itzamnaaj B'alam III. Great Skull continued to be an important figure during the reign of this next king of Yaxchilan, as he was honored by further appearances on Lintels 14 and 58.[17]

That these people did not take the *k'uhul ajaw* title suggests that they lacked the authority to do so. In the case of Great Skull of Yaxchilan, the proposed interim leader remained alive and in favor with the true successor, who changed his name from Chel Te' Chan K'inich to Itzamnaaj B'alam III and bore the *k'uhul ajaw* title at his accession. Given this information, it seems plausible to suggest that for the Classic Maya there was a period when the title of *k'uhul ajaw* was set aside and individuals other than the heir designate could govern. This is not to say that the heir designate played no role: the rarity of interim leaders in the inscriptions probably suggests the primacy of the heir designate in political and religious affairs or a desire to minimize the role of nonregnal elites in governance (at least in the inscriptions, if not in point of fact). Arguably, however, the institution of *k'uhul ajaw* was temporarily frozen following the burial of the dead king. Perhaps a similar situation existed for lesser offices, although information is lacking.

In addition to representing times of political conflict or flux at Classic Maya sites, interregnums could account for a variety of practices. Shorter ones may have accommodated preparation times for burial rites and accessions; the coronation of a new divine king probably involved the organizational gathering not only of family members but also of subordinate lords from other sites as well as supernatural witnesses, courtiers, and possibly the public. It seems possible that there was also a religious base to this idea of an interregnum: with all the "traveling" a deceased ruler's soul needed to accomplish prior to rebirth, it seems reasonable that the Classic Maya would have kept track of the time between the beginning of the *och b'ih* or *k'a'ay u sak* "flower" *ik'il* event and the triumphant emergence from the Underworld. Certainly we have seen the deceased ruler depicted as victorious on numerous monuments, such as on the aforementioned Temple 14 Tablet at Palenque; here a posthumous K'inich Kan B'alam is entering his cave (*och u ch'een*) while iconographically he stands dressed as the Maize

God above the surface of the Underworld. Detracting from this argument is the time between the death of K'inich Kan B'alam and this posthumous event: over three years, in contrast to the less than three months it took his successor, K'inich K'an Joy Chitam II, to take the reigns of power at Palenque. Whatever the actual function of an interregnum was, however, the time between the death of a ruler and the accession of his successor was a period of reorganization, both in the way the living viewed the deceased and in the way the mourners reorganized their religious and political landscape.

ROYAL FUNERALS: PUBLIC OR PRIVATE?

As we have seen throughout this study, monumental efforts in grave preparation and tomb reentry required the physical labor of subordinates and the ceremonial activities of Classic Maya rulers or their immediate families. The question of whether these activities were conducted in the privacy of the Acropolis or in the "public" sphere of the site core is an important one. Knowing whether death was a public or private affair allows us to view how the death of a royal individual affected the daily activities of courtiers, nonroyal elites, servants, and other individuals living and working within the confines of the ceremonial and political heart of a Classic Maya site. If we look at where Classic Maya rulers and their family members are buried, they are set either within symbolic "households" (such as the North Acropolis at Tikal, in a pattern fitting elite and nonelite strategies for interment) or in the vicinity of large funerary structures.[18] Spatially, some of the latter are located at great distances from an Acropolis or palace complex, while others are more centrally located. Interments like Piedras Negras Burial 13 or Tikal Burial 177, for example, are too distant from the restricted courts of an Acropolis to have been conducted in extreme privacy—barring, of course, the wholesale removal from the site core of undesirable persons. Bodies going into these and other tombs were being carried across rivers, down monumental staircases into large open expanses, or across major causeways. Add to these all of the burials housing bodies that had to be carried up and down highly visible architectural features, the commission of grave furniture in craft workshops, the noise and activity of stones being moved for funerary monuments, and the arrival of dignitaries such as the lord of Maasal at Tikal—who probably had his own retinue as well—and we have a situation where death is both public knowledge and publicized event. Likewise, we cannot assume a direct-line route to the funerary structure for the body: as Stephen Houston has pointed out, bodies may have been carried over causeways and the like in roundabout ways. Perhaps the most critical evidence for publicity stems from the fact that rulers and royal individuals were typically buried in *separate* funerary structures and *not* in domestic platforms, as per the burials of lesser elites and commoners. Houston has noted a departure from this general practice at Piedras Negras, where Ruler 3 seems to have been set within the living space of the royal family.[19]

The death of the individual in Tomb 3 of Palenque Structure 18-A is a case in point for a public burial. Here there was a body belonging to an individual who was important enough to warrant treatment analogous to that given to K'inich Janaab' Pakal I, complete with psychoduct, funerary mask, and other accoutrements of royalty. This body, if it departed from the Acropolis and was taken in a direct line to Structure 18-A, would have to have been carried between 200 and 250 meters. Complicating this picture is an Acropolis staircase, a bridge over the Otulum River, and rough terrain winding around Temple 14, the Temple of the Sun, the Temple of the Cross, and a series of terraces leading to the final destination. While some of these structures may not have been extant at the time Tomb 3 was commissioned (we are unsure as to the precise date; see Chapter 4), the general picture is clear: the transport of a royal body out of the Acropolis was likely not a secret event, even if performed at night. Comparatively, the coronation of a new ruler could hardly have taken place in privacy, so why should this have been the case with the death of a lord or a *k'uhul ajaw*? Spatially, a dead *k'uhul ajaw* was leaving the royal sphere of the Acropolis for the last time; we might envision a long, public procession produced as an occasion rather than a simple event. This is not to say that all royal burials were—or even needed to be—public events, only that the publicity of royal death must have been an issue in Maya funerary rites.

Out of necessity, however, the death of a king was the beginning of a political drama in which many individuals would take part: courtiers, petty nobles, royal widows, and prospective heirs.[20] Drawing on a model used by Peter Metcalf and Richard Huntington for states and chiefdoms in Southeast Asia,[21] we might view the participation of Classic Maya individuals as influenced by sociopolitical obligations and by religious necessities. Given that nobles, widows, and heirs were clearly part of a hierarchical system surmounted by the dead king, their failure to take part in the drama of a royal funeral would no less than sever or debilitate their ties to power and royal community. How far down the social ladder such participation was required is debatable, but for the heir apparent and his immediates, the death of the king would have been an opportunity to consolidate the unity of the political body. Likewise, royal death—for the living heir—provided an occasion to demonstrate the power and the wealth of a site. In commissioning grave goods or architecture,[22] an heir could justifiably demonstrate that he was the only individual with the resources and labor force on hand to create a proper funeral for a king. Flexing "moral authority" on a sitewide basis, the heir who could demonstrate the ability to mobilize the community justified his position. But royal death was not just an occasion for ennoblement on the kingly level. For individuals who could not accede to the highest office, royal death would have provided an ideal forum for each participant to affirm or advance sociopolitical standing. Royal death would have been one of the only opportunities for individuals to demonstrate their abilities, associations, and ambitions in a group setting at a politically and emotionally vulnerable time.

If we view the Classic Maya political system as personified by the *k'uhul ajaw,* then the death of its most important member had cosmological as well as sociopolitical implications for both the royal family and the body politic. The royal death was the archetypical death, the death that embodied the sum of beliefs about the afterlife, the ancestors, and the process of life itself. Nonregnal family members likewise drew upon a shared system of belief that was called into question at their deaths. This crisis of faith, most prominently felt at the death of a *k'uhul ajaw,* needed to be resolved via a demonstration by successive rulers that the religious and political systems remained unchanged (or even bettered). This demonstration is what we are seeing in the production of funerary monuments, hieroglyphic epitaphs, and commemoratory activities, including tomb reentry. To conclude that this crisis, at the very moment when the body and soul(s) of the deceased ruler were in transition, was completely obscured from the public eye seems absurd. Likewise, subsequent funerary rites—such as the ancestral activities detailed in the preceding chapter—could have been events incorporating numerous elites. Certainly in the case of Piedras Negras Ruler 2 and his deceased father, it is ludicrous to conjecture that only a handful of participants surrounded and affirmed the living king during rites designed to demonstrate his efficacy and continuity of office. No doubt other expressions of ancestor veneration, as mentioned in Chapter 3, were performed in more private or restricted locales depending on their purpose and on local religious practices.

BODIES AND MONUMENTS

Where a royal body was buried depended largely on local conceptions of the "genealogy of place." Structure A-5 at Uaxactun, for example, appears to have been an attempt to define a specific space for the ancestors. Yet these same ancestors lent social and political prestige to the geographic areas in which they were housed; royal tombs defined what areas of the site were most prestigious, exceedingly exclusive, or thoroughly sacred. Such burials impacted—and were impacted by—settlement as well as architectural patterns, reflecting and shaping the ways in which living kings could construct and renew the site core. Social pressure by the larger political establishment, as well as the desires of a newly installed ruler, influenced where kingly and subsequent royal burials were constructed. Such pressures are most manifest in sudden changes or long continuations of burial practice, as in the shift in prestigious burial grounds at Tikal from the Mundo Perdido complex to the North Acropolis during the Early Classic. Just as places fell into favor and disfavor—not to mention disuse—in the Classic Maya world, it seems likely that the relative prominence of certain ancestors could increase or diminish in the eyes of the body politic. This is not to say that physically "abandoned" ancestors were wholly forgotten, but as new rulers and their descendants came to power, they certainly reshaped the hierarchy of the dead. Individuals like K'inich Kan B'alam II of Palenque or Bird Jaguar IV of Yaxchilan, for example, were heavily concerned with reshaping the past in their own image; they created "new" and "better" places for the veneration of (their) key ancestors. Such shaping would obviously have affected the larger political establishment as well as the built environment in which it worked. A new funerary monument—or a new "house" in an old place—is thereby a snapshot of where the site was in its political and social development.

The setting of a ruler into such a funerary structure was a reintegrative process, the transformation from a newly lifeless corpse to a venerated ancestor. If the model for death and kingship patterned above truly represents the general situation in Classic Maya political relations, the beginning of this transformation also corresponded to the "transfer" or "leaving" of the office of *k'uhul ajaw*. The fate of the body *was* the fate of the office, with the state of that office and its relationship to site dynamics represented by the tomb and its surrounding structure(s). It remains for the paragraphs below to explore how the fate of the body also mirrored the fate of the soul: despite the probability of numerous souls in Classic Maya belief, all were ultimately tied to the fortunes of the corpse.

CORPSES, SOULS, AND MOURNERS IN TRANSITION

It can be argued that Classic Maya funerary rites, along the lines first proposed by Maurice Bloch for the Merina of Madagascar, organized the society of the living.[23] The entombment of a royal ancestor within a funerary monument involved a process of transformation that defined old relationships and produced new ones. Because that monument helped to define the royal identities of both the dead king and his living body politic—which would soon welcome another ruler to the *k'uhul ajaw* fold—it follows that the society of the dead could structure the society of the living.[24] The centers of Classic Maya sites were, in a sense, "orchards of ancestors" where specific individuals would be called upon to legitimize the ruling dynasty or supervise important religious and political events. If kingship ultimately rested in their hands, or at least under the aegis of ancestral protection, then the process of creating a new ancestor via funerary rites was a pivotal series of moments in which belief systems as well as political systems were challenged.

Meeting this challenge were sets of rites occurring in distinct stages that, I would propose, correspond to changing relationships between the royal corpse, the royal soul(s), and the royal mourners. In a scheme advanced by Robert Hertz but later modified by Peter Metcalf and Richard Huntington for dealing with this tripartite arrangement, the relationship between corpse and mourners is essentially one that reaffirms the social order.[25] The status of the deceased is manifested in the scale of burial rites and funerary monuments that, in turn, serve the interests of the living relatives. The relationship between corpse and soul is more symbolic; Hertz demonstrates for Indonesian populations a "kind of symmetry or parallelism between the condition of the body . . . and the condition of the soul," reflected in forms of mortuary rites as well as in eschatology.[26] Ties between souls and mourners involve changes in the social identity of the deceased: death involves the gradual extinction of the social person and his or her reintegration into society a memory or an ancestor.

In some respects, Hertz's tripartite approach serves the royal Classic Maya case remarkably well. Funerary monuments and elaborate burial rites do serve the interests of the living and the deceased, affirming the social order through monumentalization. As Metcalf and Huntington have noted, corpses are often made larger than life so that their names (and by extension, their selves or souls) retain power. We have seen numerous parallels between corpses and souls in this work. Corpses become skeletal relics, with bodies decomposing as living souls become ancestors. The body of the living king changes from a person to an object, with his bones used in ancestral rites, forming the foundation for an ancestor shrine, or kept by his descendants as heirlooms. The soul(s) of the king leaves the body, undergoing a journey, and becomes "available" for conjuring or communication. The social identity of a Classic Maya ruler as a ruler is extinguished permanently; in the words of the Classic Maya kings at Copan (Stela A), the dead ruler is *ma ajaw*, "not lord." His title is *not* carried with him to the Underworld or the afterlife. These instances also correspond loosely to Arnold van Gennep's idea of "liminality":[27] we have seen the repetitive nature of mortuary rites, particularly with the use of "sealing" fire, at various points in the burial and postinterment process.

Yet the above model weakens when we view the principles and practices of Classic Maya ancestor veneration. There seem to be multiple "liminal" periods, that is, numerous points at which corpses, souls, and mourners are in transition. The status of the deceased, as well as his or her relationship to descendants, can be reinterpreted and reorganized a number of times. We see this in the practice of tomb reentry. The ruler does undergo an immediate process whereby his social identity is extinguished: his society reorganizes itself around a new successor. But the "wound" of his passing is reopened with the removal of capstones, the entry of fire, and the reaffirmation of royal legitimacy vis-à-vis ancestral authority. In situations like that related for Yo'nal Ahk I of Piedras Negras, tomb reentry seems almost like a second death or a reintroduction of the dead king to the process of death, grief, and mourning. This situation provokes an interesting question: Is a royal individual reincorporated into society as a formalized ancestor prior to tomb reentry, or is the "gradual extinction" of the social person somewhat extended to beyond the first "liminal" stage? We know that most royal tombs in the Maya lowlands, including some found at Piedras Negras, were not reentered; prominent rulers are depicted as ancestors on monuments almost immediately after their deaths, as "support" for their legitimate heirs. We might therefore view the "reintroduced" dead king as a tool, couched in religious terms, for the support of his reigning descendant, as per the argument put forth by McAnany.[28] Yet as much as the dead king served the interests of the body politic, the body politic bent to the authority of the dead king. Royal space was defined as much by the dead as by the living. These dead surely aided the body politic at times when the supreme "moral authority" of a site was threatened by loss. Royal death was not only a crisis but also an opportunity: the ancestral basis of divine kingship was reaffirmed, and the society of ancestors was revived to receive another member.

GUIDE TO APPENDIXES

APPENDIX 1. BURIAL STRUCTURES AND CONTEXTS

BEDROCK   burial chamber excavated into bedrock

APPENDIX 2. BODY PREPARATIONS AND FUNERARY ACTIVITIES

A	adult
B/P	bier or platform
BUN	body in bundle
E	east
E/D	entered or disturbed
EX	extended
F	female
FL	flexed
L	layers of chert and/or obsidian
LFT	left
M	male
MI	multiple interments
MM	mosaic mask
N	north
NE	northeast
ORTN	grave orientation
PO/PU	pot over skull/pot under skull
POS	position
RP	presence of red paint
S	south
SE	southeast
SEC	secondary burial
SC	shell cradle
SOS	shell over skull
SL	shell lines
STD	seated

SU   supine
W   west

APPENDIX 3. GRAVE GOODS

CER   ceramic vessels and *incensarios*
CO   figurines and other nonvessels of ceramic manufacture
CU   pendants, stuccoed vessels, or other "unique" ceramic materials
JBDEP   jade beads, disks, earflares, and pendants
JFP   jade figurines and plaques
SBDEP   shell beads, disks, earflares, and pendants
WCS   whole or carved shells
CHOB   chert or obsidian blades, lancets, or artifacts of similar type
CHOBS   specialized chert or obsidian artifacts, such as eccentrics
GSUS   ground stone or unidentified stone artifacts
FR   faunal remains, including bones, teeth, antlers, and carapaces
PYH   pyrite and hematite artifacts, including beads
PMAR   pearls and other marine artifacts, not including stingray spines
TP   textiles, pelts, or similar remains
S   stingray spines or portions thereof
C   remains of codices
M   shell, jade, or other mosaics, including masks
CC   remains of copal or charcoal
IND   indeterminate

Note: The appendixes are designed to demonstrate architecture, context, and numbers of artifacts relative to royal burials from different sites. Burials and artifacts, of course, can be divided in different ways to demonstrate different types of information (e.g., faunal remains being classified according to animal or minimum number of individuals); for reasons of space and focus I have chosen to place the objects of the appendixes in their current arrangement. Specific data on interments and grave furniture are derived from the following sources:

Altar de Sacrificios   Smith (1971)
Altun Ha   Pendergast (1979, 1981, 1982, 1990)
Baking Pot   Welsh (1988)
Calakmul   Folan et al. (1995); Folan and Lopez (1996); Carrasco Vargas et al. (1999)
Caracol   A. Chase and D. Chase (1987, 1996a); D. Chase (1994); D. Chase and A. Chase (1994, 1996, 1998)
Copan   Fash (1991b); Fash et al. (1992); Fash et al. (2001); W. L. Fash and B. Fash (2000); Sharer (1996, 1997a, 1997b, 2000, 2002); Sharer et al. (1999)
Dos Pilas   Demarest and Houston (1989–1994); Demarest et al. (1991); Demarest (1997)
Holmul   Merwin and Vaillant (1932)

La Joyanca	Gámez Díaz (2003)
Lamanai	Pendergast (1981)
La Milpa	Hammond et al. (1996)
Mountain Cow	Thompson (1931)
Palenque	Ruz Lhuillier (1952, 1958, 1961, 1965, 1968, 1973); Robertson (1983, 2000); Tiesler Blos et al. (2002); González Cruz (n.d.)
Piedras Negras	W. Coe (1959); Barrientos, Escobedo, and Houston (1997); Escobedo and Alvarado (1997); Houston et al. (1998); Houston et al. (1999); M. Child and J. Child (2000); Houston et al. (2000); Fitzsimmons et al. (2003)
Río Azul	Adams (1984, 1986a, 1999); Carlsen (1986, 1987); Steele (1986); Hall (1989); Ponciano (1989)
Santa Rita Corozal	D. Chase and A. Chase (1986, 1988, 1998)
Tamarandito	Valdés (1997)
Tikal	W. Coe and Broman (1958); Shook (1958); Shook et al. (1958); Adams et al. (1961); Satterthwaite, Broman, and Haviland (1961); Satterthwaite (1963); Trik (1963); Hellmuth (1976); W. Coe (1990, 1996); Harrison (1999)
Tonina	Becquelin and Baudez (1979, 1982); Becquelin and Taladoire (1990)
Uaxactun	R. E. Smith (1937); A. L. Smith (1950); Valdés (1982); Valdés, Fahsen, and Escobedo (1999)
Yaxchilan	García Moll (1975, 1996, 2004); Juárez Cossio and Pérez Campa (1990a, 1990b); Tate (1992)

Site	Burial Name or No.	Name of Person in Burial	Date (Ad)
Altar de Sacrificios	128	Unknown	700–771
Altun Ha	A-1/2	Unknown	475–525
Altun Ha	TA-1/1	Unknown	525–575
Altun Ha	TB-4/7	Unknown	550–650
Altun Ha	TB-4/6	Unknown	550–650
Altun Ha	TB-4/2	Unknown	650–700
Altun Ha	TB-4/1	Unknown	750–800
Altun Ha	TB-4/5	Unknown	750–800
Altun Ha	TB-4/3	Unknown	800–825
Baking Pot	B5	Unknown	700–900
Calakmul	Str. III-Tomb 1	Unknown	500–600
Calakmul	Str. II-Tomb 4	Yuknoom Yich'aak K'ahk'	672–731
Calakmul	Str. VII-Tomb 1	Unknown	ca. 750
Caracol	Str. B20-4th Tomb 4	Wife of K'an I?	537
Caracol	Str. B19-2nd	Lady Batz' Ek'?	634
Caracol	Str. A3	Unknown	696
Copan	VII-27 (Hunal)	K'inich Yax K'uk' Mo'	ca. 437
Copan	Motmot	Unknown	ca. 437
Copan	Margarita	Wife of K'inich Yax K'uk' Mo'?	ca. 437
Copan	Burial V-6	Unknown	400–600
Copan	XXXVII-1	Unknown	ca. 437–465
Copan	XXXVII-2	Unknown	ca. 437–465
Copan	Sub-Jaguar Tomb	Waterlily Jaguar (Ruler 7)?	ca. 550
Copan	XXXVII-4	Smoke Imix (Ruler 12)	695
Copan	Tomb 1	Unknown	600–900
Dos Pilas	30	Itzamnaaj K'awiil (Ruler 2)	726
Dos Pilas	20	Lady of Cancuen	741
Holmul	B1	Unknown	200–600

Structure	Context	Burial Type	Lining	Bedrock
Str. A-III	ceremonial platform	crypt	stone	no
Str. A-1	founder, temple	cist	stone	no
Str. A-1	temple	tomb	stone	no
Str. B-4	temple	tomb	stone	no
Str. B-4	temple	crypt	stone	no
Str. B-4	temple	crypt	stone	no
Str. B-4	temple	tomb	stone	no
Str. B-4	temple	tomb	stone	no
Str. B-4	temple	crypt	stone	no
Str. A, Group 2	temple	cist	stone	no
Str. III, Room 6	palace	crypt	stone	no
Str. II, 2B-sub	founder, temple	tomb	stone	no
Str. VII	temple	tomb	stone	no
Str. B20-2nd	temple	tomb	stone	no
Str. B19-2nd	temple	tomb	stone	no
Str. A3	temple	tomb	stone	no
Yehnal	founder, residence-temple	tomb	stone	no
Motmot	plaza	shaft tomb	stone	no
Margarita	founder, temple	tomb	stone	no
Str. 10L-26	plaza	crypt	stone	no
Motmot	plaza	crypt	stone	no
Motmot	plaza	crypt	stone	no
Sub-Jaguar	ceremonial platform	tomb	stone	no
Chorcha/Str. 10L-26	founder, temple	tomb	stone	no
"El Cementerio" Group	plaza	tomb	stone	no
Str. L5-1	founder, temple	tomb	stone	yes
Str. L4-41	palace	tomb	stone	yes
Str. B, Group II, Room 1	temple	simple	simple	no

(*continued*)

APPENDIX I
(*continued*)

Site	Burial Name or No.	Name of Person in Burial	Date (Ad)
La Joyanca	23	Unknown	250–600
Lamanai	N9-56/1	Unknown	500
La Milpa	B11.67	Unknown	400–500
Mountain Cow	6	Unknown	650–750
Mountain Cow	8	Unknown	650–750
Palenque	Str. 15-T1	Unknown	600–900
Palenque	Str. 16-T1	Unknown	600–900
Palenque	"Red Queen"	Unknown	600–700
Palenque	TOI-1	K'inich Janaab' Pakal I	683
Palenque	TOC Tomb 1	Unknown	684–711
Palenque	TOC Tomb 2	Unknown	684–711
Palenque	TOC Tomb 3	Unknown	684–711
Palenque	T18-E1	Unknown	ca. 721–736
Palenque	T18-E2	Unknown	ca. 721–736
Palenque	T18-E3	Unknown	ca. 721–736
Palenque	T18A-E1	Unknown	ca. 721–736
Palenque	T18A-E2	Unknown	ca. 721–736
Palenque	T18A-E3	Unknown	ca. 721–736
Piedras Negras	110	Unknown	450–600
Piedras Negras	10	Unknown	600–900
Piedras Negras	5	K'inich Yo'nal Ahk II (Ruler 3)	639
Piedras Negras	13	Ruler 4	757
Piedras Negras	82	? Ahk Ch'ok K'in Ajaw (Nighttime Turtle)	630–750
Río Azul	T1	"Ruler X"	250–600
Río Azul	T19	Unknown	250–600
Río Azul	T23	Unknown	250–600
Santa Rita Corozal	T1	Great Scrolled Skull	250–600
Tamarandito	Str. 44 Tomb	Chanal B'alam	ca. 761
Tikal	125	Yax Ehb' Xook?	ca. 90
Tikal	177	Unknown	250–600
Tikal	22	Unknown	ca. 400

Structure	Context	Burial Type	Lining	Bedrock
G. Guacamaya Op. 124-S15	ceremonial platform	crypt	stone	no
Str. N9-56	founder, temple	tomb	stone	no
Str. 1	plaza	tomb	stone	yes
Mound A, Plaza II	household shrine	tomb	stone	no
Mound A, Plaza II	household shrine	crypt	stone	no
Str. 15	founder, temple	tomb	stone	no
Str. 16	founder, temple	tomb	stone	no
Temple XIII	founder, temple	tomb	stone	no
TOI (Temple of the Inscriptions)	founder, temple	tomb	stone	no
TOC (Temple of the Cross)	temple	tomb	stone	no
TOC	temple	tomb	stone	no
TOC	temple	tomb	stone	no
Str. 18	temple	crypt	stone	no
Str. 18	temple	crypt	stone	no
Str. 18	temple	crypt	stone	no
Str. 18A	temple	crypt	stone	no
Str. 18A	temple	crypt	stone	no
Str. 18A	founder, temple	tomb	stone	yes
Str. R-8	temple	tomb	stone	yes
Str. U-3	plaza	crypt	stone	no
Str. J 5	ceremonial platform	tomb	stone	no
Str. O-13	plaza	tomb	stone	no
Str. K-3	ceremonial platform	tomb	stone	no
Str. C1A	temple	tomb	cut rock	yes
Str. C1B	temple	tomb	cut rock	yes
Str. C1C	temple	tomb	cut rock	yes
Str. 7-3rd	temple	tomb	stone	no
Str. 44	temple	tomb	stone	no
Str. 5D-22-6th/ 5D-Sub 7	founder, ceremonial platform	crypt	cut rock	no
Str. 5D-71	palace platform	crypt	stone	no
Str. 5D-26	temple	crypt	stone	no

(continued)

APPENDIX I
(continued)

Site	Burial Name or No.	Name of Person in Burial	Date (Ad)
Tikal	10	Yax Nuun Ayiin I (Curl Snout)	ca. 400
Tikal	48	Siyaj Chan K'awiil II (Stormy Sky)	456
Tikal	160	Chak Tok Ich'aak II (Jaguar Paw)	508
Tikal	200	Wak Chan K'awiil (Double Bird)?	562
Tikal	195	Animal Skull	ca. 628
Tikal	23	Nuun Ujol Chaak (Shield Skull)?	ca. 679
Tikal	24	Unknown	ca. 680
Tikal	116	Jasaw Chan K'awiil I (Ruler A)	734
Tikal	196	Yik'in Chan K'awiil (Ruler B)?	ca. 746
Tikal	77	Jasaw Chan K'awiil II?	ca. 869
Tonina	IV-6	Unknown	600–910
Tonina	VIII-2	Unknown	600–910
Tonina	VIII-1a	Unknown	600–910
Uaxactun	PNT 191	Unknown	250–300
Uaxactun	A6	Unknown	250–300
Uaxactun	A29	Siyaj K'ahk' (Smoking Frog)	402
Uaxactun	A31	? (Bat Mahk'ina)	ca. 426–463
Uaxactun	C1	Unknown	500–600
Uaxactun	A22	Ruler A-22	ca. 504
Uaxactun	A20	Ruler A-20	ca. 534
Uaxactun	A23	Unknown	ca. 554–562
Uaxactun	A2	? (Ch'ik'in Chakte')	ca. 759
Yaxchilan	Tomb 2	Itzamnaaj B'alam II	734
Yaxchilan	Tomb 3	Lady K'ab'aal Xook	700–800

Structure	Context	Burial Type	Lining	Bedrock
Str. 5D-34	temple	tomb	cut rock	yes
Str. 5D-33-3rd	founder, temple	tomb	cut rock	yes
Str. 7F-30	household shrine	tomb	cut rock	yes
Str. 5D-22	temple	tomb	stone	no
Str. 5D-32	temple	tomb	stone	yes
Str. 5D-33	temple	tomb	cut rock	yes
Str. 5D-33	temple	tomb	stone	no
Temple 1	founder, temple	tomb	stone	yes
Str. 5D-73	ceremonial platform	tomb	stone	no
Str. 5D-11	temple	tomb	stone	no
Str. E5-13	temple	crypt	stone	no
Str. J7-5	ceremonial platform	crypt	stone	no
Str. J7-5	ceremonial platform	crypt	stone	no
Str. E-10	founder, temple	tomb	stone	no
Str. A-1	ceremonial platform	crypt	stone	no
Str. A-5	founder, temple	tomb	stone	yes
Str. A-5	temple	tomb	stone	no
Str. C-1	temple	crypt	stone	no
Str. A-5	temple	tomb	cut rock	yes
Str. A-5	temple	crypt	stone	no
Str. A-5	temple	crypt	stone	no
Str. A-1	ceremonial platform	crypt	stone	no
Temple 23	temple	tomb	stone	no
Temple 23	founder, temple	tomb	stone	no

Site	Burial Name or No.	Name of Person in Burial	Date (Ad)	Ortn	Pos
Altar de Sacrificios	128	Unknown	700–771	E	EX/SU
Altun Ha	A-1/2	Unknown	475–525	E	EX/SU
Altun Ha	TA-1/1	Unknown	525–575	S	EX/SU
Altun Ha	TB-4/7	Unknown	550–650	S	EX/SU
Altun Ha	TB-4/6	Unknown	550–650	S	EX/SU
Altun Ha	TB-4/2	Unknown	650–700	S	EX/SU
Altun Ha	TB-4/1	Unknown	750–800	S	EX/SU
Altun Ha	TB-4/5	Unknown	750–800	S	EX/SU
Altun Ha	TB-4/3	Unknown	800–825	N/A	N/A
Baking Pot	B5	Unknown	700–900	S	EX/SU
Calakmul	Str. III-Tomb 1	Unknown	500–600	N/A	EX/SU
Calakmul	Str. II-Tomb 4	Yuknoom Yich'aak K'ahk'	672–731	E	EX/SU
Calakmul	Str. VII-Tomb 1	Unknown	ca. 750	N/A	SEC
Caracol	Str. B20-4th Tomb 4	Wife of K'an I?	537	N/A	N/A
Caracol	Str. B19-2nd	Lady Batz' Ek'?	634	STD	N/A
Caracol	Str. A3	Unknown	696	N	EX
Copan	VII-27 (Hunal)	K'inich Yax K'uk' Mo'	ca. 437	S	EX/SU
Copan	Motmot	Unknown	ca. 437	STD	N/A
Copan	Margarita	Wife of K'inich Yax K'uk' Mo'?	ca. 437	S	EX/SU
Copan	Burial V-6	Unknown	400–600	STD	N/A
Copan	XXXVII-1	Unknown	ca. 437–465	S	EX/SU
Copan	XXXVII-2	Unknown	ca. 437–465	S	EX/SU
Copan	Sub-Jaguar	Waterlily Jaguar (Ruler 7)?	ca. 550	N/A	N/A
Copan	XXXVII-4	Smoke Imix (Ruler 12)	695	S	EX/SU
Copan	Tomb 1	Unknown	600–900	N/A	N/A
Dos Pilas	30	Itzamnaaj K'awiil (Ruler 2)	726	E	EX/SU

Age/Sex	E/D	RP	L	BUN	B/P	SL	SC	SOS	PO/PU	MM	MI
A/F					yes				over		
Y	yes									yes	
A/M											
A/M					yes						
A/M											
A/M											
A/M	yes										
A	yes										
A	yes										
A											
A/M		yes	yes		yes				under	yes	
A/M											
A/M											
A											
A/F	yes										
A	yes										
A/M	yes	yes			yes						
A/F	yes										yes
A/F	yes	yes			yes						
A/M											
A/M											
A/M											
Unknown		yes			yes						
A/M		yes	yes	clay	yes	yes					yes
Unknown											yes
A/M							yes				

(continued)

APPENDIX 2
(continued)

Site	Burial Name or No.	Name of Person in Burial	Date (Ad)	Ortn	Pos
Dos Pilas	20	Lady of Cancuen	741	E	EX/SU
Holmul	B1	Unknown	200–600	S	FL/LFT
La Joyanca	23	Unknown	250–600	E	EX/SU
Lamanai	N9-56/1	Unknown	500	S	EX/SU
La Milpa	B11.67	Unknown	400–500	S	EX/SU
Mountain Cow	6	Unknown	650–750	N/A	N/A
Mountain Cow	8	Unknown	650–750	N/A	N/A
Palenque	Str. 15-T1	Unknown	600–900	N/A	N/A
Palenque	Str. 16-T1	Unknown	600–900	N/A	N/A
Palenque	"Red Queen"	Unknown	600–700	N	EX/SU
Palenque	TOI-1	K'inich Janaab' Pakal I	683	N	EX/SU
Palenque	TOC Tomb 1	Unknown	684–711	N/A	N/A
Palenque	TOC Tomb 2	Unknown	684–711	N/A	N/A
Palenque	TOC Tomb 3	Unknown	684–711	N/A	N/A
Palenque	T18-E1	Unknown	ca. 721–736	N/A	N/A
Palenque	T18-E2	Unknown	ca. 721–736	N/A	N/A
Palenque	T18-E3	Unknown	ca. 721–736	N/A	N/A
Palenque	T18A-E1	Unknown	ca. 721–736	N/A	N/A
Palenque	T18A-E2	Unknown	ca. 721–736	N/A	N/A
Palenque	T18A-E3	Unknown	ca. 721–736	N	EX/SU
Piedras Negras	110	Unknown	450–600	N	EX
Piedras Negras	10	Unknown	600–900	N	N/A
Piedras Negras	5	K'inich Yo'nal Ahk II (Ruler 3)	639	N	EX/SU
Piedras Negras	13	Ruler 4	757	N	EX
Piedras Negras	82	? Ahk Ch'ok K'in Ajaw (Nighttime Turtle)	630–750	N/NE	EX/SU
Río Azul	T1	"Ruler X"	250–600	N/A	N/A
Río Azul	T19	Unknown	250–600	E	EX/SU

Age/Sex	E/D	RP	L	BUN	B/P	SL	SC	SOS	PO/PU	MM	MI
A/F											
A											
A/M											
A		yes		clay							
A/M											
Unknown											yes
Unknown	yes										yes
Unknown											
Unknown	yes										
A/F		yes								yes	yes
A/M		yes								yes	yes
Unknown			yes								
Unknown			yes								
Unknown			yes							yes	
Unknown	yes										
Unknown											
Unknown											
Unknown	yes										
Unknown	yes										
A/M		yes									yes
A							yes				yes
Unknown	yes										yes
A/M							yes				yes
A/M	yes										
A/M											
Unknown	yes	yes		yes							
A/M		yes		yes	yes						

(continued)

APPENDIX 2
(continued)

Site	Burial Name or No.	Name of Person in Burial	Date (Ad)	Ortn	Pos
Río Azul	T23	Unknown	250–600	E	EX/SU
Santa Rita Corozal	T1	Great Scrolled Skull	250–600	S	EX/SU
Tamarandito	Str. 44 Tomb	Chanal B'alam	ca. 761	N/A	EX/SU
Tikal	125	Yax Ehb' Xook?	ca. 90	E	EX/SEC
Tikal	177	Unknown	250–600	N/A	N/A
Tikal	22	Unknown	ca. 400	N/A	N/A
Tikal	10	Yax Nuun Ayiin I (Curl Snout)	ca. 400	N/A	EX
Tikal	48	Siyaj Chan K'awiil II (Stormy Sky)	456	STD	EX/SEC
Tikal	160	Chak Tok Ich'aak II (Jaguar Paw)	508	N	EX/SU
Tikal	200	Wak Chan K'awiil (Double Bird)?	562	N/A	N/A
Tikal	195	Animal Skull	ca. 628	N/A	N/A
Tikal	23	Nuun Ujol Chaak (Shield Skull)?	ca. 679	N/A	N/A
Tikal	24	Unknown	ca. 680	N/A	N/A
Tikal	116	Jasaw Chan K'awiil I (Ruler A)	734	N	EX/SU
Tikal	196	Yik'in Chan K'awiil (Ruler B)?	ca. 746	W	EX
Tikal	77	Jasaw Chan K'awiil II?	ca. 869	N	EX/SU
Tonina	IV-6	Unknown	600–910	N	EX/SU
Tonina	VIII-2	Unknown	600–910	N	EX/SU
Tonina	VIII-1a	Unknown	600–910	N	EX/SU
Uaxactun	PNT 191	Unknown	250–300	N	EX/SU
Uaxactun	A6	Unknown	250–300	N	FL
Uaxactun	A29	Siyaj K'ahk'	402	E	EX/SU

Age/Sex	E/D	RP	L	BUN	B/P	SL	SC	SOS	PO/PU	MM	MI
A/M		yes	yes	yes	yes						
A/M											
A/M											
A/M		yes									
A/M											
A/M											
A/M		yes				yes	yes				yes
A/M											yes
A/M						yes		yes		yes	
A/M											
A/M				yes		yes	yes				
A/M		yes	yes	yes	yes	yes	yes				
A/M					yes	yes	yes				
A/M			yes		yes	yes	yes				
A/M			yes			yes	yes	yes			
A/F		yes	yes						over		
A/M	yes	yes	yes								yes
A/F		yes									
A/M											
A/F											
A/M											
A/M											

(*continued*)

APPENDIX 2
(*continued*)

Site	Burial Name or No.	Name of Person in Burial	Date (Ad)	Ortn	Pos
Uaxactun	A31	? (Bat Mahk'ina)	ca. 426–463	E	EX/SU
Uaxactun	C1	Unknown	500–600	STD, W	N/A
Uaxactun	A22	Ruler A-22	ca. 504	E	EX/SU
Uaxactun	A20	Ruler A-20	ca. 534	E	EX/SU
Uaxactun	A23	Unknown	ca. 554–562	N	EX/SU
Uaxactun	A2	? (Ch'ik'in Chakte')	ca. 759	N	EX/SU
Yaxchilan	2	Itzamnaaj B'alam II	734	E	N/A
Yaxchilan	3	Lady K'ab'aal Xook	700–800	S/SE	EX/SU

Age/Sex	E/D	RP	L	BUN	B/P	SL	SC	SOS	PO/PU	MM	MI
A/M											
A/M										yes	
A/M											
A										yes	
A											
A/M											
A/M				yes				yes			
A/F				yes				yes			

Site	Burial Name or No.	Date (AD)	CER	CO	CU	JBDEP	JFP	SBDEP
Altar de Sacrificios	128	700–771	4	31	10	481	0	594
Altun Ha	A-1/2	475–525	9	5	0	0	3	2808
Altun Ha	TA-1/1	525–575	14	1	4	660	16	3552
Altun Ha	TB-4/7	550–650	1	0	4	152	3	124
Altun Ha	TB-4/6	550–650	4	0	4	102	9	118
Altun Ha	TB-4/2	650–700	3	0	2	37	11	159
Altun Ha	TB-4/1	750–800	6	0	0	285	3	434
Altun Ha	TB-4/5	750–800	0	0	0	0	1	0
Altun Ha	TB-4/3	800–825	2+	0	0	146+	7+	0
Baking Pot	B5	700–900	0	7	1	2	2	0
Calakmul	Str. III-Tomb 1	500–600	7	0	3	322	3	8252
Calakmul	Str. II-Tomb 4	672–731	4	0	10	IND	0	0
Calakmul	Str. VII-Tomb 1	ca. 750	10	0	0	2147+	20	
Caracol	Str. B20-4th Tomb 4	537	15	0	2	0	0	0
Caracol	Str. B19-2nd	634	3	0	5	IND	0	0
Caracol	Str. A3	696	8	0	0	0	0	0
Copan	VII-27 (Hunal)	ca. 437	12+	0	1	4	2	IND
Copan	Motmot	ca. 437	1	0	0	IND	0	0
Copan	Margarita	ca. 437	IND	0	1	IND	0	IND
Copan	Burial V-6	400–600	IND	0	1	IND	0	100+
Copan	XXXVII-1	ca. 437–465	2	0	1	2	0	4
Copan	XXXVII-2	ca. 437–465	1	0	0	0	1	0
Copan	Sub-Jaguar	ca. 550	16	0	12	IND	0	IND
Copan	XXXVII-4	695	52	0	2	IND	IND	IND
Copan	Tomb 1	600–900	7	1	5	IND	0	0
Dos Pilas	30	726	2	0	4	68	5	366
Dos Pilas	20	741	3	0	4	65	0	76
Holmul	B1	200–600	18	1	1	2	0	IND
La Joyanca	23	250–600	3	0	0	0	0	10
Lamanai	N9-56/1	500	2	0	0	2+	0	0V
La Milpa	B11.67	400–500	5	0	0	18+	1	IND
Mountain Cow	6	650–750	25	0	0	4	0	13

WCS	CHOB	CHOBS	GSUS	FR	PYH	PMAR	TP	S	C	M	CC
0	14	0	1	0	1	0	1	26	0	0	
10	20	0	1	27	1	IND	0	0	0	1	
6	27	24	0	2	499	79	1	13	1	0	
6	IND	26	0	31	2	4+	33+	3	0	0	yes
12+	1	19	3	0	98+	2	1	0	0	0	
23	56	10	1	58	141	1	0	6	0	0	
13	27	4	1	0	132	7+	0	2	0	0	
0	0	3	0	0	0	0	0	0	0	0	
0	0	16	0	0	0	0	0	0	0	0	
3	19	0	1	7	1	0	1	0	0	0	
100+	0	0	0	0	0	0	3+	1	0	3	
IND	0	0	0	IND	0	0	4+	0	0	2+	
IND	6	0	0	1+	0	1	1+	0	0	0	
0	0	0	1	0	0	0	0	0	0	0	yes
0	0	0	0	0	0	0	0	0	0	0	yes
0	0	0	0	13+	0	0	0	0	0	0	yes
0	0	0	0	5	0	0	0	4	0	2+	
0	0	0	IND	IND	0	0	1	0	0	0	
0	0	0	0	IND	3+	IND	5+	IND	0	0	
2	0	0	0	0	1	0	0	0	0	0	
0	2	0	0	2	0	0	0	0	0	0	
0	0	0	0	0	0	0	0	0	0	0	
2+	0	0	0	0	0	0	IND	IND	0	1	
19	2	0	IND	0	0	IND	7+	1	1	0	
1	0	0	0	4	0	0	0	0	0	0	
18	0	0	0	0	0	2	0	0	0	0	
0	0	0	0	0	0	0	0	0	0	0	
2	0	0	1	1	0	0	1	1	0	0	
1	0	0	76	1	0	0	0	0	0	0	
0	0	0	0	0	0	0	IND	0	0	1	yes
0	0	2	0	0	0	0	2	0	0	0	
1	IND	1	1	0	0	0	0	0	0	0	

(*continued*)

APPENDIX 3
(*continued*)

Site	Burial Name or No.	Date (AD)	CER	CO	CU	JBDEP	JFP	SBDEP
Mountain Cow	8	650–750	19	0	0	0	0	0
Palenque	Str. 15-T1	600–900	0	0	0	0	0	0
Palenque	Str. 16-T1	600–900	0	0	0	0	0	1
Palenque	"Red Queen"	600–700	3	0	0	IND	IND	IND
Palenque	TOI-1	683	8	0	0	876+	2	0
Palenque	TOC Tomb 1	684–711	1	0	0	IND	0	0
Palenque	TOC Tomb 2	684–711	0	0	1	IND	0	0
Palenque	TOC Tomb 3	684–711	2+	0	0	IND	0	IND
Palenque	T18-E1	ca. 721–736	0	0	0	0	0	0
Palenque	T18-E2	ca. 721–736	2	0	0	28	4	0
Palenque	T18-E3	ca. 721–736	0	0	0	IND	2	0
Palenque	T18A-E1	ca. 721–736	0	1	0	133	0	0
Palenque	T18A-E2	ca. 721–736	2	0	0	23	0	0
Palenque	T18A-E3	ca. 721–736	6	0	0	25	0	6
Piedras Negras	110	450–600	5	0	0	73	0	23
Piedras Negras	10	600–900	1	3+	0	51	0	9
Piedras Negras	5	639	2	0	0	161+	27	219
Piedras Negras	13	757	1	1	0	86	4	166
Piedras Negras	82	630–750	1	0	0	36	3	0
Río Azul	T1	250–600	0	0	0	81	0	95
Río Azul	T19	250–600	13	0	4	0	0	0
Río Azul	T23	250–600	23	1	0	6	0	0
Santa Rita Corozal	T1	250–600	8	0	0	2	6	200+
Tama-randito	Str. 44 Tomb	ca. 761	8	0	1	3+	0	0
Tikal	125	ca. 90	0	0	0	0	0	0
Tikal	177	250–600	3	0	2	0	0	0
Tikal	22	ca. 400	12	0	4	0	IND	0
Tikal	10	ca. 400	25	0	7	0	1	1

WCS	CHOB	CHOBS	GSUS	FR	PYH	PMAR	TP	S	C	M	CC
3	0	0	0	0	0	0	0	0	0	0	
0	0	0	0	0	0	0	0	0	0	0	
0	0	0	0	0	0	0	0	0	0	0	
1	4	0	4	0	0	IND	0	0	0	1+	yes
3	0	1	9	3	1	5	2	0	0	1	
0	0	1	0	1	0	0	1	0	0	0	
0	0	0	1	0	0	0	1	0	0	0	
0	0	0	1	1	0	0	1	1	0	0	
0	0	0	0	0	0	0	0	0	0	0	
1	1	3	0	0	0	2	0	0	0	1	
0	0	0	0	0	0	0	0	0	0	1	
2	9	0	2	0	0	0	0	0	0	1	
27	96	0	0	1	1	0	0	0	0	1	
0	0	0	3	0	0	0	0	0	0	1	
11	0	0	22	27	3	0	0	0	0	1	
0	IND	0	0	0	0	0	0	0	0	0	yes
24	0	0	66	8+	1	0	1+	21	0	2	
0	7	0	9	22	129	0	0	6	0	2	yes
0	1	0	0	2	0	0	1	6	0	0	
0	0	0	0	49	0	1	0	0	0	1	
1	0	0	16	0	0	0	7+	3	0	0	yes
1	5	10	7	10	0	0	7+	2	0	0	
5	3	1	1	3+	1	0	3	1	0	0	
1	0	2	0	0	0	0	0	1	0	0	
0	0	0	0	0	0	0	0	0	0	0	
0	0	0	0	0	0	0	0	0	0	1	
1	1	0	1	3	0	0	0	0	0	0	
3	0	0	0	15+	0	0	0	9	0	0	

(continued)

APPENDIX 3
(*continued*)

Site	Burial Name or No.	Date (AD)	CER	CO	CU	JBDEP	JFP	SBDEP
Tikal	48	456	27	0	3	105+	0	0
Tikal	160	508	10	0	3	11	1	2
Tikal	200	562	0	0	6	0	0	0
Tikal	195	ca. 628	0	0	4	IND	IND	6
Tikal	23	ca. 679	11	0	1	IND	1	IND
Tikal	24	ca. 680	4	0	2	2	2	IND
Tikal	116	734	2	0	19	178	2	1
Tikal	196	ca. 746	23	0	22	0	1	0
Tikal	77	ca. 869	1	0	6		1	
Tonina	IV-6	600–910	16	0	0	0	0	0
Tonina	VIII-2	600–910	3	0	0	1	1	0
Tonina	VIII-1a	600–910	4	0	1	3	0	0
Uaxactun	PNT 191	250–300	0	0	0	0	0	0
Uaxactun	A6	250–300	0	0	0	1	0	0
Uaxactun	A29	402	28	0	1	4	0	0
Uaxactun	A31	ca. 426–463	19	0	0	18	1	2
Uaxactun	C1	500–600	6	0	0	180	1	26
Uaxactun	A22	ca. 504	34	0	1		2	0
Uaxactun	A20	ca. 534	6	0	2	104	0	0
Uaxactun	A23	ca. 554–562	0	0	4	3	0	0
Uaxactun	A2	ca. 759	0	0	1	1	0	0
Yaxchilan	Tomb 2	734	5	0	1	484	0	9
Yaxchilan	Tomb 3	700–800	34	0	IND	436	0	0

WCS	CHOB	CHOBS	GSUS	FR	PYH	PMAR	TP	S	C	M	CC
IND	3	0	2	IND	0	0	0	IND	0	0	
18	24	42	0	4	0	0	1	1	0	2	
0	0	0	0	0	0	0	0	0	0	0	
0	0	0	2	0	0	1	9	1	0	0	
IND	0	0	0	IND	0	IND	3	1	0	0	
0	0	0	0	0	IND	IND	2	1	0	0	
40+	0	0	1	89	0	0	3+	5	0	4	
IND	0	0	0	0	0	0	2	2	0	2	
1+	IND	0	0	0	0	6	1	0	0	0	
0	0	0	1	0	0	0	0	0	0	0	
3	0	0	0	5	0	0	0	0	0	0	
0	0	0	0	0	0	0	0	0	0	0	
2	0	0	0	0	0	0	0	2	0	0	
1	0	0	0	0	0	0	0	1	1	0	
17	0	0	0	0	1	2	0	1	0	0	yes
10	4	1	0	3	0	0	2	0	0	0	
0	4	0	0	0	0	0	0	0	0	1	
4	0	0	0	2	0	0	1	1	0	0	yes
1	0	0	0	2	0	0	1	0	0	1	yes
0	0	0	0	0	0	0	0	1	0	0	yes
IND	0	0	0	3	0	0	0	1	0	0	
6	8	2	2	18	0	2	1	86	0	1	
1	34	0	0	109	0	0	IND	0	0	0	

NOTES

CHAPTER ONE

1. Metcalf and Huntington (1991).

2. Robert Chapman and Klavs Randsborg (1981) have provided a thorough account of the evolution of the archaeology of death. Likewise crucial is Pearson (1999).

3. Geertz (1973, 94–98).

4. Van Gennep (1960).

5. Hertz (1997).

6. Perhaps the most widely cited of these are two works by Victor Turner, *The Forest of Symbols* (1967) and *The Ritual Process* (1969). Others include Jack Goody, *Death, Property, and the Ancestors* (1962); Miles, "Socioeconomic Aspects of Secondary Burial" (1962); Maurice Bloch, *Placing the Dead* (1971); and Maurice Bloch and Jonathan Parry, *Death and the Regeneration of Life* (1981).

7. In addition to the numerous sources cited by Chapman, Kinnes, and Randsborg (1981) and Pearson (1999), see Hallam, Hockey, and Howarth (1999); McAnany, Storey, and Lockard (1999); and Rakita and Buikstra (2001).

8. Notable exceptions and key works on Classic Maya death as well as ancestor veneration include Ruz Lhuillier (1968); Welsh (1988); McAnany (1995); Schele and Mathews (1998); Eberl (1999); and Houston, Stuart, and Taube (2006).

9. For example, see Hall (1988) and Storey (1992).

10. Useful sources on these points include Freidel (1989); McAnany (1995); Fitzsimmons (1998); Schele and Mathews (1998); Stuart (1998); Houston and Taube (2002); and Kunen, Galindo, and Chase (2002);. It should be noted that Eberl (1999) has also suggested three basic phases of Maya death ritual, I was unable to procure a copy of this work, but reference to his arguments can be found in Cucina and Blos (2006).

11. Ucko (1962, 38–54).

12. Metcalf and Huntington (1991, 112).

13. Durkheim (1965).

14. Table adapted from Metcalf and Huntington (1991, fig. 1).

15. Van Gennep (1960, 42).

16. Hertz (1960, 30).

17. Metcalf and Huntington (1991, 30).

18. Turner (1967, 94).

19. Metcalf and Huntington (1991, 33).

20. Van Gennep (1960, 146).

21. Goody (1962) and Metcalf (1982).

22. Such ennoblement, however, did take place in pre-Columbian Mesoamerica in the form of captive sacrifice.

23. Metcalf and Huntington (1991, 112).

24. Ibid., 151.

25. Bloch (1971).

26. Metcalf and Huntington (1991, 151).

27. Bell (1992, 96).

28. Taube (1988).

29. Mock (1998).

30. This is the convention used by Simon Martin and Nikolai Grube in their *Chronicle of the Maya Kings and Queens* (2000). It is based in part on the last recovered date from the Maya lowlands—otherwise known as the southern lowlands or Peten—at the site of Tonina.

31. Fitzsimmons (1998). See also Eberl (1999) and Fitzsimmons (2002, 41–53).

32. Although we might attribute these weeks to secular delays in tomb construction—indeed there are cases from Tikal to support this—other factors may have been involved, as we will soon see in case examples from Piedras Negras and Quirigua.

33. Metcalf and Huntington (1991, 112).

34. Coe (1988, 222–235).

35. As John Monaghan has noted, "Religions do not operate with seamless and systematic regularity and . . . any depiction of 'reality' will bring with it special problems, if not contradictions" (2000, 29). As a result, we must remember that general patterns and ideas are just that—general—and are always modified by individual circumstances as well as site variability.

36. Tozzer (1941, 131–132).

37. For the Lacandon, see McGee (1990). For Zinacantan, consult Vogt (1969 and 1970b). Other useful sources include Bunzel (1952), Colby (1976), Tedlock (1982), and Watanabe (1992).

38. See Roys (1967, 1965), as well as Marín Arzápalo (1987).

39. Barrera Vásquez (1991).

40. Stuart and Fitzsimmons (n.d.).

41. Roys (1965, 4).

42. These sources are nevertheless of paramount importance to all Maya scholarship. The most comprehensive sources on the Classic Maya Underworld to date are Hellmuth (1987) and Grube and Nahm (1994).

43. McAnany (1995). It should be mentioned here that McAnany was the first to identify ancestral veneration in the reentry of royal tombs.

44. For example, see Pendergast (1979, 1982, and 1990); Eberl (1999); and Fitzsimmons (2006).

45. Fitzsimmons (1998, 277).

46. See Schele and Mathews (1998, fig. 3.26) and Stuart (1998).

47. Evans-Pritchard (1948); Kantorowicz (1957); Giesey (1960); Deng (1972); Binski (1996).

48. Tozzer (1941, 131).

CHAPTER TWO

1. López Austin (1988, 313).

2. A quote from San Miguel Tzinacapan echoes a similar concept: "We eat from the earth / because of this the Earth eats us" (Knab 1979, 130).

3. Florentine Codex (VI, 115), translation by López Austin (1988, 314).

4. Fernández de Oviedo (1991).

5. There is a wealth of information on the earth personified. Some noteworthy publications, ranging from archaeology to sociocultural anthropology, include Hunt (1977, 130); Lupo (1981, 246); León-Portilla (1987, 414); López Austin (1988, 56–68); Wilson (1995, 53–54); Monaghan (2000, 27; 1995, 98); Peterson, McAnany, and Cobb (2005); and Stone (2005).

6. Stephen Houston, personal communication, 2002. Iconographically, this imagery overlaps with scenes of rebirth involving turtles, crocodiles, ballcourts, and maize plants. It is unclear whether ballcourts served as metaphors for the earth's surface, although they have well-recognized ties to Underworld imagery. Sources from the colonial and modern periods portray the earth as a maize field that is cubical, square, or simply quadripartite. Sometimes these ideas are maintained alongside the "turtle" model. See Vogt (1969, 298); Nash (1970, 5); McGee (1990, 23); and Miller and Taube (1993, 84).

7. Holland (1963, 303–304); Vogt (1969, 37–38).

8. Coe (1988) and McAnany (1995).

9. Freidel, Schele, and Parker (1993, fig. 4:27); Houston, Stuart, and Taube (2006, 186).

10. Quenon and Le Fort (1997). Although their analysis centers on the tonsured Maize God, there is some overlap with the foliated version. For more on these versions, see Taube (1985, 171–181), who has demonstrated that the god of this cycle is equivalent to the father of the Hero Twins of the *Popol Vuh*.

11. Stuart and Fitzsimmons (n.d.).

12. Stephen Houston, personal communication, 2002.

13. Quenon and Le Fort (1997, 891).

14. Taube (1993, 67).

15. Edmonson (1971); Tedlock (1985); Florescano (1993, 1994).

16. Throughout this work I use the most recent Maya incarnations of king names; for ease of identification, I also provide their most common published nicknames or former names.

17. David Stuart, personal communication, 2002.

18. Pérez Martínez et al. (1996, 58).

19. Miller and Taube (1991, 108).

20. Miller and Martin (2004, 52). For further discussion on Classic Maya body aesthetics, see Taube (1985) and Houston, Stuart, and Taube (2006, 45–48).

21. Miller and Taube (1991, 108–109).

22. Bunzel (1952, 54); Vogt (1969, 35).

23. López Austin (1988, 313).

24. Monaghan (2000, 37–38). See also Hunt (1977, 89) and Houston, Stuart, and Taube (2006, 127).

25. Stephen Houston and David Stuart (personal communication, 2002) believe that this **-i** is a reflex of Common Mayan **-ik**, a marker of single argument predicates; they suggest that all intransitives are basically CVC-**i** forms.

26. Laughlin (1975, 109–110); Antonio et al. (1996, 134–135); Pérez Martínez et al. (1996, 33–34); Ramírez Pérez, Montejo, and Díaz Hurtado (1996, 114–115).

27. Stephen Houston, personal communication, 2002.

28. Proskouriakoff (1963, 149–167; 1964, 177–202); Freidel, Schele, and Parker (1993, 440); Houston and Taube (2000, 267).

29. For the soul as breath or wind, see Thompson (1970, 73); Furst (1976, 160–172); López Austin (1988, 232–236); Hanks (1990, 86); and Houston and Taube (2000). For discussion on the *cham* glyph as exhalation, see Fitzsimmons (2002, 42–43) and Houston, Stuart and Taube (2006, 145–146).

30. David Stuart and Alexandre Tokovine, personal communications, 2002.

31. Houston and Taube (2000, 267).

32. Stuart (n.d.); see also Houston, Stuart, and Taube (2006, 147–148).

33. Houston and Taube (2000, 267).

34. Houston, Stuart, and Taube (2006, 149).

35. Proskouriakoff (1963, 162–163).

36. This discovery is mentioned in Schele and Looper (1996); David Stuart's contribution is mentioned in Freidel, Schele, and Parker (1993).

37. Laughlin (1975, 131).

38. Houston and Taube (2000, 267).

39. Barrera Vásquez (1991, 712).

40. David Stuart (personal communication, 2002) has demonstrated that the **-na** suffix, which often accompanies the "flower" glyph, is actually a variant of *ik'*.

41. Schele (1988, 294–317).

42. Stephen Houston, personal communication, 2002.

43. This is mentioned in Houston and Taube (2000, 267); see also Houston, Stuart, and Taube (2006, 143).

44. Laughlin (1975); McGee (1990, 108); Miller and Taube (1991, 74); Ajpacaja Tum et al. (1996); Pérez Martínez et al. (1996). For further discussion on these themes, see also Fitzsimmons (2002, 45–46) and Houston, Stuart, and Taube (2006, 143–144).

45. Grube (2004, 59–76); Kerr (n.d.b).

46. Stephen Houston, personal communication, 2002.

47. Fitzsimmons (1998); Stuart (1998).

48. Laughlin (1975, 65).

49. Vogt (1969, 461–462).

50. Barrera Vasquez (1991).

51. This is mentioned in Schele (1999).

52. Laughlin (1975, 80).

53. Maldonado Andrés, Ordóñez Domingo, and Ortiz Domingo (1986, 30); Barrera Vasquez (1991, 46); Ajpacaja Tum et al. (1996, 25).

54. Something similar, involving changes of state, lives on in the beliefs of contemporary Lacandones, who see death as a change from one *level* of existence to another, a reversal of form and a reversal of life. See McGee (1990, 108).

55. Stephen Houston, personal communication, 2002.

56. Martin and Grube (2000, 145).

57. David Stuart, personal communication, 2002.

58. I have not conflated *och* and *ha'* together here for a variety of reasons, the major one being that there are only a few examples of this phrase.

59. Coe (1978); Robicsek and Hales (1981); Schele and Miller (1986); Hellmuth (1987); Taube (1993); Reents-Budet (1994); Quenon and Le Fort (1997).

60. Stuart and Houston (1994).

61. Stuart (2000a).

62. Schele and Miller (1986, 270).

63. Stuart (1988, 190).

64. Stephen Houston, personal communication, 2002.

65. Examples not already cited include Foster (1944); Saler (1964); Redfield and Villa Rojas (1972); Gossen (1975); and Wilson (1995).

66. Monaghan (2000, 28).

67. Calvin (1997, 868–883).

68. Houston and Stuart (1998, 92).

69. Vogt (1969, 369–370).

70. Bunzel (1952, 269); McGee (1990, 107); Wilson (1995, 143–144).

71. Guiteras Holmes (1961, 125).

72. López Austin (1988, 205).

73. Earle (1986, 170).

74. López Austin (1988, 205). The Kekchi term for "soul," *muhel,* also bears shadowy associations; as observed by Wilson (1995, 143), its root, *mu,* actually means "shadow."

75. The *tonalli,* located in the head, is most specifically tied to "name or reputation." See Furst (1995, 110).

76. Álvarez Heidenreich (1976).

77. Torquemada, cited in López Austin (1988, 323).

78. Houston and Stuart (1998, 85). These concepts have subsequently been elaborated upon by Houston, Stuart, and Taube (2006, 57–81).

79. See Fitzsimmons (2002, 58–59) and Houston, Stuart, and Taube (2006, 79–81) for more on *k'uh(ul)* and concepts of self.

80. Tozzer (1941, 131).

81. McAnany (1995, 37–38).

82. Tozzer (1907); Coggins and Shane (1984, figs. 174–176, 199); Welsh (1988, 216 and table 11); McAnany (1995, 36–37).

83. Stuart and Houston (1999). See also Houston, Stuart, and Taube (2006, fig. 1.54).

84. Cross-culturally, there are similar ideas of traveling souls, souls independent from personality, and "soul-loss"; we might look to South Asian, North American, and Greek examples for comparisons. Many of these soul studies derive from the early work of Ernst Arbman (1926, 1927). Other examples include Hultkrantz (1953); Alver (1971); Láng (1973); and Bremmer (1983).

85. Monaghan (2000, 29). Other sources that support this include Hvidtfeldt (1958); Alcorn (1984); López Austin (1988); Galinier (1990); Clendinnen (1991); and Monaghan (1995).

86. Wilson (1995, 73–74).

87. García de León (1969, 1976).

88. López Austin (1988, 230–231).

89. Bunzel (1952, 150–153); Nash (1970, 131); Redfield and Villa Rojas (1970, 119); Vogt (1970b, 222); McGee (1990, 106–119).

90. López Austin (1988, 323).

91. Ibid., 234.

92. Wisdom (1974, 372–374).

93. López Austin (1988, 323).

94. Guiteras Holmes (1961, 139–140); Vogt (1969, 222). Guiteras Holmes reports that the period is usually nine days rather than three.

95. Bunzel (1952, 150); LaFarge (1965, 44 and 140).

96. Schele and Miller (1986, 268).

97. Grube and Nahm (1994); Calvin (1997).

98. Vogt (1970b, 372–373).

99. Holland (1963, 111); Hermitte (1970, 105); Gossen (1993, 432); Monaghan (1998).

100. Vogt (1969); Gossen (1975).

101. Calvin (1997, 876).

102. Martin and Grube (2000, 185).

103. Ibid., 81.

104. Guiteras Holmes (1961, 300).

105. Ibid.

106. Stuart (2003).

107. Schele and Mathews (1998); Martin and Grube (2000).

108. We do not necessarily need to have one uniform, monolithic view of this place: it is almost certain that different sites contributed in different ways to the "Classic Maya" view of the Underworld. At the same time, sources tend to agree on its basic attributes, so we cannot retreat from the problem of creating a basic understanding of the Underworld.

109. Schele and Freidel (1990).

110. For example, see López Austin (1988, 331–336); Fash (1991b, 122); Joyce (1992, 497–505); and Garber et al. (1998, 127).

111. Miller and Taube (1991, 177).

112. Thompson (1929); Houston, Robertson, and Stuart (2000).

113. Schele and Freidel (1990, 1991); Houston and Stuart (1998).

114. Edmonson (1971); Tedlock (1985).

115. Schele and Miller (1986); Hellmuth (1987); Grube and Nahm (1994); Miller and Martin (2004).

116. Schele and Miller (1986, 267).

117. Ibid., 267–268.

118. Miller and Martin (2004, 59).

119. The rooster seems similar to the aforementioned owl. Dogs do appear in the cast of Underworld characters, although their specifics roles and characteristics are unknown.

120. Schele and Freidel (1990, 67). Schele and Freidel make a case for a Classic Maya World Tree; further research on the nature and frequency of such *axis mundi* references in Maya iconography would be key to studies of Classic Maya religion.

121. McGee (1990, 107).

122. Vogt (1969, 222).

123. Tozzer (1941, 131–132).

124. Guiteras Holmes (1961); Redfield and Villa Rojas (1970); López Austin (1988); McGee (1990).

125. Taube (1993, 72).

126. Schele and Miller (1986, 267).

127. Taube (2003).

128. One notable exception may be K'inich Janaab' Pakal I of Palenque, who wears a skirt similar to that worn by the Foliated Maize God on his Sarcophagus Lid. Yet it is clear that he is in transition, and not yet a fully fledged "ancestor."

129. Stephen Houston, personal communication, 2002.

130. We will see more of this in Chapters 3 and 4.

131. Inside the solar and lunar imagery is a deity whose forehead is labeled with a "flower"; this is the soul of the deceased. We shall return to the lid and Berlin vessel in Chapter 3. For the deceased as maize, see Houston, Stuart, and Taube (2006, 194–195).

132. Somewhat in between is the case of Tikal Stela 29, which bears the earliest ancestral imagery in the Classic Maya lowlands. There we see a floating head—clearly not deified, however—watching over a ruler in the manner of Tikal Stela 31. See also McAnany (1998, 284–285).

133. At Palenque, we find solar deification as well as transformation into local gods (GI and GIII) and ancestral plants. Outside of Palenque and the Berlin vessel, however, there are no known depictions of ancestors as plants, suggesting that such ideas were local to the western lowlands.

134. Vogt (1969, 222–223).

135. Taube (1983).

136. Fitzsimmons (2004); Stephen Houston and Karl Taube, personal communication, 2004.

137. Fash (1991b); Christopher Jones, cited in Harrison (1999, 68); Sharer et al. (1999); Martin and Grube (2000, 165–169).

CHAPTER THREE

1. Schele and Looper (1996); Martin and Grube (2000).

2. Grube, Schele, and Fahsen (1991).

3. Martin and Grube (2000, 22). There is a further wrinkle in these events that I will describe in Chapter 6.

4. We have no way of addressing the ancient olfactory aesthetic, but some type of embalming may have been practiced by the Classic Maya. See Weiss-Krejci (2003).

5. A. L. Smith (1937, 1950); R. E. Smith (1937).

6. W. Coe (1959, 120); Becquelin and Baudez (1979, 133); Andrews IV and Andrews V (1980, 314); Tourtellot III (1988); Longyear (1989, 35 and 40).

7. Ruz Lhuillier (1968); Welsh (1988).

8. A. L. Smith (1950, 88).

9. Ruz Lhuillier (1968, 165–167); Welsh (1988, 215–218).

10. Ruz Lhuillier (1958).

11. Ringle (1996).

12. Ruz Lhuillier (1961).

13. Welsh (1988, 18).

14. There is one other Early Classic example of a rock-cut tomb in the form of Burial A22 at Uaxactun. See Welsh (1988).

15. Ruz Lhuillier (1973).

16. Ruz Lhuillier (1958, 204–208); Fash et al. (2001).

17. At Río Azul it is written as *och-i ha'*. See Chapter 1, note 24, for more on this grammatical construction.

18. Hall (1989, 92–93).

19. Adams (1986b).

20. Fash (1991b, 100–112).

21. Fash et al. (2001).

22. Pendergast (1979, 1982, 1990).

23. D. Chase and A. Chase (1998, 304).

24. Mathews (1979).

25. Demarest et al. (1991); Demarest (1993, 1997).

26. David Stuart, personal communication, 2001.

27. Ruz Lhuillier (1958, 204–208); Sharer et al. (1999).

28. Stromsvik (1941).

29. M. Coe (1988).

30. Fitzsimmons (1998); Stuart (1998).

31. Schele and Mathews (1998, 127).

32. Cohodas (1991).

33. Cohodas (1985).

34. W. Coe (1990).

35. Weiss-Krejci (2006, 71–88).

36. Thompson (1931, 254–256); Becquelin and Baudez (1979, 1982); Eberl in Cucina and Blos (2006); Ciudad Ruiz (2003); Iglesias Ponce de León (2003).

37. Tiesler Blos, Cucina, and Romano Pacheco (2002); Tiesler Blos and Cucina (2003).

38. Similar cut marks, probably produced while the bodies were fleshed, have been observed in the Preclassic at Cuello, in Burials 9 and 109. Saul and Saul (1991).

39. There is also scant evidence that bodies could be stripped of their flesh before interment; Dzibilchaltun Burial 385-1, a crypt burial, contained an individual who was missing at least some flesh before interment.

40. Welsh (1988).

41. Weiss-Krejci (2003, 75).

42. Tozzer (1941, 130).

43. An individual in the Late Classic Calakmul Structure II, Tomb 4, seems to have been partially covered in cinnabar, then wrapped in a shroud impregnated with resin, and finally covered with a latexlike white material. See Carrasco Vargas et al. (1999).

44. Christopher Jones, cited in Harrison (1999, 68).

45. Carlsen (1986, 1987).

46. This example comes from Tomb 1 in Calakmul Structure VII, published by Folan et al. (1995). Although a preliminary analysis of these remains concluded that the individual had been intentionally defleshed and wrapped, subsequent research by Vera Tiesler (personal

communication, 2003) has demonstrated that the removal of flesh was the result of temporal and taphonomic processes.

47. Headrick (1999).

48. Spence (1923); Brotherston (1974); Boone (1989); Macías Goytia and Vackimes Serret (1990); Pohl (1994).

49. Pohl (1994, 82).

50. Durán (1967, 208); Headrick (1999, 70–72).

51. Taube (1993, 44).

52. Jorge Guillemín, cited in W. Coe (1990, 565).

53. These are Zaculeu Grave 1-18, Zacualpa Burial 8, and Lamanai Tomb N9-56/1, discussed in Wauchope (1948, 565–568); Woodbury and Trik (1953, 90); Pendergast (1981). Estella Weiss-Krejci (2006) has made a case that these clay matrices are related more to corpse preservation than to bundling.

54. For further information on bundling practices, particularly at Tikal, see McAnany (1998, 274).

55. McAnany(1998, 276–277).

56. Fitzsimmons 1998; Martin and Grube (2000, 145).

57. Martin and Grube (2000, 45).

58. Tedlock (1985). Similar behavior has been observed in the Andes; see Verano (1997).

59. W. Coe (1990).

60. Stuart (1996).

61. W. Coe (1959), Ruz Lhuillier (1968); Rebecca Storey, cited in Schele and Mathews (1998, 128); Weiss-Krejci (2006).

62. Hall (1989, 59 and 101–151); Carlsen "Tomb 19"; Carlsen "Tomb 21."

63. Sharer et al. (1999).

64. Ruz Lhuillier (1968, 166).

65. David Stuart, personal communication, 2002.

66. Red-ochre burials have been found in contexts too numerous to cite. For examples, see Ritzenthaler (1958); Faulkner (1960); Bienenfeld (1975); Morrison (1988); and Pearson (1999).

67. Harriet Beaubien, personal communication, 2002.

68. As mentioned in the introduction, these regional traits provide evidence that "royalty" cannot be defined solely by the presence or absence of certain Pan-Maya artifact types; though they serve as an indication of high status, such artifacts must be viewed within the context of local burial practices.

69. Such artifact types are not limited to royal interments, but they do occur in greater combinations and frequencies in the burials of kings and their families.

70. A. Chase (1992, 37).

71. Fitzsimmons et al. (2003).

72. W. Coe (1990, 538–540, 603–606, and 643–646); Fash et al. (2001, 11).

73. Ruz Lhuillier (1958, 204–208).

74. W. Coe (1990, 538–540).

75. We do not know if the body of a ruler was arranged on wooden or other portable supports before entry into the tomb.

76. Sharer et al. (1999); Fash et al. (2001).

77. Houston, Stuart, and Taube (2006, 123, 149).

78. Weiss-Krejci and Culbert (1995).

79. Carrasco et al. (1999, 47–58).

80. Welsh (1988, 64).

81. For more on jade mouth beads, see Fitzsimmons (2002, 194–195). It has been suggested that the various jade artifacts in Maya tombs "served to capture and store the breath soul of deceased rulers." See Houston, Stuart, and Taube (2006, 147).

82. Ruz Lhuillier (1958, 153, 166–174, 180; 1973).

83. Miller and Taube (1991, 106).

84. García Moll (2004).

85. These occur in Piedras Negras Burials 5, 13, and 82 (Fitzsimmons et al. 2003); Yaxchilan Tomb 2 (Martin and Grube 2000, 126); and Tikal Burial 116 (W. Coe 1990, 604–606).

86. For held bloodletters, see Tikal Burial 10 as well as Río Azul Tombs 19 and 23 (W. Coe 1990, 479–484; Hall 1989, 142–144, 305); for bloodletters over the pelvic area, see Tikal Burials 195 and 196, Uaxactun Burial PNT (Proyecto Nacional Tikal) 191, Dos Pilas Burial 30, and Río Azul Burial 19 (Hall 1989, 142–144; W. Coe 1990, 565, 642–646; Demarest et al. 1991, 14–28; Valdés, Fahsen, and Escobedo 1999, 26).

87. See Ruz Lhuillier (1973); Schele and Mathews (1998, 126–127); Sharer (2000, 2002).

88. See Arlen Chase and Diane Chase, cited in Grube (1994). Nevertheless, we do find female interments with stingray spines over the pelvic area: Uaxactun Burial PNT 191 is a good example of this. See Valdés, Fahsen, and Escobedo (1999, 26).

89. Stephen Houston, personal communication, 2002.

90. Sharer (2000).

91. W. Coe (1990, 604–606).

92. A number of shells were found over the body in the Early Classic Uaxactun Burial A-31, although the lines are not clear; see Valdés, Fahsen, and Escobedo (1999, 50).

93. Elite interments at San José, Uaxactun, Tikal, Altun Ha, and Altar de Sacrificios likewise contain individuals with shells over their skulls; see Welsh (1988, table 39).

94. Welsh notes that fewer bowl-over-skull burials occur in his sample of Copan, Piedras Negras, Palenque, and Tonina interments, although he attributes this to the comparatively smaller number of residences excavated at these sites.

95. An elite interment at Uaxactun, Burial E6, contained a variation of this practice: a metate was placed over the skull instead of a bowl; see Welsh (1988, table 35).

96. Welsh (1988, table 111).

97. Welsh (1988, 192).

98. W. Coe (1990, 479–484).

99. W. Coe (1959, 124–125).

100. Tiesler Blos and Cucina (2003); Vera Tiesler Blos (2004); Andrea Cucina and Vera Tiesler Blos (2006).

101. Welsh (1988, table 102).

102. Weiss-Krejci and Culbert (1995, 105).

103. Clemency Coggins, cited in Harrison (1999, 85).

104. Birds, for example, can be found as messengers, indicators of paradisiacal places, oracles, and even alter egos of deities in Classic Maya iconography. Taube (2004); Houston, Stuart, and Taube (2006, 229–244).

105. Incidentally, dogs are found in Classic burials at the highland site of Kaminaljuyu and at Postclassic Zaculeu; see Ruz Lhuillier (1968, 167).

106. Miller and Taube (1991, 114–115).

107. W. Coe (1959, 124); Houston et al. (1998).

108. Mary Miller and Simon Martin (2004, 44).

109. See Chapter 4 for additional information on Classic Maya dances.

110. Edmonson (1971, 243).

111. This elderly man may be a supernatural consort of the Moon Goddess, given the proliferation of deer imagery on these vessels.

112. This practice has ties to the Motmot burial at Copan; see *Tomb Re-Entry* in Chapter 5. The ties between sacrifice and death will be further elaborated in Chapter 6.

113. McAnany (1995, 31–33).

114. Tozzer (1941, 129–130).

115. Bunzel (1952, 150).

116. Guiteras Holmes (1961, 150); LaFarge (1965, 140–142); Vogt (1969, 222); Redfield and Villa Rojas (1970, 200).

117. LaFarge (1965, 141–142); Vogt (1969, 217–220).

118. These burials include the royal Río Azul Tomb 23, Tikal Burials 22 and 196, and Copan Burial XXXVII-4, as well as the high-status interments within Yaxchilan Tomb VII and Río Azul Tomb 12. Refer to Hall (1989, 121–124); W. Coe (1990, 307–309, 642–646); Juárez Cossio and Pérez Campa (1990b); Fash et al. (2001).

119. These include Tikal Burials 125, 10, and 200; the Margarita burial at Copan; and Caracol burials in Structures A3 and B19-2nd. See W. Coe (1990, 339, 479–480, 405); D. Chase (1994); Harrison (1999, 78).

120. Stuart (1998).

121. Cuevas García (2003); Houston, Stuart, and Taube (2006, 149).

122. Ruz Lhuillier (1961, 1973); Cucina and Tiesler Blos (2006, 108–111).

123. W. Coe (1990, 336–339).

124. Ruz Lhuillier (1973).

125. Pendergast (1982).

126. Hall (1989, 308).

127. William L. Fash, personal communication, 2002; Zachary Hruby, personal communication, 2003.

128. W. Coe (1990, 481, 538–540).

129. M. Coe (1988, 227).

130. See "Jades and Celts," above, and Hall (1989, 308).

131. Schele and Miller (1986).

132. Hall (1989, 124).

CHAPTER FOUR

1. McAnany (1995, 96–97).

2. Ibid., 97.

3. Gillespie (2002). With reference to ancestors and memory in archaeological contexts, see also Hendon (2000); Joyce (2001, 2003); Meskill (2003).

4. Ruz Lhuillier (1965, 1968); Welsh (1988); Freidel (1989); McAnany (1995).

5. Patricia McAnany, drawing upon the work of D. G. Saile, has suggested that royal ancestors provided a sense of "home," extending beyond residence to the site proper. See Saile (1985) and McAnany (1998, 274). A wealth of sources is available on land ownership and ancestral structures worldwide. For examples, see Barth (1987); Marcus and Flannery (1996); and Bacquart (2002).

6. McAnany (1995, 45).

7. Sharer et al. (1999); Jane Buikstra, cited in Martin and Grube (2000, 193).

8. One example from the Motmot capstone displays him as a Maya lord, echoing the behavior of Siyaj Chan K'awiil at Tikal forty years earlier. See Freidel, Schele, and Parker (1993, 121–123).

9. Excavations in the Northwest Group Plaza, directed by William Fash and James Fitzsimmons, have uncovered a Preclassic monument that demonstrates the early vitality of the Copan polity; see also Schele and Freidel (1990, 309–310); Fash (1991b, 76–79, 87).

10. Temple 26 was actually co-opted as a second "founder" structure by succeeding generations of Maya rulers, who were once again tied to K'inich Yax K'uk' Mo' and his origins. See Martin and Grube (2000, 193–211).

11. Sharer (1997b); Sharer et al. (1999); Martin and Grube (2000, 195).

12. This name appears elsewhere at Copan in connection with Underworld locations, on both Stela D and the Motmot marker; Schele and Mathews (1998, 166).

13. William L. Fash, personal communication, 1998.

14. The so-called Xukpi stone is actually part of this chamber, and it bears a poorly understood text with a date in AD 437.

15. Sharer et al. (1999); Sharer (2000, 2002).

16. Martin and Grube (2000, 195).

17. Fash (1991b, 100).

18. Agurcia Fasquelle and Fash (1991); Schele and Mathews (1998); Martin and Grube (2000).

19. Schele and Mathews (1998, 50).

20. Waxaklajuun Ub'aah K'awiil carefully buried Rosalila with a new structure, Purpura. Ricardo Agurcia, cited in Martin and Grube (2000, 204).

21. Fash (1991b, 80–84, 172).

22. Fash (1991b); Martin and Grube (2000, 194).

23. Fash (1991b, 106–113).

24. Harrison (1999).

25. Laporte and Fialko (1995)

26. Laporte and Fialko (1995); Martin and Grube (2000, 28–29).

27. Christopher Jones, cited in Harrison (1999, 68).

28. Temple I and its successors were not, of course, wholly divorced in layout or geography from earlier works.

29. Stuart (2000a).

30. Martin and Grube (2000, 37).

31. The main plaza and Structure LD-49 at Dos Pilas, as well as the massive Acropolis at Tonina, were unmistakably formative to most further developments at those sites.

32. Haviland (1968); Laporte and Vega de Zea (1987); Webster (1989); Schele and Freidel (1990); Fash (1991b); Andrews V and Fash (1992); McAnany (1995).

33. McAnany (1995, 96–97).

34. Pendergast (1979, 1982, 1990).

35. McAnany (1998).

36. See Stuart (1998).

37. Reise (1984).

38. Alternatively, this may be an indication that the true heirs of Yax Ehb' Xook were back in power: a disruption in that original line in 317 may have seen the rise of a new lineage, that of Chak Tok Ich'aak I, who was deposed—in part—by the father of Siyaj Chan K'awiil II. See Martin and Grube (2000, 27).

39. McAnany (1995, 11). For Africa, see Fortes (1987, 71); for Asia, see Freedman (1970).

40. Martin and Grube (2000, 53).

41. Houston and Stuart (2000, 55).

42. Stuart and Fitzsimmons (n.d.).

43. Guiteras Holmes (1961); LaFarge (1965); Vogt (1969); Tedlock (1982).

44. Houston and Stuart (2000).

45. For example, refer to Martin (1999, 4–5); Martin and Grube (2000, 73).

46. Ricoeur (1984, 87).

47. David Stuart, cited in Martin and Grube (2000, 127).

48. Martin and Grube (2000, 129).

49. Tate (1992, 192).

50. It is often difficult to tell the difference between ancestors, historical figures, gods, or other supernaturals. Many circular stone altars at Tonina, for example, mention ancestors who may or may not be represented by the accompanying iconography.

51. Although the Reina Roja royal tomb lacks a large vaulted stairway, excavations and analyses of this burial, as yet ongoing, are demonstrating striking similarities with the layout and furniture of the tomb of K'inich Janaab' Pakal I.

52. To date, Linda Schele and Peter Mathews (1998, 110–124) have provided the most extensive analysis of the Lid.

53. Schele and Mathews (1998, 11).

54. Ibid., 112.

55. It is unclear whether one or both of his parents held power at Palenque during these troubled times. As Linda Schele and David Freidel have argued, it is possible that the ruler prior to Pakal—having taken the name of an ancestral deity who was the mother of the Palenque Triad, the three supernatural patrons of the site—was actually Lady Sak K'uk'. An alternative explanation has been that K'an Mo' Hix actually took this progenitor title, which was male rather than female (see David Stuart, cited in Martin and Grube 2000, 161).

56. McAnany (1995, 76–77).

57. A similar series of painted figures may surround the individual within the "frescoed tomb" discovered in Palenque Temple XX in 1999.

58. Schele and Mathews (1998, 130).

59. Schele and Miller (1986, 76–77).

60. Ibid., 48–49.

61. K'inich Kan B'alam I and K'inich K'an Joy Chitam II are later deified as GIII and GI, respectively.

62. Schele and Mathews (1998, 109).

63. Stephen Houston and Karl Taube, personal communication, 1999. Looking at this scene, we see a shorthand depiction of the patron of the month Sip, an individual that has been linked by Stuart (1988) to royal blood. The sign for "zero" or "nothing" is also shown, and this sign can be found on the Sarcophagus Lid at Palenque in connection with depictions of sacred space. Houston, Stuart, and Taube (2006, 156) have suggested that this breath is "solar breath"; if so, this would be a further tie between death and solar rebirth.

64. Ruz Lhuillier (1961).

65. Both structures contain psychoducts, stone boxes bearing disarticulated adolescents, and similar chert celts within the interments.

66. Folan et al. (1995, 321–322).

67. Houston and Stuart (1996); Stuart (1996).

68. Working among the Huichol, Peter Furst has noted that bones are considered to be the soul of a person, the "part that never dies but lives on into eternity" (cited in Robertson 1983, 61). See also Vogt (1976, 18–19); Carlson and Eachus (1977); Burkhart (1989, 125); Galinier (1990, 163); Sandstrom (1991, 258–260); Lupo (1995, 112–113); and Monaghan (2000).

69. Mock (1998, 115).

70. Stross (1998, 32).

71. Stuart (1998, 417–418).

72. D. Chase and A. Chase (1986, figs. 14 and 23); Karl Taube, cited in Houston (1998, 352).

73. Houston (1998, 349–352); Taube (1998, 429–430).

74. McAnany (1998, 271); Taube (1998, 433).

75. For examples, see Freidel (1989); Vogt (1998); Walker (1998).

76. Taube (1998, 464).

77. Ibid., 466.

78. Martin and Grube (2000, 195).

79. McAnany(1998). See also Leventhal (1983).

80. McAnany (1995, 33–34).

81. William Coe (1959, 77); Becquelin and Baudez (1979, 175); Sharer and Ashmore (1979); W. Coe (1990, 541); Becker (1992); D. Chase and A. Chase (1998, 324).

82. Pendergast (1979, 106); W. Coe (1990).

83. Martin and Grube (2000, 201–204).

84. D. Chase (1994).

85. For example, see Stuart (1998).

86. Stuart (2000a); Stuart and Fitzsimmons (n.d.).

87. The bleeding jaw of the skull ornament and the o' of her headdress tie her to Tlaloc and Aj K'ahk' O' Chaak, respectively.

88. Edmonson (1971, 83).

89. Martin and Grube (2000, 125).

90. García Moll (1996).

91. Martin and Grube (2000, 127).

92. Bryan Just, personal communication, 2004.

93. D. Chase and A. Chase (1998, 311).

94. Ibid., 324.

CHAPTER FIVE

1. Another reentry may have occurred at Yaxchilan, performed for Lady K'ab'aal Xook in 729. There is a passage on Yaxchilan Lintel 28 that states: *och k'ahk' sak ? witznal tu muktun ix k'ab'aal xook,* "fire-entering at [the] white ? stone place, at her tomb, Lady K'ab'aal Xook." Given that Lintel 28 was located in Temple 24, and that the burial of Lady K'ab'aal Xook in Temple 23 was not reported as entered, this passage may alternatively refer to fire entering her ancestral shrine, rather than her tomb. For Pakal at Palenque, we do not know if or when this tomb was entered, although the presence of a vaulted stairway suggests that the chamber was created with visitation in mind. For the AD 799 burial at Tonina in Table 5, it is unclear whether this is truly Ruler 1 or simply a Late Classic namesake. See Martin and Grube (2000).

2. D. Chase (1994, 126).

3. For example, Burials IV-1, IV-3, IV-6, and IV-8 each had multiple phases of interments. Given their close relationship, we might characterize the situation in Tonina Structure IV as evidence for a Postclassic lineage compound.

4. The *el naah* rite performed for Piedras Negras Ruler 4 on Panel 13, observed in Burial 13, and the *och k'ahk'* ceremony for the woman in the Motmot tomb at Copan, recorded on the Motmot marker, obviously involved similar processes. However, it seems likely that these phrases refer to different types of burning within graves.

5. Martin and Grube (2000, 143–144).

6. Anaya Hernández, Guenter, and Mathews (2001).

7. Houston et al. (1998); Houston et al. (2000).

8. Child and Child (2000); Fitzsimmons et al. (2003).

9. Houston et al. (1998); Golden (2002).

10. Martin and Grube (2000, 142–143).

11. This sequence was published in Fitzsimmons (1998).

12. Although the exact location of his tomb has not been found, there are indications that it is in the South Group. Stephen Houston, personal communication, 2000.

13. LaFarge (1965, 34).

14. Bunzel (1952, 300).

15. Lines 650–734 in Edmonson (1971, 212–213).

16. Given the circumstances surrounding the burial of Ruler 3, as discussed below, it seems likely that the tomb of Ruler 2 was *not* opened.

17. Houston et al. (1999); Houston et al. (2000).

18. More on Burial 82 can be found in Fitzsimmons et al. (2003), and the second adolescent in question is discussed by W. Coe (1959) with respect to Burial 10.

19. Molina Solís (1896). See also Spence (1947); Reynolds (1956); Bode (1961); Kurath and Martí (1964); Méndez Cifuentes (1967).

20. McArthur (1977).

21. Fash and Fash (2000).

22. Fash and Fash (2000); Stuart (2000a); Karla Davis-Salazar, personal communication, 2000.

23. Storey (1992).

24. Stephen Houston, personal communication, 2003.

25. William Fash, personal communication, 2002.

26. D. Chase and A. Chase. (1998, 303).

27. Martin and Grube (2000, 194–195).

28. Houston (1996).

29. This may indeed be the "four macaw place" mentioned in the text.

30. Schele and Mathews (1998, 144).

31. Taking place in 589 for an otherwise unidentified ruler, Chak B'olon Chaak, this "firing" is recorded on a looted panel from the town of Emiliano Zapata. The protagonist of these events is unknown as well. See Martin and Grube (2000, 179).

32. Ibid., 184–189.

33. Patricia McAnany (1998, 274) has described one such mausoleum at K'axob (Burial 2), which consisted of interments representing a wide range of ages and sexes.

34. Blom (1923); Blom and LaFarge (1926).

35. Merwin and Vaillant (1932).

36. McAnany (1998).

37. This is something we have already seen at Early Classic Tikal in examples like Burial 48, which contained the remains of a king (secondary burial) and two subordinates (primary burials).

38. D. Chase and A. Chase (1998).

39. Ibid., 304.

40. Freidel, Schele, and Parker (1993, 139–140).

41. Heyden and Gendrop (1975).

42. D. Chase and A. Chase (1998, 300).

43. Freidel, Schele, and Parker (1993, 138–145).

44. A. Chase and D. Chase (1987); D. Chase (1994, 27).

45. A. Chase and D. Chase (1987, 12).

46. A. Chase and D. Chase (1987); D. Chase (1994, 27); D. Chase and A. Chase (1998).

47. Sharer et al. (1999).

48. Grube and Schele (1993); translation and some alterations by author.

49. Martinez et al. (1996, 119).

50. Grube and Schele (1993). Simon Martin and Nikolai Grube (2000, 46) have suggested that Maasal corresponds to the site of Naachtun, well to the north of Uaxactun and traditionally under the influence of Calakmul.

51. Jones and Satterthwaite (1982, 37).

52. Kubler (1961); Stuart (1998).

53. Welsh (1988, 216 and tables 99–104); Massey and Steele (1997); Andrew Scherer, personal communication, 2002.

54. Fitzsimmons and Fash (2003).

55. The above bone processing is not typically reported in royal interments but is rather a feature of burials or partial interments interpreted as sacrifices. Royal remains are not usually found with cut marks or even indications of flaying, as in the skull pit at Colha', where the heads of thirty individuals were set within a layered pit. That cache has been interpreted as the result of a religious sacrifice in which victims were "decapitated, skinned or butchered, possibly displayed on ceramic bowls or plates, and [the heads] buried in a location that probably had religious or political significance" (Massey and Steele 1997, 76).

56. Tozzer (1941, 120–123).

57. Mock (1998, 115).

58. Welsh (1988, 216); D. Chase and A. Chase (1994); Massey and Steele (1997).

59. Blom (1923); Ruz Lhuillier (1958); Ringle (1996).

60. At Dzibilchaltun, ceramic bowls substituted for heads and faces. Welsh (1988, 216).

61. Martin and Grube (2000, 109).

62. It would not be at all surprising to learn that such an item was akin to a fragment of a *tonalli*, an object much like the reliquaries of medieval Europe. Patricia McAnany (1995, 37) has observed images of masks in the Madrid Codex that seem to serve as proxies for ancestors.

63. This is what Schele and Freidel (1990, 243) call the *tok' pakal*.

64. In medieval Europe, such a hierarchical view of the body and its parts was a pervasive aspect of royal burials; by analogy, we might further examine the presence of such views among the Maya. See Binski (1996, 55) and Weiss-Krejci (2004).

65. Tozzer (1941, 131).

66. Headrick (1999).

67. McAnany (1995, 36–37).

68. Tozzer (1907).

69. Vogt (1969); Nash (1970); McAnany (1995).

70. Houston, Stuart, and Robertson (1999).

71. A. Chase (1992); D. Chase (1994); A. Chase and D. Chase (1996a, 1996b).

72. Grube, Lacadena, and Martin (2003). David Freidel and Stanley Guenter (2006) have likewise suggested that communion with ancestors through bones and relics did occur during the Classic Period and that the bones and relics provide evidence for a practice that "falls squarely into the province of shamanism as defined globally."

CHAPTER SIX

1. Metcalf and Huntington (1991, 163).

2. Houston et al. (1999).

3. Schele and Miller (1986, 265).

4. Houston and Stuart (2000, 55).

5. Ibid.

6. Houston et al. (1999).

7. McAnany (1995, 125–128).

8. Martin and Grube (2000, 151, 222).

9. Metcalf and Huntington (1991, 173).

10. For more on royal interregnums, see Markus Eberl (1999).

11. Houston (1983).

12. Proskouriakoff (1993).

13. McAnany (1995, 149).

14. Martin and Grube (2000, 172).

15. Ibid., 33.

16. Ibid., 127–128.

17. Ibid., 135.

18. Ruz Lhuillier (1968); Welsh (1988).

19. Stephen Houston, personal communication, 2002.

20. Metcalf and Huntington (1991, 134).

21. Ibid., 136–151.

22. One of the great unanswered questions in Maya archaeology is the degree to which rulers were habitually involved in the creation of their own tombs. The idea that rulers prepared for their own deaths with the creation of funerary chambers seems logical, given the size and scale of funerary monuments, and is clearly represented by the Margarita chamber at Copan. However, if we remember that death among the Maya was not necessarily viewed as "natural" in the Western sense, but was possibly the byproduct of trickery on the part of the lords of the Underworld, then preparing for death with a funerary monument would seem pessimistic at least.

23. Bloch (1971).

24. Metcalf and Huntington (1991, 83).

25. Hertz (1960); Metcalf and Huntington (1991, 179–184).

26. Hertz (1960, 45).

27. Van Gennep (1960).

28. McAnany (1995, 143–144).

REFERENCES

Adams, Richard E. W.
  1984 (gen. ed.) *Río Azul Project Reports No. 1, Final 1983 Report.* San Antonio: Center for Archaeological Research.
  1986a The Río Azul Archaeological Project: Introduction and summary, 1984. In *Río Azul Project Reports No. 2, the 1984 Season,* ed. Richard E. W. Adams, 1–17. San Antonio: Center for Archaeological Research.
  1986b Río Azul: Lost city of the Maya. *National Geographic Magazine* 169 (4): 420–451.
  1999 *Río Azul: An Ancient Maya City.* Norman: University of Oklahoma Press.
Adams, Richard E. W., Vivian L. Broman, William R. Coe, William A. Haviland Jr., Rubén E. Reina, Linton Satterthwaite, Edwin M. Shook, and Aubrey S. Trik
  1961 *Tikal Reports Nos. 5–10.* Philadelphia: University Museum, University of Pennsylvania.
Adams, Richard E. W., and John L. Gatling
  1964 Noreste del Petén: Un nuevo sitio y un mapa arqueológico regional. *Estudios de Cultura Maya* 4:99–118.
  1986 Northeastern Peten: A new site and a regional archaeological map. In *Rio Azul Project Reports No. 2,* ed. Richard E. W. Adams, 193–210. San Antonio: Center for Archaeological Research.
Agrinier, Pierre, and Gareth W. Lowe
  1960 *The Mound 1 Tombs and Burials.* Papers of the New World Archaeological Foundation 8 (7). Provo, Utah: Brigham Young University.
Agurcia Fasquelle, Ricardo, and William L. Fash
  1991 Maya artistry unearthed. *National Geographic* 190 (3): 94–105.
Ajpacaja Tum, Pedro Florentino, Manuel Isidro Chox Tum, Francisco Lucas Tepaz Raxuleu, and Diego Adrián Guarchaj Ajtzalam
  1996 *Diccionario K'iche'.* Antigua, Guatemala: Proyecto Lingüístico Francisco Marroquín.
Alcorn, Janis
  1984 *Huastec Mayan Ethnobotany.* Austin: University of Texas Press.
Alvarez Heidenreich, Laurencia
  1976 Breve estudio de las plantas medicinales en Hueyapán, Morelos. *Estudios sobre Etnobotánica y Antropología Médica* 1:13–28.
  1987 *La enfermedad y la cosmovisión en Hueyapan, Morelos.* Mexico City: Instituto Nacional Indigenista (hereafter INI).

Alver, Bente G.

1971   Conceptions of the living human soul in the Norwegian tradition. *Temenos* 7:7–33.

Anaya Hernández, Armando, Stanley Guenter, and Peter Mathews

2001   An inscribed wooden box from Tabasco, Mexico. Mesoweb article posted at http://www.mesoweb.com/ reports/box/index.html.

Anderson, Patricia K.

1983   Maya cosmology: Quadripartite or dualistic? Master's thesis, Department of Geography, Western Illinois University, Macomb.

Andrews, E. Wyllys IV, and E. Wyllys Andrews V

1980   *Excavations at Dzibilchaltun, Yucatan, Mexico.* MARI Publication 48. New Orleans: Middle American Research Institute, Tulane University.

Andrews, E. Wyllys V, and Barbara W. Fash

1992   Continuity and change in a royal Maya residential complex at Copan. *Ancient Mesoamerica* 3 (1): 63–88.

Antonio, Diego de, Francisco Pascual, Nicolás de Pedro, Carmelino Fernando Gonzales, Santiago Juan Matías

1996   *Diccionario del Idioma Q'anjob'al.* Antigua, Guatemala: Proyecto Lingüístico Francisco Marroquín (PLFM).

Arbman, Ernst

1926   Untersuchungen zur primitiven seelenvorstellungen mit besonderer rücksicht auf indien 1. *Le Monde Oriental* 20:85–222.

1927   Untersuchungen zur primitiven seelenvorstellungen mit besonderer rücksicht auf indien 2. *Le Monde Oriental* 21:1–185.

Aries, Philippe

1981   *The Hour of Our Death.* Trans. Helen Weaver. New York: A. Knopf.

Artes, Federico

1893   *Description of the Peten Department.* Pamphlet. *El Guatemalteco* 23 (16). Guatemala City, Guatemala.

Ashmore, Wendy, and Pamela L. Geller

2001   Social dimensions of mortuary space. Paper presented at the 66th Annual Meeting of the Society for American Archaeology, New Orleans.

Bacquart, Jean-Baptiste

2002   *The Tribal Arts of Africa.* London: Thames and Hudson.

Ball, Joseph

1983   Teotihuacan, the Maya, and ceramic interchange: A contextual perspective. In *Highland-Lowland Interaction in Mesoamerica: Interdisciplinary Approaches,* ed. Arthur G. Miller, 125–146. Washington, D.C.: Dumbarton Oaks.

Barrera Vásquez, Alfredo

1991   (ed.) *Diccionario Maya: Maya-Español, Español-Maya.* Mexico City: Editorial Porrúa.

Barrientos Q., Tomás, Héctor L. Escobedo, and Stephen D. Houston

1997   PN1: Excavaciones en la Estructura O-13. In *Proyecto Arqueológico Regional Piedras Negras: Informe Preliminar No. 1, Primera Temporada 1997,* ed. Héctor L. Escobedo and Stephen D. Houston, 1–20. Report produced for the Instituto de Antropología e Historia (hereafter IDAEH), Guatemala City.

Barth, Fredrik
  1987 *Cosmologies in the Making: A Generative Approach to Cultural Variation in Inner New Guinea.* Cambridge: Cambridge University Press.

Barthel, Thomas
  1968 El complejo "emblema." *Estudios de Cultura Maya* 7:159–193.

Baudez, Claude F.
  1994 *Maya Sculpture of Copan: The Iconography.* Norman: University of Oklahoma Press.

Becker, Marshall J.
  1971 The identification of a second plaza plan at Tikal, Guatemala, and its implications for ancient Maya social complexity. Ph.D. diss., University of Pennsylvania, Philadelphia.
  1988 Caches as burials, burials as caches: The meaning of ritual deposits among the Classic Period lowland Maya. In *Recent Studies in Pre-Columbian Archaeology,* ed. Nicholas J. Saunders and Oliver de Montmollin, 117–134. BAR International Series. Oxford: Archaeopress.
  1992 Burials as caches; caches as burials: A new interpretation of the meaning of ritual deposits among the Classic Period lowland Maya. In *New Theories on the Ancient Maya,* ed. E. C. Danien and Robert Sharer, 185–196. University Museum Monograph 77. Philadelphia: University of Pennsylvania.

Becquelin, Pierre, and Claude F. Baudez
  1979 *Tonina, Une Cite Maya du Chiapas: Tome I.* Collection Etudes Mesoamericaines 6 (1). Paris: La mission archéologique et ethnologique française au Mexique.
  1982 *Tonina, Une Cite Maya du Chiapas: Tome III.* Collection Etudes Mesoamericaines 6 (2). Paris: La mission archéologique et ethnologique française au Mexique.

Becquelin, Pierre, and Eric Taladoire
  1990 *Tonina, Une Cite Maya du Chiapas: Tome IV.* Collection Etudes Mesoamericaines 6 (4). Paris: La mission archéologique et ethnologique française au Mexique.

Beetz, Carl P., and Linton Satterthwaite
  1981 *The Monuments and Inscriptions of Caracol, Belize.* University Museum Monograph 45. Philadelphia: University of Pennsylvania.

Bell, Catherine
  1992 *Ritual Theory, Ritual Practice.* New York: Oxford University Press.

Berlin, Heinrich
  1958 Glifo "emblema" en las inscripciones mayas. *Journal de la Société des Américanistes* 47:111–119.

Beyer, Hermann
  1908 The symbolic meaning of the dog in ancient Mexico. *American Anthropologist* 10:419–422.

Bienenfeld, Paula F.
  1975 Gilde Site, a red ochre burial site in Shiawassee County. *Michigan Archaeologist* 21 (3–4): 153–160.

Binford, Lewis R.
  1971 Mortuary practices: Their study and their potential. In *Approaches to the Social Dimensions of Mortuary Practices,* ed. J. Brown, 6–29. Memoir of the Society for American Archaeology 25. Providence, R.I.: Brown University.

Binski, Paul

    1996   *Medieval Death: Ritual and Representation.* Ithaca, N.Y.: Cornell University Press.

Bloch, Maurice

    1971   *Placing the Dead: Tombs, Ancestral Villages, and Kinship Organization in Madagascar.* London: Seminar Press.

Bloch, Maurice, and Jonathan Parry

    1981   *Death and the Regeneration of Life.* Cambridge: Cambridge University Press.

Blom, Franz

    1923   *Las Ruinas de Palenque.* Mexico City: INAH.

Blom, Franz, and Oliver LaFarge

    1926   *Tribes and Temples: A Record of the Expedition to Middle America Conducted by the Tulane University of Louisiana in 1925.* Vol. 1. New Orleans: Tulane University.

Bode, Barbara

    1961   *The Dance of the Conquest of Guatemala.* MARI Publication 27. New Orleans: Middle American Research Institute, Tulane University.

Boone, Elizabeth Hill

    1989   Image of Huitzilopochtli: Changing Ideas and Visual Manifestations of the Aztec God. In *Imagination of Matter: Religion and Ecology in Mesoamerican Traditions,* ed. David Carrasco, 51–82. BAR International Series 515. Oxford: Archaeopress.

Brady, James E., and Andrea Stone

    1986   Naj Tunich: Entrance to the Maya Underworld. *Archaeology* 39 (6): 18–25.

Bremmer, Jan

    1981   *The Early Greek Concept of the Soul.* Princeton, N.J.: Princeton University Press.

Bricker, Victoria R.

    1986   *A Grammar of Mayan Hieroglyphs.* MARI Publication 56. New Orleans: Middle American Research Institute, Tulane University.

    1994   Mortuary practices in the Madrid Codex. In *Seventh Palenque Round Table, 1989,* ed. Virginia M. Fields, 195–200. San Francisco: Pre-Columbian Art Research Institute.

Brotherston, Gordon

    1974   Huitzilopochtli and what was made of him. In *Mesoamerican Archaeology: New Approaches,* ed. Norman Hammond, 155–166. Austin: University of Texas Press.

Buikstra, Jane, Douglas Price, James Burton, and Lori Wright

    2000   The Early Classic royal burials at Copán: A bioarchaeological perspective. A paper presented at the symposium Understanding Early Classic Copán (E. Bell, M. Canuto, and R. Sharer, organizers) at the Annual Meeting of the Society for American Archaeology, Philadelphia.

Bunzel, Ruth

    1952   *Chichicastenango: A Guatemalan Village.* Publication No. 22. Seattle: American Ethnological Society, University of Washington Press.

Burkhart, Louise

    1989   *The Slippery Earth: Nahua-Christian Moral Dialog in Sixteenth-Century Mexico.* Tucson: University of Arizona Press.

Butler, Mary

    1977   The Kekchi spirit world. In *Cognitive Studies of Southern Mesoamerica,* ed. Helen

Neuenswander and Dean E. Arnold, 36–65. Dallas: Summer Institute of Linguistics Museum of Anthropology.

Calvin, Inga

1997   Where the Wayob live: A further examination of Classic Maya supernaturals. In *Maya Vase Book 5: A Corpus of Rollout Photographs of Maya Vases,* ed. Justin Kerr, 868–883. New York: Kerr Associates.

Carlsen, Robert

1986   Analysis of the Early Classic period textile remains—Tomb 19, Río Azul, Guatemala. In *Río Azul Reports No. 2, the 1984 Season,* ed. Richard E. W. Adams, 122–155. San Antonio: Center for Archaeological Research.

1987   Analysis of the Early Classic period textile remains from Tomb 23, Río Azul, Guatemala. In *Río Azul Reports No. 3, the 1985 Season,* ed. Richard E. W. Adams, 152–160. San Antonio: Center for Archaeological Research.

Carlson, Ruth, and Francis Eachus

1977   The Kekchi spirit world. In *Cognitive Studies in Southern Mesoamerica,* ed. Helen Neuenswander and Dean Arnold, 38–65. Summer Institute of Linguistics Museum of Anthropology Publication 3. Dallas: Summer Institute of Linguistics.

Carr, Christopher

1995   Mortuary practices: Their social, philosophical-religious, circumstantial, and physical determinants. *Journal of Archaeological Method and Theory* 2:105–200.

Carrasco Vargas, Ramón, Sylviane Boucher, Paula Alvarez González, Vera Tiesler Bios, Valeria García Vierna, Renata García Moreno, and Javier Vázquez Negrete

1999   A dynastic tomb from Campeche, Mexico: New evidence on Jaguar Paw, a ruler from Calakmul. *Latin American Antiquity* 10:47–58.

Cederroth, Sven, Claes Corlin, and Jan Lindstrom

1988   *On the Meaning of Death: Essays on Mortuary Rituals and Eschatological Beliefs.* Uppsala Studies in Cultural Anthropology 8. Stockholm: Almqvist and Wiksell.

Chapman, Anne

1982   *Los hijos de la muerte: El universo mítico de los Tolupan-Jicaques (Honduras).* Mexico City: Instituto Nacional de Antropología e Historia (INAH).

Chapman, Robert, Ian Kinnes, and Klavs Randsborg

1981   *The Archaeology of Death.* Cambridge: Cambridge University Press.

Chapman, Robert, and Klavs Randsborg

1981   Approaches to the archaeology of death. In *The Archaeology of Death,* ed. Robert Chapman, Ian Kinnes, and Klavs Randsborg, 1–24. Cambridge: Cambridge University Press.

Chase, Arlen F.

1985   Troubled times: The archaeology and iconography of the Terminal Classic southern lowland Maya. In *Fifth Palenque Round Table,* ed. Merle Greene Robertson, 103–114. San Francisco: Pre-Columbian Art Research Institute.

1992   Elites and the changing organization of Classic Maya society. In *Mesoamerican Elites: An Archaeological Assessment,* ed. Diane Z. Chase and Arlen F. Chase, 30–49. Norman: University of Oklahoma Press.

Chase, Arlen F., and Diane Z. Chase

1987   *Investigations at the Classic Maya City of Caracol, Belize, 1985–1987.* PARI Monograph 3. San Francisco: Pre-Columbian Art Research Institute.

1996a The causeways of Caracol. *Belize Today* 10 (3/4): 31–32.

1996b A mighty Maya nation: How Caracol built an empire by cultivating its "middle class." *Archaeology* 49 (5): 66–72.

Chase, Arlen F., Nikolai Grube, and Diane Z. Chase

1991 *Three Terminal Classic Monuments from Caracol, Belize.* Research Reports on Ancient Maya Writing 36. Washington, D.C.: Center for Maya Research.

Chase, Diane Z.

1986 Caches and censerwares: Meaning from Maya pottery. In *A Pot for All Reasons: Ceramic Ecology Revisted,* ed. Charles Kolb and Louana Lackey, 81–104. Philadelphia: Laboratory of Anthropology, Temple University.

1994 Human osteology, pathology, and demography as represented in the burials of Caracol, Belize. In *Studies in the Archaeology of Caracol, Belize,* ed. Diane Z. Chase and Arlen F. Chase, 123–138. PARI Monograph 7. San Francisco: Pre-Columbian Research Institute.

Chase, Diane Z., and Arlen F. Chase

1986 *Offerings to the Gods: Maya Archaeology at Santa Rita Corozal.* Orlando: University of Central Florida.

1988 *A Postclassic Perspective: Excavations at the Maya Site of Santa Rita Corozal, Belize.* PARI Monograph 4. San Francisco: Pre-Columbian Research Institute.

1994 Maya veneration of the dead at Caracol, Belize. In *Seventh Mesa Redonda de Palenque, 1989,* Vol. 8, ed. Virginia M. Fields, 53–60. San Francisco: Pre-Columbian Research Institute.

1996 Maya multiples: Individuals, entries, and tombs in Structure A-34 of Caracol, Belize. *Latin American Antiquity* 7:61–79.

1998 Architectural context of caches, burials, and other ritual activities. In *Function and Meaning in Maya Architecture,* ed. Stephen Houston, 299–332. Washington, D.C.: Dumbarton Oaks.

Cheek, Charles D., and Rene Viel

1983 Sepulturas. In *Introducción a la arqueología de Copán, Honduras,* ed. Claude F. Baudez, 551–609. Tegucigalpa, Honduras: Instituto Hondureño de Antropología e Historia.

Child, Mark, and Jessica Child

2000 Excavaciones en la Estructura R-8. In *Proyecto Piedras Negras: Informe Preliminar No. 4, Cuarta Temporada 2000,* ed. Héctor L. Escobedo and Stephen D. Houston, 389–402. Guatemala City: IDAEH.

Ciudad Ruiz, Andrés

2003 La tradición funeraria de las Tierras Altas de Guatemala durante la etapa prehispánica. In *Antropología de la eternidad: La muerte en la cultura maya,* ed. Andrés Ciudad Ruiz, M. Humberto Ruz Sosa, and M. Josefa Iglesias Ponce de León, 77–112. Madrid: Sociedad Española de Estudios Mayas (hereafter SEEM).

Clendinnen, Inga

1991 *Aztecs: An Interpretation.* Cambridge: Cambridge University Press.

Closs, Michael D.

1985 The dynastic history of Naranjo: The middle period. In *Fourth Palenque Round Table,* ed. Merle Greene Robertson, 65–78. San Francisco: Pre-Columbian Art Research Institute.

Coe, Michael D.

1956   The funerary temple among the Classic Maya. *Southwestern Journal of Anthropology* 12 (4): 387–394.

1973   *The Maya Scribe and His World.* New York: Grolier Club.

1978   *Lords of the Underworld.* Princeton, N.J.: Princeton University Press.

1988   Ideology of the Maya tomb. In *Maya Iconography,* ed. Elizabeth P. Benson and Gillett G. Griffin, 222–235. Princeton, N.J.: Princeton University Press.

1989   The Hero Twins: Myth and image. In *The Maya Vase Book: A Corpus of Rollout Photographs of Maya Vases,* Vol. 1, ed. Justin Kerr, 161–184. New York: Kerr and Associates.

Coe, William R.

1959   *Piedras Negras Archaeology: Artifacts, Caches, and Burials.* Philadelphia: University Museum, University of Pennsylvania Monographs.

1990   *Excavations in the Great Plaza, North Terrace, and North Acropolis of Tikal.* Tikal Report No. 14, Vols. 1–6. Philadelphia: University Museum, University of Pennsylvania Monographs.

1996   *Excavations in the East Plaza of Tikal.* Tikal Report No. 16, Vols. 1 and 2. Philadelphia: University Museum, University of Pennsylvania Monographs.

Coe, William R., and Vivian L. Broman

1958   *Excavations in the Stela 23 Group.* Tikal Report Nos. 1–4. Museum Monograph No. 15. Philadelphia: University Museum, University of Pennsylvania Monographs.

Coggins, Clemency

1975   Painting and drawing styles at Tikal. Ph.D. diss., Harvard University.

1988   Classic Maya metaphors of death and life. *RES: Anthropology and Aesthetics* 16:64–84.

Coggins, Clemency, and Orrin C. Shane

1984   *Cenote of Sacrifice.* Austin: University of Texas Press.

Cohodas, Marvin

1985   Public architecture of the Maya lowlands. *Cuadernos de Arquitectura Mesoamericana* 6:51–58.

1991   Ballgame imagery of the Maya lowlands: History and iconography. In *The Mesoamerican Ballgame,* ed. Vernon Scarborough and David Wilcox, 251–288. Tucson: University of Arizona Press.

Colas, Pierre Robert

1998   Ritual and politics in the Underworld. *Mexicon* 20:99–104.

Colby, Benjamin N.

1976   The anonymous Ixil—bypassed by the Postclassic? *American Antiquity* 41:74–80.

Cucina, Andrea, and Vera Tiesler Blos

2006   The companions of Janaab' Pakal and the "Red Queen" from Palenque, Chiapas. In *Janaab' Pakal of Palenque: Reconstructing the Life and Death of a Maya Ruler,* ed. Vera Tiesler and Andrea Cucina, 102–125. Tucson: University of Arizona Press.

Cuevas García, Martha

2003   Ritos funerarios de los dioses-incensarios de Palenque. In *Antropología de la eternidad: La muerte en la cultura maya,* ed. Andrés Ciudad Ruiz, Mario Humberto Ruz Sosa, and M. Josefa Iglesias Ponce de León, 317–336. Madrid: SEEM.

Culbert, T. Patrick

1993   *The Ceramics of Tikal: Vessels from the Burials, Caches, and Problematical Deposits.* Tikal Report No. 25, Part A. Philadelphia: University Museum, University of Pennsylvania Monographs.

Dacus, Chelsea

2005   Weaving the past: An examination of bones buried with an elite Maya woman. Master's thesis, Department of Art History, Southern Methodist University, Dallas, Texas.

Davoust, Michel

2001   Venus cycle used in the throne text of Temple XIX at Palenque. *PARI Journal* 2 (1): 23–24.

Demarest, Arthur

1993   The violent saga of a Maya kingdom. *National Geographic Magazine* 183 (2): 94–111.

1997   The Vanderbilt Petexbatun Regional Archaeological Project 1989–1994. *Ancient Mesoamerica* 8 (2): 209–227.

Demarest, Arthur, Héctor Escobedo, Juan A. Valdés, Stephen Houston, Lori Wright, and Katherine Emery

1991   Arqueología, epigrafía y el descubrimiento de una tumba real en el centro ceremonial de Dos Pilas, Petén, Guatemala. *U Tz'ib* 1:14–28.

Demarest, Arthur, and Stephen Houston

1989–1994   *El Proyecto Arqueológico Regional Petexbatún: Primera–Sexta Temporadas.* Guatemala City: IDAEH.

Deng, Francis M.

1972   *The Dinka of the Sudan.* New York: Holt, Rinehart and Winston.

Duetting, Dieter

1979   Birth, inauguration, and death in the inscriptions of Palenque, Chiapas, Mexico. In *Tercera Mesa Redonda de Palenque, 1978,* Vol. 4, ed. Merle Greene Robertson and Donnan C. Jeffers, 183–214. Palenque, Mexico: Pre-Columbian Art Printers.

1981   Life and death in Mayan hieroglyphic inscriptions. *Zeitschrift für Ethnologie* 106:185–228.

Durán, Fray Diego de

1967   *Historia de las Indias de Nueva España e Islas de la Tierra Firme.* Mexico City: Editorial Porrúa.

Durkheim, Émile

1965   *The Elementary Forms of the Religious Life.* Trans. Joseph W. Swain. New York: Free Press. (Orig. pub. 1912.)

Earle, Duncan

1986   The metaphor of the day in Quiché: Notes on the nature of everyday life. In *Symbol and Meaning beyond the Closed Community: Essays in Mesoamerican Ideas,* ed. Gary Gossen, 155–172. Albany, N.Y.: Institute for Mesoamerican Studies, SUNY Albany.

Eberl, Markus

1999   Tod und begräbnis in der Klassischen Maya-Kultur. Master's thesis, Philosophische Fakultät, Rheinische Friedrich-Wilhelms-Universität, Bonn.

2000   Death and conceptions of the soul. In *Maya: Divine Kings of the Rain Forest,* ed. Nikolai Grube, 310–321. Cologne, Germany: Koenemann Verlagsgesellschaft mBH.

Edmonson, Munro S.

    1971   *The Book of Counsel: The Popol Vuh of the Quiche Maya of Guatemala.* MARI Publication 35. New Orleans: Middle American Research Institute, Tulane University.

Escobedo, Héctor L., and Carlos Alvarado

    1997   PN1: Excavaciones en la Estructura O-13. In *Proyecto Arqueológico Piedras Negras: Informe Preliminar No. 1, Segunda Temporada 1998,* ed. Héctor L. Escobedo and Stephen D. Houston, 1–20. Guatemala City: IDAEH.

Escobedo, Héctor L., Tomás Barrientos, and F. Marcelo Zamora

    2001   The high and the mighty: Temples and mortuary pyramids at Piedras Negras. Paper given at the 66th Annual Meeting of the Society for American Archaeology in New Orleans.

Evans-Pritchard, Edward Evan

    1948   *The Divine Kingship of the Shilluk of the Nilotic Sudan.* Cambridge: Cambridge University Press.

Fahsen, Federico

    1986   Algunos aspectos sobre el texto de la Estela 31 de Tikal. *Mesoamerica* 11:135–154.

Fash, William L.

    1991a Lineage patrons and ancestor worship among the Classic Maya nobility: The case of Copan Structure 9N-82. *Sixth Palenque Round Table,* 1986. Norman: University of Oklahoma Press.

    1991b *Scribes, Warriors, and Kings.* London: Thames and Hudson.

    2001   Religion and human agency in ancient Maya history: Tales from the Hieroglyphic Stairway. *Cambridge Archaeological Journal* 12 (1): 5–19.

Fash, William L., and Barbara W. Fash

    2000   Teotihuacan and the Maya: A Classic heritage. In *Mesoamerica's Classic Heritage: From Teotihuacan to the Aztecs,* ed. David Carrasco, Lindsay Jones, and Scott Sessions, 433–464. Boulder: University Press of Colorado.

Fash, William L., Harriet F. Beaubien, Catherine E. Magee, Barbara W. Fash, and Richard V. Williamson

    2001   Trappings of kingship among the Classic Maya: Ritual and identity in a royal tomb from Copan. In *Fleeting Identities: Perishable Material Culture in Archaeological Research,* ed. Penelope B. Drooker, 152–169. Carbondale: Center for Archaeological Investigations, Southern Illinois University.

Fash, William L., Richard Williamson, Carlos R. Larios, and Joel Palka

    1992   The Hieroglyphic Stairway and its ancestors: Investigations of Copan Structure 10L-26. *Ancient Mesoamerica* 3:105–115.

Faulkner, Charles H.

    1960   The Red Ochre culture: An early burial complex in northern Indiana. *Wisconsin Archeologist* 41 (2): 35–49.

Fernández de Oviedo y Valdés, Gonzalo

    1991   *Historia general y natural de las Indias, islas y tierra-firme del Mar Océano.* Vol. 11. Asunción del Paraguay: Editorial Guaranía.

Fitzsimmons, James

    1995   Classic Maya anniversary glyphs at two sites: Piedras Negras and Yaxchilan. Report for the National Endowment for the Humanities Younger Scholar's Grant (REF:FI-27563–95).

1998   Classic Maya mortuary anniversaries at Piedras Negras, Guatemala. *Ancient Mesoamerica* 9:271–278.

1999   PN40: Excavaciones en el Grupo N/O, Estructuras N-7 y N-10. In *Proyecto Piedras Negras: Informe Preliminar No. 3, Tercera Temporada 1999*, ed. Héctor L. Escobedo and Stephen D. Houston. Guatemala City: IDAEH.

2002   Death and the Maya: Language and archaeology in Classic Maya mortuary ceremonialism. Ph.D. diss., Harvard University.

2004   Social death in Classic Maya texts. Paper presented at the European Maya Meetings in Madrid.

2006   Tomb re-entry among the Classic Maya: Archaeology and epigraphy in mortuary ceremonialism. In *Jaws of the Underworld: Life, Death, and Rebirth among the Ancient Maya,* ed. Pierre R. Colas, Geneviéve LeFort, and Bodil Liljefors Persson, 35–42. Acta Mesoamericana 16. Möckmühl, Germany: Verlag Anton Saurwein.

Fitzsimmons, James L., and William L. Fash

2003   Susaj b'aak: Muerte y ceremonia mortuoria en la Plaza Mayor de Copán. In *Antropología de la eternidad: La muerte en la cultura maya,* ed. Andrés Ciudad Ruiz, Mario Humberto Ruz Sosa, and M. Josefa Iglesias Ponce de León, 299–316. Madrid: SEEM.

Fitzsimmons, James L., Andrew Scherer, Stephen D. Houston, and Héctor Escobedo

2003   Guardian of the Acropolis: The sacred space of a royal burial at Piedras Negras, Guatemala. *Latin American Antiquity* 14 (3): 449–468.

Florescano, Enrique

1993   *El mito de Quetzalcoatl.* Mexico City: Fondo de Cultura Económica.

1994   *Memoria mexicana.* Mexico City: Fondo de Cultura Económica.

Folan, William J., and Abel Morales López

1996   Calakmul, Campeche, Mexico: La Estructura II-H, sus entierros y otras funciones ceremoniales y habitacionales. *Revista Española de Antropología Americana* (Madrid) 26:9–28.

Folan, William J., Joyce Marcus, Sophia Pincemin, María del Rosario Domínguez Carrasco, Laraine Fletcher, and Abel Morales López

1995   Calakmul: New data from an ancient Maya capital in Campeche, Mexico. *Latin American Antiquity* 6 (4): 310–334.

Fortes, Meyer

1987   *Religion, Morality, and the Person: Essays on Tallensi Religion.* Cambridge: Cambridge University Press.

Foster, George

1944   Nagualism in Mexico and Guatemala. *Acta Americana* 2 (1–2): 87–103.

Fought, John G.

1972   *Chorti (Mayan) Texts.* Philadelphia: University of Pennsylvania Press.

Freedman, Maurice

1970   Ritual aspects of Chinese kinship and marriage. In *Family and Kinship in Chinese Society,* ed. Maurice Freedman, 163–188. Stanford: Stanford University Press.

Freidel, David A.

1989   Dead kings and living temples: Dedication and termination rituals among ancient Maya. In *Word and Image in Maya Culture,* ed. William F. Hanks and Don S. Rice, 233–243. Salt Lake City: University of Utah Press.

1992 The trees of life: Ahau as idea and artifact in Classic Lowland Maya civilization. In *Ideology and Pre-Columbian Civilizations*, ed. Arthur Demarest and Geoffrey W. Conrad, 115–133. Santa Fe, N.M.: School of American Research Press.

Freidel, David A., and Stanley Guenter

2006 Shamanic practice and divine kingship in Classic Maya civilization. Paper given at the University of Pennsylvania Maya Weekend, Philadelphia.

Freidel, David A., Linda Schele, and Joy Parker

1993 *Maya Cosmos: Three Thousand Years on the Shaman's Path*. New York: William Morrow.

Furst, Jill L. M.

1993 *The Natural History of the Soul in Ancient Mexico*. New Haven, Conn.: Yale University Press.

Furst, Peter T.

1976 Fertility, vision quest, and auto-sacrifice: Some thoughts on ritual blood-letting among the Maya. In *The Art, Iconography, and Dynastic History of Palenque, Part III: Proceedings of the Segunda Mesa Redonda de Palenque*, ed. Merle Greene Robertson, 181–193. Pebble Beach, Calif.: Pre-Columbian Art Research Institute, Robert Louis Stevenson School.

Galinier, Jacques

1990 *La mitad del mundo: Cuerpo y cosmos en los rituales otomíes*. Mexico City: Universidad Nacional Autónoma de México (hereafter UNAM) and INI.

Gámez Díaz, Laura Lucía

2003 Áreas rituales en complejos residenciales de la región de las Tierras Bajas mayas: El grupo guacamaya del sitio arqueológico La Joyanca, Petén. Licenciatura thesis, Universidad de San Carlos, Guatemala City.

Garber, James F., W. David Driver, Lauren A. Sullivan, and David M. Glassman

1998 Bloody bowls and broken pots. In *The Sowing and the Dawning: Termination, Dedication, and Transformation in the Archaeological and Ethnographic Record of Mesoamerica*, ed. Shirley Boteler Mock, 125–133. Albuquerque: University of New Mexico Press.

García de León, Antonio

1969 El universo de lo sobrenatural entre los nahuas de Pajapán, Veracruz. *Estudios de Cultura Nahuatl* 8:279–311.

1976 *Pajapán, un dialecto mexicano del Golfo*. Mexico City: Instituto Nacional de Antropología e Historia (hereafter INAH).

1993 Tiempo mítico, tiempo verbal, tiempo histórico. *Boletín de Antropología Americana* 28:31–42.

García Moll, Roberto

1975 Primera temporada arqueológica en Yaxchilán, Chiapas. *INAH Boletín* 12:3–12.

1996 Yaxchilán, Chiapas. *Arqueología Mexicana* 4 (22): 36–45.

2004 Tombs 2 and 3 at Yaxchilan, Chiapas. In *Courtly Art of the Ancient Maya*, ed. Mary Miller and Simon Martin, 264–267. London: Thames and Hudson.

Gates, William

1935 *Arte y diccionario en lengua Cholti: A Manuscript Copied from the Libro Grande of Fr. Pedro Morán of about 1625*. Maya Society Publication 9. Baltimore: Maya Society.

Geertz, Clifford
1973   *The Interpretation of Cultures.* New York: Basic Books.
Giesey, Ralph E.
1960   *The Royal Funeral Ceremony in Renaissance France.* Geneva, Switzerland: Librairie E. Droz.
Gillespie, Susan D.
2003   Body and soul among the Maya: Keeping the spirits in place. *Archaeological Papers of the American Anthropological Association* 11 (1): 67–78.
Golden, Charles
2002   Bridging the gap between archaeological and indigenous chronologies: An investigation of the Early Classic/Late Classic divide at Piedras Negras, Guatemala. Ph.D diss., University of Pennsylvania, Philadelphia.
Goldstein, Lynne G.
1981   One-dimensional archaeology and multidimensional people: Spatial organization and mortuary analysis. In *The Archaeology of Death,* ed. Robert Chapman, Ian Kinnes, and Klavs Randsborg, 53–69. Cambridge: Cambridge University Press.
González Cruz, Arnoldo
n.d.   The Red Queen. Description of 1994 burial inside Temple XIII; located at www.mesoweb.com/palenque/features/red_queen/01.htm.
Goody, Jack
1962   *Death, Property, and the Ancestors.* Stanford: Stanford University Press.
Gordon, George B.
1896   *Prehistoric Ruins of Copan, Honduras: A Preliminary Report of the Explorations by the Museum, 1891–1895.* Memoirs of the Peabody Museum of American Archaeology and Ethnology 1 (1). Cambridge: Peabody Museum, Harvard University.
1913   *The Book of Chilam Balam of Chumayel.* University Museum Anthropological Publications 5. Philadelphia: University of Pennsylvania.
Gossen, Gary H.
1974   *Chamulas in the World of the Sun: Time and Space in a Maya Oral Tradition.* Cambridge: Harvard University Press.
1975   Animal souls and human destiny in Chamula. *Man* 10 (3): 448–461.
1993   On the human condition and the moral order: A testimony from the Chamula Tzotzil Maya of Chiapas, Mexico. In *South and Mesoamerican Native Spirituality: From the Cult of the Feathered Serpent to the Theology of Liberation,* ed. Gary H. Gossen, 414–435. New York: Crossroad Publishing.
Graham, Ian
1972   *The Hieroglyphic Inscriptions and Monumental Art of Altar de Sacrificios.* Papers of the Peabody Museum of American Archaeology and Ethnology 64 (2). Cambridge: Peabody Museum, Harvard University.
1982   *Corpus of Maya Hieroglyphic Inscriptions, Volume 3, Part III: Yaxchilan.* Cambridge: Peabody Museum, Harvard University.
1996   *Corpus of Maya Hieroglyphic Inscriptions, Volume 7, Part I: Seibal.* Cambridge: Peabody Museum, Harvard University.
Graham, Ian, and Eric von Euw
1977   *Corpus of Maya Hieroglyphic Inscriptions, Volume 3, Part I: Yaxchilan.* Cambridge: Peabody Museum, Harvard University.

Grube, Nikolai

1992   Classic Maya dance: Evidence from hieroglyphs and iconography. *Ancient Meso-america* 3:201–218.

1994   Epigraphic research at Caracol, Belize. In *Studies in the Archaeology of Caracol, Belize,* ed. Diane Z. Chase and Arlen F. Chase, 83–122. PARI Monograph 7. San Francisco: Pre-Columbian Art Research Institute.

1996   Palenque in the Maya world. In *Eighth Palenque Round Table, 1993,* ed. Merle Greene Robertson, 1–13. San Francisco: Pre-Columbian Art Research Institute.

1998   Observations on the Late Classic interregnum at Yaxchilan. In *The Archaeology of Mesoamerica,* ed. Warrick Bray and Linda Manzanilla, 116–127. London: British Museum Press.

2004   Akan—the god of drinking, disease and death. In *Continuity and Change: Maya Religious Practices in Temporal Perspective,* ed. Daniel D. Graña Behrens et al., 59–76. Acta Mesoamericana 14. Markt Schwaben, Germany: Verlag Anton Saurwein.

Grube, Nikolai, Alfonso Lacadena, and Simon Martin

2003   Chichen Itza and Ek Balam: Terminal Classic inscriptions from Yucatan. In *Notebook for the 27th Maya Hieroglyphic Forum at Texas,* ed. Nikolai Grube, 2–25. Austin: University of Texas Press.

Grube, Nikolai, and Simon Martin

1998   *Notebook for the 22nd Hieroglyphic Forum at Texas: Deciphering Maya Politics.* Austin, Texas: Maya Workshop Foundation.

Grube, Nikolai, and Werner Nahm

1994   A census of Xibalba: A complete inventory of Way characters on Maya ceramics. In *The Maya Vase Book: A Corpus of Rollout Photographs of Maya Vases,* Vol. 4, ed. Justin Kerr, 686–715. New York: Kerr Associates.

Grube, Nikolai, and Linda Schele

1988   *Cu-Ix, the Fourth Ruler of Copan and His Monuments.* Copan Notes 40. Austin, Texas: Copan Mosaics Project, Instituto Hondureño de Antropología e Historia.

1993   *Naranjo Altar 1 and Rituals of Death and Burials.* Texas Notes on Pre-Columbian Art, Writing, and Culture No. 54. Austin: The Center for the History and Art of Ancient American Culture, Art Department, University of Texas.

Grube, Nikolai, Linda Schele, and Federico Fahsen

1991   Odds and ends from the inscriptions of Quirigua. *Mexicon* 13 (6): 106–112.

Guiteras Holmes, Calixta

1961   *Perils of the Soul: The Worldview of a Tzotzil Indian.* New York: Free Press of Glencoe.

Hall, Grant

1989   Realms of death: Royal mortuary customs and polity interaction in the Classic Maya lowlands. Ph.D. diss., Harvard University, Cambridge.

Hallam, Elizabeth, Jennifer Hockey, and Glennys Howarth

1999   *Beyond the Body: Death and Social Identity.* London: Routledge.

Hammond, Norman

1981   Pom for the ancestors: A re-examination of Piedras Negras Stela 40. *Mexicon* 3 (5): 77–79.

Hammond, Norman, and Theya Molleson

1994   Huguenot weavers and Maya kings: Anthropological assessment versus documentary record of age at death. *Mexicon* 16 (4): 75–77.

Hammond, Norman, Gair Tortellot III, Sara Donaghey, and Amanda Clarke
    1996   Survey and excavation at La Milpa, Belize, 1996. *Mexicon* 28 (1): 8–11.

Hanks, William F.
    1990   *Referential Practice: Language and Lived Space among the Maya.* Chicago: University of Chicago Press.

Harrison, Peter D.
    1999   *The Lords of Tikal: Rulers of an Ancient Maya City.* London: Thames and Hudson.

Haviland, William A.
    1968   Ancient lowland Maya social organization. In *Archaeological Studies in Middle America,* 93–117. New Orleans: Middle American Research Institute, Tulane University.
    1981   Dower houses and minor centers at Tikal, Guatemala: An investigation into the valid units in settlement hierarchies. In *Lowland Maya Settlement Patterns,* ed. Wendy Ashmore, 89–117. Albuquerque: University of New Mexico Press.
    1985   Population and social dynamics: The dynasties and social structure of Tikal. *Expedition* 27 (3): 34–41.

Headrick, Annabeth
    1999   The street of the dead . . . it really was: Mortuary bundles at Teotihuacan. *Ancient Mesoamerica* 10 (1): 69–85.

Hellmuth, Nicholas M.
    1976   *Tikal Copan Travel Guide.* Guatemala City: Asociación para la Investigación Antropológica en América Latina.
    1987   *The Surface of the Underwaterworld: Iconography of the Gods of Early Classic Maya Art in Peten, Guatemala.* Vols. 1 and 2. Culver City, Calif.: Foundation for Latin American Anthropological Research.

Henderson, Lucia
    2001   Dishes of death: Rebirth and cosmic intersection in the burial ceramics of Ruler 12. Senior thesis, Harvard University, Cambridge.

Hendon, Julia
    2000   Having and holding: Storage, memory, knowledge, and social relations. *American Anthropologist* 102 (1): 42–53.

Hermitte, Maria Esther
    1970   *Poder sobrenatural y control social en un pueblo maya contemporáneo.* Mexico City: Instituto Indigenista Interamericano.

Hertz, Robert
    1960   A contribution to the study of the collective representation of death. In *Death and the Right Hand,* trans. Rodney Needham and Claudia Needham, 63–71. New York: Free Press.

Heyden, Doris, and Paul Gendrop
    1975   *Pre-Columbian Architecture of Mesoamerica.* New York: Harry N. Abrams.

Holland, William R.
    1963   *Medicina maya en los altos de Chiapas: Un estudio del cambio socio-cultural.* Mexico City: Instituto Nacional Indigenista.

Houston, Stephen D.
    1983   On Ruler "6" at Piedras Negras, Guatemala. *Mexicon* 5 (5): 84–86.

1987   The inscriptions and monumental art of Dos Pilas, Guatemala. Ph.D. diss., Yale University, New Haven, Conn.

1993   *Hieroglyphs and History at Dos Pilas: Dynastic Politics of the Classic Maya.* Austin: University of Texas Press.

1996   Symbolic sweatbaths of the Maya: Architectural meaning in the Cross Group at Palenque, Mexico. *Latin American Antiquity* 7 (2): 132–151.

1998   Classic Maya depictions of the built environment. In *Function and Meaning in Classic Maya Architecture,* ed. Stephen Houston, 333–372. Washington, D.C.: Dumbarton Oaks.

1999   Classic Maya religion: Beliefs and practices of an ancient American people. *BYU Studies* 38 (4): 43–72.

Houston, Stephen D., and Thomas Cummins

1998   Body, presence, and space in Andean and Mesoamerican rulership. Paper presented at Ancient Palaces of the New World: Form, Function, and Meaning, Dumbarton Oaks, Washington, D.C.

Houston, Stephen, Héctor Escobedo, Mark Child, Charles Golden, Richard Terry, and David Webster

2000   In the land of the turtle lords: Archaeological investigations at Piedras Negras, Guatemala. *Mexicon* 22 (5): 97–110.

Houston, Stephen, Héctor Escobedo, Donald Forsyth, Perry Hardin, David Webster, and Lori Wright

1998   On the River of Ruins: Explorations at Piedras Negras, Guatemala, 1997. *Mexicon* 20 (1): 16–22.

Houston, Stephen, Héctor Escobedo, Perry Hardin, Richard Terry, David Webster, Mark Child, Charles Golden, Kitty Emery, and David Stuart

1999   Between mountains and sea: Investigations at Piedras Negras, Guatemala, 1998. *Mexicon* 21 (1): 10–17.

Houston, Stephen D., and Peter Mathews

1985   *The Dynastic Sequence of Dos Pilas, Guatemala.* Pre-Columbian Art Research Institute Monograph 1. San Francisco: Pre-Columbian Art Research Institute.

Houston, Stephen D., John Robertson, and David Stuart

2000   The language of Classic Maya inscriptions. *Current Anthropology* 41 (3): 321–356.

Houston, Stephen D., and David Stuart

1996   Of gods, glyphs, and kings: Divinity and rulership among the Classic Maya. *Antiquity* 70:289–312.

1998   The ancient Maya self: Personhood and portraiture in the Classic Period. *RES: Anthropology and Aesthetics* 33:73–101.

2000   Peopling the Classic Maya court. In *Royal Courts of the Ancient Maya,* ed. Takeshi Inomata and Stephen D. Houston, 54–83. Norman: University of Oklahoma Press.

Houston, Stephen D., David Stuart, and John Robertson

1999   Classic Mayan language and Classic Maya gods. In *Notebook for the 23rd Maya Hieroglyphic Forum at Texas,* ed. Linda Schele, Part II, 63. Austin: University of Texas Press.

Houston, Stephen, David Stuart, and Karl Taube

2006   *The Memory of Bones: Body, Being, and Experience among the Classic Maya.* Austin: University of Texas Press.

Houston, Stephen, David Stuart, Claudia Wolley, and Lori Wright
    1991   A death monument: Dos Pilas Throne 1. Manuscript on file, Department of Anthropology, Brigham Young University, Provo, Utah.
Houston, Stephen, and Karl Taube
    2000   An archaeology of the senses: Perception and cultural expression in ancient Mesoamerica. *Cambridge Archaeological Journal* (UK) 10 (2): 261–294.
Hultkrantz, Ake
    1953   *Conceptions of the Soul among North American Indians.* Stockholm: Ethnographical Museum of Sweden.
Hunt, Eva
    1977   *The Transformation of the Hummingbird: Cultural Roots of a Zinacantan Mythical Poem.* Ithaca, N.Y.: Cornell University Press.
Huntington, Richard
    1973   Death and the social order: Bara funeral customs (Madagascar). *African Studies* 32:65–84.
Hvidtfeldt, Arild
    1958   *Teotl and Ixiptlatli: Some Central Conceptions in Ancient Mexican Religion.* Copenhagen: Munksgaard.
Iglesias Ponce de León, María Josefa
    2003   Contenedores de cuerpos, cenizas y almas: El uso de las urnas funerarias en la cultura maya. In *Antropología de la eternidad: La muerte en la cultura maya,* ed. Andrés Ciudad Ruiz, M. Humberto Ruz Sosa, and M. Josefa Iglesias Ponce de León, 209–254. Madrid: SEEM.
Inomata, Takeshi
    1997   The last day of a fortified Classic Maya center: Archaeological investigations at Aguateca, Guatemala. *Ancient Mesoamerica* 8 (2): 337–351.
Johnston, Kevin
    1984   A commentary on the hieroglyphic inscriptions of Piedras Negras, Guatemala. Master's thesis, Department of Anthropology, University of Texas, Austin.
Jones, Christopher, and Linton Satterthwaite
    1982   *The Monuments and Inscriptions of Tikal: The Carved Monuments.* Tikal Report 33, Part A. University of Pennsylvania Monographs. Philadelphia: University Museum.
Joyce, Rosemary A.
    1991   Ideology in action: Classic Maya ritual practice. In *Ancient Images, Ancient Thought: The Archaeology of Ideology,* ed. A. Sean Goldsmith, Sandra Garvie, David Selin, and Jeannette Smith, 497–505. Proceedings of the 23rd Annual Chacmool Conference. Calgary, Canada: University of Calgary Press.
    2001   Burying the dead at Tlatilco: Social memory and social identities. *Archaeological Papers of the American Anthropological Association* 10 (1): 12–26.
    2003   Concrete memories: Fragments of the past in the Classic Maya present (AD 500–1000). In *Archaeologies of Memory,* ed. Ruth Van Dyke and Susan E. Alcock, 104–126. Oxford: Blackwell Publishing.
Juárez Cossio, Daniel, and Mario Pérez Campa
    1990a   Exploraciones en la pequeña Acrópolis, Yaxchilán, Chiapas. *Boletín del Consejo de Arqueología,* 140–146.
    1990b   Proyecto Yaxchilán: Acrópolis Oeste. *Boletín del Consejo de Arqueologia,* 154–156.

Kantorowicz, Ernst

 1957 *The King's Two Bodies.* Princeton, N.J.: Princeton University Press.

Kelley, David Humiston

 1972 The Nine Lords of the Night. *Contributions of the University of California Archaeological Research Facility* (Department of Anthropology, Berkeley) 16:53–68.

 1976 *Deciphering the Maya Script.* Austin: University of Texas Press.

 1985 The Lords of Palenque and the Lords of Heaven. In *Fifth Palenque Round Table, 1983.* Vol. 7, ed. Virginia M. Fields, 235–239. San Francisco: Pre-Columbian Art Research Institute.

Kerr, Justin

 1989 *The Maya Vase Book: A Corpus of Rollout Photographs of Maya Vases.* Vol. 1. New York: Kerr Associates.

 1990 *The Maya Vase Book: A Corpus of Rollout Photographs of Maya Vases.* Vol. 2. New York: Kerr Associates.

 1992 *The Maya Vase Book: A Corpus of Rollout Photographs of Maya Vases.* Vol. 3. New York: Kerr Associates.

 1997 *The Maya Vase Book: A Corpus of Rollout Photographs of Maya Vases.* Vol. 5. New York: Kerr Associates.

 n.d.a Kerr Maya vase archives. Digital photos of Maya vases on FAMSI website at http://famsi.saiph.com:9500/dataSpark/maya.

 n.d.b The transformation of Xbalanqué or the many faces of God A'. FAMSI paper at http://www.famsi.org/mayavase/jkarticles/xbalanque/xbalanque.htm.

Kidder, Alfred V., Jesse D. Jennings, and Edwin M. Shook

 1946 *Excavations at Kaminaljuyu, Guatemala.* Carnegie Institution of Washington, Publication 561. Washington, D.C.: Carnegie Institution.

Knab, Tim

 1979 Talocan Talmanic: Supernatural beings of the Sierra de Puebla. In *Actes du XLII Congrès International des Américanistes,* 6:127–136. Paris: Congrès du Centenaire.

Kowalski, Jeff Karl

 1986 Uxmal: A Terminal Classic Maya capital in northern Yucatan. In *City States of the Maya: Art and Architecture,* ed. Elizabeth P. Benson, 138–171. Denver: Rocky Mountain Institute for Pre-Columbian Studies.

Kubler, George A.

 1961 The design of space in Maya architecture. In *Studies of Ancient American and European Art: The Collected Essays of George Kubler,* ed. Thomas F. Reese, 242–255. New Haven, Conn.: Yale University Press.

Kunen, Julie L., Mary Jo Galindo, and Erin Chase

 2002 Pits and bones: Identifying Maya ritual behavior in the archaeological record. *Ancient Mesoamerica* 13 (2): 197–211.

Kurath, Gertrude Prokosch, and Samuel Martí

 1964 *Dances of the Anáhuac.* Chicago: Aldine Publishing.

Kurbjuhn, Kornelia

 1985 Man in the turtle, man in the snail: A study of occupants of turtle and snail shells in Maya art. In *Fifth Palenque Round Table, 1983,* ed. Merle Greene Robertson and Virginia M. Fields, 159–170. San Francisco: Pre-Columbian Art Research Institute.

LaFarge, Oliver
    1965   *Santa Eulalia: The Religion of a Cuchumatan Indian Town.* Chicago: University of Chicago Press.

Láng, Janos
    1973   The concept of psyche. *Acta Ethnographica Academiae Scientiarum Hungaricae* 22:171–197.

Laporte, Juan Pedro, and Vilma Fialko
    1995   Un reencuentro con Mundo Perdido, Tikal, Guatemala. *Ancient Mesoamerica* 6 (2): 41–94.

Laporte, Juan Pedro, and Lilian Vega de Zea
    1987   Aspectos dinásticos para el clásico temprano de Mundo Perdido, Tikal. In *Primer simposio mundial sobre epigrafía maya,* ed. Asociatión Tikal, 127–140. Guatemala City: Ministerio de Cultura y Deportes.

Las Casas, Bartolomé de
    1967   *Apologetica historia sumaria.* Edited by Edmundo O'Gorman. Mexico City: Instituto de Investigaciones Históricas, UNAM.

Laughlin, Robert M.
    1975   *The Great Tzotzil Dictionary of San Lorenzo Zinacantán.* Washington, D.C.: Smithsonian Institution Press.

León-Portilla, Miguel
    1987   *Toltecáyotl: Aspectos de la cultura náhuatl.* Mexico City: Fondo de Cultura Económica.

Leventhal, Richard M.
    1983   Household groups and Classic Maya religion. In *Prehistoric Settlement Patterns: Essays in Honor of Gordon R. Willey,* ed. Evon Z. Vogt and Richard M. Leventhal, 55–76. Cambridge: Peabody Museum, Harvard University; and Albuquerque: University of New Mexico Press.

Looper, Matthew G.
    1992   The "Canoe Gods." *Texas Note 31.* Austin: Center of the History and Art of Ancient American Culture, Art Department, University of Texas at Austin.
    1996   Documentation of sculptures at Quiriguá, Guatemala. Report submitted to FAMSI, located at http://www.famsi.org/reports/95015/index.html.

Longyear, John M.
    1989   *Copan Ceramics: A Study of Southeastern Maya Pottery.* Carnegie Institution of Washington Publication 597. Washington, D.C.: Carnegie Institution.

López Austin, Alfredo
    1988   *The Human Body and Ideology: Concepts of the Ancient Nahuas.* Vol. 1. Trans. Thelma Ortiz de Montellano and Bernard Ortiz de Montellano. Salt Lake City: University of Utah Press.

Lupo, Alessandro
    1981   Conoscenze astronomiche e conocezioni cosmologiche dei huave di San Mateo del Mar. *L'Uomo* 5 (2): 267–314.
    1995   *La tierra nos escucha: La cosmología de los nahuas a través de las súplicas rituales.* Mexico City: INI.

Macías Goytia, Angelina, and Katina Vackimes Serret
    1990   Proyecto cuenca de Cuitzeo. *Boletín del Consejo de Arqueología* 1989:71–81.

Maler, Teobert

1896   Seibal and Altar de Sacrificios. *Globus* 70 (10): 149–150.

1901   *Researches in the Central Portion of the Usumatsintla Valley: Report of Explorations for the Museum, 1898–1900.* Memoirs of the Peabody Museum of American Archaeology and Ethnology 2. Cambridge: Peabody Museum, Harvard University.

1908   *Exploration of the Upper Usumacintla and Adjacent Regions.* Memoirs of the Peabody Museum of American Archaeology and Ethnology 4 (1). Cambridge: Peabody Museum, Harvard University.

Maldonado Andrés, Juan, Juan Ordóñez Domingo, and Juan Ortiz Domingo

1986   *Diccionario Mam.* Antigua, Guatemala: Proyecto Lingüístico Francisco Marroquín.

Marcus, Joyce

1973   Territorial organization of the lowland Classic Maya. *Science* 180:911–916.

1976   *Emblem and State in the Classic Maya Lowlands.* Washington, D.C.: Dumbarton Oaks.

Marcus, Joyce, and Kent Flannery

1996   *Zapotec Civilization.* London: Thames and Hudson.

Marcus, Joyce, and William Folan

1994   Una estela más del siglo V y nueva información sobre Pata de Jaguar, gobernante de Calakmul, Campeche, en el siglo VII. *Gaceta Universitaria Año IV* No. 15–16, Campeche, Mexico.

Marín Arzápalo, Ramón (trans.)

1987   *El ritual de los bacabes.* Mexico City: UNAM.

Martin, Simon

1995   New epigraphic data on Maya warfare. Paper presented at the Primera Mesa Redonda de Palenque, Nueva Epoca, 1995, Palenque, Mexico.

1996   Tikal's "star war" against Naranjo. In *Eighth Palenque Round Table,* ed. Merle Greene Robertson, 223–235. San Francisco: Pre-Columbian Art Research Institute.

1999   The queen of Middle Classic Tikal. *PARI Newsletter* 1999:4–5.

2000   Los señores de Calakmul. *Arqueología Mexicana* 7 (42): 40–45.

Martin, Simon, and Nikolai Grube

2000   *Chronicle of the Maya Kings and Queens: Deciphering the Dynasties of the Ancient Maya.* London: Thames and Hudson.

Massey, Virginia K., and D. Gentry Steele

1997   A Maya skull pit from the Terminal Classic period, Colha, Belize. In *Bones of the Maya,* ed. Stephen L. Whittington and David M. Reed, 62–77. Washington, D.C.: Smithsonian Institution Press.

Mathews, Peter

1979   Souverains. In *Tonina; Une Cité Maya du Chiapas,* ed. Pierre Becquelin and Claude Baudez, 3:1381–1383. Mexico City: Centre d'Etudes Mexicaines et Centraméricaines.

1983   *Tonina.* Corpus of Maya Hieroglyphic Inscriptions 6 (1). Cambridge: Peabody Museum of Archaeology and Ethnology, Harvard University.

1985   Early Classic monuments and inscriptions. In *A Consideration of the Early Classic Period in the Maya Lowlands,* ed. Gordon R. Willey and Peter Mathews, 5–55. IMS Monograph No. 10. Albany: Institute for Mesoamerican Studies, State University of New York.

n.d.   The inscription on the back of Stela 8, Dos Pilas, Guatemala. Manuscript in possession of the author.

Mayer, Karl Herbert

1978   *Maya Monuments: Sculptures of Unknown Provenance in Europe.* Trans. Sandra L. Brizee. Ramona, Calif.: Acoma Books.

1980   *Maya Monuments: Sculptures of Unknown Provenance in the United States.* Trans. Sandra L. Brizee. Ramona, Calif.: Acoma Books.

1984   *Maya Monuments III: Sculptures of Unknown Provenance.* Berlin: Verlag Karl-Friedrich von Flemming.

1986   *Maya Monuments: Sculptures of Unknown Provenance in Middle America.* Berlin: Verlag Karl-Friedrich von Flemming.

1987   *Maya Monuments IV: Sculptures of Unknown Provenance.* Berlin: Verlag Karl-Friedrich von Flemming.

1989   *Maya Monuments: Sculptures of Unknown Provenance.* Supplement 2. Graz, Austria: Verlag von Fleming.

McAnany, Patricia A.

1995   *Living with the Ancestors: Kinship and Kingship in Ancient Maya Society.* Austin: University of Texas Press.

1998   Ancestors and the Classic Maya built environment. In *Function and Meaning in Classic Maya Architecture,* ed., Stephen D. Houston, 271–298. Washington, D.C.: Dumbarton Oaks.

McAnany, Patricia A., Rebecca Storey, and Angela K. Lockard

1999   Mortuary ritual and family politics at Formative and Early Classic K'axob, Belize. *Ancient Mesoamerica* 10 (1): 129–146.

McArthur, Harry S.

1977   Releasing the dead: Ritual and motivation in Aguacatec dances. In *Cognitive Studies of Southern Mesoamerica,* ed. Helen L. Neuenswander and Dean E. Arnold, 6–35. Dallas: Summer Institute of Linguistics Museum of Anthropology.

McGee, R. Jon

1984   The influence of prehispanic Maya religion in contemporary Lacandon ritual. *Journal of Latin American Lore* 10 (2): 175–187.

1990   *Life, Ritual, and Religion among the Lacandon Maya.* Belmont, Calif.: Wadsworth Publishing.

1997   Narrative structure of Lacandon creation mythology. *Latin American Indian Literatures Journal* 13 (1): 1–22.

Méndez Cifuentes, Arturo

1967   *Baile de la pach.* Folklore de Guatemala, No. 3. Guatemala City: Departamento de Arte Folklórico Nacional.

Merwin, Raymond E., and George C. Vaillant

1932   *The Ruins of Holmul.* Memoirs of the Peabody Museum of American Archaeology and Ethnology 3 (2). Cambridge: Peabody Museum, Harvard University.

Meskill, Lynn

2003   Memory's materiality: Ancestral presence, commemorative practice and disjunctive locales. In *Archaeologies of Memory,* ed. Ruth Van Dyke and Susan E. Alcock, 34–55. Oxford: Blackwell Publishing.

Metcalf, Peter

 1981 Meaning and materialism: The ritual economy of death. *Man* 16:563–78.

 1982 *A Borneo Journey into Death: Berawan Eschatology from Its Rituals.* Philadelphia: University of Pennsylvania Press.

Metcalf, Peter, and Richard Huntington

 1991 *Celebrations of Death: The Anthropology of Mortuary Ritual.* Cambridge: Cambridge University Press.

Miles, Douglas J.

 1965 Socioeconomic aspects of secondary burial. *Oceania* 35 (3): 161–174.

Miller, Julia C.

 2000 Proyecto de las Cruces field report: Spring 2000. *PARI Journal* 1 (1): 25–26.

Miller, Mary Ellen

 1986 Copan: Conference with a perished city. In *City States of the Maya: Art and Architecture,* ed. Elizabeth P. Benson, 72–109. Denver: University Press of Colorado.

 1991 Some observations on the relationship between Yaxchilan and Piedras Negras. Paper presented at the Seventh Texas Symposium, Austin.

Miller, Mary Ellen, and Simon Martin

 2004 *Courtly Art of the Ancient Maya.* London: Thames and Hudson.

Miller, Mary Ellen, and Marco Samayoa

 1998 Where maize may grow: Jade, chacmools, and the Maize God. *RES: Anthropology and Aesthetics* 33:54–72.

Miller, Mary Ellen, and Linda Schele

 1986 *The Blood of Kings: Dynasty and Ritual in Maya Art.* Fort Worth, Texas: Kimbell Art Museum.

Miller, Mary Ellen, and Karl Taube

 1991 *The Gods and Symbols of Ancient Mexico and the Maya.* London: Thames and Hudson.

Mock, Shirley Boteler

 1998 Preface to *The Sowing and the Dawning: Termination, Dedication and Transformation in the Archaeological and Ethnographic Record of Mesoamerica,* ed. Shirley B. Mock, 3–18. Albuquerque: University of New Mexico Press.

Molina Solís, Juan Francisco

 1896 *Historia del descubrimiento y conquista de Yucatán.* Mérida, Mexico: Imp. E. Caballero.

Monaghan, John

 1995 *The Covenants with Earth and Rain: Exchange, Sacrifice, and Revelation in Mixtec Society.* Norman: University of Oklahoma Press.

 1998 The person, destiny, and the construction of difference in Mesoamerica. *RES: Anthropology and Aesthetics* 33:137–146.

 2000 Theology and history in the study of Mesoamerican religions. In *Handbook of Middle American Indians, Supplement 6: Ethnology,* ed. John D. Monaghan and Barbara W. Edmonson, 24–49. Austin: University of Texas Press.

Morán, Francisco

 1695 Arte en lengua cholti, que quiere decir lengua de milperos. Photographic copy, Latin American Library, Tulane University, New Orleans. Facsimile edition by Gates (1935).

Morley, Sylvanus G.

1920   *The Inscriptions at Copan.* Carnegie Institution of Washington Publication 219. Washington, D.C.: Carnegie Institution.

1937–1938   *The Inscriptions of Peten.* Carnegie Institution of Washington Publication 437. Washington, D.C.: Carnegie Institution.

Morrison, Dennis Michael

1988   Red ochre find at 20IS8, Oscoda, Michigan. *Michigan Archaeologist* 34 (3): 63–68.

Nash, June

1970   *In the Eyes of the Ancestors: Belief and Behavior in a Maya Community.* New Haven: Yale University Press.

Newsome, Elizabeth A.

1998   The ontology of being and spiritual power in the stone monument cults of the lowland Maya. *RES: Anthropology and Aesthetics* 33:115–136.

Niehoff, Arthur H.

1959   Beads from a red ochre burial in Ozaukee County. *Wisconsin Archaeologist* 40:25–28.

O'Shea, John

1984   *Mortuary Variability: An Archaeological Investigation.* New York: Academic Press.

Pásztory, Esther (gen. ed.)

1978   *Middle Classic Mesoamerica, A.D. 400–700.* New York: Columbia University Press.

Pearson, Mike Parker

1999   *The Archaeology of Death and Burial.* College Station: Texas A&M University Press.

Pendergast, David

1979   *Excavations at Altun Ha, Belize: 1964–1970.* Vol. 1. Toronto, Canada: Royal Ontario Museum Publications in Archaeology.

1981   Lamanai, Belize: Summary of excavation results, 1974–1980. *Journal of Field Archaeology* 8:29–53.

1982   *Excavations at Altun Ha, Belize: 1964–1970.* Vol. 2. Toronto, Canada: Royal Ontario Museum Publications in Archaeology.

1990   *Excavations at Altun Ha, Belize: 1964–1970.* Vol. 3. Toronto, Canada: Royal Ontario Museum Publications in Archaeology.

Pérez Martínez, Vitalino, Federico García, Felipe Martínez, and Jeremías López

1996   *Diccionario del Idioma Ch'orti'.* Antigua, Guatemala: Proyecto Lingüístico Francisco Marroquín.

Peterson, Polly A., Patricia A. McAnany, and Allan B. Cobb

2005   De-fanging the earth monster: Speleotherm transport to surface sites in the Sibun Valley. In *Stone Houses and Earth Lords: Maya Religion in the Cave Context,* ed. Keith M. Prufer and James E. Brady, 225–248. Boulder: University Press of Colorado.

Pohl, John M. D.

1994   *The Politics of Symbolism in the Mixtec Codices.* Nashville, Tenn.: Vanderbilt University.

Ponciano, Erick M.

1989   Informe final y lista global de artefactos tumba 25, Río Azul, Petén, Guatemala.

In *Rio Azul Project Reports 4,* ed. Richard E. W. Adams, 175–188. San Antonio: Center for Archaeological Research.

Proskouriakoff, Tatiana

1950   *A Study of Classic Maya Sculpture.* Carnegie Institution of Washington Publication 593. Washington, D.C.: Carnegie Institution.

1960   Historical implications of a pattern of dates at Piedras Negras, Guatemala. *American Antiquity* 25:454–475.

1963   Historical data in the inscriptions of Yaxchilan, Parts I–II. *Estudios de Cultura Maya* 3:149–167.

1964   Historical data in the inscriptions of Yaxchilan, Parts I–II. *Estudios de Cultura Maya* 4:177–201.

1993   *Maya History.* Austin: University of Texas Press.

Quenon, Michel, and Geneviéve Le Fort

1997   Rebirth and resurrection in Maize God iconography. In *Maya Vase Book 5: A Corpus of Rollout Photographs of Maya Vases,* ed. Barbara Kerr and Justin Kerr, 884–902. New York: Kerr Associates.

Quirarte, Jacinto

1976   The Underworld jaguar in Maya vase painting: An iconographic study. *New Mexico Studies in Fine Arts* 1:20–25.

1979   The representation of Underworld processions in Maya vase painting: An iconographic study. In *Maya Archaeology and Ethnohistory,* ed. Norman Hammond and Gordon R. Willey, 116–148. Austin: University of Texas Press.

Ragon, Michel

1988   *The Space of Death: A Study of Funerary Architecture, Decoration, and Urbanism.* Charlottesville: University of Virginia Press.

Rakita, Gordon, and Jane Buikstra

2001   Corrupting flesh: Re-examining Hertz's perspective on mummification and cremation. Paper presented for the 66th Annual Meeting of the Society for American Archaeology, New Orleans.

Ramírez Pérez, José, Andrés Montejo, and Baltazar Díaz Hurtado

1996   *Diccionario del idioma jakalteco.* Antigua, Guatemala: Proyecto Lingüístico Francisco Marroquín.

Randsborg, Klavs

1980   *The Viking Age in Denmark.* London: Duckworth.

Rathje, William

1970   Lowland Classic Maya socio-political organization: Degree and form in time and space. Ph.D. diss., Harvard University, Cambridge, Mass.

Redfield, Robert, and Alfonso Villa Rojas

1970   *Chan Kom: A Maya Village.* Washington, D.C.: Carnegie Institution of Washington.

Reents-Budet, Dorie

1994   *Painting the Maya Universe: Royal Ceramics of the Classic Period.* Durham, N.C.: Duke University Press.

Reise, Berthold

1982   Die Popol Vuh Peten platte. *Indiana* 7:143–157.

1984   Hel hieroglyphs. In *Phoneticism in Maya Hieroglyphic Writing,* ed. John Justeson and Lyle Campbell, 263–286. IMS Monograph No. 9. Albany: Institute for Meso-american Studies, State University of New York.

Renfrew, Colin A.

1983   The social archaeology of megalithic monuments. *Scientific American* 249:152–163.

Reynolds, Dorothy

1956   Danzas guatemaltecas. *Americas* (Pan American Union, Washington, D.C.) 2:31–35.

Ricoeur, Paul

1984   *Time and Narrative.* Vol. 1. Trans. Kathleen McLaughlin and David Pellauer. Chicago: University of Chicago Press.

Ringle, William M.

1988   *Of Mice and Monkeys: The Value and Meaning of T1016, the God C Hieroglyph.* Research Reports of Ancient Maya Writing No. 18. Washington, D.C.: Center for Maya Research.

1996   Birds of a feather: The fallen stucco inscription of Temple XVIII, Palenque, Chiapas. In *Eighth Palenque Round Table, 1993,* ed. Merle Greene Robertson, 45–61. San Francisco: Pre-Columbian Art Research Institute.

Ritzenthaler, Robert E.

1958   A Red Ochre burial in Ozaukee County. *Wisconsin Archeologist* 39:115–120.

Rivard, Jean J.

1965   Cascabeles y ojos del dios maya de la muerte, Ah Puch. *Estudios de Cultura Maya* 5:75–92.

Robertson, Merle Greene

1983   *The Sculpture of Palenque.* Vol. 1, *The Temple of the Inscriptions.* Princeton, N.J.: Princeton University Press.

1985a   *The Sculpture of Palenque.* Vol. 2, *The Early Buildings of the Palace and the Wall Painting.* Princeton, N.J.: Princeton University Press.

1985b   *The Sculpture of Palenque.* Vol. 3, *The Late Buildings of the Palace.* Princeton, N.J.: Princeton University Press.

1991   *The Sculpture of Palenque.* Vol. 4, *The Cross Group, the North Group, the Olvidado, and Other Pieces.* Princeton, N.J.: Princeton University Press.

2000   New discovery of a tomb at Palenque. *PARI Journal* 1 (1): 1–2.

Robichaux, Hubert R.

1990   The hieroglyphic texts of Rio Azul, Guatemala. Master's thesis, University of Texas at San Antonio.

Robicsek, Francis

1972   *Copan: Home of the Mayan Gods.* New York: The Museum of the American Indian.

Robicsek, Francis, and Donald M. Hales

1981   *The Maya Book of the Dead: The Ceramic Codex.* Charlottesville: University of Virginia Art Museum.

Roys, Ralph L.

1965   *Ritual of the Bacabs.* Norman: University of Oklahoma Press.

1967   *The Book of Chilam Balam of Chumayel.* Norman: University of Oklahoma Press.

Ruz Lhuillier, Alberto

1952   Exploraciones arqueológicas en Palenque 1949. *INAH Anales* 4 (32): 49–60.

1958 Exploraciones arqueológicas en Palenque 1953–1956. *INAH Anales* 10 (39): 69–299.

1961 Exploraciones arqueológicas en Palenque 1957–1958. *INAH Anales* 14 (43): 35–112.

1965 Tombs and funerary practices of the Maya lowlands. In *Handbook of Middle American Indians*, Vol. 2: *Archaeology of Southern Mesoamerica, Part 1*, ed. Gordon R. Willey, 441–461. Austin: University of Texas Press.

1968 *Costumbres funerarias de los antiguos mayas.* Mexico City: UNAM.

1973 *El Templo de las Inscripciones, Palenque.* Colección Científica Arqueológica 7. Mexico City: INAH.

Sabloff, Jeremy

1975 *Excavations at Seibal: The Ceramics.* Memoirs of the Peabody Museum of American Archaeology and Ethnography 13 (2). Cambridge: Peabody Museum, Harvard University.

Saile, David G.

1985 The ritual establishment of home. In *Home Environments,* ed. Irwin Altman and Carol M. Werner, 87–111. New York: Plenum Press.

Saler, Benson

1964 Nagual, witch and sorceror in a Quiché village. *Ethnology* 3 (3): 305–328.

Sandstrom, Alan

1991 *Corn Is Our Blood: Culture and Ethnic Identity in a Contemporary Aztec Indian Village.* Norman: University of Oklahoma Press.

Satterthwaite, Linton, Jr.

1934–1936 *Piedras Negras Preliminary Papers, Nos. 1–3, 5.* Philadelphia: University Museum, University of Pennsylvania.

1937 Identification of Maya temple buildings at Piedras Negras. *Publication of the Philadelphia Anthropological Society, Vol. 1: 25th Anniversary Studies,* ed. Daniel S. Davidson, 161–177. Philadelphia: University of Pennsylvania Press.

1943 Introduction. *Piedras Negras Architecture, Pt. 1, No. 1.* Philadelphia: University Museum, University of Pennsylvania.

1952 *Piedras Negras Archaeology: Architecture, Part VI, Unclassified Buildings and Substructures, No. 4: Structure O-7.* Philadelphia: University Museum, University of Pennsylvania.

1958 Five newly discovered carved monuments at Tikal and new data on four others. In *Tikal Reports Nos. 1–4,* ed. Edwin M. Shook, William R. Coe, Vivian L. Broman, and Linton Satterthwaite, 85–150. Museum Monograph No. 15. Philadelphia: University Museum, University of Pennsylvania.

1963 Note on hieroglyphs on bone from the tomb below Temple I, Tikal. *Expedition* 6:18–19.

1964 Dates in a new Tikal hieroglyphic text as Katun-Baktun Anniversaries. *Estudios de Cultura Maya* 4:203–222.

Satterthwaite, Linton, Vivian L. Broman, and William A. Haviland

1961 Miscellaneous investigations. In *Tikal Reports Nos. 5–10,* ed. Linton Satterthwaite, Vivian L. Broman, and William A. Haviland, 149–170. Museum Monograph No. 20. Philadelphia: University Museum, University of Pennsylvania.

Saul, Julie M., and Frank P. Saul

1991 The Preclassic population of Cuello. In *Cuello: An Early Maya Community in Belize,* ed. Norman Hammond, 134–158. Cambridge: Cambridge University Press.

Saxe, Arthur A.

1971   Social dimensions of mortuary practices in a Mesolithic population from Wadi
Halfa, Sudan. In *Approaches to the Social Dimensions of Mortuary Practices*, ed. James A.
Brown, 39–57. Memoir of the Society for American Archaeology 25. Washington,
D.C.: Society for American Archaeology.

Schele, Linda

1974   Observations on the cross motif at Palenque. In *Primera Mesa Redonda de Palenque,
Pt. 1*, ed. Merle Greene Robertson, 41–61. Pebble Beach, Calif.: Robert Louis Stevenson School.

1975   Accession iconography of Chan-Bahlam in the Group of the Cross at Palenque.
In *Segunda Mesa Redonda de Palenque, Part III*, ed. Merle Greene Robertson, 41–70.
Palenque, Chiapas, Mexico: Pre-Columbian Art Research Center.

1982   *Maya Glyphs: The Verbs*. Austin: University of Texas Press.

1985   The Hauberg Stela: Bloodletting and the mythos of Maya rulership. In *Fifth
Palenque Round Table, 1983*, ed. Virginia M. Fields, 135–149. San Francisco: Pre-
Columbian Art Research Institute.

1988   The Xibalba Shuffle: A Dance after Death. In *Maya Iconography*, ed. Elizabeth P.
Benson and Gillett G. Griffin, 294–317. Princeton, N.J.: Princeton University Press.

1991a   An epigraphic history of the western Maya region. In *Classic Maya Political History*, ed. T. Patrick Culbert, 72–101. Cambridge: Cambridge University Press.

1991b   *Notebook for the Fifteenth Maya Hieroglyphic Workshop at Texas*. Austin: Institute
of Latin American Studies, University of Texas.

1992a   The founders of lineages at Copan and other Maya sites. *Ancient Mesoamerica*
3:135–145.

1992b   *Notebook for the Sixteenth Maya Hieroglyphic Workshop at Texas*. Austin: Institute
of Latin American Studies, University of Texas.

1999   *Notebook for the Twenty-third Maya Hieroglyphic Forum at Texas, Parts I and II*.
Austin: Institute of Latin American Studies, University of Texas.

Schele, Linda, and David A. Freidel

1990   *A Forest of Kings: The Untold Story of the Ancient Maya*. New York: William
Morrow.

1991   The Courts of Creation: Ballcourts, Ballgames, and Portals to the Maya Otherworld. In *The Mesoamerican Ballgame*, ed. Vernon L. Scarborough and David R.
Wilcox, 289–315. Tucson: University of Arizona Press.

Schele, Linda, and Nikolai Grube

1991   *Speculations on Who Built the Temple under 11*. Copan Notes 102. Austin, Texas:
Copan Mosaics Project, Instituto Hondureño de Antropología e Historia.

Schele, Linda, and Matt Looper

1996   *Notebook for the Twentieth Maya Hieroglyphic Forum at Texas*. Austin: Institute of
Latin American Studies, University of Texas.

Schele, Linda, and Peter Mathews

1979   *The Bodega of Palenque*. Washington, D.C.: Dumbarton Oaks.

1991   Royal visits and other interesting relationships among the Classic Maya. In *Classic Maya Political History*, ed. T. Patrick Culbert, 226–252. Cambridge: Cambridge
University Press.

1998   *The Code of Kings: The Language of Seven Sacred Maya Temples and Tombs.* New York: Simon and Schuster.

Schele, Linda, and Mary Miller

1986   *The Blood of Kings: Dynasty and Ritual in Maya Art.* Fort Worth, Texas: Kimbell Art Museum.

Schele, Linda, and David Stuart

1986   *Butz'-Chaan, the 11th Successor of the Yax-K'uk'-Mo' Lineage.* Copan Notes 14. Austin, Texas: Copan Mosaics Project, Instituto Hondureño de Antropología e Historia.

Schellas, Paul

1904   *Representation of Deities of the Maya Manuscripts.* Papers of the Peabody Museum of American Archaeology and Ethnology 4 (1). Cambridge: Peabody Museum, Harvard University.

Scherer, Andrew, and Lori Wright

2000   Los esqueletos de Piedras Negras: Reporte Preliminar No. 4. In *Proyecto Arqueológico Piedras Negras, Informe Preliminar No. 4, Cuarta Temporada 2000,* ed. Héctor Escobedo and Stephen Houston, 553–558. Guatemala City: IDAEH.

Scherer, Andrew, Cassidy Yoder, and Lori Wright

1999   Los esqueletos de Piedras Negras: Reporte Preliminar No. 3. In *Proyecto Arqueológico Piedras Negras, Informe Preliminar No. 3, Tercera Temporada 1999,* ed Héctor Escobedo and Stephen Houston, 387–400. Guatemala City: IDAEH.

Sharer, Robert J.

1988   Quirigua as a Classic Maya center. In *The Southeast Classic Maya Zone,* ed. Elizabeth Boone and Gordon Willey, 31–65. Washington, D.C.: Dumbarton Oaks.

1990   *Quirigua: A Classic Maya Center and Its Sculptures.* Durham, N.C.: Carolina Academic Press.

1996   Patterns of architectural growth in the Early Classic Copan Acropolis. Paper presented at the 61st Annual Meeting of the Society for American Archaeology, New Orleans.

1997a   Early Copan Acropolis Program 1995–1997 field seasons: Latest findings at Copan, Honduras. Report submitted to FAMSI, located at http://www.famsi.org/reports/sharer/sharer.htm.

1997b   *Yax K'uk' Mo' and Copan's Early External Connections.* Early Copan Acropolis Paper 11. Philadelphia: University Museum, University of Pennsylvania.

2000   Early Copan Acropolis Program 2000 season. Report submitted to FAMSI, located at http://www.famsi.org/reports/sharer3/sharer3.htm.

2002   Report of the 1996 field season of the Early Copán Acropolis Program. Report submitted to FAMSI, located at http://www.famsi.org/reports/sharer96/sharer96.htm.

Sharer, Robert J., and Wendy Ashmore

1979   *Quirigua Reports.* Vol. 1, *Papers 1–5.* University Museum Monograph 37. Philadelphia: University of Pennsylvania.

Sharer, Robert J., Loa Traxler, David Sedat, Ellen Bell, Marcello Canuto, and Chris Powell

1999   Early Classic architecture beneath the Copan Acropolis. *Ancient Mesoamerica* 10:3–23.

Shook, Edwin M.

　1958　Field director's report: The 1956 and 1957 seasons. In *Tikal Reports Nos. 1–4,* ed. Edwin M. Shook, William R. Coe, Vivian L. Broman, and Linton Satterthwaite, 1–22. Museum Monograph No. 15. Philadelphia: University Museum, University of Pennsylvania.

Shook, Edwin M., William R. Coe, Vivian L. Broman, and Linton Satterthwaite (eds.)

　1958　*Tikal Reports Nos. 1–4.* Philadelphia: University Museum, University of Pennsylvania.

Shyrock, Andrew J.

　1987　The Wright Mound reexamined: Generative structures and the political economy of a simple chiefdom. *Midcontinental Journal of Archaeology* 12:243–268.

Smith, Augustus Ledyard

　1937　*Structure A-XVIII, Uaxactun.* Carnegie Institution of Washington Publication 483, No. 20. Washington, D.C.: Carnegie Institution.

　1950　*Uaxactun, Guatemala: Excavations of 1931–1937.* Carnegie Institution of Washington Publication 588. Washington, D.C.: Carnegie Institution.

　1971　*Excavations at Altar de Sacrificios: Architecture, Settlement, Burials and Caches.* Papers of the Peabody Museum of American Archaeology and Ethnology 62 (2). Cambridge: Peabody Museum, Harvard University.

Smith, Augustus Ledyard, and Gordon R. Willey

　1964–1968　*Seibal Preliminary Reports 1–5.* Cambridge: Peabody Museum, Harvard University.

Smith, Robert E.

　1937　*A Study of Structure A-I Complex at Uaxactun, Peten, Guatemala.* Carnegie Institution of Washington Publication 456, No. 19. Washington, D.C.: Carnegie Institution.

Sosa, John R.

　1988　The Maya sky, the Maya world: A symbolic analysis of Yucatec Maya cosmology. Ph.D. diss., State University of New York at Albany.

Spence, Lewis

　1923　*The Gods of Mexico.* London: T. F. Unwin.

　1947　*Myth and Ritual in Dance, Game and Rhyme.* London: Watts.

Steele, D. Gentry

　1986　The skeletal remains from Rio Azul, 1984 season. In *Rio Azul Reports No. 2, the 1984 Season,* ed. Richard Adams, 117–121. San Antonio: Center for Archaeological Research.

Stone, Andrea

　1995　*Images from the Underworld: Naj Tunich and the Tradition of Maya Cave Painting.* Austin: University of Texas Press.

　2005　Scribes and caves in the Maya lowlands. In *Stone Houses and Earth Lords: Maya Religion in the Cave Context,* ed. Keith M. Prufer and James E. Brady, 135–148. Boulder: University Press of Colorado.

Storey, Rebecca

　1992　*Life and Death in the Ancient City of Teotihuacan: A Modern Paleodemographic Synthesis.* Tuscaloosa: University of Alabama Press.

Stromsvik, Gustav

1941 Substela caches and stela foundations at Copan and Quirigua. *Contributions to American Archaeology* 7 (37): 63–96.

Stross, Brian

1998 Seven ingredients in Mesoamerican ensoulment: Dedication and termination in Tenejapa. In *The Sowing and the Dawning,* ed. Shirley Boteler Mock, 31–39. Albuquerque: University of New Mexico Press.

Stuart, David

1985 The inscription on four shell plaques from Piedras Negras, Guatemala. In *Fourth Palenque Round Table,* ed. Merle Greene Robertson, 175–184. San Francisco: Pre-Columbian Art Research Institute.

1988 Blood symbolism in Maya iconography. In *Maya Iconography,* ed. Elizabeth P. Benson and Gillett G. Griffin, 175–221. Princeton, N.J.: Princeton University Press.

1990 Hieroglyphic miscellanea. Manuscript on file, Department of Anthropology, Harvard University, Cambridge.

1992 Hieroglyphs and archaeology at Copan. *Ancient Mesoamerica* 3:169–184.

1994 The texts of Temple 26: Analysis of a Classic Maya dynastic shrine at Copan. Manuscript on file, Department of Anthropology, Harvard University, Cambridge.

1995 A study of Maya inscriptions. Ph.D. diss., Vanderbilt University, Nashville, Tenn.

1996 Kings of stone: A consideration of stelae in ancient Maya ritual and representation. *RES: Anthropology and Aesthetics* 29/30:148–71.

1997 Kinship terms in Maya inscriptions. In *The Language of Maya Hieroglyphs,* ed. Martha Macri and Anabel Ford, 1–11. San Francisco: Pre-Columbian Research Institute.

1998 "The fire enters his house": Architecture and ritual in Classic Maya texts. In *Function and Meaning in Classic Maya Architecture,* ed. Stephen D. Houston, 373–425. Washington, D.C.: Dumbarton Oaks.

1999 The new inscriptions of Temple XIX. Paper presented at the 1999 Palenque Round Table, Palenque, Mexico.

2000a The arrival of strangers: Teotihuacan and Tollan in Classic Maya History. In *Mesoamerica's Classic Heritage: From Teotihuacan to the Aztecs,* ed. David Carrasco, Lindsay Jones, and Scott Sessions, 465–513. Boulder: University Press of Colorado.

2000b Ritual and history in the stucco inscription from Temple XIX at Palenque. *PARI Journal* 1 (1): 13–19.

2003 Los ciudades de Hixwitz. Paper presented for the XVI Simposio de Investigaciones Arqueológicas, Museo Nacional de Arqueología y Etnología, Guatemala City.

n.d. The ajaw as flower. Manuscript in possession of the author.

Stuart, David, and James Fitzsimmons

n.d. Conjuring and creating: Some operating principles of Classic Maya rituals. Unpublished manuscript in possession of the authors.

Stuart, David, and Stephen Houston

1994 *Classic Maya Place Names.* Studies in Pre-Columbian Art and Archaeology 33. Washington, D.C.: Dumbarton Oaks.

Stuart, George

1997 The royal crypts of Copan. *National Geographic* 192 (6): 68–93.

Tainter, Joseph R.

1975   Social inference and mortuary practices: An experiment in numerical classification. *World Archaeology* 7:1–15.

Tate, Carolyn E.

1992   *Yaxchilan: The Design of a Maya Ceremonial City.* Austin: University of Texas
Press.

Taube, Karl A.

1983   The Teotihuacan spider woman. *Journal of Latin American Lore* 2:107–189.

1985   The Classic Maya maize god: A reappraisal. In *Fifth Palenque Round Table,* ed.
Virginia M. Fields, 171–181. San Francisco: Pre-Columbian Art Research Institute.

1988   The ancient Yucatec New Year festival: The liminal period in Maya ritual and
cosmology. Ph.D. diss., Yale University, New Haven, Conn.

1992   *The Major Gods of Ancient Yucatan.* Studies in Pre-Columbian Art and Archaeology No. 32. Washington, D.C.: Dumbarton Oaks Research Library and Collection.

1993   *Aztec and Maya Myths.* Austin: University of Texas Press.

1998   The jade hearth: Centrality, rulership, and the Classic Maya temple. In *Function
and Meaning in Maya Architecture,* ed. Stephen Houston, 427–478. Washington, D.C.:
Dumbarton Oaks.

2000   The Classic Maya gods. In *Maya: Divine Kings of the Rain Forest,* ed. Nikolai
Grube, 262–277. Cologne, Germany: Koenemann Verlagsgesellschaft mbH.

2001   The breath of life: The symbolism of wind in Mesoamerica and the American
Southwest. In *The Road to Aztlan: Art from a Mythic Homeland,* ed. Virginia M. Fields
and V. Zamudio-Taylor, 102–123. Los Angeles: Los Angeles County Museum of Art.

2003   La iconografía de los murales de San Bartolo, Guatemala. Paper presented for the
XVI Simposio de Investigaciones Arqueológicas en Guatemala, Museo Nacional de
Arqueología y Etnología de Guatemala.

2004   Flower mountain: Concepts of life, beauty, and paradise among the Classic
Maya. *RES: Anthropology and Aesthetics* 45:69–98.

Tedlock, Barbara

1982   *Time and the Highland Maya.* Albuquerque: University of New Mexico Press.

Tedlock, Dennis

1985   *Popol Vuh: The Mayan Book of the Dawn of Life.* New York: Simon and Schuster.

Thompson, Edward H.

1895   Palenque. *Proceedings of the American Antiquarian Society* 10 (1): 191–194.

Thompson, J. Eric S.

1929   Maya chronology: Glyph G of the Lunar Series. *American Anthropologist*
31:223–231.

1931   *Archaeological Investigations in the Southern Cayo District, British Honduras.* Anthropological Series 17–3, Field Museum of Natural History Publication 301. Chicago: University of Chicago Press.

1960   *Maya Hieroglyphic Writing: An Introduction.* Norman: University of Oklahoma
Press.

1962   *A Catalog of Maya Hieroglyphs.* Norman: University of Oklahoma Press.

1970   *Maya History and Religion.* Norman: University of Oklahoma Press.

Tiesler Blos, Vera

2004   Maya mortuary treatments of the elite: An osteotaphonomic perspective. In *Con-*

tinuity and Change: Maya Religious Practices in Temporal Perspective, ed. Daniel Graña Behrens, Nikolai Grube, Christian M. Prager, Frauke Sachse, Stefanie Teufel, and Elisabeth Wagner, 143–156. Acta Mesoamericana 14. Markt Schwaben, Germany: Verlag Antón Saurwein.

Tiesler Blos, Vera, and Andrea Cucina

2003 Sacrificio, tratamiento y ofrenda del cuerpo humano entre los mayas del Clásico: Una mirada bioarqueológica. In *Antropología de la eternidad: La muerte en la cultura maya,* ed. Andrés Ciudad Ruiz, M. Humberto Ruz Sosa, and M. Josefa Iglesias Ponce de León, 337–354. Madrid: SEEM.

Tiesler Blos, Vera, Andrea Cucina, and Arturo Romano Pacheco

2002 Vida y muerte del personaje en el Templo XIII-sub Palenque: Culto funerario y sacrificio humano. *Mexicon* 24 (4): 75–78.

Tourtellot, Gair, III

1988 Developmental cycles of households and houses at Seibal. In *Household and Community in the Mesoamerican Past,* ed. Richard Wilk and Wendy Ashmore, 97–120. Albuquerque: University of New Mexico Press.

Tozzer, Alfred Marston

1907 Survivals of ancient forms of culture among the Mayas of Yucatan and the Lacandones of Chiapas. *15th International Congress of Americanists, 1906, Quebec, Tome II,* 283–288. Quebec City, Quebec: International Congress of Americanists.

1941 *Landa's Relación de las Cosas de Yucatán.* Papers of the Peabody Museum of American Archaeology and Ethnology 18. Cambridge: Peabody Museum, Harvard University.

Trik, Aubrey

1963 The splendid tomb of Temple I at Tikal, Guatemala. *Expedition* 6:2–18.

Turner, Victor

1967 *The Forest of Symbols.* Ithaca, N.Y.: Cornell University Press.

1969 *The Ritual Process.* Chicago: University of Chicago Press.

Ucko, Peter J.

1962 The interpretation of prehistoric anthropomorphic figurines. *Journal of the Royal Anthropological Institute of Great Britain and Ireland* 92 (1): 38–54.

Urcid, Javier

1993 *Bones and Epigraphy: The Accurate Versus the Fictitious?* Texas Note 42. Austin: Center of the History and Art of Ancient American Culture, Art Department, University of Texas at Austin.

Valdés, Juan Antonio

1982 Uaxactun: Recientes investigaciones. *Mexicon* 8 (6): 125–128.

1997 Tamarandito: Archaeology and regional politics in the Petexbatún region. *Ancient Mesoamerica* 8:321–335.

Valdés, Juan Antonio, Federico Fahsen, and Héctor L. Escobedo

1999 *Reyes, tumbas y palacios: La historia dinástica de Uaxactun.* Centro de Estudios Mayas, Cuaderno 25. Mexico City: UNAM; Guatemala City: Instituto de Antropología de Guatemala.

van Gennep, Arnold

1960 *The Rites of Passage.* Trans. Monika A. Vicedom and Solon T. Kimball. Chicago: University of Chicago Press.

Verano, John

1997   Human remains from Tomb 1, Sipán, and their social implications. *Antiquity* 71 (273): 670–682.

Villela, Khristaan D.

1991a   *The Death of Lady Wak Chan Tzuk of Naranjo Recorded at Dos Pilas.* Texas Note 18. Austin: Center of the History and Art of Ancient American Culture, Art Department, University of Texas at Austin.

1991b   *Early Notices on the Maya Paddler Gods.* Texas Note 17. Austin: Center of the History and Art of Ancient American Culture, Art Department, University of Texas at Austin.

Vogt, Evon Z.

1966   Ancestor worship in Zinacantan religion. *International Congress of Americanists* 36:281–285.

1969   *Zinacantan: A Maya Community in the Highlands of Chiapas.* Cambridge: The Belknap Press of Harvard University Press.

1970a   Human souls and animal spirits in Zinacantan. In *Éxchanges et Communications: Mélanges offerts a Claude Lévi-Strauss a l'occasion de son 60éme anniversaire,* ed. Jean Pouillon and Pierre Maranda, 1148–1167. The Hague, Netherlands: Editions Mouton.

1970b   *The Zinacantecos of Mexico.* New York: Holt, Rinehart and Winston.

1976   *Tortillas for the Gods: A Symbolic Analysis of Zinacanteco Rituals.* Cambridge: Harvard University Press.

1998   Zinacanteco dedication and termination rituals. In *The Sowing and the Dawning,* ed. Shirley Boteler Mock, 21–30. Albuquerque: University of New Mexico Press.

Walker, Debra Selsor

1998   Smashed pots and shattered dreams. In *The Sowing and the Dawning,* ed. Shirley Boteler Mock, 81–98. Albuquerque: University of New Mexico Press.

Watanabe, John M.

1992   *Maya Saints and Souls in a Changing World.* Austin: University of Texas Press.

Wauchope, Robert

1948   *Excavations at Zacualpa, Guatemala.* MARI Publication 14: 565–568. New Orleans: Middle American Research Institute, Tulane University.

Webster, David

1989   The house of the Bacabs: Its social context. In *The House of the Bacabs, Copan, Honduras,* ed. David Webster, 5–40. Studies in Pre-Columbian Art and Archaeology 29. Washington, D.C.: Dumbarton Oaks.

1997   Studying Maya burials. In *Bones of the Maya,* ed. Stephen L. Whittington and David M. Reed, 3–14. Washington, D.C.: Smithsonian Institution Press.

Weiss-Krejci, Estella

2003   Victims of human sacrifice in multiple tombs of the ancient Maya: A critical review. In *Antropología de la eternidad: La muerte en la cultura maya,* ed. Andrés Ciudad Ruiz, Mario Humberto Ruz Sosa, and M. Josefa Iglesias Ponce de León, 355–382. Madrid: SEEM.

2004   Mortuary representations of the noble house: A cross-cultural comparison between collective tombs of the ancient Maya and dynastic Europe. *Journal of Social Archaeology* 4 (3): 368–404.

2006   The Maya corpse: Body processing from Preclassic to Postclassic times in the

Maya highlands and lowlands. In *Jaws of the Underworld: Life, Death, and Rebirth among the Ancient Maya*, ed. Pierre Colas, Geneviève LeFort, and Bodil Liljefors Persson, 71–88. Acta Mesoamericana 16. Schwaben, Germany: Verlag Anton Saurwein.

Weiss-Krejci, Estella, and T. Patrick Culbert

1995 Preclassic and Classic burials and caches in the Maya lowlands. In *The Emergence of Lowland Maya Civilization,* ed. Nikolai Grube, 101–116. Acta Mesoamericana 8. Möckmühl, Germany: Verlag Anton Saurwein.

Wells, E. Christian

1998 PN26: Excavaciones en el área habitacional en la Plaza del Grupo Noroeste, Estructura F-2. In *Proyecto Arqueológico Piedras Negras, Informe Preliminar No. 2, Segunda Temporada 1999,* ed. Héctor Escobedo and Stephen Houston, 143–156. Guatemala City: IDAEH.

1999 PN33: Investigaciones en un conjunto residencial del Cuadrante U. In *Proyecto Arqueológico Piedras Negras, Informe Preliminar No. 3, Tercera Temporada 1999,* ed. Héctor Escobedo and Stephen Houston, 65–104. Guatemala City: IDAEH.

Welsh, W. Bruce M.

1988 *An Analysis of Classic Lowland Maya Burials.* Bar International Series 409. Oxford: Archaeopress.

Willey, Gordon

1974 The Classic Maya hiatus: A rehearsal for the collapse? In *Mesoamerican Archaeology: New Approaches,* ed. Norman Hammond, 417–430. Austin: University of Texas Press.

1975–1990 (gen. ed.) *Excavations at Seibal, Department of Peten, Guatemala.* Memoirs of the Peabody Museum of American Archaeology and Ethnology 14–17. Cambridge: Peabody Museum, Harvard University.

Willey, Gordon, and Augustus Ledyard Smith

1969 *The Ruins of Altar de Sacrificios, Department of Peten, Guatemala, An Introduction.* Papers of the Peabody Museum of American Archaeology and Ethnology 62 (1). Cambridge: Peabody Museum, Harvard University.

Wilson, Richard

1995 *Maya Resurgence in Guatemala: Q'eqchi' Experiences.* Norman: University of Oklahoma Press.

Winters, Diane

1988 A study of the fish-in-hand glyph, T714: Part I. In *Fifth Palenque Round Table,* ed. Merle Greene Robertson, 233–245. Pebble Beach, Calif.: Robert Louis Stevenson School.

Wisdom, Charles

1974 *The Chorti' Indians of Guatemala.* Chicago: University of Chicago Press.

Woodbury, Richard B., and Aubrey S. Trik

1953 *The Ruins of Zaculeu, Guatemala.* Richmond: University of Virginia Press.

Zender, Marc, and Joel Skidmore

2000 On the new Palenque ruler's name. *PARI Journal* 1 (1): 20.

INDEX

Note: Italic page numbers indicate figures and tables. Plate numbers indicate plates.

Adams, Richard E. W., 68–69

afterlife: amalgamations of Christian and native conceptions of, 12–13; bifurcated nature of, 52; *cham* as root for words, 26; Classic Maya beliefs about, 11, 15; and Classic Maya royalty, 15, 53, 57, 58–59; cultural attitudes toward, 2; and deification of ancestors, 57; ethnographic data on, 3, 10, 59; and Merina funeral rites, 6; and nonroyal elite, 59; and royal death, 180; souls' afterlife journeys, 43, 48, 177, 182; and status levels, 16

Agurcia, Ricardo, 108

Ahau day name, 28

ajaw "lord," 27–28, 29, 47

Akan, 31

alligators, as metaphor for earth, 67

Altar de Sacrificios: bone "use" evidence, 167; and bowl coverings, 92; burial patterns of, 12; and burning patterns, 75; and sealing tombs, 103; and shell artifacts, 218n93; and wooden or stone platforms, 85

Altar de Sacrificios Burial 128, 92

Altun Ha: bone "use" evidence, 167; burial patterns of, 12, 135; and caches, 103; and jade and shell offerings, 71, 87; and mirrors, 97; and multiple interments, 93; and new construction of royal interments, 115; and sealing tombs, 103; and

shell artifacts, 90, 218n93; and wooden or stone platforms, 85

Alvarez Heidenreich, Laurencia, 40

ancestors: and Bird Jaguar IV, 120–123, 125, 129, 176, 181; as celestial bodies, 53, 55; Classic Maya royalty as, 53, 58–59; deification of, 57, 58, 122, 123, 127, 129, 215n133; effect of royal death on, 180; ethnographic data on, 10; and founders, 105–106, 107, 117, 118, 122–123, 134; and genealogy of place, 180–181; inequality of, 60; kingship concentrated in ancestral spirit, 172; and landscape, 127; and legitimacy, 171, 181, 182, 183; and lineage rights, 123; masks serving as proxies for, 225n62; Maya residence as receptacle of, 105; and monuments, 119–120, 123, 134, 141, 171; physical representations of, 42; and power hierarchies, 119; religious and political role of, 142; and tomb reentry, 144

ancestor veneration: and caches, 103, 135; and Classic Maya religion, 2; in Classic Maya texts, 13, 15; and cults of personality, 117–120; and dancing, 155–156; and disturbed burials, 16; and face removal, 168; and liminality, 182; and lineage mountains and caves, 18; nature of, 15–16; and offerings, 135, 149; and Piedras Negras, 155; and political manipulation, 171; and portable representations, 169, 225n72; and reshaping of past, 181; and Rosalila Temple, 111, 115; and royal death, 180; and soul, 13; structures for, 134–135, 181; and tomb reentry, 210n43

ancestral bundles, 78, 80, 172

ancestral effigies, 41, 42, 78, 168, 172

ancestral relics, 75

ánima, 42, 43

animal spirit-companion: and concepts of death, 13, 15; and concepts of souls, 39, 42–43; and soul-loss, 39. *See also way* "coessences" or "animal spirit companions"

anthropological theory, and ethnographic information, 3

anthropophagy, and maize consumption, 25

Arbman, Ernst, 213n84

archaeological anthropology, 10

archaeology: and ancestor veneration, 155; and animation of buildings, 132; and *b'aah*, 41; and burial sequences, 97; and Classic Maya death rituals, 10; and Classic Maya iconographic records, 3; and Classic Maya ideology, 11; and Co-pan Motmot burial, 159; and determining means of coloring, 82; ethnographic parallels used in, 3; and founder model, 106; and funerary rituals, 61; of *och k'ahk'*, 156; and royal interment, 70; and study of death, 1; and tomb reentry, 142, 145, 162; and Underworld, 48

autonomy/society tension, 4

-aw, 26

axis mundi, 132, 133, 137. *See also* World Tree

Aztecs: and afterlife, 59; and ancestor bundles, 78, 80, 172; concept of Underworld, 50, 52; and death of children, 17; and *ihiyotl*, 43, 44; and layers of Underworld, 49; and maize, 25; and sealing tombs, 103; and souls, 40–41; and *tlatoani*, 43

Aztec Templo Mayor, 70

b'aah "self, person, head," 41, *41,* 42, 47, 48, 131, 168

B'alam Quitze, 80

ballcourts, 72, 159, 211n6

bank-likal muk'ta vits "senior large mountain," 46

Bara (in Madagascar), 6

Batz Chan Mat, 66, 101

Beaubien, Harriet, 83, 110

bedrock, and tomb construction, 66–67

belief systems: and Classic Maya religion, 2, 35; and Classic Maya Underworld, 53; evolving nature of, 11; and funerary rites, 181; and phrasing of death, 11, 28, 29–31, 33–39; similarities and differences in Maya lowlands, 16; and souls, 39–42; and Underworld, 10

Bell, Catherine, 6

Berawan (in Borneo), 4–5

Berlin vessel: and ancestors as plants, 127, 215n133; and bundling, 76; depiction of funerary rites on, 61, *62;* and Maize God, 57, 215n131

bih "road," 33

Bird Jaguar III of Yaxchilan, 120

Bird Jaguar IV of Yaxchilan: and ancestors, 120–123, 125, 129, 176, 181; and legitimacy claims, 175; and Yoaat B'alam II, 177

birds: avian remains, 96; and human-animal associations, 96, 218n104

Bloch, Maurice, 181

Blom, Franz, 161, 167

bloodletting artifacts, 88, *89,* 90, 96, 218n88

bloodletting bowls, and ancestor veneration, 15

bloodletting rites: and ancestors, 122; and conjuring, 139, 148; and obsidian, 88; and *tuun*-binding, 81

Blood Woman, 139

body politic versus body natural, and royal succession, 16, 172

body preparations: body processing, 74–75; and funerary ritual, *194–201*

body/soul relationship: and changing societal roles and relations, 6–7; and corpse, 2, 5, 171, 181–183; and death rituals, 1–2, 5, 182; and liminality, 7, 182

Bolon K'uh (Nine God), 108, 220n12

Bolon-K'uhnal, 49

Bonampak, 97

bone needles, as bloodletting artifacts, 90

The Book of Chilam Balam of Chumayel, 13

Borneo: Goody's and Metcalf's fieldwork in, 5–6; Hertz's fieldwork in, 1–2, 4–5

bowl coverings, 92–93

breath: breath of life and breath of death contrasted, 31, 44; fragrant flowers connected with, 27; jade artifacts representing, 87, 88, 218n81; and phrasing death, 28–31; solar breath, 222n63; souls connected with, 27; white flower breath phrases, 11, 13, 28, *28*, 29–31, 34, 38, 42, 43, 44, 47–48, 177. *See also ik' "*breath, life, spirit"

breath escaping from nostrils as *t'ab'ay*, 27, plate 4

bundling: ancestor bundles, 78, 80, 172; and body processing, 75, 76–81; and Calakmul, 76, 216–217n46; god bundles, 78, 79, *79;* incorporation of artifacts in, 80–81, *80;* and king's continued rule after death, 172; and localizing remains of deceased ruler, 81; mortuary bundles, 81; and mummy bundles, 76–77; and painting, 81, 82; remains of cremated bundles, 78; and Río Azul, 76

Bunzel, Ruth, 24, 44, 100

burial patterns: of Altun Ha, 12, 135; and burial sequences, 97–98, 100–101; of Dzibilchaltun, 12, 216n39; and human sacrifice, 2, 65, 74, 75; of Tikal, 12, 180

burials: classification schemes for, 64; as collections of ideas, 97; and genealogy of place, 180; intrusive burials, 67–68; lapse of time between death and interment, 61–64; primary burials, 162; red ochre in, 82, 217n66; red-paint burials, 81–83, 164; regional and temporal nature of, 83; secondary burials, 5, 79, 162; stone-platform burials, 85; verbs used for, 34

burial structures: summary of, *188–193. See also* funerary structures; tomb construction; tombs

burning patterns: and ancestor shrines, 135–137; and Caracol, 101, 135, 136–137; and conjuring, 137; and Copan, 101, 110,

135; and royal interments, 75, 101; and sealing tombs, 101–102, 137, 142, 159; and tomb reentry, 159–160. *See also* fire

Butz' Chan, 166

caches, 71, 72, 102–103, 135, 158

Calakmul: and bundling, 76, 216–217n46; and burning patterns, 75; and ceramic vessels, 87; and jade artifacts, 87; and psychoducts, 131; and royals missing body parts, 75; and shell artifacts, 90; *way* of, *45,* 47, plates 6–7

Calakmul Structure II, Tomb 4, 216n43

Calakmul Structure III, 87, 130–131

Calakmul Structure VII, 87

Calakmul Structure VII, Tomb I, 78, 216–217n46

Calvin, Inga, 46

"canoe" glyph, 35, 37, 38

Caracol: and ancestor shrines, 135; and bloodletting artifacts, 90; and burning patterns, 101, 135, 136–137; and caches, 158; and familial mausoleums, 161–162; finger-bowl caches of, 167; and interregnum, 176; jade and shell offerings in, 71; and *sakb'ih*, 33; and sealing tombs, 103; and tomb reentry, 142, 144–145, 162; and *way,* 47

Caracol Stela 6, 142, *143*

Caracol Structure A3, 219n119

Caracol Structure A34, 162

Caracol Structure B19–2nd, 136, *136*, 164, 219n119

Caracol Structure B20, 90, 113–114, 137, 163–164

Caracol Structure B20–2nd, 72, 137

Caracol Structure B20–3rd, 163

Caracol Structure B20–4th, 163

Carlsen, Robert, 76, 81

carved bloodletter, and identification of royal interments, 11

carved ornaments, 88

Castillo, Chichén Itzá, 49

caves: and ancestor veneration, 18; as entrances to Underworld, 71; as faces of gods, 42; and lithics for sealing tombs,

103–104; marine objects alluding to, 90; and Maya art and architecture, 18; mirrors associated with, 96; replicated within funerary structures, 18; tombs as, 71–72, 104, 132

celestial bodies, Classic Maya royalty as, 53, 55

cenotaphs, 141

ceramics in large quantity, and identification of royal interments, 11, 83, 84

ceramic vessels: and burial sequences, 98, *99;* and Classic Maya Underworld, 49–50, 52, 87; and death as sacrifice, 60; and entrance to Underworld, 149, *150;* and grave furniture, 85, 87; and headdresses, 133; and *ihiyotl,* 47–48; and Maize God, 53, 57, 215n131; and *och ha',* 68; rebirth imagery of, 83; ritually important skeletal elements in, 167; and royal interments, 83; and souls' journeys, 48; and watery bands, 50, 61, 71; and watery resting places, 35, 70; and *way,* 46, 47–48

ceremonial duties, and interment, 90

ceremonial platforms, and royal interments, 65

Chaak (Maya god of lightning): and Bird Jaguar IV, 121; and ceramic vessels, 88; Classic Maya royalty impersonating, 57; and death rituals, 8; depictions of, 20, 21, plate 2; and tomb reentry, 149

ch'ab' ak'ab' "penance-darkness": and ancestor veneration, 15; and conjuring ceremonies, 137; and power hierarchies, 118–119, 170

Chak Suutz', 115

Chak Tok Ich'aak I (Jaguar Paw) of Tikal, 36, 112–113

Chak Xib Chaak, 59, 127, 129

chambers, definition of, 65

cham "death verb," 26–27, *26,* 29, 31, 37, 42, 43

cham-hol "dried-up corn silk," 26

cham-i "death verb," 26, 37, 38, 211n25

cham-i ti ? tuun "at/to (the) ? stone," 37

Chan Ahk of Hix Witz, 31, 37

change and transformation: in ceramic vessels, 87, 96; from dead state to ancestral state, 67, 181; and death as phased, 60; and escape from Underworld, 53; and liminality, 5; and *och,* 31, 33–35; and *och ha',* 35–36, 43; and phrasing of death, 38; and royal interment, 181; and sealing tombs, 104

ch'anul "shadow," 39, 46, 47

Chapman, Robert, 209n2

Chase, Arlen, 137, 141, 162, 163, 169

Chase, Diane, 136, 137, 141, 144–145, 162, 163, 169

Chax Xib Chaak, Classic Maya royalty impersonating, 53

ch'ay ik' "extinguished breath," 28

ch'een "cave," 71

Chichén Itzá, Castillo, 49

Chichicatenango, 100, 151

chocolate, 87

ch'ok "sprout," 22, 57

Ch'orti': and *b'i'r,* 33; and *cham,* 26; and *k'a,* 28–29; and "night air," 43, 44; and *sak ik',* 13

Christianity: and evolving nature of Classic Maya religion, 12–13; and god eating, 25; influence of, 48

chuchajaw, 100, 101

ch'uhlel "inner souls, of the earth": and *b'aah,* 41, 42, 47; and cinnabar or hematite as symbolic blood, 82; divisions of, 39–40; and eating of the earth, 25; and ideas of self, 42, 131; and maize plants, 24; stages of, 43; and *tonalli,* 40–41; as type of soul, 39, 48

cinnabar: as decoration for wooden or stone platforms, 85; and painting royal bodies, 81, 82, 83, 164; and textiles, 84; and tomb reentry, 158, 159

cist, as term, 64

Classic Maya: art and architecture, 18, 48, 82, 83; cities of, 7, *8;* as people of corn, 22; royal focus of inscriptions, 10

Classic Maya Death Gods: and causes of death, 50; and *kis,* 31; and *u'uk ha' nal,* 35; and *way,* 47

Classic Maya ideology: general patterns of, 11, 210n35; and maize, 25, 57; Ruz Lhuillier on, 2; and souls, 41

Classic Maya religion: archaeological evidence and iconographic records, 3; and belief systems, 2, 35; and conjuring, 137, 139–140; continuity in, 15; evolving nature of, 11, 12–13, 57; and hieroglyphs, 2; and interregnum, 177; and physical representations of ancestors, 42; and royal succession, 179; Ruz Lhuillier on, 2; and temple-house-censer model, 133; and World Tree, 214n120

Classic Maya royalty: and afterlife, 15, 53, 57, 58–59; as celestial bodies, 53, 54; death and accession dates at Classic Maya sites, 173–175; death and burial dates of Classic Maya Rulers, 63; death as causal result of trickery, soul-loss, or active choice, 50, 226n22; as embodiment of temple, 133; as focus of inscriptions, 10–11; and Hero Twins, 53; as impersonating deities, 53, 57; individual and theoretical views of kingship, 172; and k'uhul in title, 41; moral authority of, 170, 171, 179, 183; multiple deaths and souls for, 58; portraits representing self, 42; portrayed as Maize Gods, 22, 23, 25, 57; problem of royal death, 171; and process of transformation into ancestor, 16; rationale for death, 25; religious and political role of, 170; subordinates of, 170, 171, 176, 177, 179; and use of term royal, 11–12; and way, 46–47; writing death, 25–31, 33–39. See also dead kings/successors relationship

Classic Maya Underworld: conceptions of, 13, 14, 16, 48, 214n108; iconographic depictions of, 15; inhabitants of, 50, 52, 214n119; layers of, 48, 49–50, 52, 70; and lithics for sealing tombs, 103, 104; Lords of the Underworld as captives, 50, 51; solar mythology of, 13; tests of, 52, 53, 59; watery associations of, 35, 37, 50, 61, 70, 90, 92, 158; and way, 50; and wayoob', 46.

See also Otherworld; Underworld; Upperworld; Xibalba

clays: and body processing, 75, 78; clay whistles and child interments, 65; and Smoke Imix, 85

Codex Borgia, 103

Codex Vaticanus, 49

Coe, Michael, 11, 72, 74, 81, 93, 97, 103, 135

Colha', 167

Colonial Period sources: and Classic Maya Underworld, 15; and concepts of mortality, 17; and metaphors for earth, 211n6

conjuring ceremonies: and appearance of ancestors, 167; creatures summoned in, 159; and dressing as supernaturals to be conjured, 139; and proximity to ancestors, 137; soul of king available for, 182; and tomb reentry, 149, 158; verbal and physical gestures in, 148

copal, and sealing tombs, 101, 137

Copal Groups 9N-8, 115

Copal Groups 10L-2, 115

Copan: and ancestor shrines, 135; and bloodletting artifacts, 90; and bowl coverings, 218n94; and bundling, 76; and burning patterns, 101, 110, 135; and ceramic vessels, 87; and Classic Maya royalty, 53; classification scheme for burials, 64; early vitality of polity, 108, 220n9; and fire in sealing tombs, 101; and founders, 110–111, 115, 122; and interregnums, 172, 175, 176; local burial patterns, 12; and observation of royal anniversaries, 7; and painting royal bodies, 83; place-names of, 49; Rosalila Temple, 58, 59; and sealing tombs, 103; and self and temple, 133; studies on, 107–108; and textiles, 85; and tomb reentry, 142; and wooden or stone platforms, 85; and wrapped monumental stones, 81

Copan Altar Q, 57, 58, 111, 152

Copan Altar T, 19, 21

Copan Burial XXXVII-4: and burial sequences, 97; and burning patterns, 135–136; and clay casing, 78; and emergence from Underworld, 70, 71; and layering of artifacts, 84; marine objects in, 70; and sealing tomb with fire, 219n118; and Temple 26, 112; as tomb of Smoke Imix, 70; and watery descent themes, 68; wooden bier in, 85

Copan Hieroglyphic Stairway, 28, 136, 156

Copan Hunal interment, 85

Copan Margarita complex: and burning patterns, 135, 219n119; and cave-like interior passages, 72; and commemoration of dead, 135; and "Dazzler" vessel, 133; and jade and other artifacts near pelvis, 88, 90; and painting royal bodies, 82, 164; rulers' participation in creation of, 226n22; and sealing tomb, 104; and site core, 108, 110; and stone-platform burials, 85

Copan Motmot burial, 70, 145, 156–160, 157, 219n112, 223n4

Copan Ruler 2, 160

Copan Stela A, 53, 166, 182

Copan Stela C, 159

Copan Stela H, 22, 23, 42

Copan Sub-Jaguar interment, 85

Copan Temple 16, 108, 109, 111

Copan Temple 26, 108, 109, 111–112, 136, 141, 156, 220n10

Copan Temple 33, 70

corpse: and body/soul relationship, 2, 5, 171, 181–183; and society/autonomy tension, 4

cranial bones, curation of, 42

cremation, 74, 75, 78, 142

crocodiles, as metaphor for earth, 18, 67, 211n6

crypts: definition of, 64; preferences in, 65–66; and specific body treatments, 74

Cucina, Andrea, 93

Cuello Burial 9, 216n38

Cuello Burial 109, 216n38

Culbert, T. Patrick, 11, 12, 87, 96

cut marks, and evisceration, 75, 216n38

dancing, 155–156

"Dazzler" vessel, 110, 133, 134

dead kings/successors relationship: and afterlife, 15; and ancestor status, 16, 171, 181, 182, 183; and burial of dead king, 177; and continuation of symbolic rule of dead king, 172, 176; and crisis of abandoned kingship, 171–172; and death and accession dates, 172, 173–175, 175–176; and interregnums, 172, 175–178; and k'uhul ajaw, 176, 177, 180; and passing of the torch, 152; and postmortem dissension, 175

death: as birth, 82–83; concepts of, 13, 212n54; concurrent models of, 17; earth as realm of, 17, 18; fleshless skull representing, 26; and floral issue, 29; as form of sacrifice, 59–60; representation of, 16; royal death as archetypal death, 180, 183; and social values, 1; solution to problem of royal death, 171; split between physical and spiritual sides of, 34, 83; as vegetative process, 23, 25; writing of, 25–31, 33–39

death and transformation on K1182, 99, plate 8

"death-eye" prefix, 26

death process: Classic Maya beliefs about, 11, 33; and ochb'ih, 35

death rituals: Hertz on, 1–2, 4–5, 7, 10, 171, 181; and hieroglyphic and iconographic decipherment, 2–3; liminal period in, 1–2, 4–5; as mirrors of changing societal roles and relations, 6; performance aspect of, 155; and preparations for interment, 61–64; tripartite structure of, 1, 4, 182

deer: and ceramic vessels, 98, 219n111; and Copan Motmot burial, 158, 159; and Río Azul, 69–70

disarticulated skeletons, and burial of K'inish Ahkal Mo' Naab' III, 66

disturbed burials, 16. See also tomb reentry

dogs, 50, 96, 219n105

Dos Pilas: and founders, 115, 117; and sealing tombs, 103; and shell artifacts, 92

Dos Pilas Burial 30 of Structure L5-1, 66, 71

Dos Pilas Panel 19, 148

Dos Pilas Stela 3, 151
Dos Pilas Stela 25, *28*
Dos Pilas Structure LD-49, 220n31
dressing, and interment, 76–81
Durkheim, Émile, 1, 3–4
Dzibanche, and *och ch'een*, 71
Dzibilchaltun: bone "use" evidence, 167;
    and bowls replacing faces and skulls, 92;
    burial patterns of, 12, 216n39; and burn-
    ing patterns, 75; classification scheme
    for burials, 64; and royals missing body
    parts, 75
Dzibilchaltun Burial 385–I, 216n39

earflares, and identification of royal inter-
    ments, 11, 83
Early Classic Río Hondo vase, *36*
earth: conceptions of, 18, 67, 211n6;
    metaphors for, 18–19, 22, 64, 67, 211n6; as
    realm of death, 17, 18; temple construc-
    tion as making new surface for earth, 68
Earth Lord, sale of soul to, 39
effigies: ancestral effigies, 41, 42, 78, 168;
    god effigies, 9; kingship transferred to,
    172, 176; mortuary effigy boxes, 41, 168;
    and *tonalli*, 40–41; wooden effigies, 41,
    42, 168
el naah "house-censing," 101, 154–155, 163
el naah tu mukil "his tomb is house-censed,"
    145, 147, 223n4
el naj tu mukil "house censing at his tomb,"
    72
El Peru, 18, 70, 87
El Peru Stela 3, 18
embalming, 64, 74–75, 82, 215n4
embedded mythology, *ochb'ih* as, 35
English royal model, 172
ennoblement, and political ends of tripartite
    structure, 6
epigraphy: and ancestor veneration, 155;
    and *b'aah*, 41; and Classic Maya death
    rituals, 3, 10, 17; and Classic Maya
    ideology, 11; and concepts of death, 13;
    and founder model, 106; and funerary
    rituals, 61; and identification of rulers,
    88; and *k'a'ay u sak* "flower" *ik'il*, 29; and

models of death rituals, 7; and *och h⟨*
    68; and *och k'ahk'*, 101; of *och k'ahk'*, 1⟨
    Sarcophagus Lid, 125; and tomb reen⟨
    142, 145; and tombs as houses, 72; an⟨
    Underworld, 48
episodic funerary behavior, ethnographi⟨
    data on, 10
Escobedo, Héctor, 155
ethnographic information: and afterlife,
    10, 59; and animation of buildings, 13
    and anthropological theory, 3; applic⟨
    bility of, 12–13; and burial sequences,
    100; and death rituals, 2; and power
    hierarchies, 119; on souls, 39; and tom⟨
    reentry, 151; and tombs as houses, 72;
    Underworld, 52
ethnohistoric information: and animatio⟨
    of buildings, 132; applicability of, 12–⟨
    and burial sequences, 98; and *ch'ab'-
    ak'ab'* phrase, 15; and concepts of deat⟨
    13; and death rituals, 2; and souls, 41;
    Underworld, 52
Evans-Pritchard, Edward E., 172
evisceration, 74–75

face removal, 65, 75, 168
familial mausoleums, 161–162
Fash, Barbara, 158
Fash, William L., 70, 107, 158, 220n9
fasting, 97–98, 155
faunal remains, 96
Fernández de Oviedo y Valdés, Gonzalo⟨
fire: and sealing tombs, 101, 182. *See also*
    burning patterns
fire drills, 166
Fitzsimmons, James, 84, 118–119, 220n9
Florentine Codex, 17
flowers: and Classic Maya ideology, 11; ja⟨
    artifacts representing, 88; metaphor of
    exhaling flower, 28, 29–31; souls con-
    nected with, 27, 28; white flower breat⟨
    phrases, 11, 13, 28, *28*, 29–31, 34, 38, 42,
    43, 44, 47–48, 177
founders: and ancestors, 105–106, *107*,
    117, 118, 122–123, 134; of Classic Maya
    lowlands, 105–106, *107*, 112–117; and co⟨

petition for dominance, 120; funerary structures of, 106–107; and legitimacy, 122; and ritual power, 119

fragrant flowers, breath connected with, 27

Frazer, James George, 172

Freidel, David, 48, 141, 162, 214n120, 221n55, 225n72

Frieze of the Dream Lords, 47

funerary ceramics, and tests of Classic Maya Underworld, 52

funerary chambers: arrangement of, 97, 123; private nature of, 129; and roles of dead, 125

funerary ritual: and body preparations, *194–201;* depictions of, 61, 146; public nature of, 178–180; scale of, 182; and social structure, 5–6, 181. *See also* mortuary practice

funerary structures: animation of, 132, 142; of founders, 106–107; and pan-lowland Maya practices, 65; preferences for, 65, 129; and royal interments, 178, 181; rulers' participation in creation of, 226n22; and status of deceased, 182. *See also* tomb construction; tombs

Furst, Peter, 222n68

GI of Palenque Triad, 55, 129, 215n133. *See also* Maize God

GII of Palenque Triad, 55, 129

GIII of Palenque Triad, 55, 71, 129, 215n133

García Moll, Roberto, 140

gender: and bloodletting artifacts, 90, 218n88; similarity in interments, 65

Gendrop, Paul, 162

God A: aspect of, 166; Classic Maya royalty impersonating, 57; depiction of, *20,* plate 2

God A': aspect of, 166; depiction of, *31, 32,* plate 5

god bundles, 78, 79, *79*

god effigies, 79

God L, 50

gods: death caused by, 39; pool of souls kept by, 40; and skin or bark, 42, 68; wrapped as bundles, 78, 79, *79. See also specific gods*

Goody, Jack, 5–6

grave furniture: and bloodletting artifacts, 88, *89,* 90; and bowl coverings, 92–93; in burial of K'inish Ahkal Mo' Naab' III, 66; and burial sequences, 97–98, 100–101; and ceramic vessels, 85, 87; and Classic Maya Underworld, 49; commissioning of, 178; and faunal remains, 96; and jade artifacts, 87–88; and mirrors, pyrite, and hematite, 96–97; regional and local patterns in, 83, 84; and shell and other marine artifacts, 90, *91,* 92; similarity in, 65; and textiles and other layering, 84–85, 158; and tomb reentry, 142; wooden or stone platforms, 85, 217n75

grave goods: and Classic Maya ideology, 11; commissioning of, 179; Ruz Lhuillier on, 2; and status level, 16; summary of, *202–207;* supporting data for, 3; and tomb reentry, 145, 164

gravemakers, 64–68

Great Skull of Yaxchilan, 177

Grube, Nikolai: on Bird Jaguar IV, 120; on bone "use" evidence, 168; on Caracol Structure B19–2nd, 136; on Classic Period, 210n30; on Maasal, 224n50; on *ochb'hiiy,* 34; and Piedras Negras Stela 40, 154; on psychoducts, 130; on royal succession, 176–177; and Tikal Altar 5, 165; and Tonina, 160; on waiting for interment, 64; on *way,* 46

Guenter, Stanley, 221n55

Guillemín, Jorge, 78

Guiteras Holmes, Calixta, 39, 40, 47, 214n94

Ha' K'in Xook, 154, 171

Hall, Grant, 68, 81, 103–104

Hatzcap Ceel, 74

headdresses, 133, 138

Headrick, Annabeth, 76–77

Heidegger, Martin, 119

heirlooms: and body processing, 75; and effigies, 41, 42; jewelry, 169

Hellmuth, Nicholas, 35

hematite: and grave furniture, 96–97; and
    painting royal bodies, 81, 82, 83, 164
Hero Twins: and iconography, 121; journey
    taken by Classic Maya royalty compared
    to, 53; and Maize God, 19, 22, 52; as
    primordial cultivators, 19, 21; and resur-
    rection and rebirth, 159; *way* compared
    to, 47; and Xibalba, 23, 52
Hertz, Robert: critiques and revisions of
    model of, 6; on death rituals, 1–2, 4–5,
    7, 10, 171, 181; on physical and spiritual
    aspects of death, 83, 182; and transition
    to ancestor status, 16
Heyden, Doris, 162
hieroglyphs: and *cham*, 31; and Classic Maya
    religion, 2; and color red, 82; and death
    expressions, 34; and funerary rituals, 61,
    146; and identification of royal inter-
    ments, 11; of Paddler Gods, 37; and Pie-
    dras Negras, 146; and tomb reentry, 142
hijillo "night air," 43, 44
Holmul, and mausoleums, 161–162
Hombre de Tikal statue, 176
Ho-Noh-Chan, 49
house dedications, and tomb reentry, 145
household interments, 2
household shrines, 65
Houston, Stephen: on *b'aah*, 41; on breath,
    souls, and fragrant flowers, 27; on *cham*,
    211n25; on Classic Maya heirlooms, 42;
    on death phrases, 37; on earth metaphor,
    19, 211n6; on floral issue, 29; on funer-
    ary structures, 178; on *k'uhul ajaw*, 119;
    on moral authority of royalty, 170, 171;
    and Piedras Negras excavation, 155; and
    portable representations, 169; on power
    hierarchies, 118, 170; on royal interments,
    178–179; and royal power as fiery essence,
    170–171; on *sakb'ih*, 33; on solar breath,
    222n63; on sweatbath imagery, 158; on *ti
    ? tuun*, 38; on *u'uk ha' nal*, 35
Huitzilopochtli, 78
human sacrifice: and bone processing,
    224n55; bones taken from burial, 167;
    and burial patterns, 2, 65, 74, 75; Clas-
    sic Maya royal burials unassociated

with, 10–11; and face removal, 168; and
    multiple interments, 93; and *och ch'een*,
    71; scene from K4013, *150;* and sealing
    tomb, 102
humiliated gods, disrobing of, 76
Hun Ajaw, *21*, plate 3
Hunal tomb, 82
Hun Hunahpu, 22
Huntington, Robert, 5, 6, 10, 170, 172, 179,
    181–182

iconography: and ancestor veneration, 16;
    and *b'aah*, 41; of birds, 218n104; and
    bloodletting artifacts, 88; and ceramic
    vessels, 87; and Classic Maya death ritu-
    als, 3, 10; and Classic Maya religion, 2;
    in Classic Maya tombs, 22–23; of Classic
    Maya Underworld, 15; and Copan
    Motmot burial, 159; deified ancestors in,
    57; and faunal remains, 96; of feasting
    or dancing, 97; and founders, 115; and
    funerary rituals, 61; and god bundles, 78;
    and headdresses, 133; and K'ahk' Tiliw
    Chan Yoaat, 62; and *k'uhul*, 41; and
    models of death rituals, 7; monumental
    iconography, 48; and mortuary bundles,
    81; and obsidian celts, 88; and *och ha'*, 35;
    and *och witz*, 163; of Piedras Negras, 146;
    and portal, 158; and *sak*, 29; of Sarcopha-
    gus Lid, 125; and supernatural figures,
    137; and *tis*, 44; of tombs as caves, 71; and
    tombs as portals, 70; in tombs of Río
    Azul, 68, 69, 70; and watery bands, 92
ihiyotl "night air, death air," 43, 44, 47–48
ik' "breath, life, spirit," 13, 15, 26–27, 28, 29,
    31, 42, 44, 126
Inca, 172
incense, 87, 137, 142, 154–155, 156, 158, 163
incense burners, 133, 159
India, 4
individual autonomy/societal integration,
    and Durkheim, 3–4
Indonesia, 3, 4, 6
inner soul, concept of, 39
interment: and bodies stripped of flesh,
    216n39; bundling as preparatory rite for,

79; child interments, 65; and dressing,
76–81; individual or local strategies for,
3; multiple interments, 65, 93, *94*, 95–96,
95, 161–162, 164; nonroyal elite interments, 59, 178; and painting royal bodies,
81–83; successive interment, 162; timing
and ritual process, 72, 74, 100; waiting for, 61–64, 100; within residential
platforms, 105. *See also* royal interments
interregnums, 172, 175–178
in teuhtli, in tlazolli "the dust, the filth," 17
intrusive burials, as sowing or planting acts,
67–68
Itzamnaaj, 60, 110–111
Itzamnaaj B'alam II, 117, 120–122, 137, 140,
175
Itzamnaaj B'alam III, 177
Itzamnaaj K'awiil (Ruler 2) of Dos Pilas:
cave as tomb of, 71; death and burial
dates of, *63*; time period before interment, 62; and tomb firing, 160

jade artifacts: as bloodletting artifacts, 90;
in burial of K'inish Ahkal Mo' Naab'
III, 66; changes in use of, 96; in royal
interments, 83
jade mosaic masks, and royal interments,
65, 88
jades in large quantity, and identification of
royal interments, 11, 83, 84, 87–88
Jaguar God of the Underworld: Classic
Maya royalty impersonating, 53, *54*, 57;
and death rituals, 8; depiction of, *20*,
plate 2; and tomb reentry, 147, 149, 166
jaguar phalanges, and pelts, 85
jaguars: and human-animal associations,
96; representation of, 88
Jakalteko, 26
Jasaw Chan K'awiil I (Ruler A): capture of
god bundle of Calakmul deity, 79; and
construction of funerary temples, 112;
and marine objects, 90; and power hierarchies, 118; and Tikal Altar 5, 165–166;
and Tikal Burial 23, 74
Jester God, 69
Jones, Christopher, 112, 165

Joy Chitam Ahk, 147
Just, Bryan, 140
juuntahn sak "flower" *ik'* "precious white
flower breath," 30

k'a-a-yi, 28
k'a'ay "to end, terminate, or finish," 28–29
k'a'ay u sak "flower" *ik'il* "it finishes, his
white flower breath": and interregnum,
177; and phrasing of death, 11, 13, 28, *28*,
29–31, 38, 42, 43, 44, 47–48
k'a'ay u sak "flower" *ik u tis* "it finishes, his
flower breath, his flatulence," 30–31, *30*,
37, 44, 47
K'ahk' Joplaj Chan K'awiil, 117, 175
K'ahk' Tiliw Chan Yoaat (Cauac Sky) of
Quirigua: death and burial dates of,
63–64, *63*; death of, 62; and founders,
106, 117; funeral of, 61–62; and interregnum, 176; rule of, 62; time period before
interment, 64; and transfer of power,
171
K'ahk' Ujol K'inich II of Caracol, 169, 176
Kan B'alam as the Jaguar God of the Un-
derworld, *54*
Kanhobal, 26, 44, 100
K'an II, 137, 176
K'an Joy Chitam II, 129, 221n61
Kan Mo' B'alam, 116–117, 129
K'an Mo' Hix, 125, 221n55
k'a'pes "to terminate, finish, or arrest," 29
k'atin bak, 52
k'awiil, 46, 55, 57, 127, 129, 137, 139
K'awiil Chan K'inich, 116–117
K'axob', 106
Kekchi: and maize, 25; and souls, 39, 42,
213n74
kingship: theoretical views of, 172. *See also*
Classic Maya royalty; dead kings/suc-
cessors relationship
K'inich Ahkal Mo' Naab' III (Chaacal III,
Akul Anab III), 66, 101, 130, 176
K'inich Ajaw, the Night Sun, 69, 70, 111, 122
K'inich Ajaw, the Sun God, 53, *54*, 57–59,
66, 88, 110–111, 122
K'inich B'aaknal Chaak, 160

K'inich B'alam, and El Peru Stela 3, 18

K'inich Ich'aak Chapat, 160–161

K'inich Janaab' Pakal I of Palenque: agrarian metaphors on tomb of, 127–128; and ancestral inequality, 60; and bloodletting artifacts, 88, 90; and burial sequences, 98; disarticulated skeletons in tomb of, 66; and emergence from Underworld, 70; in fetal position, 83; and founders, 106; and funerary rites, 101; and human sacrifice, 102; and iconographic use of offering bowl, 87; and *juuntahn sak* "flower" *ik'* "precious white flower breath," 30; plan view of tomb, *102;* and power hierarchies, 118; and red-paint burials, 81–82; roles of, 125; and royal interment, 179; and Sarcophagus Lid of Pakal, 16, 57, 58, *58,* 59–60, *59,* 83, 123, *124,* 125–127, *126, 128,* 129–130, 215n128; and sealing tomb, 102–103; stucco figures from tomb, 55, *56;* tomb design of, 67, 129–130; tomb layout as ballcourt, 72; and tomb reentry, 223n1; widow of, 66

K'inich Kan B'alam I of Palenque, 53, 71, 129, 221n61

K'inich Kan B'alam II of Palenque, 53, 123, 129, 177–178, 181

K'inich K'an Joy Chitam II of Palenque, 53, 54, 176, 178

K'inich Tajal Wayib', 108

K'inich Tatb'u Skull II, 120

K'inich Yax K'uk' Mo' of Copan: and ancestral inequality, 60; building of, 156; dynasty of, 157; as founder, 107–108, 110–112, 117; humanistic ancestral images of, 58; as Maya lord, 108, 220n8; and mortuary headdress, 133; solar ancestral images of, 53, 58, *59;* and Teotihuacan, 108, 111–112; and tomb reentry, 158

K'inich Yo'nal Ahk I (Ruler 1) of Piedras Negras: and burial sequences, 98; and death and dynastic succession, 16; and death rituals, 7–8, 10; monuments built by, 146, *147;* and tomb reentry, 145, 147–149, 151–152, 155

K'inich Yo'nal Ahk II (Ruler 3) of Piedras Negras: marriage of, 152; and mirrors, 97; and multiple interments, 93, *95;* and psychoduct, 130; reign of, 152, 154

K'inich Yo'nal Ahk III of Piedras Negras, 154

kis "flatulence," 31

Kisin, 52

Kubler, George, 166

k'uh "god," 41

k'uhul ajaw "holy lord," 81, 101, 119, 176, 177, 180, 181

k'uhul "holy," 41, 70, 82, 83, 158

K'uk' Mo', 176

Lacandon: and changes of state, 212n54; and Death God, 31; and soul-loss concept, 13; and souls, 39; and Upperworld, 52; and wooden effigies, 168

Lady Batz' Ek' of Caracol, 136–137

Lady Ik' Skull, 120, 121, 122

Lady K'ab'aal Xook, 117, 120, 137, 139–140, 141, 167, 223n1

Lady K'atun Ajaw, 152

Lady Olnal, 58, *128*

Lady Sak K'uk', 125, 129, 221n55

Lady Tuun Kaywak, 26, 164–166

Lady Tz'akb'u Ajaw, 66

LaFarge, Oliver, 44, 161

Lamanai, 78, 103

Landa, Diego de, 52, 75, 167, 168

landscape: and ancestors, 127; as changed by the dead, 35; creation of new features on, 67, 68, 115, 141; and genealogy of place, 105–106, 115, 122; relationship of Classic Maya to, 22, 24; and royal interment, 70; and sealing tombs, 104; and site core, 106, 118; and visible reminders of territorial inheritance, 105

Late Classic Period, social change during, 61

layering in tombs, 84–85, 158

Le Fort, Geneviéve, 18, 22, 211n10

life force, 131

lightning, and lithics for sealing tombs, 103

liminality: and body/soul relationship, 7, 182; and change, process, and passage, 5;

liminal period in death rituals, 1–2, 4–5;
liminal period in transition ceremonies,
4; and royal succession, 176; static view
of, 5; and Yucatecan New Year festivals, 7
Lineage of the Lords of Totonicapan,
151–152
lithics, for sealing tombs, 103–104
Lo Dagaa in West Africa, 6
López Austin, Alfredo, 17, 40, 44
Lunar Series, Glyph G, 49

ma ajaw "not lord," 182
Maasal, 164, 165, 166, 224n50
Madagascar, 3, 4, 6, 181
Madrid Codex, 31, 42
maize: and anthropomorphism, 24; human qualities attributed to, 23–24; and
iconography of Classic Maya tombs,
22–23, *24,* 55; and individual from El
Peru, 19; jade artifacts representing, 87;
life cycle of Classic Maya royalty likened
to, 67; maize plants as metaphor for
earth, 211n6; mythological and symbolic
attributes of, 17; as source of life and
death, 17, 28, 57
maize consumption: and anthropophagy,
25; and consuming death, 17, 24–25, 57
Maize God: burial as planting seeds of
future ancestral rebirth, 67; and ceramic
vessels, 53, 57, 215n131; Classic Maya
royalty portrayed as, 22, *23,* 25, 57; death
and resurrection cycle of, 18–19, 22,
23, 36, 50, 53, 55, 57, 70, 76, 88, 125, 159,
211n10; and Hero Twins, 19, 22, 52; and
multiple interments, 95; and *och ha',* 35;
and Temple of the Inscriptions, 126–127,
129; and turtles, 19, *21,* 22; and *u'uk ha'
nal,* 35; and *way,* 47
Mam, 39, 46, 119
marine objects: and royal interments, 90, *91,*
92; and textiles, 84; in tomb of Smoke
Imix, 70. *See also* shell artifacts
Martin, Simon: on Bird Jaguar IV, 120;
on bone "use" evidence, 168; on Caracol Structure B19–2nd, 136; on Classic
Period, 210n30; on Maasal, 224n50; mir-

ror as idealized turtle carapace, 97; on
ochb'ihiiy, 34; and Piedras Negras Stela
40, 154; on psychoducts, 130; on royal
succession, 176–177; and Tonina, 160; on
waiting for interment, 64
Mascarones Structure at Copan, 67
masked façade, 162–164
masks: in bundles, 80–81; and gods, 42; and
mosaics, 65, 88, 92, 168; relationship to
bowls, 93; and royal interments, 83, 179;
serving as ancestors' proxies, 225n62;
uses of, 92
Mathews, Peter, 16, 55, 71, 72, 125, 127, 130
Maya lords being reborn as trees, Berlin
vessel, *62*
Maya lord with mourners, Berlin vessel, *62*
Maya lowlands: artifactual remains and
anthropology of death, 2; belief systems
of, 16; crypts and chambers characterizing royal interments in, 64; founders
of, 105–106, *107,* 112–117; grave typologies for, 2; and lineage customs, 105; and
Maize God, 53; regional traditions of,
83; and souls, 41; tradition of centralized
kingship in, 10
McAnany, Patricia: on ancestor veneration,
16, 171, 210n43; on feasting, 98; on garden themes, 127; and genealogy of place,
105–106, 115; on Holmul, 161–162; masks
serving as ancestors' proxies, 225n62;
on mortuary effigy boxes, 41–42; on
multiple interments, 224n33; and postmortem conflicts, 175; on royal ancestors,
220n5; on seated bundles, 79; on shrines
to commemorate dead, 135; on tomb
reentry, 183; on wooden effigies, 168
McArthur, Harry S., 155
McLeod, Barbara, 28
mercury, 158
Merina (in Madagascar), 6
Merwin, Raymond E., 161
Metcalf, Peter, 5–6, 10, 170, 172, 179, 181–182
-mi, 26
Mictlan, 17
migrations, and ancestor bundles, 80
Miller, Mary, 22, 96, 97

mirrors, 96–97

Mixtecs, 77, 78

Mock, Shirley Boteler, 7, 167, 168

Mok Chi (God A'), 31, *32*, plate 5

Molina Solís, Juan Francisco, 155

Monaghan, John, 25, 39, 42, 210n35

"Moon Jaguar" of Copan, 110

morality: as acquired attribute, 17; moral authority of Classic Maya royalty, 170, 171, 179, 183

mortality: conceptions of, 17, 50; cultural attitudes toward, 2; and maize cycle, 23, 25

mortuary bundles, 81

mortuary effigy boxes, and souls, 41, 168

mortuary practice: anthropology of, 1; and fasting, 97–98; and individual versus theoretical views of kingship, 172; Ruz Lhuillier on, 2; temporal and spatial variations in, 61; and Underworld, 48; visibility outside royal sector, 16. *See also* burial patterns; funerary ritual

mosaics: and identification of royal interments, 11, 83; introduction of, 96; and masks, 65, 88, 92, 168; and pyrite, 96

Motagua Valley of Quirigua, 62

mountains, 18

mountain temples, imagery of, 18

mourners and mourning: and body/soul relationship, 2, 5, 171, 181; and ceramic vessels, 61, 98; and interregnum, 178; and wailing, 61, 98

muhel "shadow," 213n74

muhkaj "he/she is buried," 34, 38, 64

muk tuun (stone burial), 158

multiple interments, 65, 93, *94*, 95–96, *95*, 161–162, 164

mythology: and attributes of maize, 17; embedded mythology, 35; solar mythology, 13; of Underworld, 48, 49

Nahm, Werner, 46

Nahuatl, 40, 43

Naranjo, 115, 166

natural features, supernatural aspects of, 18

Ndembu of southern Africa, 5

Nebaj, 75

Nicaraos, 17

nonelite groups, 16, 59

obsidian, and sealing tombs, 103

obsidian blades: as bloodletting artifacts, 90; and identification of royal interments, 11, 83, 84, 88

obsidian celts, 88

ochb'ihaj "[the] road is entered," 34

ochb'ihiiy "[he] road-entered," 33–34, 152

ochb'ih "road-entering": and interregnum, 177; and phrasing of death, 11, 31, 33–37, *33*, *37*, 38, 42, 43; and Sarcophagus Lid, 125–126, *126*

och ch'een "cave-entering," as journey of soul into a tomb, 71

och ha' "water-entering": and change and transformation, 35–36, 43; and epigraphy, 68; and iconography, 35; and Maize God, 35, 47; and phrasing of death, 31, *33*, 35–37, *37*, 38, 213n58; physical remains of royalty subjected to, 71; and Underworld, 35, 38

och'ihiiy u sak "flower" *ik'* "[the] road was entered [by] his white "flower breath," 34

och k'ahk' "fire-entering," 31, 35, 101, 156–160

och k'ahk' tu mukil "fire enters into his tomb," 145, 156, 223n4

och witz "mountain-entering," 163

okol k'in, 58

`ol ahk "heart of the turtle," 18

1-Banak 8-Banak, and death rituals, 8

onyx vessel from Hix Witz, *38*, 48

orientation: patterns of, 12; preferences for, 65, 83; Ruz Lhuillier on, 2; supporting data for, 3

Otherworld: and ancestors, 122; and Classic Maya royalty, 53; and mirrors, 97; Underworld confused with, 48; and *way,* 47

Paddler Gods, 19, 35, 37, 50

painting royal bodies, and interment, 81–83

Palenque: and ancestors as plants, 123, 127, 215n133; and bowl coverings, 218n94; burial patterns of, 12; and Classic Maya royalty, 53, 57–58; and faunal remains,

96; and founders, 117; and *k'a'ay u sak* "flower" *ik'il*, 29–30; and maize iconography, 24; and mausoleums, 161; and mosaics, 92; and multiple interments, 95–96; and obsidian celts, 88; and painting royal bodies, 83; and *sak b'aknal chapat*, 46; Sarcophagus Lid of Pakal, 16, 57, 58, *58*, 59–60, *59*, 123, *124*, 125–127, *126*, *128*, 129–130, 215n128; Temple of the Cross, *24;* Temple of the Inscriptions, 48; and textiles, 84–85; and tomb reentry, 145

Palenque Group IV, 115

Palenque Tablet XIV, 57

Palenque Temple 14, 71, 177

Palenque Temple 18, 65, 66, 167

Palenque Temple 18–A: and human sacrifice, 102; and jade celts, 88; and multiple interments, 96; and psychoduct, 130, 179; and royal interment, 179; and tomb as cave, 72

Palenque Temple 18–A, Tomb I, 66

Palenque Temple 18–A, Tomb 3, 67

Palenque Temple XIII-sub, 75

Palenque Temple XX, 221n57

Pan-Maya practice, Welsh's proposed patterns of, 2

Parker, Joy, 162

pearls, and identification of royal interments, 11, 83

Pendergast, David, 71, 115, 135

people of corn, Classic Maya as, 22

perceptual psychology, and Classic Maya religion, 2

Period Endings: ceremonies for, 137, 142; and tomb reentry, 157; tying or wrapping in conjunction with, 80

physical beauty, Maya view of, 22

Piedras Negras: and ancestor veneration, 155; bedrock used in tomb construction, 66–67; and bloodletting artifacts, 88, *89*, 90; and bowl coverings, 218n94; burial patterns of, 12; classification scheme for burials, 64; death rituals of, 8, 10; and faunal remains, 96; Maya inscriptions of, 7; and mirrors, 97; and *muhkaj*, 34; and *ochb'ihiiy*, 33; role of dead in wed-

ding and birthday celebrations, 79; and royal transfer of power, 171; and sealing tombs, 103; and tomb reentry, 142, 145–149, 151–152, 154–156, 183

Piedras Negras Burial 5, 68, *95*, 154

Piedras Negras Burial 13, 145, 178, 223n4

Piedras Negras Burial 82, 85, *86*, *89*, 155

Piedras Negras Burial 110, 146, 162

Piedras Negras Panel 2, 8, *9*

Piedras Negras Ruler 2: and ancestor veneration, 16; and building program, 146; death date of, 33–34, 64; and death rituals, 8; and *ochb'ihiiy*, 33–34; time before interment, 62; and tomb reentry, 147, 158

Piedras Negras Ruler 3, 146, 179

Piedras Negras Ruler 4: and ancestor veneration, 154; death and burial dates of, *63;* and mirrors, 97; and royal succession, 175; time period before interment, 62

Piedras Negras Ruler 7, 154, 155, 160, 171, 175

Piedras Negras Stela I, 125, 152, *153*

Piedras Negras Stela 8, 52, 155

Piedras Negras Stela 40, 76, 77, 130, 131, 154, 155, 222n63

Piedras Negras Structure O-13, 154, 155

pilgrimages, and ancestor bundles, 80

pimienta (*Pimienta dioica*), 76

place-names, and layers of Underworld, 49

places or sites, and *way*, 46

plaques, 88

Plumeria alba "white plumeria," 29

Pohl, John, 78

Popol Vuh: on Classic Maya Underworld, 13, 15, 49–50, 52–53; and conjuring, 139; depictions of roads, 33; on fasting, 97–98; Hero Twins of, 19, 22, 23, 53; and Itzamnaaj, 110; maize imagery in, 23; and sealing tombs, 103; and *way*, 47; and Xbalanque, 31

Postclassic Chichén Itzá, 42

Postclassic Quiche Maya Xibalba, 48

postprocessual theory, and study of death, 1

power hierarchies: and founders, 105–108, 110–117, 119, 120; institutional transfers of power, 171, 179; and kingship and lineage, 105–106, 118, 129; and Piedras

Negras, 145–146; and ritual power, 119, 170, 171; royal power as fiery essence, 170–171; and subordinates of royalty, 170, 171, 176, 177, 179
primary burials, 162
processual theory, 1
Proskouriakoff, Tatiana, 28, 146
psychoducts, 129–131, 154, 164, 222n65
púhle'n alma' "untying the dead," 156
puluuy u tz'itil "[it] burns, his long object," 154
pyrite, 96–97
pyrite mosaics, 96–97

Quenon, Michel, 18, 22, 211n10
Quiche: and ancestor bundles, 80; and maize, 24, 25; mortuary rites of, 100; and souls, 39, 40, 43, 44, 58
Quirigua, 34, 62, 133, 171
Quirigua Zoomorph G, *34, 63*

Rain God, 52
Randsborg, Klavs, 209n2
rebirth: and Classic Maya ideology, 11; and color red, 82, 83; and Hero Twins, 159; of Maize God, 18–19; and metaphors for earth, 211n6; resurrection distinguished from, 22; vegetative depictions of, 25
red ochre in burials, 82, 217n66
red-paint burials, 81–83, 164
red pigments, and identification of royal interments, 11, 83
Red Queen, tomb of, at Temple XIII-sub, Palenque, 75
religion: and death rituals, 5; evolution of, 11; modern Maya religion, 24; sociology of, 3–4. *See also* Classic Maya religion
Renaissance France, and kingship, 172
Resbalón, and *och ha'*, 68
resins, as preservatives, 75, 216n43
resurrection: Maize God's death and resurrection cycle, 18–19, 22, 23, 36, 50, 53, 55, 57, 70, 76, 88, 125, 159, 211n10; rebirth distinguished from, 22
Ricoeur, Paul, 119–120
Ringle, William, 66, 167

Río Azul: and dressing, 76; and fire in sealing tombs, 101; and *och ha'*, 68, 216n17; painted tombs of, 68–69; and painting royal bodies, 81; and rock-cut tombs, 66; and sealing tombs, 103; and shell artifacts, 92; and stingray spines, 88; and tomb construction, 67; and water bands, 36, 71; and wooden or stone platforms, 85
Río Azul Tomb 1, 68–70, *69*, 82–83
Río Azul Tomb 12, 219n118
Río Azul Tomb 19, 68, 69, 76, *77*, 81
Río Azul Tomb 23, 68, 76, 81, 101, 104, 219n118
The Ritual of the Bacabs, 13
rock-cut tombs, 66, 67, 216n14
Rosalila Temple, Copan, 58, *59*, 110–111, *110*, 115, 135, 162, 220n20
royal, use of, as term, 11–12
royal identities, 171, 181, 182
royal interments: and burning patterns, 75, 101; cut marks and human sacrifice, 75; and founders, 112; and funerary structures, 178, 181; identification of, 11–12, 65, 83, 84, 87–88, 217n69; location of, 178; and marine objects, 90, *91*, 92; and masks, 83, 179; orientation and positioning patterns of, 83; textiles in, 84–85
royal succession. *See* dead kings/successors relationship
royalty. *See* Classic Maya royalty
Ruz Lhuillier, Alberto: on Classic Maya, 2, 11–12; on painting royal bodies, 81, 82; studies of funerary practices, 65; and Temple 18 at Palenque, 66, 167

Saile, D. G., 220n5
sak b'aknal chapat "white bone house centipede," 46
sakb'ih "white road," 33
sak ik' "white breath," 30
sak-ik' "wind coming from the west," 13
sak nikte' "white plumeria," 29
sak "white," 29, *29*
San Bartolo, Preclassic murals of, 53
San José, and shell artifacts, 218n93
San Miguel Tzinacapan, 211n2

scene of sacrifice from K4013, *150*

Schele, Linda: on ancestors representing sequence of rulers, 127; on buildings as living features, 141; on Lady Sak K'uk', 221n55; on layout of Pakal's tomb, 72; on Maize God, 55; on masked façade, 162; on organization of labor, 125; on psychoducts, 130; and Tikal Altar 5, 165; on transition to ancestor status, 16; on Underworld-Otherworld question, 48; on weaving implements in burial, 90; on World Tree, 214n120

Schellas God A, 31, 149

seated bundling, 79

secondary burials, 5, 79, 162

Segovia, Victor, 130

Seibal: and bowl coverings, 92; burial patterns of, 12; classification scheme for burials, 64; and founders, 115, 116–117; and observation of royal anniversaries, 7; and tomb firing, 160

self: bones serving as discrete portions of, 166, 168; multiple spiritual or supernatural entities in, 47, 131; and soul, 40–42; tomb as house for, 72, 131, 132–133. *See also b'aah* "self, person, head"

Seven-Black-Yellow-Place, Tonina Monument 69, *19*

sexual activity, and consuming death, 17

shaft tombs, 156–157

Sharer, Robert, 62, 82, 90, 110, 164

shell artifacts: in burial of K'inish Ahkal Mo' Naab' III, 66; changes in use of, 96; and high-status interments, 65; and royal interments, 84, 217n69. *See also* marine objects

Shilluk, 172

single versus multiple interments, preference for, 65

site administration: and *k'uhul ajaw*, 176; and subordinates of kings, 170, 176

site core: of Copan, 108, *109;* kings' construction and renewal of, 180; and Maya landscape, 106, 118; and royal interments, 178; royal life in, 135

site layout, and Classic Maya ideology, 11

Site Q, 37

Siyaj Chan K'awiil II (Stormy Sky), 36, 66, 74, 79, 177, 220n8

Siyaj Chan K'inich of Tikal, 176–177

Siyaj K'ahk', 36, 112, 113–114

skeletal mutilation: and burial patterns, 2; and evisceration, 74–75

skeletal remains: and animation of buildings, 131–132, 166; associations with specific skeletal elements, 168; and tomb reentry, 144, 145, 149, 158, 159, 164, 166–169

skeleton position, preferences for, 65, 83

skull removal: preference for, 65; and tomb reentry, 167

skulls, and bowl coverings, 92

Sky Xul, 62, 171, 176

Smith, Augustus L., 64, 65

Smith, Robert E., 64

Smoke Imix (God K) of Copan: and burning patterns, 135–136; death and burial dates of, *63;* and Temple 26, 112; time period before interment, 62; tomb of, 70, 85

social order: and corpse/mourners relationship, 181–182; and death of ruler, 171; divine kings as symbols of perpetuity in, 170; and monumentalization, 182

social status, royal death as opportunity for advancement in, 179–180

social structure, and funerary ritual, 5–6, 181

social values, and death, 1

sociocultural anthropology, 1, 5, 10

sociology of religion, and Durkheim, 3–4

sólön "unwinding," 155–156

soul-loss concept, 13–14, 39, 213n84

souls: afterlife journeys of, 43, 48, 177, 182; and animation of buildings, 131–132; and body/soul relationship, 2, 5, 171; breath connected with, 27; concept of, 39–42; cross-cultural studies of, 213n84; divisions of, 39–40; flowers connected with, 27, 28; and flowery exhalations, 31; gods' examination of, 52; and mortuary effigy boxes, 41, 168; and *och ha'*, 36; relationship of corpse to, 182; and *t'ab'ay,*

27; traveling outside of body, 39, 44, 131; types of, 39, 131. *See also ch'uhlel* "inner souls, of the earth"

Spondylus shells, 90, 92

status level, and grave goods, 16

stelae caches, and symbolic caves, 72

stingray spines: and ancestor veneration, 15; as bloodletting artifacts, 88, 90; and identification of royal interments, 11, 65, 83

Storey, Rebecca, 81, 158

Stuart, David: on *ajaw*, 27–28; on *b'aah*, 41; on breath phrases, 30–31; on *cham*, 211n25; on cinnabar or hematite as symbolic blood, 82; on Classic Maya heirlooms, 42; on Copan Motmot burial, 157; on fire for house dedications, 132; on Jaguar God costume, 166; on *k'uhul ajaw*, 119; on *ochb'ih*, 33; on *och ch'een* and human sacrifice, 71; on *och k'ahk'* and *el naah*, 156; on power hierarchies, 118–119, 170; and royal power as fiery essence, 170–171; on Sarcophagus Lid of Pakal, 57; on Sip, 222n63; on tendrils of breath, 27; on *u'uk ha' nal*, 35; on variant of *ik'*, 212n40; on Yaxchilan, 120

Sudan, 172

Sunraiser Jaguar, 63–64

supernatural world: distinction from Underworld, 48; lack of distinction from natural world, 18. *See also* conjuring ceremonies

sweatbaths, 158, 159

symbolism, and Classic Maya ideology, 11

t'ab'ay "[it] ascends," 27, *27*, plate 4

Tajoom Uk'ab' Tuun, 146, 147

Tamarandito, 117

Tarascans, 77–78

Tate, Carolyn, 121

Taube, Karl: on breath, 27; death and floral issue, 29; on headdresses, 133; on liminality, 7; on mirrors, 96; on origins of corn, 22; on solar breath, 222n63; on temple as hearth, 132

Temple of the Cross, Palenque: and bed-

rock, 67; and jade celts, 88; layering in, 84–85; maize personified on, *24;* Tomb 1, 84; Tomb 2, 71–72, 84

Temple of the Inscriptions, Palenque: animation of, 132; and bedrock, 67; and dynastic claims, 125; interior passages of, 72; internal shrines of, 104; internal tablets of, 123; jade artifacts in, 66, 88; and levels of Underworld, 49; long-term use of, 135; and Maize God, 126–127; and psychoduct, 130; public face versus private nature of funerary chamber, 129; role of K'inich Jannaab' Pakal I in construction, 141; and sealing tombs, 96, 102

temple-pyramids: and self-glorification, 129; tomb and crypt locations inside, 65; tombs in alignment with, 67

temples: and ancestors, 122; and headdresses, 133; as imposition of new mountain on landscape, 67; mountain temples, 18; as natural features, 115; purpose of, 141; and royal interments, 65; and self, 133

Teotihuacan: fall of, 61; and K'inich Yax K'uk' Mo' of Copan, 108, 111–112; and mummy bundles, 76–77; and Piedras Negras, 146, 149; and shaft tombs, 158; studies of, 2

tests of Classic Maya Underworld, 52, 53, 59

textiles, in royal interment, 84–85

teyolia (animistic entity), 42–43, 44, 48

13 Kawak House, 64, 171

13 Sky Owl, 50

Tiesler Blos, Vera, 93, 216–217n46

Tikal: and ancestor shrines, 135; and bloodletting artifacts, 88, *89,* 90; and bowl coverings, 92; and bundling, 76, 93; burial patterns of, 12, 180; and burning patterns, 101, 135; and ceramic vessels, 85, 87; and Classic Maya royalty, 53; and faunal remains, 96; and fire in sealing tombs, 101; and foreign intrigue, 108; and founders, 112–113, 115, 122; and interregnums, 175, 176–177; and mosaic masks, 92; and multiple interments, 93, *94;* and *och ha'*, 68; and painting royal bodies, 83; and rock-cut tombs, 66; and royals missing body parts, 75; and *sakb'ih,* 33; and sealing tombs, 103; and self and temple, 133; and shell artifacts, 92, 218n93; site core, 112, *113;* and textiles, 84–85; and tomb construction, 67, 210n32; and *way,* 47; and wooden or stone platforms, 85

Tikal Altar 5, 26, *27,* 164–166, *165*

Tikal Burial 10, 82, *94,* 96, 97, 103, 135, 219n119

Tikal Burial 22, 219n118

Tikal Burial 23, 72, *73,* 74, 84, 85, 103

Tikal Burial 48, 79, 167, 224n37

Tikal Burial 80, 81

Tikal Burial 85, 112, 167

Tikal Burial 116: and bedrock, 66; and bloodletting artifacts, *89;* and bowl covering, 92; and "canoe" glyph, 37; and layering, 84; and marine objects, 84, 90, *91;* and *och ha',* 35, *36;* and watery bands, 70; and *way,* 47

Tikal Burial 125, 76, 85, 102, 112, *114,* 219n119

Tikal Burial 177, 178

Tikal Burial 195, 66, 78, *80*

Tikal Burial 196, 84, 219n118

Tikal Burial 200, 219n119

Tikal Mundo Perdido complex, 112–113, 115, 180

Tikal North Acropolis, 112–113, 135, 178, 180

Tikal Stela 16, 164, 165, *165,* 166

Tikal Stela 29, 215n132

Tikal Stela 31, 36, *37,* 117, 176, 215n132

Tikal Structure 4D-33–2nd, 74

Tikal Temple I, 49, 135, 220n28

Tikal Temple 33, 74

tis "flatulence," 44, 47, 48

Tlacaelel (Aztec king), 78

tlatoani, 43

Tliliuhquitepec, 78

Toda of India, 4

Tohil, 80

tomb construction: and bedrock, 66–67; and Classic Maya ideology, 11; generation of location for, 68; and K'inich Janaab' Pakal I, 67; order of events for, 72; preferences in, 65; reinterpretation of carving tombs, 66; rulers' involvement in, 226n22; and shaft tombs, 157; supporting data for, 3; and Tikal, 67, 210n32; and tomb reentry, 162

tomb entering rituals, 2

tomb firing pattern, 10, 160, 224n31

tomb reentry rites: and ancestor veneration, 210n43; and bone processing, 164–166, 224n55; bones taken from burial, 166–169; and chronology of tomb activities, 84; and conjuring ceremonies, 149, 158; false reentry, 162–164; hypothetical order of events, 148–149; and multiple interments, 93; and painting royal bodies, 81–83, 164; patterns of, 145–149, 151–152, 154–156; phrases associated with, 145; reentered royal tombs of Classic Maya lowlands, *144;* and royal interment, 101; and status of deceased, 182; tomb firing pattern, 10, 160, 166, 224n31

tomb reuse: and burial practices, 83; and multiple interments, 65, 93, *94,* 95–96, *95,* 161–162, 164

tombs: as caves, 71–72, 104, 132; as centers of religious and political activity, 68; chronology for tomb activities, 84; definition of, 64, 65; as entrances to Underworld, 71; floors as watery surfaces, 71; floral fragrance as symbolic of vitality of kings, 28; as house for self, 72, 131, 132–133; maize iconography in, 22–23; placing body in, 34; rock-cut tombs, 66, 67, 216n14; sealing of, 64, 101–104, 137, 142, 182; shaft tombs, 156–157; as Underworld surfaces, 68–71; vaulted tombs, 11, 67; watery bands decorating, 36, 68, 70, 71; as watery realms, 90

Tonacacuauhtitlan, 17

tonalli "shadow," 40–44, 47, 131, 213n75, 225n62

Tonina: and ancestors, 221n50; and bowl coverings, 218n94; and bundling, 76; burial patterns of, 12; and *cham,* 26; classification scheme for burials, 64; and founders, 115, 117; Frieze of the Dream Lords, 47; and *k'a'ay u sak* "flower" *ik'il*, 29, 30; and *och witz*, 38; and painting royal bodies, 83; and self and temple, 133; and tomb firing, 160, 224n31; and tomb reentry, 142, 145, 223n3

Tonina Burial IV-6, 79

Tonina Burial VIII-2, 81, 82

Tonina Burial VII-Ia, 81, 82

Tonina MNAH Disk, *28*

Tonina Monument 69, 18, *19*

Tonina Monument 161, *161*

Topoxte, 75

Tortuguero, 90, 117

Tozzer, Alfred M., 168

transformation. *See* change and transformation

tripartite structure: and cultural values, 6; of death rituals, 1, 4, 182; political ends of, 6; of transition ceremonies, 1, 4, *4*

Turner, Victor, 5, 7

turtles: and Maize God, 19, *21*, 22; as metaphor for earth, 18, 64, 67, 211n6; mirror as idealized turtle carapace, 97; tombs as hearts of turtles, 70

Turtle Tooth, 147

tuun "stone," 81

Tzeltal, 39

Tzotzil: and *b'e*, 33; and *cham*, 26; and *ch'anul*, 46, 47; and *ch'ay 'ik*, 28; and death as supernatural, 50; and eating of the earth, 25; and *k'a'ay*, 29; and maize plants, 24; mortuary rites of, 100; and *och*, 31; and power hierarchies, 119; and souls, 39, 40, 41, 43, 44, 58; and Underworld, 52

Tzutujil, 39, 119

tzuultaq'as "earth deities," 42

Uaxactun: and ancestor shrines, 135; and bowl coverings, 218n95; burial patterns of, 12; and burning patterns, 75; and faunal remains, 96; and founders, 112, 113–114, 115; and mosaic masks, 92; and multiple interments, 93; rock-cut tomb of Burial A22, 216n14; and royals missing body parts, 75; and sealing tombs, 103; and shell artifacts, 92, 218n93

Uaxactun Burial A20, 92, 167

Uaxactun Burial A-31, 218n92

Uaxactun Burial CI, 79, 80, 92, 167

Uaxactun Burial E6, 218n95

Uaxactun Structure A-5, 113–114, 115, 180

Ucko, Peter, 3

u jol k'uhil "his skull god," 167

Uk-Ek-K'an, 49

Ukit Kan Le'k, 169

Underworld: ballcourts associated with, 72; caves as entrances to, 71; and Classic Maya beliefs, 10; and *och ha'*, 35, 38; place-names affiliated with Quirigua, 62; rebirth and resurrection distinguished, 22; supernaturals of, 2; tombs as entrances to, 71; tombs as Underworld surfaces, 68–71. *See also* Classic Maya Underworld; Otherworld; Upperworld; Xibalba

Underworld scene, *14*, plate 1

Upperworld, 48, 49, 50, 52

u tis "his flatulence," 43, 47

u'uk h' nal "Place of Seven Water," 35

Vaillant, George C., 161

van Gennep, Arnold: adaptations of work, 6; on death as phased, 60; on death rituals, 1, 2, 4, 10; on liminality, 5, 182; and society/autonomy tension, 4; and transition to ancestor status, 16; on tripartite structure of transition ceremonies, 1, 4, 5, 7

vaulted tombs, 11, 67

vegetation, jade artifacts representing, 87, 88

vinahel "heavens," 52

Vogt, Evon, 24, 39

Vucub Hunahpu, 22

wailing, 61, 98

Wak Chan K'ahk', death of, Tonina Monument 69, *19*

war: and ancestral bundles, 78, 80; captives of, 76, 166, 167; and god effigies, 79

water, jade artifacts representing, 87

watery bands: caches representing, 71; and ceramic vessels, 50, 61, 71; and death phrases, 35–36, *36;* and shell artifacts, 92; and tombs, 36, 68, 70, 71

Waxak Banak Hun Banak, 147, 149

Waxaklajuun Ub'aah K'awiil (18 Rabbit): erection of Copan Stela C, 159; impersonating deities, 57; K'ahk' Tiliw Chan Yoaat's capture of, 62, 175; as Maize God on Copan Stela H, 22, *23,* 42; and Rosalila Temple, 111, 220n20

way "coessences" or "animal spirit companions": and *ch'anul,* 46; Classic Maya *way* killing other *way, 45,* 47, plates 6–7; cosmological role of, 50; and faunal remains, 96; ties to specific individual, 44, 46–47, 48

wayhel eater, 47

wayoob', 46

weaving implements, 90

Weiss-Krejci, Estella, 11, 12, 74, 75, 81, 87, 96

Welsh, W. Bruce M.: on bowl coverings, 92, 218n94; on Classic Maya, 2, 12; on grave furniture, 83; on rock-cut tombs, 66; and royals missing body parts, 75, 167, 168; studies of funerary practices, 65

West Africa, 6

witz (Earth Lord), 13

witz (mountain), 111, 115, 132, 163–164

wooden effigies, 41, 42, 168

wooden or stone platforms, 85, 217n75

World Tree, 17, 125, 214n129. *See also axis mundi*

Xbalanque, 31

Xibalba: and Hero Twins, 23, 52; House of Bats in, 49; House of Knives in, 49; inhabitants of, 49–50; lack of glyph for, 15; and Maize God, 22; summons from lords of, 52; Underworld confused with, 48. *See also* Classic Maya Underworld

yaktaaj ajawlel "the leaving/transferring of his kingship," 171

Yax B'alam, *21,* plate 3

Yaxchilan: Classic Maya royalty as celestial bodies, 53, 58; and conjuring ceremonies, 137, 139; and faunal remains, 96; and fire in sealing tombs, 101; and royal succession, 175, 177; and sealing tombs, 103; and tomb reentry, 223n1

Yaxchilan Lintel 12, 46

Yaxchilan Lintel 14, 46, 148, *148,* 177

Yaxchilan Lintel 25, 137, *138,* 139–140, *140,* 167

Yaxchilan Lintel 27, A2–B2, *28*

Yaxchilan Lintel 27, G2, *28*

Yaxchilan Lintel 58, 177

Yaxchilan Stela 1, 121

Yaxchilan Stela 4, 121, *121*

Yaxchilan Stela 6, 121

Yaxchilan Stela 10, 121

Yaxchilan Stela 11, 121

Yaxchilan Stela 14, *29*

Yaxchilan Temple 23, 139–140, *140,* 141

Yaxchilan Temple 24, 135, 140, 141

Yaxchilan Tomb 2, 88

Yaxchilan Tomb VII, 219n118

Yax Ehb' Xook of Tikal: and ancestral inequality, 60; and Burial 125, 112, *114;* disrobing of, 76; and founders, 117, 221n38; as K'inich Ajaw, *54*

Yaxha' Chaak, 147, 149

Yax Nuun Ayiin of Tikal: and faunal remains, 96; lineage of, 112–113; and multiple interments, 93; and red-paint burials, 81–82; and rock-cut tombs, 66; and royal succession, 176, 177; solar ancestral images of, 53

Yax Pasaj Chan Yoaat of Copan, 71, 111

yichaan ajaw "uncle of the lord," 177

Yoaat B'alam I of Yaxchilan, 117

Yoaat B'alam II of Yaxchilan, 117, 175, 177

Yo'nal Ahk I of Piedras Negras, 182

Yucatan: and burning patterns, 75; ethnohistoric information on, 12–13; and masked façades, 162–163; and Underworld, 52; and wooden effigies, 42, 168

Yucatec: and Death God, 31; and "entering" verbs, 33; mortuary rites of, 100; New

Year festivals, 7; and *okol k'in*, 58; and power hierarchies, 119; and *sak-ik'*, 13; and *sak nikte'*, 29

Yuknoom Yich'aak K'ahk', 79, 168

Zacualpa, 78

Zaculeu, 78

Zinacantecos, 13, 42, 52, 58

zoomorphic heads, and Río Azul, 69